Pioneering theories in nursing

Pioneering theories in nursing

edited by

Austyn Snowden,
Allan Donnell and Tim Duffy

QUAY
BOOKS

A division of MA Healthcare Ltd

Note

*Healthcare practice and knowledge are constantly changing and developing
as new research and treatments, changes in procedures, drugs and equipment become available.*

*The author and publishers have, as far as is possible, taken care to confirm that the information complies with
the latest standards of practice and legislation.*

Quay Books Division, MA Healthcare Ltd, St Jude's Church, Dulwich Road, London SE24 0PB

British Library Cataloguing-in-Publication Data
A catalogue record is available for this book

© MA Healthcare Limited 2010
ISBN-10: 1 85642 4006; ISBN-13: 978 1 85642 4004

Printed by CLE, Huntingdon, Cambridgeshire

Contents

Foreword

Sir George Castledine

Questions are often asked about the historical basis of nursing and too often people assume that there is little more to our evolution than Florence Nightingale. This book demonstrates that there is more to nursing theorists than many would care to appreciate.

It is about our heritage, our culture, our body of knowledge and most of all about the people who have formed and developed theories of nursing. Much of their work is based on what they have experienced and the circumstances that have existed during their lifetime practising, studying and thinking about nursing. Their efforts give us purpose and direction and most of all make us think about what it is we are doing when we say we practise nursing. We should be proud of our heritage and our past because by looking back and reading what these pioneers in nursing have to say we realise the richness of our roots and the value of our academic thinkers to the development of our profession.

At times, nursing, although practised over the centuries, is little understood and often simplified without thinking about what it is that gives us our direction and discipline. There are those who believe that such theorists are a waste of time; that it is not necessary in today's world to bother about the past. There is a danger of too much political interference and management direction of what it is we must do for the organisation rather than for our patients. Specialisation of healthcare is leading us towards a medicalised model where nurse specialists and advanced practitioners are seen more as mini-doctors, medical assistants or technicians.

This is, therefore, a very timely book which should be compulsive reading for all nursing students and serious professional registered nurses. For students it will give an idea of the basis of nursing and the different ways it can be interpreted in various settings. As for the qualified nurse it is good to have a source that can be dipped into to explore aspects of nursing forgotten or lost in the 'rat' race to meet targets and satisfy the whims of others.

Theories may be viewed as visions giving intellectual insight into phenomena, but for maximum significance and impact they should be explanatory and predictive in nature so as to guide professional practice. This book examines 27 theorists and their work in a simplified and creative way. The book is divided into five discrete but innovative sections and readers are encouraged to explore the theorists through their biography, a summary of their writing, the theories themselves and their application to practice. We are then taken on to look at their links to other theorists and their influence in general. Key dates are given to help trace the significant times that influenced the theorist and the text is easy to follow, motivating one to read on and learn more.

The approach is ideal for the casual reader because of the simplified way the information is presented; yet for those who want to explore the subject in more depth there are excellent references for further reading.

I am extremely happy to recommend this book to all nurses and to those who want an introductory guide as to what is the true basis of nursing. I am sure it will become an invaluable reference and essential reading for all undergraduate and certain postgraduate courses. It certainly deserves high recognition and the authors should be congratulated on an excellent piece of work.

I strongly urge you to read this book and immerse yourself in the historical and essential roots of nursing theory and practice.

Austyn Snowden

Austyn Snowden has 25 years of international mental health nursing experience, mostly in the care of the older adult. He is a specialist practitioner in gerontological nursing and an independent prescriber and has just completed a PhD developing a theory of how competence is developed within the field of prescribing. The PhD also led to the development of concurrent analysis, a novel method of qualitative research.

Over the past four years Austyn has developed an international reputation within the field of non-medical prescribing. He is a regular speaker at national and international nurse prescribing events and is a peer reviewer for numerous journals on the topic. He is a member of the editorial boards of Quay Books and the journal *Nurse Prescribing*, and is the author of *Prescribing and mental health nursing*, a well-reviewed textbook on medicine management in mental health nursing. He has also had numerous peer-reviewed journal articles and book chapters published on subjects such as classification of mental illness, ethics and originality. He is currently a lecturer in mental health nursing at the University of West of Scotland and a research fellow in psychological care and treatment. In partnership with Macmillan cancer support and NHS Ayrshire and Arran he is currently evaluating a project on distress management in cancer services.

Allan Donnell

Allan Donnell is a Senior Lecturer and Programme Leader for the Pre-Registration Mental Health Nursing Programmes at the University of the West of Scotland. Allan trained as a schoolteacher at Craigie College of Education in Ayr but following several summer jobs as a nursing assistant in Dykebar Hospital in Paisley decided that his interest lay in mental health nursing and he left teaching to study for his RMN. This he obtained in 1982 when he returned to Dykebar Hospital as a staff nurse in a rehabilitation unit. His nursing career was spent in the West of Scotland between Dykebar and the Argyll and Bute Hospitals where he was Charge Nurse for long-stay and rehabilitation units

and where he gained some experience in community psychiatric nursing.

Whilst on secondment to Argyll and Clyde Health Board in a quality assurance position it became clear that education was his real passion and Allan was successful in obtaining a nurse tutor's position at Argyll Renfrewshire and Dumbarton College of Nursing and Midwifery. At that time he also obtained his BSc in Nursing Studies at Glasgow Caledonian University and subsequently his Masters in Nursing (Education) at Glasgow University.

Recently Allan has returned to Ayr and now works at the University of the West of Scotland's campus in the town. He continues to be interested in how students learn the skills required to help people with mental health problems and in particular how empathy and engagement skills can be taught and developed.

Tim Duffy

Until recently Tim Duffy has been the Director of Distance Learning within the School of Health, Nursing and Midwifery at the University of the West of Scotland. He is a qualified social worker and specialised in working with people with alcohol and drug-related problems. For six years he was National Training Officer with responsibility for training social work and healthcare personnel to develop strategies to help motivate clients and patients of all ages to reduce problems related to alcohol and drug use.

Since 1995 he has supported the development, delivery and evaluation of a range of undergraduate and post-graduate distance learning programmes including the BSc in Nursing Studies (with Gerontology). In this role he has supported academic staff to develop and deliver distance learning teaching materials for students in 28 countries.

Tim's PhD study evaluated the impact of a Self-Administered Motivational Instrument (the SAMI) in a UK Higher Education setting. He has researched student learning styles and approaches to study, student motivation, methods of supporting students online and student retention. Tim is now a full-time researcher specialising in psychosocial interventions within a wide range of health and social care settings.

Mandy Allison

Mandy Allison is 47 years old and recently graduated as a Mental Health Nurse from the University of the West of Scotland. Formerly, Mandy lived in the City of London where she had worked in organisational development and training over a 20-year period. It was while working on a project for Marie Curie Cancer Care, that Mandy realised she wanted to be a nurse. Mandy is a regular contributor on the readers' panel at the *Nursing Standard* where she has recently had several reflections published.

John Atkinson

John Atkinson is a community nurse by background. Originally from London, he has lived and worked in Scotland since 1984. His clinical and academic work has mainly focused on caring for marginalised people, including the homeless, prisoners and those with HIV. He has also undertaken environmental and human health work in Malawi. Since 1999 he has worked at the University of the West of Scotland (previously the University of Paisley) as senior lecturer, Associate Dean and Professor of Community Health and Postgraduate Studies. He has published widely and his academic website is at http://myprofile.cos.com/atkinson22.

Margaret M Brown

Margaret M Brown is a Lecturer in Mental Health Nursing within the School of Health, Nursing and Midwifery at the University of the West of Scotland. Margaret is a Registered Nurse in Mental Health and has worked for a number of years in a wide range of mental healthcare settings, finally specialising in the care of the older adult with mental healthcare needs. She also worked for five years as a lecturer/practitioner before moving to a full-time educational role. She has had an enduring interest in the practical application of nursing theories into the care setting and led a group of mental health nurses who successfully implemented Peplau's theory in community mental health nursing across a wide range of specialist teams. Margaret teaches mental health nursing and the care of the older adult in both pre-registration and post-registration courses and her research interests include the mental healthcare needs of older adults and the care of the person with advanced dementia.

Yvonne Christley

Yvonne Christley was born in Dublin and completed undergraduate and graduate studies at the Queen's University Belfast, the University of Ulster and Glasgow Caledonian University. She is a Registered Nurse and has enjoyed a varied career in clinical practice, research and education. After spending a number of years specialising in cardiothoracic intensive care Yvonne integrated her passion for nursing and research by moving to the Royal College of Nursing as a Policy Advisor. Whilst in this post she specialised in public health, primary care and independent sector policy research and produced numerous policy position papers in these areas on behalf of nurses and nursing.

Over the next few years Yvonne continued to gain experience and knowledge undertaking research which culminated in her appointment to the Glasgow Centre of Population Health (GCPH). While at the GCPH she was a key member of the team responsible for the groundbreaking Glasgow Community Health and Wellbeing Research and Learning Programme. Yvonne is currently a lecturer at the University of the West of Scotland and has a special interest in research and public health. She is completing a PhD on the emotional health and wellbeing of people suffering from chronic fatigue syndrome.

Valerie Douglas

Valerie Douglas is a Lecturer at the University of the West of Scotland. She is a Registered Nurse and Midwife with a wide range of clinical experience which includes emergency care, midwifery, neonatal nursing and community nursing. She worked as a clinical teacher in pre- and post-registration nursing for about four years before doing a teacher training course at Strathclyde University, Glasgow from 1992 to 1993. During her time in nurse education, she has been involved in curriculum development of a Diploma/BSc in Nursing, the development of post-registration nursing modules on infection control and caring for the older adult in the community.

Valerie has a special interest in research and disaster/major incident preparedness. She initiated a collaborative approach with three Health Boards and the Scottish Ambulance Service to develop two disaster management modules at the University of Paisley. Valerie was responsible for the coordination of these modules from 2003 to 2007. These modules were accessed by paramedics and registered nurses. In 2008, she carried out a study on the contribution of community nurses to major incident management

Throughout her nursing career Valerie has always been interested in the application of nursing theories as a vehicle for enhancing patient care.

Lorraine Duers

Lorraine Duers (nee Keenan) is a Lecturer in Adult Nursing within the School of Health, Nursing and Midwifery at the University of the West of Scotland (UWS). She is a Registered General Nurse who qualified from Glasgow Royal Infirmary in 1983. It was on qualifying that she became increasingly interested in the Roper, Logan and Tierney model of nursing and its application within the practice areas. Other professional qualifications include midwifery and health visiting. As a health visitor, she became team leader and lead nurse for clinical governance and also set up a nurse-led asthma clinic within the practice to which she was attached. She is also a Registered Nurse Prescriber. In 2002, she made the transition from practice into higher education and became a registered teacher. Within UWS she is involved in the Staff Student Liaison Committee and admissions team and co-ordinates a year 1 module on reflection for nursing practice. Academic qualifications include a BSc in Health Studies, Postgraduate Diploma in Asthma and an MSc in Nursing and Applied Education. At present she is undertaking EdD studies, exploring the place and purpose of formative assessment within the student nurse curriculum.

Kathleen Duffy

Kathleen Duffy is a Senior Lecturer, Department of Adult Nursing and Health within the School of Health at Glasgow Caledonian University. She is a qualified nurse and a Registered Nurse Teacher. Following completion of her initial nursing degree Kathleen worked as a staff nurse within acute medicine. She then undertook a general intensive care nursing course working within a cardiothoracic unit before returning to acute medicine as a ward sister. After completing a post-graduate certificate in education, she undertook her Masters degree in Nursing. Kathleen has a long-standing interest in mentorship, student support and practice-based education issues. Her expertise in the area of mentorship and practice-based assessment is recognised both locally and nationally as a result of her Nursing and Midwifery Council scholarship and PhD work around the issues of failing to fail. She was awarded her PhD in 2006 for a thesis entitled 'Weighing the balance: A grounded theory study of the factors that influence the decision regarding the assessment of students' competence in practice'. She is currently involved in research exploring experiences of students who are failing in clinical practice, enhancing the learning environment and student retention.

Raymond Duffy

Raymond Duffy is currently a Nurse Lecturer in Gerontology at the University of the West of Scotland. He has been a Nurse Lecturer since 1995 initially teaching pre-registration adult nursing. Since 2001 he has been teaching post-registration gerontology courses. He is also an experienced distance learning and online learning tutor who has developed and written a number of eLearning and distance learning modules for his current employer. He is a member of the Higher Education Academy and also the Royal College of Nursing Older People's Forum and Respiratory Nurse Forum. Since 2002 he has been a Member of Alzheimer's Scotland NHS and Community Health Care Committee. He is also a Committee Member of the British Computing Society Health (Scotland) Specialist Group.

Brian Johnston

Brian Johnston is a Lecturer within the School of Health, Nursing and Midwifery at the University of the West of Scotland. He is a Registered Nurse and has specialised in the care of older people.

Brian joined the University of the West of Scotland in 2009. Prior to taking up post he has a held a variety of posts including working as a Community Psychiatric Nurse for older people, Clinical Nurse Manager within an Assessment Unit for older people and most recently the Older People's Services Co-ordinator within a primary care setting.

During his nursing career Brian has been interested in how services are developed and delivered to older people, particularly how health and social care services work together. He is particularly focused on how these services are targeted to vulnerable individuals with the greatest needs. This interest allowed Brian to be involved in a few secondments including working as a project manager with NHS Education for Scotland on the Joint Future agenda and more recently to work on a community-based project to develop a protocol that supports vulnerable people with the administration of prescribed medication.

Anne Kay

Anne Kay is a Mental Health Nursing Lecturer in the School of Health, Nursing and Midwifery at the University of the West of Scotland. She worked for a number of years as a mental health nurse in a variety of clinical environments including care of the elderly, acute admissions and rehabilitation. Anne has worked in nurse education since 1985, initially as a clinical teacher and now as a lecturer. She has been responsible for introducing a wide range of subjects to the curriculum. Her teaching is focused in pre-registration where she has been commended for her innovative approach to student development. She is currently responsible for a module entitled 'Becoming a person', which focuses on the development of vulnerability or resilience across the lifespan and contains a strong emphasis on the child and young person within the context of the family. Her research interests include critical thinking, reflection in nursing, the arts in nursing, and communication skills.

Kenny Keegan

Kenny Keegan is a Mental Health Nursing Lecturer in the School of Health, Nursing and Midwifery at the University of the West of Scotland.

He worked as a mental health nurse for 17 years in a wide variety of clinical environments including care of the elderly, rehabilitation, acute, and forensic mental healthcare. During the 1990s he worked in several seconded research posts within Lanarkshire Health Board and authored and co-authored three major reports concerning service development for severe and enduring mental health needs. Now a qualified higher education teacher he has taught within the pre- and post-registration nursing programmes at the University of the West of Scotland since 2002. His teaching and research interests include ethics, schizophrenia, student nurse reflection, learning and portfolio development.

Angela Kydd

Angela Kydd is a Senior Lecturer in Gerontology within the School of Health, Nursing and Midwifery at the University of the West of Scotland. She is a qualified general and mental health nurse, specialising in the care of older people. She joined the University of the West of Scotland in 1995. During this time she has designed and delivered modules at degree, honours and masters level in gerontology. She has also designed a gerontology programme for the World Health Organization and has taught in Finland, Sweden and Slovenia. She is a visiting professor at the College of Nursing in Jesenice, Slovenia.

For six years she was programme leader for the Nurse Specialist in Gerontological Nursing honours course and for three years was programme manager for an Erasmus Intensive Programme. She was programme lead for three years for the Overseas Nursing Programme and has been a co-ordinator of one of the on-line degree research modules. She has also designed and delivered workshops on aspects of best practice for the care of older people for hospitals, NHS 24, and care homes.

Since 2005, she has been involved in teaching, evaluation and research. One evaluation centred on the effectiveness of a rapid response team in a Scottish Health Board and one for Alzheimer's Scotland on evaluating the process of a training for trainers programme on palliative care and dementia. Her research has included work with colleagues in Sweden on healthcare beliefs of women with diabetes and she is currently working with colleagues from the US, Slovenia and Sweden on attitudes towards healthcare professionals who work with older people.

Angela has run a gerontology interest group for 11 years in the Paisley campus and has recently started one in the Hamilton campus. This is a multi-professional group that meets three times a year to share good practice in the care and well-being of older people.

Angela's PhD study, which was completed in 2006, was on the policy and practice of older people classed as 'delayed discharges'. She has a keen interest in frail older people and has developed a Masters module in frailty which will run in February 2010.

Angela is an active member of the Sigma Theta Tau organisation and a steering group member of the British Society of Gerontology (Scotland), she is also a steering group member of NHS Health Scotland Mental Health and Well Being in Later Life Group.

Glenn Marland

Glenn Marland is Senior Lecturer and Vice Chair of the Mental Health Subject Development Group, within the School of Health, Nursing and Midwifery at the University of the West of Scotland. He is a registered

mental health nurse and has spent most of his career in nurse education. He is committed to team building, innovative curriculum development and effective liaison with stakeholders. His special interests are mental health promotion, research, writing for publication and management and leadership.

Glenn's PhD study explored patterns of medicine taking decision making in people with a diagnosis of schizophrenia in comparison to those with asthma and epilepsy.

Billy Mathers

Billy Mathers is a Lecturer in Mental Health Nursing at the University of the West of Scotland. After qualifying as a mental health nurse he then trained in counselling. Thereafter he worked in forensic units for several years and later as a community psychiatric nurse (CPN) in east London. In his early research he studied the changing role of the CPN in newly formed community mental health teams and the role of the CPN in community depot clinics. This research has been presented at conferences both nationally and internationally.

He commenced working in higher education in 1995 and was for many years module leader for both pre-registration and post-registration mental health nursing programmes. Billy's Doctor in Education study evaluated a training programme for acute mental health nurses and examined ways to increase their therapeutic clinical involvement. He is currently campus lead in the pre-registration mental health nursing programme and campus mental health lead in the mentorship programme.

Gerry McGhee

Gerry McGhee is a Mental Health Lecturer within the School of Health, Nursing and Midwifery at the University of the West of Scotland. He is a registered mental health nurse who specialised in community psychiatry, working as a community psychiatric nurse for eight years. He entered education in 1989 qualifying as a Registered Nurse teacher in 1990. During his time in nurse education he has worked at both undergraduate and postgraduate levels, as well as delivering a variety of in-service training programmes within the NHS.

In 1994 Gerry graduated from the University of Glasgow with a Masters in Nursing specialising in health promotion. During the mid to late 1990s he specialised in this topic, teaching the health promotion theme within the new Project 2000 diploma courses. He has a strong interest in maternal mental health, a subject he taught across all the undergraduate courses.

Gerry's PhD study examined the relationship that developed between a professional care worker and a carer of a person with dementia. He currently has a significant input into the research culture within the University of the West of Scotland, both teaching research methods to undergraduate and postgraduate students as well as supervising students at Masters and PhD levels.

Mary Milligan

Mary Milligan is a Senior Lecturer within the School of Health, Nursing and Midwifery, University of the West of Scotland. She is also currently Vice-chair of the Adult Nursing Subject Development Group within the School.

A Registered Nurse, Mary has worked in nurse education since 1985 and is programme leader for the Diploma of Higher Education in Nursing by open learning, a programme for experienced first and second level nurses. Since 1995 she has been involved in the development and implementation of a process of accrediting experience-derived learning and she is interested in the influence of experiential learning on professional judgement.

Mary is also interested in the influence of perceived boundaries on recruitment, retention, professional development and career progression. Her doctoral study concerned enrolled nurses' experiences of conversion to first level and she is currently involved in the development and evaluation of two modules designed for potential applicants to pre-registration nursing programmes, First Steps to Nursing and Personal Qualities for Nursing.

Stuart Milligan

Stuart Milligan is a member of the team of cancer and palliative care lecturers at the University of the West of Scotland. He is also also employed by Ardgowan Hospice, Greenock as hospice education facilitator. His employment history has included spells as a research biologist (during which he obtained his PhD) and 15 years of nursing practice (including experience in surgical, hospice and community specialist palliative care nursing). In his current role, Stuart is responsible for the delivery of a range of modules at graduate and postgraduate levels. At Ardgowan Hospice, he provides an education service for over 80 staff and contributes to the training of the hospice's considerable team of volunteers.

Stuart plays an active role in developing palliative care in his own locality and further afield. He is currently involved in delivering training on end-of-life care pathways to district nurses and GPs. He advises on the planning and delivery of palliative care services. He also gives talks to community groups, patient groups and schools on topics such as spiritual health and healthy grieving. He is active in palliative care research and has published work on oral care and spirituality. His current research interest is breakthrough pain.

Maria Pollard

Maria Pollard is a Midwife Lecturer and Supervisor of Midwives at the University of the West of Scotland. She qualified as a nurse in 1987 and a midwife in 1990. As a registered midwife she predominantly practised in the labour suite and latterly as a practice development midwife.

Since moving into education she has been involved in the development and teaching of both pre- and pos-

registration programmes and is programme leader for the preparation of supervisors of midwives. As well as education, her main areas of interest are breastfeeding, supervision of midwives and normal childbirth.

Maria is currently studying for a doctorate in education, exploring how student midwives learn about breastfeeding. She was also recently involved in a large interdisciplinary research study on the relationship between the environment, crop elements, diet, nutrition, health and educational outcome in Malawi.

Catherine Rae

Catherine Rae is an Associate Lecturer within the School of Health, Nursing and Midwifery at the University of the West of Scotland (UWS). She is also an Associate Researcher with the Dementia Services Development Centre, Stirling University. Her research is primarily around dementia although in recent years it has included palliative care, learning disability, and dementia as well as research in other health-related areas.

At present Catherine is a distance learning tutor for the BSc Nursing Studies research module as well as undertaking research contracts within the UWS.

Sue Royce

Sue Royce is a Lecturer at the University of the West of Scotland (UWS) within the pre-registration programme and has held this post for nine years. Prior to this she was a Lecturer at Salford University where she taught within the pre- and post-registration programmes. She has been a Registered General Nurse since 1982 and held has held numerous posts within gerontology and rehabilitation, culminating in G grade sister on medical admissions for the over 60s in Lancaster. She has developed modules in the post-registration training at UWS in Respiratory Health and Rehabilitation

She has a BA from the Open University in Sociology and Philosophy and an MA in Health Care Ethics; she has recently become interested in the history of nursing having studied for some post-graduate modules in this subject. She is hoping to return to her PhD studies in the history of nursing at Manchester University in the near future. This study explores the role of the cottage hospital in Scottish rural society, and the role of the nurse within this. She is currently working on an article for publication which explores the role and influence of the nurse in the decision by the islanders to leave St Kilda.

Betty Scholes

Betty Scholes is a Lecturer in Mental Health Nursing within the School of Health, Nursing and Midwifery at the University of the West of Scotland. She is a Registered Mental Nurse and worked in the National Health Service for 20 some years. During this time she practised primarily in adult mental health in both acute in-patient services and community mental health services, working with people experiencing severe and/or enduring mental illness. Before leaving the NHS she worked as a practice education facilitator, supporting mentors and student nurses in the clinical setting. Within her clinical role she also supported the integration of outcome measurement in routine clinical practice. She moved to higher education in 2006 and teaches across the pre-registration programme for mental health nursing students.

Elaine Stevens

Elaine Stevens holds a joint appointment between Ayrshire Hospice and the University of the West of Scotland. She manages the education service at the Hospice and is the Programme Leader for the palliative care named award at degree level within the university. Elaine's main interests are loss, grief and bereavement, decision making at the end of life, pain management, communication issues and palliative day care. Before this Elaine held a number of nursing posts in hospices, including managing palliative day services. She remains lead for education and research for the Association of Palliative Day Care Leaders. Elaine is also current chair of the Palliative Nursing Forum of the Royal College of Nursing. This forum has over 8000 members and the steering group acts as a voice for palliative nurses within the UK. The steering group is regularly involved in commenting on palliative care guidance at international, national and local levels to ensure nurses influence new policies, protocols and standards.

Lesley Storrie

Lesley Storrie is currently a Senior Lecturer within the School of Health Nursing and Midwifery at the University of the West of Scotland. She is a Registered Nurse and Midwife and, following a clinical career as a nurse and midwife, has worked in education for 18 years. During this time she taught on both undergraduate and postgraduate midwifery programmes. From a background in midwifery education, the focus of her career over the last five years has been in the areas of learning and teaching and quality enhancement. She is active in module provision for both nurse and midwifery students and continues to provide consultancy on midwifery issues both internally and externally.

Lesley's doctoral studies were in the field of midwifery education, exploring the nature of knowledge in midwifery and how this affects midwives' readiness to innovate or make changes in practice. Since then her research and scholarly activity have focused on both maternity care-related issues and higher education. Her current research with colleagues relates to student learning styles. In addition she continues to have an active interest in issues related to professional registration.

Boyd Thomson

Boyd Thomson is a Lecturer in Mental Health Nursing within the School of Health, Nursing and Midwifery at the University of the West of Scotland. He is a qualified clinical and nurse teacher. Prior to entering nurse education he held a number of posts in adult and mental health nursing, being dual trained. Since entering nurse education in 1986 he has been involved in the development, delivery and evaluation of a range of undergraduate and postgraduate nursing programmes both in his own institution and as an external examiner for the University of Hertfordshire and Glyndwr University in Wales.

Boyd holds an MSc in Nursing from University of Edinburgh with a dissertation research on the perceived level of skills competence of senior pre-registration students – a comparison of attitudes of clinical staff and students. He is currently involved in the preparation for delivery of a Masters in Nursing programme for mental health nurses.

Linda Wylie

Linda Wylie is a Lecturer and Programme Leader for the BSc Midwifery course at the University of the West of Scotland. Trained as a nurse and later as a midwife in England, she has extensive clinical experience as a midwife, entering education as a midwifery lecturer in Scotland in 1993. Particular interests in midwifery are physiology and promoting normality in childbirth. Previous publications include *Essential anatomy and physiology in maternity care, the midwife's guide to key medical conditions* and as a contributor to *Care of the newborn by ten teachers*.

Introduction

This book is for student nurses and midwives, and all those qualified nurses and other professionals interested in an introduction to the theories of nursing. Understanding the thoughts of the pioneers discussed in this book will help clarify where nursing is now, how it arrived there and where it is likely to go next.

Modern nursing entails caring about people in a competent manner. It involves treating people as partners in evidence-based care. Most nurses would agree with this, but few would stop there. It is not far-fetched to imagine that 10 registered nurses in a room would generate 10 different definitions of nursing. Most will talk about care, compassion and competence. Many will talk about skills, knowledge and evidence. Others may talk about partnership, recovery, dignity and respect. More may focus on the practical application of basic nursing skills, such as addressing the activities of living. Some would talk about eliminating problems whereas others would see their role as enhancing strengths. The notion of basic nursing care would no doubt be central to a lot of these discussions, although it would be unlikely that any two nurses would come to absolute agreement over what that may entail.

This state of affairs is highly unsatisfactory to the novice nurse. It is therefore important to try and demystify nursing theory and this is why this book has been produced. The book traces the origins of nursing theories through their founders and, as such, personalises them. The result is a story instead of a dry decontextualised academic text. For example, it becomes instantly understandable why Faye Abdellah went into nursing when you consider her background. She witnessed helplessly as the Hindenburgh scorched its victims and vowed to become a nurse there and then. Hers was a vocation borne of a desire to do more to help. Her story becomes instantly more interesting given that surely most nurses enter the profession with a similar desire.

The personal aspect is therefore a strength of this book. The reader is given the context within which our selected nursing theorists worked and can relate to them better as a consequence. This may help where the theory under discussion can seem distant and difficult. Nursing theory has evolved through many stages, some of which are more comprehensible than others. As an extreme example Martha Rogers, discussed in Section Four, developed a theory of nursing in space. This appears ridiculous when decontextualised. We urge you to read the chapter yourself and see if you still hold the same opinion afterwards.

Another strength of this book is its structure. While we appreciate that none of these theorists would likely consider him or herself part of any particular school of thought, for the purpose of introducing the general ideas discussed above we have separated the book into five discrete sections.

- Section 1. How did we get here? (The context for the development of the nursing profession)
- Section 2. How do I do the job? (Development of the knowledge and skills required in nursing)
- Section 3. How do I know what people need? (Understanding the problem by reviewing the patients' deficits and strengths)
- Section 4. Grand theories (How does this all fit together?)
- Section 5. What do you want me to do to help? (Working in partnership)

At this point it is important to clarify that this delineation is arbitrary and only used for the purpose of introducing these topics. No theory is just about what is needed to become a nurse or how to diagnose a nursing problem. Likewise partnership is impossible without some sort of theory as to how these aspects of care fit together. All the theorists discussed in this book could quite easily fit into some of the other sections and it is absolutely fair to say that all these nurses belong in Section 5. Nevertheless in order to understand where all these ideas come from it is a useful framework to begin discussion.

Section One

Section One discusses the pioneers such as Florence Nightingale and Mary Seacole who carved out the role of the nurse and professionalised it. These stories may surprise you. For example, Florence Nightingale's story is about great leadership and political awareness as well as the more traditionally held image of the lady and the lamp. This section is more about action and political history than theorising, but it is important to understand these antecedents. All of the following theorists also utilise political acumen and clearly directed action.

Section Two

Section Two gathers together those theorists whose primary concern was to understand what skills and knowledge were required to do the job. This is important to understand since many current guidelines and codes of conduct refer to competencies. What then, are competencies and where did they come from? Carper is considered early in this section, focusing on 'Fundamental patterns of knowing'. This is an interesting story of serendipity given that Carper never envisaged her paper would have the lasting impact it has. Maria Pollard points out that Carper's paper appeared at a time of great change in nursing, and the reader will notice this is an enduring theme throughout the book. Nursing has always been in flux, and the more enduring theories tend to capture something of that flux within the Zeitgeist.

Section Three

A cursory critical analysis of the chapters in Section Two reveals that all these authors also elucidate how they envisage the patient (the term 'patient' is maintained here where appropriate). Section Three specifically concentrates on this area. It introduces those theorists whose focus is on how to conceptualise problems for the purpose of taking action. In other words, how do I know what's wrong with this person in order to use the skills discussed in the previous section? Arguably the most famous of these theories is that of Roper, Logan and Tierney. Their model of the activities of living endures, and it is interesting to note that this journey also started with a quest to understand the nature of nursing, in this case Nancy Roper's PhD study answering the question, 'What is nursing?' in 1976.

Section Four

Section Four is the most difficult to understand. The theorists included here have taken all the ideas discussed in the preceding sections and attempted to integrate them into a coherent whole. The origins of holism are here, and these authors have been referred to as 'grand theorists'. This is because they attempt to explain everything. These authors have been criticised for trying to do too much. Nevertheless some of the most innovative and enduring ideas belong to these people. For example, we currently take for granted the idea of holism underpinning all interventions, but it first appears fully developed within nursing in the writings of Martha Rogers. Despite being criticised for some overly abstract thinking, her work is undoubtedly influential, certainly among many other theorists discussed here, and is therefore important to understand.

Section Five

Section Five goes on to discuss those theorists who have done most to integrate all the components discussed in the four previous sections and apply them in practice. As discussed above all the theories could fit into this section as the application of the theories inevitably involves some sort of partnership in action. However, these theorists have explicitly made this notion central to their theories. Barker, for example, is probably the most influential writer in mental health nursing at present, and the core of his approach is genuinely person-centred. Everything else flows from being with the individual.

Each section begins with an overview of the chapters within, summarising salient points and identifying common themes. All the chapters follow a standard structure. A short profile of the theorist with key dates is provided at the beginning. A short biography then introduces the reader to the theorist. A summary of special interests follows where it is necessary to elaborate on these. This leads onto an outline of their writings, before each theory is articulated in detail. The following part of the chapter then looks at instances of how this theory has been put into practice and what influence this process has had on the wider nursing community. Readers are then shown where they can find out more. Links to other theorists are highlighted. This gives the reader the option to follow a cross-referenced path through the book instead of the traditional linear path. In fact it is highly recommended that the reader does this in order to develop a more coherent understanding of the interconnected nature of these theories.

Of course the people in this book are not the only important nursing theorists. For example, many of the most important mental health nurse theorists, such as Tom Kitwood and Carl Rogers, are not nurses. Other major theorists, such as Jean Watson and Susan Kleiman, have not been included, despite being nurses. This is because a lot of their ideas are addressed in the book by the theorists discussed here. We understand that some may not agree with our choices. Nevertheless this book is about many of the people who have shaped nursing and midwifery as it is today. By the end of it you will have an overview of some of the greatest nursing leaders, clinicians and theorists to date. We hope they inspire you to become one of them.

Section One

How did we get here?

The context for the development of the nursing profession

Overview

This section focuses on the original pioneers of nursing. In the first three chapters this is historically evident as these nurses practised in the 19th century. Nightingale, Seacole and Robb were literally creating an original role in an environment difficult for us to fully comprehend from this distance. Women were deemed subordinate to men, and so had to overcome endemic inequality. Seacole's case is particularly striking as she was also Black. This was a period where Black people could be born into slavery. As such these opening chapters are slightly different in style from the rest of the book in order to contextualise better the extraordinary achievements of these women. None of these first three nurses were theorists as such, although the origins of most nursing theory can be found here. These nurses were trailblazers, and their stories are articulated better by providing more background than is necessary in some of the other chapters.

For example, Nightingale's time as a clinical nurse was comparatively short. She spent most of her young adult life trying to convince her sceptical family that being a nurse was an appropriate use of her talents. This is a significant discussion as nursing was seen as disreputable at the time. She got her wish at 38 and became the legendary 'lady with the lamp'. What is less well known is that she arguably did her most significant work on her return from the Crimea.

The Crimean War has been described as the first war to be reported 'as it happened' in the UK press, and as a consequence her fame rocketed as soldiers returned praising the actions of Nightingale and her nurses. She gained heroine status as a result, and, whilst rejecting personal glory, cleverly set about utilising the fame and authority she acquired.

She spent her last 50 years influencing policy in public health around the world, based on her interpretation of the best evidence available. She forged partnerships with some of the most powerful politicians and academics of her generation. What is even more extraordinary is that she did this largely from the confines of her sick bed.

Austyn Snowden's chapter on Nightingale therefore provides the reader with a greater understanding of her enduring influence by explaining why this work was important to her and how she carried it out. The drive to improve care for as many as possible permeates the actions of all the theorists in this book. Nightingale was among the first to show one way in which this could be done.

Affiliation and partnership were not always available to these early clinicians. Sue Royce comes to the conclusion that Western medicine was not ready for assertive healers like Seacole. In fact it took active steps to discourage her. Nightingale and Seacole were in Scutari at the same time, but it appears Nightingale had no role for her there. Far from being put off by this Seacole instead headed for the front line where she delivered care to soldiers on the battlefield. This persistence in the face of adversity is certainly a common theme amongst these early pioneers. There is also the sense that these women would have made their mark regardless of obstacle or profession. For example, in Robb's case a chance conversation with a colleague led her to change career from teacher to nurse. In actuality she amalgamated the two, showing another quality of these theorists: the ability to make connections. She is described in the chapter as a planner and a director, leader and teacher. Like her influential peers she travelled extensively and she influenced American nursing to a degree very similar to that accomplished in England by Nightingale. She was an extraordinary networker who always saw the value of partnership. She was tragically killed in 1910. Catherine Rae details her achievements and enduring influence.

Lastly, we are brought firmly into the 20th century with Abdellah, who was arguably the first major nursing theorist in the modern sense. Betty Scholes takes us through Abdellah's 60 year career which encompassed a massive range of nurse leadership roles. Her patient-centred approach is similar to but more complex than Henderson's Four Activities for Client Assistance theory discussed in Section Three. It also bears similarity to Orem. Possibly more influential than the theory itself however is the influence of Abdellah's perspective of nursing as a profession in its own right that should be practised within a context of evidence and scientific premise. This is another common thread throughout the book. It could be argued though that Abdellah, like Nightingale, Seacole and Robb, was more of a networker than a theorist. She was certainly intensely political and very clear on the necessity for evidence-based policy and practice based on professional standards. However, whilst we take the importance of an evidence-based profession for granted now, this was not always the case. The nurses discussed in this section laid the foundation stones for the incorporation of these ideas within the modern nursing profession.

CHAPTER I

Florence Nightingale

Austyn Snowden

Biography

Of all human sounds I think the words 'I don't know' are the saddest.
Nightingale, quoted in Cook (1913: xxiii)

There is insufficient room here to do justice to all Florence Nightingale's interests. She was a leader, innovator, politician and a nurse. She was deeply spiritual, with an extraordinary moral agenda. She was a philosopher and mathematician with a remarkable ability to grasp and retain useful information and communicate it in an articulate manner. She made connections others could not, and she put all this energy into improving the health of people around the world. In other words nursing to her was a means rather than an end in itself (McDonald, 2001). As far as she was concerned the more lives she could save the better. In order to provide both a general introduction and as much depth as possible in limited space this chapter therefore focuses on her skills as a researcher in order to better understand her lasting impact on nursing.

Florence Nightingale was born into an upper class family. She was the granddaughter of William Smith, a famous politician and abolitionist. Her mother Fanny was consequently brought up in the company of politicians and aspired to continue the social climb. Her father was born William Shore; he inherited the name Nightingale and £100 000 at the age of 21. As a child Florence preferred the company of her father who, according to Oakley (1981), was charming and funny, intelligent and engaging but also listless and bleak at times. He is credited with educating his daughters at home. This was highly unusual in Victorian society which generally held that education would make women ill, as they were considered mentally, physically and morally inferior.

In line with the spirit of the time, Florence's older sister Parthenope preferred domestic activities with her mother. Florence on the other hand enjoyed political and religious speculation with her father, sharing his humorous but gloomy outlook and gifts of analysis and abstract thinking (Boyd, 1982). By the age of six Florence was making graphs on the efficacy of prayer. She would keep a record of what she had prayed for and what had subsequently been granted in order to compare the two. Aged nine, she was reading Homer in Greek. By her early 20s she was corresponding on philosophy, theology and sanitation with some of the most powerful thinkers and public servants of her era (Bostridge, 2008). This appears to have come at a personal cost however. Florence did not believe herself to be like others, a source of some distress to her as a child. She went through a period when could not bear to be looked at for she feared others would discover the monster she believed herself to be (Holliday and Parker, 1997: 484).

Although Florence was attractive, intelligent and very popular with young men she found the life of a Victorian lady vacuous and depressing. She appears to have made significant efforts to please her mother and sister by trying to conform to societal expectations but ultimately could not bring herself to do so. She turned down an offer of marriage from Richard Monckton Milnes, a man she was clearly in love with in order to pursue what she considered to be a higher quest. During this period Nightingale

Profile

Florence Nightingale is globally considered to be the founder of modern nursing. Whilst being most often remembered as the 'lady with the lamp' for her work in the Crimea, her most significant work came after this with her tireless reform of sanitation and public health and her promotion of evidence-based nursing.

Key dates

1837	God spoke to her at Embley, but she is not clear on how to 'serve' Him.
1850/1	Attends Kaiserswerth for nurse training
1853	Her father gives her a yearly allowance of £500
1854/5	Travels to Scutari to care for wounded soldiers from Crimean War
1858	William Farr supports her application to Statistical Society of London
1859	*Notes on nursing* published
1860	The Nightingale Training School for nurses opens at St. Thomas Infirmary
1871	*Notes on lying in institutions* (her analysis of midwifery) published
1872	Red Cross founder Henri Dunant claims Nightingale's work influenced his ideas
1894	Isobel Hampton Robb delivers paper written by Nightingale to Worlds Fair in Chicago
1907	November, King Edward VII bestows the Order of Merit, the first time the Order is given to a woman

accompanied her mother on her goodwill visits to the sick and found these visits both meaningful and satisfying. It is likely her interest in caring developed here (Smith, 1981) and there are records of her going alone into the local village to help the sick as best she could (Bostridge, 2008).

Around her 17th birthday Florence had the first of four religious revelations. The notion of nursing being a 'calling' can be traced to her statement

God spoke to me and called me to His service.

Although initially unsure how to follow this calling, by the time she was 24 she realised she wanted to become a nurse. Her mother fiercely opposed this idea however, and for the next 15 years attempted to dissuade Florence from pursuing this course. This becomes more understandable given that most nurses at the time were men who had a reputation for drunkenness and dishonesty. During this time Florence furtively studied public health and hospital statistics (Spiegelhalter, 1999) and wrote her book *Suggestions for thought,* which is discussed later in this chapter. This activity proved therapeutic and encouraged her to follow her 'calling'. In 1851 and 1852 she travelled to the Institute of Deaconesses in Kaiserswerth, Germany, to train as a nurse. Nurses learned solely through experience and Florence treated sick people, distributed medicine, and assisted during operations. She was reported to be very happy and stated:

We learned to think of our work, not ourselves.

Her family meanwhile was less happy. Parthenope particularly seemed to take great exception to her sister's 'unnatural and unsisterly behaviour' and suffered what is described as a 'nervous breakdown' (Holliday and Parker, 1997: 485) as a consequence. This paradoxically freed Florence to pursue nursing as a career due to the family doctor insisting that the sisters be kept separate for the sake of Parthenope's health. Under doctor's orders, Florence's father therefore granted Florence an allowance and hence financial independence from the family.

The Nightingales had connections at the very highest level. The family was friends and neighbour with Lord Palmerston, the prime minister of UK during the Crimean War. Florence was also supported within the war office by Sidney Herbert, another prominent politician of the time. With these powerful connections she was able to put her theories into practice, and at the age of 38 finally became the leader and inspirational nurse she wanted to be. Cook (1913) makes the point that this was not an act of 'sacrifice' on her part but a fulfilment of the desire for a life of active usefulness. She took a team of 38 nurses to Scutari and it was here that she and her famous lamp worked through the night, comforting the sick and dying from the Crimean war. The conditions were appalling. During January and February 1854 she saw 3000 soldiers die of frostbite, gangrene, dysentery and other diseases in four miles of beds 18 inches apart. She regularly worked 20 hours a day and her own quarters were vermin infested and cramped. Her impact on mortality rates is questionable and varies according to source. The uncritical view is that she reduced mortality from 43% to 2% in six months (Burney, 2008). The hostile view (Williams, 2008) is that she made matters worse by undermining the actions of the local doctors. The balanced view is that mortality reduced from 43% to 2% over the course of the war although the reduction is most likely to have been a consequence of unblocking the sewers after the first winter (Maindonald, 2004). While Nightingale realised the impact of this, as is clear in her focus on hygiene in her writing, it is not clear she was instrumental in Scutari. What is crystal clear however is the impact that her caring had on the soldiers.

The men returning home spoke glowingly of their treatment by the nurses and in particular Florence Nightingale. This turned her into a media heroine. No other war had been so extensively covered by the press and Nightingale's actions were a potent antidote to the public relations disaster the war had become (Williams, 2008). Nightingale was quick to recognise the power this brought and used it to garner better equipment and supplies. She contracted a near fatal illness (probably brucellosis, an infectious disease largely transmitted by contaminated animal products) the following May, and despite being urged to go home remained in Scutari convalescing until the last soldier had gone home, 21 months after her arrival.

While Nightingale clearly understood and used the power she had gained through becoming a media heroine, there is equally compelling evidence to suggest that she did not enjoy the status personally. Scholars of Nightingale (Bostridge, 2005) believe celebrity would not have sat comfortably with her notion of religious servitude. She refused the receptions planned in her honour on return from the Crimea and instead became an invalid, retiring to bed for the rest of her life. Her illness has been the subject of historical speculation. Some authors believe it to be an extension of the brucellosis she contracted in the Crimea, whilst others believe there to have been nothing wrong at all (Woodham-Smith, 1951). Wisner et al. (2005) believe her to have been a lifelong sufferer of bipolar illness with psychotic features. Mackowiak and Batten (2008) make a solid case for post-traumatic stress disorder, although this does not explain her pre-morbid personality.

She most certainly complained of anorexia, fatigue, depression, dyspnoea and palpitations. It is certain that, in being thwarted by her family and being exposed to thousands of soldiers dying, she felt the stress now believed to be causal in most psychiatric problems (Kingdon and Turkington, 2004). This did not stop her working, however, and she wrote prolifically to the Queen, the Government and any influential doctors to carry on her reforms. Although she is most remembered as the 'lady with the lamp', she spent the following 50 years influencing nursing reform, sanitisation and hospital design in Britain and beyond (Mackowiak and Batten 2008: 1160), India in particular. She died aged 90, having made a significant contribution to public health worldwide.

Special interest: Some key concepts

In order to understand Nightingale's focus it is important to understand the wider context within which caring was conceptualised in the early 19th century. Around the turn of the century the study of medicine had radically altered for the first time in nearly 2000 years. Prior to this time medicine had broadly followed the Galenic principles of the four humours (Bynum, 2008). This idea that health equated to balance was grounded in ancient Greek ideas of sickness and health (Elstad and Torjuul, 2009), where sickness was understood in terms of excess or lack of one of the four humours: black bile, yellow bile, phlegm and blood. Physicians practising Galenic medicine were therefore concerned with the whole body in a general sense in order to rebalance the system. Anything requiring local intervention at specific sites of the body, such as boils and broken bones, were the remit of the surgeon. Florence Nightingale's life spans the demise of this way of thinking and this is probably why traces of it remain in her writing (Nightingale, 1849/1980: 99).

The demise of Galenic medicine was gradual. However, much of it can be understood as an extension of what happened after the French Revolution. The revolution had stripped physicians of their authority but not their necessity. The French, realising that they still needed medical attention, put the previously disparate components of medicine together under one broad umbrella (Bynum, 2008: 46). Medicine subsequently became concerned not just with the whole but also with the specific. While not entirely new medicine came to embrace three principles:

- Physical diagnosis
- Pathologico-clinical correlation
- The use of large numbers of cases to elucidate diagnostic categories and to evaluate therapy.

This is important as our current systems of diagnosis and disease classification have their origins here. The International Classification of Diseases (ICD) is about to release its 11th edition (Sartorious, 2009). This is a massive worldwide collaborative effort coordinated by the World Health Organisation (WHO). However, it started its life as the International Classification of Death in 1893 (WHO, 2009). The groundwork for this project had been done largely by the Statistical Society of London. Florence Nightingale was the first woman member of this organisation (Spiegelhalter, 1999) and therefore has a place as one of the founders of modern concepts of disease.

Statistics played a massive part in Nightingale's life. She developed her love of mathematics as a child and continued to see it as a source of ultimate understanding. This belief was spiritual according to Spiegelhalter (1999). She was deeply influenced by the Belgian mathematician Adolphe Quetelet who advanced the idea that nature and the physical environment could be understood in mathematical terms. Nature could therefore be ultimately understood through proper statistical analysis (Kudzma, 2006). This concept sat well with Nightingale and in 1870 she expressed the belief that statistics reveal 'the character of God' and that there was a

Links with other theorists

Florence Nightingale has links, in particular, with Mary Seacole (*see Chapter 2*), Isobel Hampton Robb (*see Chapter 3*), Hildegard Peplau (*see Chapter 26*) and Virginia Henderson (*see Chapter 11*).

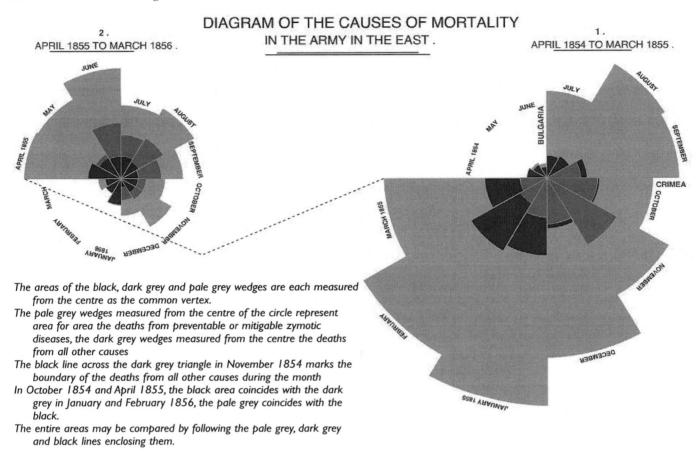

The areas of the black, dark grey and pale grey wedges are each measured from the centre as the common vertex.

The pale grey wedges measured from the centre of the circle represent area for area the deaths from preventable or mitigable zymotic diseases, the dark grey wedges measured from the centre the deaths from all other causes

The black line across the dark grey triangle in November 1854 marks the boundary of the deaths from all other causes during the month

In October 1854 and April 1855, the black area coincides with the dark grey in January and February 1856, the pale grey coincides with the black.

The entire areas may be compared by following the pale grey, dark grey and black lines enclosing them.

Figure 1.1. Reproduction of a Florence Nightingale polar chart. Reproduced courtesy of Zachary Forest Johnson.

subsequent duty to apply 'statistics to the reform of the world' (Diamond and Stone, 1981). Even when she was exhausted, believing herself to have only a short time to live, 'the sight of long columns of figures was perfectly reviving to her' (Spiegelhalter, 1999: 47 quoting Florence's cousin Hilary Bonham Carter). It is easy to see why she was referred to as the 'passionate statistician' (McDonald, 2001).

One of her greatest assets was to combine her understanding of the need for statistics with her ability to communicate them in a manner likely to be meaningful to policy makers. To this end she developed the use of specific types of pie charts (polar area charts) to illustrate her findings. *Figure 1.1* shows all causes of mortality being greatly reduced in her second year in the Crimea (on the left) as opposed to the first. A month-by-month breakdown of mortality by cause illustrates instantly what may not have been read in detail by policy makers. The dark grey segments are deaths by wounds and the pale grey segments deaths by preventable disease. The black segments entail other causes.

She worked closely with William Farr for over 20 years (Kudzma, 2006) and it was Farr who suggested she join the Statistical Society of London. Their partnership enabled her to simultaneously extend her interests to comparisons of military and civilian death rates and also ensure her analyses were valid. Farr sent her statistical summaries of civil hospital data across the

British Empire and she sent him her observations of the British Army (Cope, 1958). The purpose of this and other collaborations was to understand better the depth of the issues the statistics referred to in order to infer appropriately from them. In this respect she clearly understood the limitation of general statistics and the subsequent potential for bias and misinterpretation. The following issues remain prescient today:

- Inadequate control for the type of patient under study (comparing different groups while assuming they are equivalent).
- Data manipulation (only reporting supportive or negating data).
- The use of single outcome measures (such as mortality, without describing the type and context of the mortality).

These issues took centre stage during an attempt to use evidence to demonstrate the necessity for trained nurses (McDonald, 2001). A previous study had provided evidence that mortality rates had not dropped as a consequence of deploying trained nurses. However, this conclusion (only reporting negating data) was based on non-randomised interventions (inadequate control) where the trained nurses looked after the most complex cases and hence those that were more likely to die (use of a single outcome measure).

In other words the statistics in this study were misleading. They did not compare like with like and therefore the conclusions were incomplete. At the time Nightingale pointed out that the mortality rate of any institution would primarily have been down to its sanitation, the severity of the cases treated and the type of treatment offered. Only if these were comparable could any assumptions be made on the efficacy of nursing.

A similar issue applied to studies in midwifery at the time (McDonald, 2006). A Parisian study had shown a higher mortality rate among women treated by trained midwives in comparison to those giving birth at home. This was taken as evidence of the inefficacy of midwifery but Nightingale again strongly challenged this assumption. Hindsight showed that, as she had predicted, hygiene was a more fundamental factor. It was custom at the time for midwives in Paris to conduct or attend the autopsy of women who died in childbirth. While the autopsies provided no useful information they ensured that further women would be infected. Hand washing would have significantly reduced mortality rates.

This desire to get to the heart of the matter in order to improve care permeated her work. Florence Nightingale above all else was interested in accumulating data to approximate the truth as she understood it. In this she can rightly be regarded as one of the originators of evidence-based nursing (McDonald, 2001).

Summary of writings

Nightingale wrote extensively. She wrote thousands of letters. of which over 14 000 remain (Bostridge, 2008) and this body of work is known to be one of the most voluminous written by any single individual (Agnew, 1958). The *Collected works of Florence Nightingale* series edited by Lynn McDonald runs to 16 volumes. References are provided at the end of the chapter for the interested reader to access some of these primary sources. By way of introduction her first two books will be the focus of discussion here.

Her first book, *Suggestion for thought,* was a rambling three volume tome. The first volume entailed an outline for a new philosophical religion including the development of a sisterhood for educated women. The second volume entailed research into religious psychology and the third volume focused on issues of morality. The overarching theme of these volumes is that God works through people in order to perfect them (Holliday and Parker, 1997). It is from the second volume that the novel Cassandra was taken. In this she asks,

> *Why is it that women have passion, intellect, moral activity, and a place in society where not one of these three can be exercised?*

She refers to women feeling as if they are going mad due to the fact that they have nothing to do all day (Woodham-Smith, 1951).

Cassandra is almost certainly autobiographical, although Nightingale herself denied this when questioned directly. Cassandra is a character from Greek mythology who is provided with the gift of prophecy by Apollo. When Cassandra refuses Apollo's romantic advances he places a curse on her, ensuring that no-one will believe or heed her prophecies. Cassandra was therefore left with the knowledge of future events but no power to alter them. It is easy to see how Florence Nightingale could empathise with this myth of imposed powerlessness. In Cassandra she makes the point that the fictional heroines of the time had few family ties and rarely a mother. Cassandra can therefore be read as a ferocious attack on Victorian Britain from the perspective of a frustrated and thwarted prisoner of that society. On reading Cassandra for the first time Virginia Woolf considered it to be 'more

References

Agnew LR (1958) Florence Nightingale – statistician. *American Journal of Nursing* **58**: 664–5

Andrews GJ (2003) Nightingale's geography. *Nursing Inquiry* **10**(4): 270–4

Blanchard EB, Jones-Alexander J, Buckley TC, Forneris CA (1996) Psychometric properties of the PTSD checklist. *Behavioural Research and Therapy* **34**: 669–73

Bostridge M (2005) *Women of the world unite*. Available from: http://www.guardian.co.uk/books/2005/jan/29/featuresreviews.guardianreview35 [accessed 4th December 2009]

Bostridge M (2008) *Florence Nightingale, the making of an icon*. Farrar, Straus and Giroux, New York

Boyd N (1982) *Josephine Butler, Octavia Hill, Florence Nightingale. Three Victorian women who changed their world*. Macmillan, London.

Burney R (2008) T*he brilliance of Florence Nightingale*. Available from: http://www.mwaohn.org/florencenightingale.html [accessed 4th December 2009]

Bynum W (2008) T*he history of medicine: A very short introduction*. Oxford University Press, Oxford

Cohen IB (1984) Florence Nightingale. *Scientific American* **250**: 128–36.

Cook ET (1913) *The life of Florence Nightingale*. Macmillan Company, London

Cope Z (1958) *Florence Nightingale and the Doctors*. JB Lippincott, Philadelphia

Diamond M, Stone M (1981) Nightingale on Quetelet. *Journal of the Royal Statistical Society A* **144**: 66–79

Elstad I, Torjuul K (2009) The issue of life: Aristotle in nursing perspective. *Nursing Philosophy* **10**: 275–86

Goodrick E, Reay T (2010)
Florence Nightingale
endures: Legitimizing a new
professional role identity.
Journal of Management Studies
47(1): 55–84

Holliday ME, Parker DL (1997)
Florence Nightingale, feminism
and nursing. *Journal of
Advanced Nursing* **26**: 483–8

Johnson ZF (2008) *Nightingale's
roses in action*. Available
from: http://indiemaps.com/
blog/2008/10/nightingales-
roses-in-actionscript-3/ [last
accessed 19th Jan 2010]

Keith JM (1988) Florence
Nightingale: Statistician and
consultant epidemiologist.
International Nursing Review
35: 147–50

Kingdon D, Turkington D
(2004) *Cognitive therapy of
schizophrenia*. Guilford Press,
New York

Krozier B, Erb G (1987)
Fundamentals of nursing.
Addison-Wesley, Menlo Park,
CA

Kudzma EC (2006) Florence
Nightingale and healthcare
reform. *Nursing Science
Quarterly* **19**(1): 61–4

Mackowiak PA, Batten SV (2008)
Post-traumatic stress reactions
before the advent of post
traumatic stress disorder:
Potential effects on the lives
and legacies of Alexander the
Great, Captain James Cook,
Emily Dickinson and Florence
Nightingale. *Military Medicine*
173(12): 1158–63

Maindonald J (2004) This
passionate study: A dialogue
with Florence Nightingale.
Journal of Statistics Education
12(1). Available from: http://
www.amstat.org/publications/
JSE/v12n1/maindonald.html
[accessed 7th December 2009]

McDonald L (2001) Florence
Nightingale and the early
origins of evidence-based
nursing. *EBN notebook* **4**:
68–70

          ld L (2006) *Florence*

like screaming than writing' and John Stuart Mill had earlier been struck by its representation of the Victorian family as an 'instrument of tyranny' (Bostridge, 2005).

There are different versions of Cassandra, ranging from the first version that depicts a conversation between parents and their two daughters with many fantastic and imaginative asides; to the final version written in the third person and devoid of the personal. The latter version paradoxically betrays the personal aspect of the novel more than the original fictitious version according to Bostridge (2005). That is, later in her life she attempted to reword the novel in order to replace the autobiographical elements with a more general emphasis on the plight of all women at the time. In the first version the tragic heroine clearly mirrors Nightingale's position of idle confinement and welcomes death at the age of 30 (Nightingale's age at the time) as the only means of escape.

It was discussed in the previous section that Nightingale had embraced the new ideas about health care developed in France in the early 19th century. This is only true to a degree. Change does not happen all at once and, as discussed in the special interest section, late varieties of Galenic medicine persisted for some time (Elstad and Torjuul, 2009). For example, Nightingale was taught 'cupping' at Kaiserworth in mid-century, a technique used by Galen in Roman times that entailed placing heated cups on a patient's back to draw blood. As a general principle she continued to believe, like Galen, that nature, not medical intervention, played the largest part in healing. The first part of *Notes on nursing* clearly states her philosophy:

> *As a general principle…all disease…is more or less a reparative process, not necessarily accompanied with suffering: an effort of nature to remedy a process of poisoning and decay.*
>
> (Nightingale, 1848/1980: i)

In order to truly understand her philosophy of nursing, however, you have to read the whole book. Written in 1858, the style is unmistakably Victorian, full of asides and annotations, often melodramatic, and contains very little of what would currently be considered high quality evidence to support the sweeping claims. Nevertheless it is clearly passionate, articulate, humorous in places and unique in its time. Most of the book is delivered as a critique of nursing and care in general and nurses and visitors alike are berated as ignorant, unobservant nuisances to the patient who often do more harm than good. There are many pages about the benefits of fresh air and the need to understand airflow patterns through a room and its adjoining corridors. There are chapters on noise, light and personal hygiene. The theme that persists throughout however is contemporary and relevant: engaged observation is key to good nursing care. In fact this keen sense of gathering facts in order to understand and improve health pervades all her writing.

Influence

There are over 1000 published books still in print concerning the works of Florence Nightingale, more than the rest of the theorists discussed in this book put together. The books range from scholarly well-balanced analyses to sycophantic fiction. What is absolutely clear however, particularly in the centenary of her death, is the enduring existence of a remarkable legacy to nursing.

Nursing has become increasingly concerned over the last few decades with attempts to define itself. The rest of this book holds testament to this. In order to understand where we are it is necessary to know where we have been, and for many historians this question leads back to Florence

Nightingale. Even without discussing the theorists in this book there is plenty of evidence that modern nursing has roots in her work. As discussed, many place her as the originator of evidence-based nursing (Keith, 1988; McDonald, 2001; Bostridge, 2005), but there are also numerous wider claims, and more modern ideas claim to originate with Nightingale. For example Andrews (2003) argues that the study of the dynamics between nursing, space and place should be deemed the 'geography of nursing'. Andrews goes on to trace the roots of this new field of theoretical study to Florence Nightingale by reinterpreting her *Notes on nursing*. Krozier and Erb (1987) put forward the argument that the concepts of holism and patient autonomy are consistent with Florence Nightingale's vision at the turn of the century. However it should be noted that this interpretation is in sharp contrast to Young's (2009) reading of *Notes on nursing*. He believes Nightingale clearly places the nurse as expert and the patient as recipient and concludes that the book gives no directions on how to determine patient preference or understand individual experience in order to promote self-management. This he says is wholly inconsistent with modern ideas of autonomy and holism.

In these diverse interpretations of her work it can be seen she can be viewed as the originator or antithesis of modern nursing, the example for others to follow or the error for others to avoid. In many ways the plethora of writing she left has given more room than usual to provide evidence to support these conflicting perspectives. Just about any idea can be associated with her given enough searching. For example, it is true that *Notes on nursing* is inconsistent with modern concepts of choice. All literature of the time was. But it is also true that Nightingale talks as much about holistic nursing care as any modern theorist. Krozier and Erb (1987) and Young (2009) are therefore both right.

Many writers take it for granted she was a feminist, even when faced with her overtly antifeminist views. For example, see Stark's (1979) introduction to the Feminist Press publication of Cassandra. Nightingale was certainly an independent thinker and woman of extraordinary vision and privilege. She used these gifts to carve a new profession out for women. In this she was leader and inspirer of women. It is also clear however that she disapproved of the women's rights movement, believing it to be ill focused. In fact she devotes the last paragraph of *Notes on nursing* to her rejection of the ideas. She believed in being the best one can be and considered rights as subordinate. You will recall from her biography that she appeared most happy when not thinking about herself. Regardless, feminist writers often claim her as one of their own. According to Holliday and Parker (1997) she found very few women throughout her lifetime with whom she could relate and was broadly disappointed with the lack of mental power she met among women. She often referred to herself as a 'man of action' (Stark, 1979: 19).

What is most significant from these discussions is therefore the place given to Nightingale in these debates. Few argue that she was the first professional nurse as understood in modern terms and as such she has long been held up as the ideal nurse (Goodrick and Reay, 2010). Over the years, what has been highlighted about her has changed but she continues to be presented as a symbol of modern nursing, regardless of the nature of those changes.

Her enduring impact is even more extraordinary in light of her retreat from society following her return from the Crimea. That is, she very rarely saw more that one visitor at a time and so was never privy to informal discourse. Maintaining an understanding of politics sufficient to exert genuine reform from this position is remarkable. Her mathematical prowess coupled with her moral focus and strategic understanding appears to have

Nightingale: Maternal mortality and gender politics. Paper for the History of Nursing Conference of the Canadian Association for the History of Nursing June 2006, St Paul's Hospital, Vancouver, B.C. Available from: http://www.sociology.uoguelph.ca/fnightingale/Public%20Health%20Care/maternal.htm [accessed 16th December 2009]

Nightingale F (1848/1980) *Notes on nursing.* Churchill Livingstone, Edinburgh

Oakley A (1981) *Subject women.* Martin Robertson, Oxford

Rosenburg C (1992) *Explaining epidemics and other studies in the history of medicine.* Cambridge University Press, London

Sartorious N (2009) Progress in the development of ICD-11 and DSM-V classifications of mental disorders. *European Journal of Psychiatry* **24**(S1): S40

Smith FB (1981) Florence Nightingale. Reputation and power. Croom Helm, London

Spiegelhalter DJ (1999) Surgical Audit: Statistical lessons from Nightingale and Codman. *Journal of the Royal Statistical Society* **161**(1): 45–58

Stark M (1979) *Florence Nightingale's angry outcry against the forced idleness of Victorian women. Cassandra.* The Feminist Press, City University of New York

Williams K (2008) Reappraising Florence Nightingale. *British Medical Journal* 337: 1461–3

Wisner KL, Bostridge M, Mackowiak PA (2005) A case of glimmering gloom. *Pharos,* **Autumn**: 4–13

Woodham-Smith P (1951) *Florence Nightingale 1820–1910.* McGraw-Hill, New York.

World Health Organisation (2009) *History of the development of the ICD.* Available from: http://www.who.int/classifications/icd/en/HistoryOfICD.pdf

[accessed 6th December 2009]
Young N (2009) Lessons from
a Guru. *Nursing Standard*
23(19): 20–2

Where to find out more

- Cook ET (1913) *The life
  of Florence Nightingale*.
  Macmillan Company, London

Available as a free download
from: http://departments.kings.edu/
womens_history/florence.html

- http://www.sociology.uoguelph.
  ca/fnightingale/publications/
  index.htm

This website gives details of the
collective works of Florence
Nightingale meticulously gathered
by Lynn McDonald. It is the
ultimate primary source.

- http://www.gap-system.
  org/~history/Obits/Nightingale.
  html

This website contains
Nightingale's obituary in *The
Times*

- http://www.rcn.org.
  uk/development/
  researchanddevelopment/rs/
  research2010

This website contains details of the
Royal College of Nursing's 2010
conference.

been consistently coherent to policy makers of the time. She did not always
hold consistent attitudes according to Rosenburg (1992), but her relentless
pursuit of public health improvement grounded in evidence-based nursing
ensures her legend endures, given that these dual aims remain at the
forefront of nursing today.

Where to find out more

Practically every nurse theorist has a view on the impact of Florence
Nightingale. They all interpret her work from a particular perspective. For
example, I have stressed her mathematical and statistical abilities. I have not
mentioned her vast impact on nurse education at all. There is therefore no
substitute for the real thing. Go to the primary sources. For example *Notes
on nursing* is only just over 100 pages and makes a fascinating read. It is
difficult not to be caught up by the energy, passion and insight this little
book offers into the life, times and ideas of the 'founder of nursing'. In the
book she covers topics from hygiene to homeopathy, women's fashion and
wallpaper. She talks about fresh air, noise and light and offers prescriptions
with the forthright certainty that what she conveys is the truth. Her ideas
are contrasted throughout with habits and practices of thoughtless people
and it is easy to see how these ideas proved seminal. The book was a huge
bestseller in its time.

Shortly after her death the family commissioned a biography. Whilst the
biography has been criticised for being biased, Cook's (1913) book *The life
of Florence Nightingale*, is extremely well thought of and easily accessible.
Its strength is in its use of primary sources that are replicated within the
book. There are examples of her handwritten letters along with portraits and
drawings of her. The introduction sets out clearly the structure of the book
and the overview provides an excellent summary of her life for those who
only want to study a particular aspect of her life.

For those interested in interpretive works there are over 1000 textbooks
and countless more websites and journal articles focused on her life and
works. I would recommend peer reviewed literature where possible, and
the references accompanying this chapter would be a good place to start.
One of the most recently critically acclaimed books was written by Mark
Bostridge. The last chapter of this book is particularly interesting as it gives
some insight into how her legend has been constructed and reconstructed
since her death.

Finally, 2010 is the centenary of her death. If you are fortunate enough to
be reading this in 2010 you will find numerous events being held around the
world in her honour. Although these are unlikely to provide a deep critical
analysis of her work they will nevertheless celebrate a unique woman and
will no doubt promote a healthy discourse. Conduct a local search to find
out times and venues near you. As an example in UK the Royal College of
Nursing is coordinating their annual international research conference to
coincide with international nurses day on 12th May, Florence's birthday.
The 2010 conference will include additional centenary events that reflect
Florence Nightingale's contribution to patient care and research.

It is unlikely, however, that 2010 will be the last celebration. Every
year has a 'week of the nurse' and this also coincides with the birthday of
Florence Nightingale. .

CHAPTER 2

Mary Seacole
Sue Royce

Biography

Mary Seacole was born in 1805 on the island of Jamaica. Her mother was a Jamaican Creole and a doctress, her father was a Scotsman in the army stationed in Kingston. Doctress literally means female doctor, however this was an alien concept for women in Europe and even within the US. The trials and tribulations of Sophia Jex-Blake, Elizabeth Garrett and others shows the difficulty women had even to gain admission to study medicine, let alone qualify as a doctor (Jex-Blake, 1970). However, for Seacole, within her native Jamaica, it was common for Creole and Afro-Caribbean women to practise medicine. The social standing that Mary's mother gained by being a doctress and the wealth she had accumulated enabled her marriage to Sergeant Grant, an Officer in the British army, to take place. During this period slavery was still in existence, and Mary's mother was held in such esteem that she was considered 'a free women'. This was extremely unusual for men of colour, even more so for women of colour. This status of free woman continued into the next generation and when Mary was born she too was considered free.

Mary's mother owned and ran a hotel/boarding house where soldiers stayed for both recreational purposes and for treatment by Mary's mother. Mary herself was very proud of her background, 'There is good Scottish blood flowing through these veins' (Seacole, 1857) and took this Scottish gene to be the cause of her drive and ambition,

Many people have traced to my Scotch blood that energy and activity which are not always found in the Creole race.

(Seacole 1857: 6)

This drive enabled her to contemplate travel, work and education that would, in other women and in more traditional settings, not have been considered appropriate or fitting for a young woman. This pride in her nationality also perhaps explains her interest in the British Empire.

In 1836 Mary married Edwin Horatio Hamilton Seacole, godson of the British Naval hero, Lord Nelson. They were married for eight years. During this time Mary describes her husband as being of a delicate nature and requiring her skills. After his death she returned to her mother's house and continued to improve her nursing/doctress skills.

In 1851 she travelled first to Panama to visit her brother who had set up hotel/boarding house and then on to Cuba, two extremely unconventional destinations for a single woman to even consider visiting, let alone stay. In Cuba she set up boarding houses/hotels by herself giving lodgings to travellers and new arrivals, as well as treating injuries of the workers and injuries incurred from the frontier-type existence that prevailed. This perhaps is the first indication of her tenacity and desire to give aid to those in need utilising her medical and nursing skills.

Whilst these were dangerous and exciting times for Mary, they gave her increased skills and understanding which were to be of great benefit to her and to those she subsequently treated in the Crimean war. It was her involvement in the care of soldiers in the Crimean war that made Mary both a national and

Mary Seacole
1805–1881

Profile

Mary Seacole was a women and an adventuress at a time when it was seen to be unfit, unwise and immoral to be travelling alone, let alone travelling and intending to make her own way in the world.

Mary was admired not just for her bravery, diligence and skills but also because she cared. This caring attitude and the way she encouraged her patients to call her mother, endeared her to those with whom she came in contact.

She was a woman of colour who despised racism of any kind. She was a person born ahead of her time.

Key dates

1826	Mary returns to Jamaica after her second visit to Britain
1833	All slaves in the British Empire are freed by a new law from William Wilberforce
1836	Mary marries Edwin Seacole
1837	Victoria is crowned
1843	Mary's hotel in Kingston is burned down
1850	Mary travels to Panama
1853	Mary tries to be recruited by Nightingale
1854	Mary sails for the Crimea to nurse British soldiers
1856	Crimean war ends
1857	Mary's book is published
1860	Nightingale starts the first acknowledged school of nursing
1867	A second fund is launched to raise money for Mary
1881	Mary Seacole dies. Her grave is in St Mary's catholic cemetery, Harrow, London

international heroine. However, her route to the Crimea was not to be an easy one. She was rejected by both the War Office and Florence Nightingale's nurses, despite the fact that she had many references from soldiers she had nursed in Jamaica and beyond. This did not deter Mary. She and a distant relative set up a general store and hotel in Balaclava, near the British camp in Crimea. They called this the British Hotel. So, at the age of 50, with her life-learned skills and a stock of medicines, she went to the battlefields to sell provisions and medicines to those who could afford to pay.

Using the money gained from selling her skills and medicines she bought more provisions and medicines to give to those in need who were unable to pay. Some army doctors were suspicious of her at first; fortunately others realised her skills and talents and utilised them fully. The talents, knowledge and skills she had accumulated during her life, in particular her knowledge of nursing patients with cholera and other infectious diseases, established her as competent and capable and the army doctors utilised her skills well. She was in the thick of the battlefield unlike Nightingale's hospital based at Scutari, which was several hundred miles away, requiring both a land and sea journey for the injured soldiers. Mary performed her duties and attended to soldiers whilst under fire and often in freezing conditions, unconcerned as to the nationality of the soldiers but working where and when care was required. It was here that she obtained the name 'Mother Seacole'.

It was WH Russell, the first modern war correspondent, who made Mary a national heroine and internationally famous. As Russell states

I trust that England will never forget one who nursed her sick and sought out her wounded to aid and succour them.

(Seacole, 1857: 3)

In 1856 the Crimean war ended. Mary found herself in financial difficulty and she and her partner were declared bankrupt. However, she had won the hearts of the British people and many public appeals were made on her behalf, including one by Queen Victoria. She returned to London where she was the toast of 19th century London society and she was awarded the Crimean medal. Her autobiography published in 1857 was a great success. In 1873 Mary was appointed as masseuse to the Princess of Wales. The Crimean war memorial, unveiled in 1859, included Nightingale but not Seacole. Her final years were spent in obscurity and she died on the 14th of November 1881. It is only recently that the enormity of her contribution to nursing has been made public and acknowledged and a memorial statue is due to be erected in London in the near future. She is a guiding light and inspiration to the nurses that followed her. Many nursing departments have buildings named after her and have created awards and funding in

her name. She is considered a national hero in Jamaica, and is also on the list of the 100 Great Black Britons.

Context

Jamaica is the largest of the Caribbean islands, 20 miles south of Cuba. Sugar plantations were the economic mainstay of the island and they spread to every parish in Jamaica by the 18th century. It was common for male British colonisers to mix with local women (Bush, 1990). Some, as did Mary's parents, mimicked the formal marriage of the West. In order to understand the society in which Mary lived one needs to understand the role of women within that society. As Bush (1990: 34) suggests there was a complex stratification of slaves, with women slaves being generally less favourably seen than their male counterparts. This was further complicated by the social hierarchy between Black and coloured, African and Creole. Most of the slave elite was male; the only female salves to be held in high esteem were midwives, doctresses or chief housekeepers. As a doctress Mary's mother was considered highly useful within the plantation hospital.

Mary's mother also used her skills with the White population, including the soldiers based there and shared her knowledge with the medical doctors at the camp. It was this aspect of her engagement within the British social system that enabled Mary's mother to acquire some degree of wealth, to marry Sergeant Grant and to be 'free' within her native Jamaica. A long and difficult battle was being fought within Europe regarding slavery. This battle had great deal to do with politics and economics, which it is not possible to do justice to here. Suffice to say Britain, in theory, agreed with the abolition of slavery. However, William Wilberforce, one of the main proponents of the anti-slavery movement (Furneaux, 2006), had contradictory expectations of what women should and should not do. It is well established that he disapproved of women anti-slavery activists such as Elizabeth Heyrick. This highlights the duplicity of society for women at this time. This belonging and yet not belonging, to be allowed to do some things but not others must have been confusing for Mary. Perhaps this explains in part her innate drive and personal aspirations. She neither chose nor wanted to be the vanguard of any movement yet no one can or would deny she was a true inspiration for nurses both past and present.

Mary chose to be an entrepreneur as this was the means by which she earned a living for herself. Whilst in England this may have been an alien concept for a woman of her social class; for a Jamaican woman it was not. Some would say she pushed forward the role of women in society, yet she would not have been comfortable with this. Others would say she was purely entrepreneurial, a charlatan even, yet money from her hotel/lodgings was used to treat those who could not afford to pay. As Mary says,

I have never thought too exclusively of money, believing rather that we were born to be happy'.

(Seacole, 1857)

This too is one of her greatest assets, the use of humour in dangerous and adverse situations. This is highlighted throughout her autobiography.

Theory

Although Mary did not write about her nursing as did other nursing theorists she did highlight many important issues. One of Mary's overriding themes and philosophies was her intolerance of racism, perhaps more specifically her distaste for those who judge people without fully understanding them. As a Jamaican Creole woman, Mary had to contend with the entrenched stereotypical representations of Black and Mulatto women from the West Indies as women of promiscuity and gross sexual appetite (Dorsey, 2000). Mary felt that she belonged to the British Empire and attempted to live up to the expectations of that society.

Whilst she still maintained her enduring spirit to explore, learn and give care where required she also had to make sufficient money in order to survive. This perhaps not only caused a dichotomy for Mary but for others as well. Poon (2007) suggests that Mary strongly identified with the British Empire; as such she felt it was her duty to discover more about it and its people. This perhaps was the inspiration for Mary to visit London in her teens. It was here that Mary first encountered racism. Whilst out exploring the capital Mary and her colleague were subject to teasing and taunted by some young children because of their colour.

I am only a little brown – a few shades duskier than the brunettes whom you all admire so much; but my companion was very dark, and a fair (if I can apply the term to her) subject to their rude wit. She was hot tempered, poor thing!

(Seacole 1857: 7).

Mary had many hurdles to overcome, not least the innate racism and racist attitudes, in particular in relation to being able to join Nightingale's nurses. It is through her dedication and persistence that she overcame these difficulties. Robinson (2005) suggests that racism, covert or open, did not lie well with Mary. In her autobiography Mary recalls an incident where an American from the south praised and gave toast to Mary for her care and hospitality, despite her colour. She responded with

Gentlemen, I return you my best thanks for your kindness in drinking my health. As for what I have done in Cruces, providence evidently made me useful, I cannot help it. But I must say that I do not altogether appreciate your friend's kind wishes with respect to my complexion. If it had been as dark as any nigger's, I should have been just as happy and as useful and as much respected by those whose respect I value and as to his offer of bleaching me, I should, even if it were practicable, decline it without any thanks. As to the society which this process might gain me admission into, all I can say is that, judging from the specimens I have met here and elsewhere, I do not think that I shall lose much by being excluded from it. So gentlemen, I drink to you and the general reformation of American manners.

(Seacole, 2004: 47)

Links with other nursing theorists

Mary Seacole has links with Florence Nightingale (*see Chapter 1*), Madeleine Leininger (*see Chapter 12*) and Jean Watson's Human Caring Theory. Watson, like Seacole, contends that caring and care of the individual is the most crucial element in the nurse–patient relationship.

References

Achterberg J (1990) *Women as Healer: A panoramic survey of the healing activities of women from prehistoric times to the present*. Shambhala Press, USA

Bostridge M (2004) Ministering on distant shores, *The Guardian Saturday Review* 14 Feb: 7

Brooke E (1995) *Women Healer: Portraits of herbalists, physicians and midwives*. Healing Arts Press, Vermont

Bush B (1990) *Slave Women in Caribbean Society 1650– 1838 the Colombia series of Caribbean studies*. Heinemann, Kingston

Dorsey J (2000) Women without history: Slavery and the international politics of Partis Sequiter Ventrem in the Spanish Caribbean. In Shepherd V, Beckles H (eds) *Caribbean Slavery in the Atlantic World: A student reader*. Ian Randle, Jamaica

Ehrenreich B, English D (1976) *Witches, midwives and nurses: A history of women healers*. Writers and Readers Publishing Cooperative, London

Fluir N (2006) *Mary Seacole's maternal personae in Victorian literature and culture*. Cambridge University Press, USA

Furneaux R (2006) *William Wilberforce*. Regent College Press, Vancouver

Gill E (2004) Chapter in Aniowu E (ed) *William Willberforce*. Regent College Press, Vancouver

Jex-Blake S (1867) *A visit to some American schools and colleges*. MacMillan, London

Jex-Blake S (1970) *Medical women: A thesis and a history*, Source Book Press, New York

Levine P (2004) *Gender and empire: Oxford history of the British empire*. Oxford

Mary's innate ability to turn a rebuke into a positive comment for the future shows her optimistic attitude to life and also indicates how she uses humour to overcome adversity. Mary did not particularly mention in her writings how she utilised this understanding of how and why different cultures needed to be understood and respected and not changed. It is difficult to ignore the fact that having been on the receiving end of racism this must surely have had some influence on her. However she utilised this knowledge in a positive and constructive manner to enlighten and enrich her practice.

On her way to meet her cousin at the battlefields she made a detour to visit Nightingale's hospital at Scutari. Fluir (2006) suggest that she did this in order to legitimise her presence and seek Nightingale's approval for being at the Crimea. Whilst there she met, talked and cared for some of the soldiers as well as talking to some of the medical staff. Nightingale's hospital was several hundred miles from the Crimean peninsula where most of the fighting took place (Wilson, 2003). It perhaps also suggests that Mary may have manipulated the meeting to highlight her skills and acceptance by others in the Crimea. She did not actually meet Nightingale as she was 'distracted by her meetings with old colleagues and caring for the wounded soldiers'. She did meet Mrs Bracebridge who intimated that there was not a place for her at Nightingale's hospital. 'Miss Nightingale has the entire management of our hospital staff, but I do not think that any vacancy...'(Seacole, 1857). Mary replied that she was bound for the front in a few days, and reflected to herself:

If it is so here, what must it be at the scene of the war – on the spot where the poor fellows are stricken down by pestilence or Russian bullets and days and nights of agony must be passed before a woman's hands can dress their wounds. I felt happy in the conviction that I must be useful three or four days nearer to their pressing wants than this.

(Seacole, 1857: 39)

It is suggested (Robinson 2006) that both Nightingale and Mrs Bracebridge thought her of dubious moral character. However, she was allowed to stay the night but was required to sleep with the washerwomen rather than with the nurses. Mary, in her own immutable manner, manages to turn this rebuff into a positive,

My experience of washerwomen the world over, is the same – that they are kind soft-hearted folks. Possibly the soap-suds they almost live in find their way into their hearts and tempers and soften them. This Scutari washerwoman was no exception to the rule, and welcomes me most heartily.

(Seacole, 1857: 86)

It is unlikely we will ever know the full truth of the matter and no doubt the conjecture will continue, but suffice to stay it must be judged on the morals and expectations of that time and not our present ones.

Practice

Reports from the Crimean war by *The Times* war correspondent William Howard Russell (Wilson, 2003) were an innovation. The public had never before had such immediate contact with or understanding of the reality of war; the bungling as well as the heroism, and the horrible dying by disease. Russell reported on the appalling conditions of the army hospitals and it was this that spurred Florence Nightingale to set up her nurses at Scutari. Also within his despatches, Russell highlighted the neglected nutritional state of the men. It was not so much that they had insufficient rations, but that each individual soldier had to prepare his own food often in difficult and dangerous situations. This was read by Soyer, a French chef (Wilson, 2003: 175) who was well known for providing food for the rich and famous. Soyer was also philanthropist and wished to help those in the battle zone. His idea was to provide steam boiler ovens to make possible mass catering for the soldiers in order to provide adequate nutrition, and one of his greatest inventions was the vegetable cake. It was whilst setting up this venture that Soyer came upon Mary Seacole. Soyer was well known to Mary through her business interests in Jamaica and they worked together to try and improve the nutrition for soldiers on the battlefield.

Here we can see Mary's ability and vision to incorporate new ideas and utilise them to ensure adequate nutrition under tremendous difficulties. In the Crimean war, like others fought before the 20th century, far more men died of disease than they did in combat. One-fifth of the casualties died on the battlefield, four-fifths from diseases such as cholera, scurvy, typhus and typhoid. This reflected the primitive medical conditions and the poor sanitation and water supplies. There are many accounts of the Crimean war and it appears military decisions meant many men were unable to recover from their wounds. Those that were recovered from the battlefields then had to wait as there were limited vehicles with which to transport them to the hospitals. Some ships in Balaclava harbour waited three weeks before transporting injured soldiers. Conditions on board deteriorated quickly (Ponting, 2005). It is like that witnessing this appalling situation spurred Mary on to help treat the men on the battlefield.

Writings

Mary was a tireless humanitarian who touched the lives of many. She has been many things to countless people both during her lifetime and after her death. She has been a true source of inspiration for both past and future nurses. It is hard to imagine that an understanding of cultural issues would have been so important for nurses today without the insight that Seacole gave us. Mary's written legacy to us is captured in her only book, *The Wonderful Adventures of Mary Seacole in Many Lands*. There are no diaries or other primary sources which have been found to date. Yet when looking at the written work she left us, we can tease out some of the significant features that show the depth of knowledge and understanding that enabled her to nurse her patients so well. Seacole intrinsically knew that it was essential to work in partnership with patients and their families. This is, in fact, the concept and ideology on which she based her nursing.

Like many women practitioners she was well aware of the psychological component to physical illness. She realised very early on in her training, under her mother's tutelage, the importance of nutrition and humour and the need to attend to the psychological well being of patients as well as their physical condition. It could be claimed that she pioneered the ideology behind patient-centred care. She understood the true nature of working 'with' the patient rather than 'at' them. She put the patient as the primary focus of the care that was required; all this whilst being at the forefront of the battlefields and being a women. There is also evidence that when she helped nurse soldiers on the battlefield she did not differentiate between them but nursed those she felt she could assist. She used the funds that she made from those who could afford to pay to provide care for those in need.

It must be understood that many of those who could afford to pay for my services did so handsomely, but the great many of my patients had nothing better to give their doctress than the thanks.

(Seacole 1857: 15)

University Press. Oxford

Ponting C (2005) *The Crimean War: The truth behind the myth*. random House, London

Poon A (2007) Comic Acts of (Be) longing: Performing Englishness in wonderful adventures of Mrs Seacole in many lands. *Victorian Literature and Culture* 35, 501-516

Porter R (1999) *The greatest benefit to mankind: A medical history of humanity from antiquity to the present*. Fontana Press. London

Robinson D (2006) From: http://www.trainingjournal.com/tj/75.html [accessed 17/06/2009]

Robinson J (2005) *Mary Seacole: the charismatic Black nurse who became a heroine of the Crimea*. Constable and Robinson Limited London

Seacole M (1857 reprinted 2004) *The wonderful adventures of Mrs Seacole in many lands: The amazing autobiography of Britain's greatest unsung heroine*. Black Classics. London

Tomey A, Alligood (2006) *Nursing theorists and their work* (3rd edn) C.V.Mosby, St Louis

Wilson AN (2003) *The Victorians*. Arrow Books, London

Where to find out more

For further information about Mary Seacole visit the following websites:

- www.maryseacole.com
- www.rcn.org.uk/development/library
- www.archive.org

Some called Mary the Nightingale of Jamaica and to some degree there where similarities between the two. However she and Florence Nightingale were as diverse as they were similar: They were both women, both from, in their own minds, privileged backgrounds, both single women, both single-minded and determined. From this point on they differ. What and how they acquired and utilised their achievements in nursing were very diverse. Gill (2004) suggests that they both saw themselves as a 'mother' figure to the soldiers. Fluir (2006) suggests that Mary did not see herself as the same as White mothers whose shoes she claimed to have filled, but that she was indifferent to their differences. Nightingale was well aware of the differences and continued to highlight them and ensure that future qualified nurses would continue to maintain these differences. Mary used her skills and understanding of the disease process to treat and alleviate suffering. Nightingale used her organisational skills, providing clean air, water, linen, food, etc. and followed orders given by medical staff in relation to treatments. Tomes and Allgood (2006) suggest that the nursing theory began with Florence Nightingale and her vision of nurses as a body of educated women at a time when most women were neither educated, nor employed. Nightingale, unlike other nurse leaders of the time, expressed firmly that she believed that nursing knowledge was distant from medical knowledge. Mary did not have Nightingale's skills of organisation but she was in the front line and her British Hotel in Balaclava was an important refuge for soldiers. The ranks who had a fear of hospitals felt more at ease with 'Mother Seacole' than in the Turkish field hospitals (Bostridge, 2004).

Why do we not have women healers like Mary Seacole today?

Women have always been healers (Ehreneich and English, 1976) but Achterburg (1990) suggests that women healers were only suitable to take up occupations such as doctor's scribe, cook and barber. As the medical profession emerged it set out to suppress female healers in order to gain access to this lucrative political and economic arena (Brooke, 1995). The thrust of the male-dominated medical profession in the Western world forced the woman's role to change to one of service only. As a consequence the numbers of women healers declined. As Mary grew up she utilised her observational skills. She reported: 'even from an early age, whatever disease was present in Kingston, be sure my poor doll soon contracted it' (Seacole 1857: 6). The knowledge that Mary had obtained was at times in advance of current medical knowledge. This was particularly noticeable in relation to infectious diseases.

> *I believe that the faculty of medicine has yet to come to the conclusion that cholera is contagious and I am not presumptuous enough to forestall them: but my people have always thought it so.*

Mary put the patient at the forefront of everything she did; she was the first to truly take on board patient-centred care, in a holistic and culturally sensitive manner. She was the first to ensure a value-based caring position for everyone under her care.

CHAPTER 3

Isabel Hampton Robb

Catherine Rae

Biography

Isabel Hampton was born in Welland, Ontario, Canada on 26 August 1860. Little is known of her early childhood. She was one of seven children born to parents who had emigrated from Cornwall, England. She had little formal education but did complete one or two years of work at St Catherine's Collegiate Institute. From this she gained a teaching certificate which allowed her to work as a public school teacher in Merritton, Ontario, at the age of 17. As her teaching certificate was due to expire a chance conversation with a colleague led to a change of career. In 1881 she entered the Bellevue Training school for Nurses in New York and received her diploma two years later in 1883.

Isabel spent two years as a nurse in St Paul's House in Rome, which was jointly run by the Protestant Episcopal Church and the Church of England and provided both British and American nurses to wealthy travellers in Rome. On returning from Rome she worked as a private duty nurse for the Conover family in South Amboy, New Jersey, until 1886 when she took up the post of superintendent of the Illinois Training School for Nurses at Cook County Hospital. In 1889 she became the first Superintendent of Nurses and Principal of the Training School at the newly opened Johns Hopkins Hospital. While she was superintendent at Johns Hopkins she wrote her nursing textbook, *Nursing: Its principles and practices* which was published in 1894. In the same year she organised the Nurses section of the International Congress of Charities, Correction and Philanthropy at the World's Fair in Chicago. It was for this she arranged to have Florence Nightingale send an address. From these activities, the American Society of Superintendents of Training Schools for Nurses was organised (this later became the National League for Nurses) and she served as its president.

In 1894 she left her post at Johns Hopkins Hospital to marry Dr Hunter Robb, an obstetrician/gynaecologist. They were married that year in London on July 11th and Isabel's wedding bouquet was given to her by Florence Nightingale. After their wedding they moved to Cleveland, Ohio and had two sons, Hampton, born 1895, and Phillip, born 1902.

Isabel Hampton Robb continued her leadership within nursing through her writing, nursing organisations and activities. In 1896 she became president of the Nurses' Associated Alumnae of the United States and Canada (later to become the American Nurses Association). She also helped found the *American Journal of Nurses*. In 1900 she wrote her book *Nursing Ethics* and in 1907 *Educational Standards for Nurses*.

She was tragically killed on April 15th 1910 in a traffic accident in Cleveland, Ohio.

Summary of writings

Isabel Hampton Robb wrote *Nursing: Its principles and practice for hospital and private use* (1894) in her early thirties while she was Superintendent of Nurses and Principal of the Training School for Nurses at St Johns Hopkins Hospital, Baltimore. She dedicated the book to her pupils at St Johns and in Chicago. The book indicated what was expected of nurses in the late 19th century and the contents included training school organisation and

Profile

Isabel Hampton Robb embodied the professional woman. Her diversity as teacher, nurse, administrator, organiser, wife and mother was evident in many areas. She was a born leader and a role model for those who would become effective in implementing change.

Isabel Hampton Robb has been recognised as the single most versatile and visionary nurse of her time. Separated by class from those with power, and limited by 19th century ideas of a women's place, Isabel Hampton Robb helped establish the professionalism of nursing.

Key dates

1883	Isabel Hampton Robb graduated from New York Training School at Bellevue Hospital
1886	Robb became superintendent of Illinois Training School, Chicago
1889	Became First Superintendent of Nurses and Principal of Johns Hopkins Training School, Baltimore, Maryland
1893	Organised nursing section at International Congress of Charities, Corrections and Philanthropy, World Columbian Exposition in Chicago
1894	Married Dr Hunter Robb. *Nursing: Its principles and practices* published
1897	First president of Nurses Associated Alumnae of the United States and Canada

(now American Nurses As-
sociation)

1899 One of the organisers of the
International
Congress of Nurses,
chaired the committee on
International Standards of
Education

1910 Died in Cleveland after being hit by a street car

curriculum, general nursing, surgical nursing, symptomology and disease. This book is unusual in that most textbooks are used to teach a subject; few give instructions about organising a school. Robb's book highlights her belief that she and others like her were founding a profession and thought the first step was to create professional schools.

In her book *Nursing ethics* (1900), Robb placed obedience at the core of nursing virtues. She said of nurses

Above all, let her remember to do what she is told to do, and no more; the sooner she learns this lesson, the easier her work will be for her, and the less likely will she be to fall under severe criticism. Implicit, unquestioning obedience is one of the first lessons a probationer must learn, for this is a quality that will be expected of her in her professional capacity for all future time.

Educational standards for nurses (1907) includes the aims, methods and spirit of the Associated Alumnae of Trained Nurses of the United States.

Other publications include papers given by her at various events throughout her career, such as the International Congress of Charities, Correction and Philanthropy between 1893 and 1909.

Theory

In order to appreciate the enormous contribution Isabel Hampton Robb made to nursing, it is necessary to look at what life was like for a typical nurse at that time. Nursing in the late 19th century was not seen as a 'respectable' job, it was seen as 'undesirable' and for women 'of questionable morals'. There was little or no training and nurses worked long hours, their day beginning at 7 a.m. and finishing at 8 p.m. On top of being responsible for up to 50 patients the nurse was expected to sweep and wash the floors, dust the patient's furniture and window sills, maintain the ward at an even temperature by bringing in a scuttle of coal for the day's business, fill the kerosene lamps, wash the windows once a week as well as making their own pen nibs (nurses' notes were seen as an important aid for doctors) (Cherry, 2008).

Robb was truly inspirational and was a significant influence in changing the face of nursing from a mostly untrained occupation to a highly skilled and well-respected medical profession with very important responsibilities.

Prior to the Robb era, no credentials were available to nurses in the USA. In the late 19th century, nurse education varied a great deal in quality and length with training programmes ranging from 6 weeks to 3 years. In 1893 at the Columbian Exposition in Chicago, Isabel Hampton lamented that,

In the absence of education and professional standards, I am sadly forced to admit that the term 'trained nurse' means anything, everything and next to nothing.

(Moody, 1938)

At a time when women had not won the vote, Isabel Hampton was committed to obtaining recognition through formalisation and uniformity of nurse training.

During her time in Europe, her duties took her to all the major cities in Italy, France and Germany (Welch, 2008). For a young woman at this time these experiences would have been invaluable and would undoubtedly have broadened her vision and scope of knowledge about nursing and its problems. These experiences would form the foundation for her future work promoting international relationships between nurses. In 1885 she returned to the USA, as Moody (1938) writes, 'with ideas enlarged, ambition kindled and energy aroused for the accomplishment of work'. She had not returned to the US for long when she was given an opportunity to put her ideas into practice. At this time, nursing schools were an easy way to increase a hospital's workforce as it used students to provide care. There was no standard curriculum or fair way to measure a student's progress, and there was no recognition that education was crucial to nurses' understanding of why they were doing what in delivering patient care (Welch, 2008). In July 1886 Isabel Hampton accepted the position of Superintendent of Nurses at the Illinois Training School for Nurses which had been established five years previously in Chicago. She soon proved herself very capable of the position which required skills in leadership and administration. At this time the school was under the control of a board of lady managers which gave Miss Hampton her first experience of working with lay women. Although apprehensive to begin with, in time she found them to be indispensable to the welfare of the hospital. The training school was contracted by Cook County Hospital, a large municipal institution, to provide nurses for some of their wards. As Moody describes,

The hospital was politically controlled which meant, with the exception of the members of the nursing department, at each change of party control, the hospital staff of employees was dismissed and a new one installed. The dismissal of the nursing staff was considered each time too, but Miss Hampton succeeded in keeping the school apart from these decisions and even managed to persuade the commissioners to agree to long-needed improvements and to allow her nurses into many more wards within the hospital.

(Moody, 1938)

It was here that Isabel Hampton showed her ability to organise and to achieve remarkable results. At her instigation and under her guidance, the plan for a graded curriculum of study and practice was put into effect. As Welch (2008) writes, 'this programme is now so established into each school for nurses that few realise it originated from a young and inexperienced nurse in her first administrative post'. In her last year in this post she brought about one of the first affiliations of a nursing school for the purpose of broadening the training of the student nurse. Moody writes,

An affiliation was begun by which it was agreed that the Illinois Training School would provide the nursing care of private patients in the Presbyterian Hospital in order that the student nurses might obtain training in the care of this type of patient which was not afforded them in their own large, free hospital. This affiliation was successful and continued for fifteen years.

(Moody, 1938)

Moody goes on to write that, under the influence of Isabel Hampton, the educational and ethical reputation of the school continued to grow. Isabel Hampton succeeded in having the practice of student nurses assigned to compulsory unpaid private duties (which earned money for the hospital or school) abolished during their training. This practice was so well established in all training schools that to bring it to an end was a truly revolutionary and pioneering step.

In 1889 Isabel Hampton resigned from the Illinois Training School to take up a similar position at the Johns Hopkins Hospital in Baltimore, Maryland. The hospital had not trained nurses before and it was here that she was able to put into practice her vision of what nurse training should be. She changed the standing of nursing from unseemly and disreputable to dignified and respectable, both professionally and socially. The Johns Hopkins School became known as a centre for 'liberal scientific teaching' and as a 'model of good methods' in nursing (Moody, 1938). Isabel followed the principles of Florence Nightingale as closely as possible. In Isabel's inaugural speech on accepting the position she stated,

...technical skill can only be acquired through a systematic course of practical and theoretical study under competent teachers.

(Moody, 1938)

Isabel maintained a high standard of excellence in relation to entrance requirements and kept the age limits (23 to 35 years) much higher than in other schools. There was a period of probation (1 month) during which the students' fitness for continuing the course was assessed. Two of the tests during this probationary month were the student's ability to take lecture notes and her ability to write legible and accurate reports regarding her patients. Miss Hampton put into place a 12-hour day, in which the student would have time off for meals and two hours for rest, study or recreation (Moody, 1938). As far as other schools were concerned this was innovative. Isabel also introduced the grading system of theory and practice which she had introduced at the Illinois Training School. She would always emphasise the quality rather than the quantity of nursing. She seemed to have found her 'niche' at the Johns Hopkins School, as Adelaide Nutting has said of her:

Planning, initiating, directing and controlling, - such activities provided for her an element in which she lived and moved with the greatest ease and freedom. She was in every sense of the word a leader by nature, by capacity, by personal attributes and qualities, by choice, and probably to some extent by inheritance and training; a follower she never was.

(Nutting, 1910)

Putting theory into practice

Isabel Hampton was responsible for preparing the programme for the nurses' section at the International Congress of Charities, Correction and Philanthropy held in 1893 in Chicago during the World's Fair. In preparing for this meeting Isabel Hampton and Florence Nightingale corresponded regularly and Isabel delivered an address at the fair sent to her by Florence. It was during the Congress that Isabel gathered together a group of prominent nurse educators of the day to discuss the formation of an organisation. It was from this group that the Society of Superintendents of Training Schools for Nurses was formed which was to exert a significant influence throughout the United States on nursing education (Noel, 1979). In 1895 at the annual convention of the American Society of Superintendents of Training Schools for Nurses, which was held in Boston, Miss Hampton gave a paper in which she advocated a three year course and eight hour day for nursing students. Ideas such as this were not only new but viewed by some as disrupting. However, Isabel felt strongly that more than an eight hour day was not only unfair to the nurse herself but she (the nurse) would be unable to give her best nursing care to her patients for longer than that period (Nutting, 1910).

It was while at Johns Hopkins Hospital that Isabel set up an affiliation with the Mt Wilson Sanatorium for Infants in order to supply the students with experience in the nursing care of infants, which at that time was unavailable at Johns Hopkins. Her interests in affiliation was shown when, through her advice, a training school in Milwaukee became the central school through which nursing was carried on in as many as eight small hospitals and sanatoria (Welch, 2008). In 1905 Isabel Hampton read a paper to the first formal meeting of the American Federation of Nurses where she expressed her view that 'necessary uniformity of training offered in schools of nursing could be best accomplished through affiliation'. According to Moody (1938) she deplored the fact that there were 'best' schools and was sure affiliation would solve many problems that some schools experienced due to lack of facilities. She was under no illusion about the feasibility of trying to improve schools by changes in hospitals and felt it was impossible to expect uniformity of education programmes without making use of outside facilities of hospitals and educational institutions. Moody writes that Isabel saw two main obstacles to the success of affiliation. She felt there would be difficulty adapting the methods of one school to that of another, and that there would be instability because the administrators of the school in need of affiliation were not offered adequate representation in the administration of the cooperative plan.

Her suggestion to address these obstacles was that of a central institute. This would necessitate

- The formation of a central committee made up of representatives from all the schools and hospitals taking part in the affiliation.
- The delegation of duties regarding administration, education and finance would be completely independent of any of the hospitals.
- The central institute, through the central committee, would have authority not only for the theory of the students but also their work in general nursing, issuing all diplomas to the students.
- All hospitals would be grouped so that each group would represent a complete course in clinical experience.

Although this plan was never completely put into effect, elements from it are still evident today. (Moody, 1938)

While still at Johns Hopkins Isabel instigated the admission of members of each successive class of graduating nurses to membership in the alumnae society of the school. Before this the alumnae society had been very exclusive and had discriminated against certain graduates of the school. During this time at Johns Hopkins Isabel wrote her book *Nursing: Its principles and practice for hospital and private use*. This book became the core text in many schools of nursing and remained so for many years. She revised the book in 1907 when she rewrote much allowing more leeway on the part of teachers who were to use the book. But she maintained her strict conservative ideas concerning hospital etiquette and nursing ethics. Her ideas on the availability of laboratories for the science course, inclusion of courses on dietetics and chemistry and the provision of an adequate number of teachers showed she had ambition far in advance of those in the majority of nursing schools of the day.

In June 1894, at St Margaret's Church in Westminster, London, Isabel Hampton married a young doctor called Hunter Robb. After her wedding she and her husband made their home in Cleveland Ohio. The nursing profession at this time did not allow nurses to continue to work after their marriage. Although Isabel ended her participation at the institution, her marriage did not terminate her interest in nursing organisation.

As Nutting (1910) said, one of her primary interests was that of uniformity – uniformity from nurses' dress to educational methods.

As previously mentioned, Robb was one of those responsible for setting up the American Society of Superintendents of Training Schools for Nurses. Her desire for uniformity could be seen as one of the main aims of the organisation was to 'secure concerted effort in improving the standards and methods in nursing education and to bring about a uniformity of curricula' (Moody, 1938). To begin with, it was only superintendents of the 'best' schools who were members. However, as time passed it became necessary to invite the superintendents of smaller schools to join as it was they who really required advice and assistance from the organisation. From its humble beginnings in 1893 this organisation grew into the large and influential body known today as the National League for Nursing (NLN). Today the NLN is an improved and relevant professional association for the 21st century. Cited by the American Society of Association Executives for the 'will to govern well', the NLN is committed to delivering improved, enhanced and expanded services to its members and championing the pursuit of quality nursing education for all types of nursing education programmes. Once this organisation was well established Robb began campaigning for an organisation for all nurses. In February 1897 Robb became the first president of this new organisation called the Associated Alumnae of Trained Nurses of the United States and Canada, a position she held until her resignation in 1902. From this organisation the present American Nurses Association developed which today represents the interests of the nation's 2.9 million registered nurses.

Influence

Isabel Hampton Robb was passionate about the recognition of the status of the nurse, and did her best to develop and maintain that status. In her support of registration for nurses, she comments that the 'professional status of the trained nurse will be defined no less sharply than that of the physician or of the lawyer' (Moody, 1938). She also felt that, 'such legislation was necessary to stimulate training schools and graduates to meet the required educational standards, and that the public would be assured competent nurses' (Moody, 1938). Her sincere feeling that something should be done is expressed in her own words when she said

> *Can we be still and let things take their own way so long as the stamp of mediocrity marks a work to which should be given the best and highest that hands, hearts, and minds of women can bring to it?*
>
> (cited in Moody, 1938)

In the years following her marriage Isabel Hampton Robb wrote her second book, *Nursing ethics*, which expresses her ideas and ideals for the conduct of nurses. During this time she also advised the management of Lakeside Hospital Training School for Nurses in Cleveland and served on its board of management until her death. She was also a member of the American Red Cross Nursing Service and a lecturer on the course established for nurses in 1898 at Teachers College, Columbia University. Robb's interest in nursing was not only national but international. She was a campaigner for women's progress at all times. In 1899 she was invited to become a member in the International Council of Women; and in 1900 became a member of the International Council of Nurses. She was a delegate at the Congress of the International Council of Nurses in London in 1909 and suggested steps should be taken to establish an International Educational Standard, and was made chairman of a committee for that purpose.

Isabel Hampton Robb is remembered as one of the great women in nursing history of the United States not just for her work on organisation and administration but also for her 'unfaltering ideals, for her ability to set a worthwhile goal and proceed towards it with no uncertainties or deviations and for her inspiration to others to achieve' (Moody, 1938). One of her favourite expressions was, 'once a nurse, always a nurse', and she truly exemplified all that is truest and best in this 'trite' phrase. She, in her own characteristic way, said,

Links to other nursing theorists

Isabel Robb has links with Florence Nightingale (*see Chapter 1*).

References

Cherry B (2008) *Contemporary nursing: Issues, trends and management*. Elsevier, London

Moody S (1938) Isabel Hampton Robb: Her contribution to nursing education. *American Journal of Nursing* **38**(10) 1131–9

Noel N (1979) *Isabel Hampton Robb: Architect of American Nursing*. Available from: http://www.geocities.com

Nutting MA (1910) Isabel Hampton Robb – Her work in organisation and education. *American Journal of Nursing* **11**: 19–25

Welch C (2008) *Brilliant, creative, dedicated, driven, inspired and inspiring: Isabel Hampton Robb 1860-1910*. Available from: www.tcneaa.org.

Where to find out more

- www.nursing.jhu.edu
The Johns Hopkins School of Nursing opened in 1889 with Isabel Hampton Robb as its first Superintendent of Nurses. This website has a detailed history of the university which includes a history of the time Robb was with the school.

- http://foundationnysnurses.org/ bellevue
The Bellevue Alumnae Centre for Nursing History is dedicated to preserving the history of nursing. This website allows the reader to explore the nursing archives, read an oral history, view an exhibit or visit the Foundation.

Acknowledgement

I am indebted to Bellevue Alumnae Centre for Nursing History for information on Isabel Robb.

The woman who would be a success as a nurse, or, in fact, in anything, who would possess the quality of thoroughness in its fullest sense, no matter what kind of work she undertakes, needs the combined qualities of a trained mind, capable hands and body – and all must be dominated by the soul.

(Moody 1938)

The obstacles Isabel Hampton Robb faced cannot be over-emphasised. She accomplished innovative goals for women and nurses despite being separated by social class from physicians, hospital administrators, trustees and 19th century attitudes of women's place in society. She possessed intelligence, the ability to motivate others, political skills and good judgement. Her vision of increasing the theoretical component of nursing education as well as limiting ward work for students changed nursing education and influenced subsequent educational models.

On Friday April 15th 1910 in Cleveland Isabel Hampton Robb died as the result of a road traffic accident. Her work continues to this day giving inspiration and opportunities for development as she herself said,

To produce a force which shall intelligently, kindly and mercifully take care of the sick and helpless.

CHAPTER 4

Faye Glenn Abdellah

Betty Scholes

Biography

Faye Glenn Abdellah was among the first nursing theorists to influence the development of nursing as a profession (Wills, 2007). She was born in New York City on March 13th 1919 to a Scottish mother and an Algerian father (Lessing, 2004). She credits an early experience with triggering her interest in nursing as a profession: 18-year-old Abdellah lived in New Jersey with her family and witnessed the explosion of the hydrogen-fuelled airship Hindenburg in 1937. She and her brother ran to the scene to try and help, and she stated in a later interview,

> *Having no training in what to do in an emergency situation, I could only view the tragedy of the poor scorched victims exiting the dirigible... It was at that moment I thought that I've got to do something. I've got to become a nurse.*

(Lessing, 2004: iv)

She went on to earn her nursing diploma from Fitkin Memorial Hospital's School of Nursing (now Ann May School of Nursing), New Jersey and worked as a staff nurse then head nurse, before moving to education and public health (Johnson and Webber, 2005).

Abdellah believed in nursing practice that was rooted in a sound research base rather than on the previous experiences of the nurse and went on to earn three further degrees from Teachers College, Columbia University. She graduated with a Bachelor of Science in Nursing Degree in 1945 and gained her first teaching post at Yale University. It was in this post that she staged a burning of the main course textbook in the university courtyard in protest at the use of an outdated, unscientific text (Lessing, 2004). Despite having to pay for the cost of the books over the next year she never regretted this act, and in a later interview commented that sometimes you have to 'create a rebellion' (McAuliffe, 1998). This rebellion marked the beginnings of Abdellah's pursuit of a scientific basis for nursing and triggered her graduate studies that lead to her receiving a Master of Arts degree in psychology in 1947. She then went on to gain a Doctor of Education in 1955, also from Columbia and carried out graduate work in the sciences at Rutgers University, New Jersey.

Abdellah combined a career as a nurse educator/researcher with a 40-year military service in the US Public Health Service Commissioned Corps. Her research path moved from early qualitative studies on the patient experience of health care to her later larger-scale quantitative studies developing the ground work for progressive patient care. She was pivotal in the development of the diagnostic-related groups, a patient categorising system adopted by the healthcare providers in the US. She was also involved in the development of nursing home standards in the US and in 1981 was appointed Deputy Surgeon General. She was the first woman and nurse to hold this post and she also served as the Chief Nursing Officer for Public Health. Her nursing role encompassed public health issues related to the elderly, AIDS and health promotion. She retired from military service in 1989 at the rank of Rear Admiral but continued with her Government role focusing on the development and funding of health policy and nurse education

Faye Glenn Abdellah

Born: March 13th 1919

Profile

Faye Glenn Abdellah's 60-year career has encompassed an extraordinary range of nursing leadership roles. She has been instrumental in bringing nurse research into the core of nursing activity and has driven the professionalisation of nursing forward through example, through focusing on the education of nurses and through the building of a science base for nursing.

Key dates

1919	Born in New York
1937	Witnessed explosion of the Hindenburg
1942	Qualified as a nurse
1945	Bachelor of Science in Nursing
1947	Master of Arts in Psychology
1955	Doctor of Education
1960	*Patient-centred approaches to nursing* published outlining '21 nursing problems'
1981	Appointed Deputy Surgeon General
1989	Retired at rank of Rear Admiral
1993	Dean of Uniform Services University of the Health Sciences Graduate School of Nursing
2000	Inducted to National Women's Hall of Fame
2002	Retired from Uniform Services University of the Health Sciences

within the US system of funding. In 1993 she became dean of the newly formed Uniform Services University of the Health Sciences Graduate School of Nursing until her retirement in 2002 (Abdellah, 2004). She has been involved in healthcare activities across the globe, acting as a consultant to international bodies such as the World Health Organisation, and countries including the Peoples Republic of China, Portugal, the Soviet Union and Japan. She has been granted many honorary doctorates, medals, and professional and academic awards and memberships. In 2000 she was inducted into the US National Women's Hall of Fame for her achievements in science. On her induction Abdellah said,

> *We cannot wait for the world to change...Those of us with intelligence, purpose and vision must take the lead and change the world. Let us move forward together!...I promise never to rest until my work has been completed.*

(UXL Encyclopaedia of World Biography, 2009)

Areas of interest

Abdellah's early interests centred on the scientific basis of nursing theory and practice, she clearly felt that the lack of nursing research limited the potential of nursing to meet the needs of patients. During Abdellah's early teaching career the role of nurses as researchers was very limited and she describes the experience of a nurse researcher in 1949 who received the following response to a research report submission from a nursing journal,

> *Nurses do not research; they are not interested in research and that furthermore research has no place in nursing.*

(Abdellah, 1969: 390)

Her desire was to see nursing move from a service and practice experience to return to the aspirations of Nightingale for a research-based profession (Abdellah and Levine, 1979) informed her career path. This desire was evident in her key interests in research and nurse education, indeed her doctoral study aimed to improve clinical education through better understanding of the patient experience (Johnson and Webber, 2005).

In a survey of 40 schools of nursing Abdellah (Johnson and Webber, 2005) identified a classification of nursing problems that informed nurse education for many years. The findings of this study provided the groundwork for the development of Abdellah's typology of 21 Nursing Problems, although this philosophy of nursing continued to be developed in response to her later research. Parse (2006) highlights that Abdellah's work promoted the perspective of keeping the focus on the patient, in keeping with her view that nursing's entire focus must be on those to whom nurses provide care.

In the late 1950s Abdellah engaged in research with Eugene Levine (Abdellah and Levine, 1957) with the perspective that the patient's perception of care could influence care delivery, giving credence to the then new term, 'patient-centred care' (Brown, 1997). This project that considered matching patient's needs, including what was considered the most patient-satisfying care, to staffing provision formed the basis of a progressive patient care programme (Abdellah and Levine, 1979). This care need-led service model with its three levels of care, ranging from intensive in-patient care, through intermediate care to home care is one that is familiar internationally (McAuliffe, 1998). Abdellah's recognition of the importance of policy and finance on the development of patient care and nursing is evident in her discussion of the outcomes of this project. She stated in her 1998 interview 'Everybody loved the ICU. We had no trouble selling that. You can document that units treating the acutely ill save thousands of lives a year.' (McAuliffe, 1998). This signalled a move to a more politically astute perspective that served Abdellah well in future campaigns to improve healthcare delivery to key groups in America.

In her role of setting standards for care homes for the elderly she developed an abiding interest in health care provision to this group and was among the first to consider gerontology a specialist field of nursing. During an interview for *Military Medicine* Abdellah describes, with evident pride, making an unfavourable comparison between the high quality of care provided to zoo animals and the poor quality of care received in nursing homes in one city that so angered the health providers she was escorted from the interview (Lessing, 2004).

It was however this unflinching ability to cut to the heart of the matter that was necessary in her role as Deputy Surgeon General. She promoted the development of information systems to support those who prescribed to the elderly, recognising that standard dosages were not appropriate for these patients and that specialised prescribing guidelines were needed to ensure safe prescribing practice (Rodin, 1984). She also worked in her role as Deputy Surgeon General to ensure that good quality relevant health information was made available to the elderly, giving advice and information on issues such as Alzheimer's disease, arthritis and general health promotion (Rodin, 1984).

Her research interests led to her involvement in national bodies supporting the development of research in nursing and in 1970 to produce a comprehensive overview of nursing research from 1955 to 1968 (Abdellah and Levine, 1979). She strove throughout her career to support the funding of nurse education beyond diploma level, striving to show the value of nurse education at baccalaureate, masters and doctoral levels, with advanced practice in key areas such as gerontology (McAuliffe, 1998), culminating in her role as dean in the graduate school at the Uniform Services University of the Health Sciences.

Summary of writings

Faye Glenn Abdellah has written extensively throughout her career, being the author or co-author of 150 publications, including journal articles, books, book chapters, reports, and monographs, and it is not possible to discuss in any depth the breadth of this work in detail here.

Her earliest journal publications were co-authored with Eugene Levine in the mid 1950s, and began the development of her concept of nursing. Her most significant early work was the book *Patient-centred approaches to nursing*, published in 1960 that outlined the application of the 21 Nursing Problems framework to nurse education and service. This work was co-authored with three colleagues, Beland, Martin and Matheny, and was updated in 1973 as *New directions in patient-centred nursing*. As important as these works were in influencing the design of nursing curricula, it is perhaps Abdellah's work with Eugene Levine on nurse research that is her most lasting written creation. The first joint publication *Better patient care through nursing research* (Abdellah and Levine, 1965) was the first research book targeted to a nursing audience and framed the activity of research as being a direct influence on nursing activity with patients. A further two editions of this work were published, the last in 1986. In 1994 Abdellah and Levine produced an updated nursing research text, *Preparing nursing research for the 21st century*, a book whose stated aim was to assess the past and present state of nursing research in the US and envisage the future of nursing research. She has authored or co-authored journal articles with topics as diverse as the human genome project and nursing care of the aged; however the common theme in much of her journal writing has been nursing research. Her written work on nursing research includes reports on studies she has carried out, such as methods of identifying covert aspects of nursing problems (Abdellah, 1957) or discussion pieces geared to addressing the development of nursing research such as, 'The human genome initiative – implications for nurse researchers' (Abdellah, 1991). A body of written work by Faye Glenn Abdellah from 1952 to 1989 can be found archived by the US National Library of Medicine encompassing many conference papers and monographs as well as *Patient-centred approaches to nursing* which are no longer in print.

Patient-centred approach to nursing theory

Abdellah's theory centred on the key concepts of patient need, described as the 21 Nursing Problems and was linked to a set of nursing roles and functions. These roles and functions are outlined below as the activities that Abdellah perceived nurses needed to undertake to identify and address nursing problems. The 21 Nursing Problems are then detailed as the core concern of these nursing roles and functions. She described the theory as a 'framework' and that term will be used within this discussion.

Abdellah could be considered as belonging to a school of thought in nursing that focused on the needs of or deficits experienced by patients, a school of thought that, although stepping away from the strictly biomedical model, remained influenced by this perspective (Meleis, 1997). Her patient-centred approach to nursing was developed to assist with nurse education and was considered applicable to both practice and education (Abdellah et al, 1960). The theory was generated inductively through Abdellah's clinical experience and her research studies carried out over a five year period (Falco, 2002). At the point of development Abdellah's framework was intended as a means of providing a clinical record for learner nurses (Johnson and Webber, 2005) and to give a more robust framework to the curriculum of nurse education which until that time was often rather unstructured (Wills, 2007). Although Abdellah's framework is referred to as '21 Nursing Problems', a term that seems rather at odds with the patient-centred stance claimed by Abdellah, the problems within the typology are those that are experienced by the patient and which the nurse, as a professional helper, can assist the patient to address. It is most strongly linked to Maslow's hierarchy of needs and Henderson's 14 basic human needs (Falco, 2002; Tomey, 2006) and Abdellah is often referred to as a needs theorist, akin to the previous work of Virginia Henderson and that of her contemporary Dorothea Orem (Meleis, 1997). Meleis (1997) discusses the idea of a Columbia school of thought, noting a similarity in influences in theory development in a group, including Abdellah, who had received their graduate education in this institution.

The typology of 21 Nursing Problems first appeared in the 1960 work *Patient-centred approaches to nursing* (Abdellah et al, 1960), in which around half of the text was devoted to the inclusion of this model in nurse education (Johnson and Webber, 2005). Abdellah and colleagues introduced the nursing roles and nursing problems typology in this 1960 framework and revised some aspects of this in the 1973 publication *New directions in patient-centred approaches to nursing* (Abdellah et al, 1973).

In order that nurses could provide the service outlined in this framework Abdellah proposed that they were required to problem solve through the identification of what she termed overt and covert nursing problems (Abdellah et al, 1960). Overt problems are those that are evident on assessment, and covert problems are problems that may be less evident but are an underlying feature of an overt problem. She also recognised that consideration of covert problems may assist in the resolution of overt problems, and proposed 10 steps to identifying these problems:

Links with other theorists

Abdellah's patient-centred approach is similar to but more complex than Virginia Henderson's 14 Activities for Client Assistance theory. It is a need-based theory and as such bears similarity in focus to both Virginia Henderson (*see Chapter 11*) and Dorothea Orem (*see Chapter 14*).

References

Abdellah F G (1957) Methods of identifying covert aspects of nursing problems. *Nursing Research* **6**: 4–23.

Abdellah FG (1969) The nature of nursing science. *Nursing Research* 18: 390–3

Abdellah FG (1991) The human genome initiative – Implications for nurse researchers. *Journal of Professional Nursing* 7: 332

Abdellah FG (2004) Establishing the Graduate School of Nursing at the Uniformed Services University of the Health Sciences. *Military Medicine.* **169**: vii–x

Abdellah FG, Beland IL, Martin A, Matheney RV (1960) *Patient-centred approaches to nursing.* McMillan, New York

Abdellah FG, Beland IL, Martin A, Matheney RV (1973) *New directions in patient-centred approaches to nursing.* 3rd edn. McMillan, New York.

Abdellah FG, Levine E (1957) Developing a measure of patient and personnel satisfaction with nursing care. *Nursing Research* 5: 100–8

Abdellah F G, Levine E (1965) *Better patient care through nursing research.* (1st edn)McMillan Publishing, New York

Abdellah FG, Levine E (1979) *Better Patient Care through Nursing Research.* 2nd edn. McMillan Publishing, New York

1. Learn to know the patient.
2. Sort out relevant and significant data.
3. Make generalisations about available data in relation to similar nursing problems presented by other patients.
4. Identify the therapeutic plan.
5. Test generalisations with the patient and make additional generalisations.
6. Validate the patient's conclusions about his nursing problem.
7. Continue to observe and evaluate the patient over a period of time to identify any attitudes and clues affecting his behaviour.
8. Explore the patient's and family's reaction to the therapeutic plan and involve them in the plan.
9. Identify how the nurse feels about the patient's nursing problems.
10. Discuss and develop a comprehensive care plan.

(Wills, 2007)

Through this process of problem identification Abdellah proposed that nursing encompassed a range of activities needed to provide a comprehensive service and would include the following, although the later revision eliminated item 3 (Falco, 2002);

1. Recognising the nursing problems of the patient.
2. Deciding the appropriate course of action to take in terms of relevant nursing principles.
3. Providing continuous care of the individual's total health needs.
4. Providing continuous care to relieve pain and discomfort and provide immediate security for the individual.
5. Adjusting the total nursing care plan to meet the patient's individual needs.
6. Helping the individual to become more self-directing in attaining or maintaining a healthy state of mind and body.
7. Instructing nursing personnel and family to help the individual do for himself that which he can within his limitations.
8. Helping the individual adjust to his limitations and emotional problems.
9. Working with allied health professions in planning for optimum health on local, state, national, and international level.
10. Carrying out continuous evaluation and research to improve nursing techniques and to develop new techniques to meet the health needs of people.

(Abdellah et al, 1960: 24–5)

Falco (2002) posits that the later revision related to the impossibility of providing continuous and total care as specified in item 3.

Abdellah and colleagues differentiated between these two aspects of the nursing role through discussion of nursing functions and nursing diagnoses (Fuller, 1997). They defined nursing diagnosis as the identification of nursing problems including the assessment of the severity and impact of those nursing problems on the patient, and nursing function as the activities needed to address these nursing problems (Wills, 2007). From this Abdellah and colleagues proposed a typology of 21 Nursing Problems, these covering a range of physiological and psychosocial needs that the nurse could be required to assist the patient with to some extent.

1. To maintain good physical hygiene, and physical comfort.
2. To promote optimal activity; exercise, rest and sleep.
3. To promote safety through the prevention of accident, injury, or other

trauma and through the prevention of the spread of infection.

4. To maintain good body mechanics and to prevent and correct deformity.
5. To facilitate the maintenance of a supply of oxygen to all body cells.
6. To facilitate the maintenance of nutrition to all body cells.
7. To facilitate the maintenance of elimination.
8. To facilitate the maintenance of fluid and electrolyte balance.
9. To recognise the physiological responses of the body to disease conditions – pathological, physiological, and compensatory.
10. To facilitate the maintenance of regulatory mechanisms and functions.
11. To facilitate the maintenance of sensory functions.
12. To identify and accept positive and negative expressions, feelings and reactions.
13. To identify and accept inter-relatedness of emotions and organic illness.
14. To facilitate the maintenance of effective verbal and nonverbal communication.
15. To promote the development of productive interpersonal relationships.
16. To facilitate the progress towards achievement and personal spiritual goals.
17. To create or maintain a therapeutic environment.
18. To facilitate awareness of self as an individual with varying physical, emotional and developmental needs.
19. To accept the optimum possible goals in the light of limitations, physical and emotional.
20. To use community resources as an aid to resolving problems arising from illness.
21. To understand the role social problems have as influencing factors in the cause of illness.

(Abdellah et al., 1960)

Putting theory into practice

When developing this framework Abdellah's initial aim was to develop a structure that learner nurses could use to record their clinical knowledge and skills development. In her first writing on this subject she devoted her discussion to the inclusion of this framework in nurse education at all academic levels (Johnson and Webber, 2005). The theory describes a focus of nursing within fields of sustenal, remedial, restorative, preventive, self-help and need deficit or excess (Abdellah and Levine, 1979; Meleis, 1997) with the goal being to assist individuals to meet their health needs and cope with their health problems. The theory focused primarily on the individual, addressing the family and society as resources that could be used by nurses to help patients in achieving their goals. Meleis (1997) describes the image of the nurse created by needs theorists such as Abdellah as

..a nurse who is active and busy working and a patient who is striving for independence. The nurse's work is focused on doing a deliberate and well planned activity.

(Meleis, 1997: 198)

Abdellah's theory is named a 'patient-centred approach' due to the aim of moving the focus of care from the disease to the individual patient (George, 2002); a focus that directed the assessment and care provision of the nurse to that person rather than the diagnosis. This linked strongly with Abdellah's progressive patient care model that saw patients being cared for according to level of need and condition rather than solely on diagnosis (Rodin, 1984). The impact of this focus on the manner of practising nursing, as being allied

Abdellah FG, Levine E (1994) *Preparing nursing research for the 21st century. Evolution, methodologies, challenges.* Springer Publishing Company, New York

Brown MI (1997) Research in the Development of Nursing Theory: The Importance of a Theoretical Framework in Nursing Research. In Nicoll LH (ed) *Perspectives on nursing theory.* 3rd edn. Lippincott, Philadelphia

Falco SM (2002) Patient-centred ppproaches Faye Glenn Abdellah. In George JB (ed) *Nursing theories. The base for professional nursing practice.* 5th edn. Prentice River, New Jersey

Fortin J (2006) Human needs and nursing theory. In Kim HS, Kollak I (eds) *Nursing theories: Conceptual and philosophical foundations.* 2nd edn. Springer, New York

Fuller SS (1997) Holistic man and the science and practice of nursing. In Nicoll LH (ed) *Perspectives on nursing theory.* 3rd edn. Lippincott, Philadelphia

George J B (2002) *Nursing theories: The base for professional nursing practice* (5th edn)Prentice River, New Jersey.

Gordon M (1998) Nursing Nomenclature and Classification System Development. *Journal of Issues in Nursing* 3(2): Manuscript 1. Available from: www.nursingworld.org/MainMenuCategories/ANAMarketplace/ANAPeriodicals/OJIN/TableofContents/Vol31998/No2Sept1998/NomenclatureandClassification.aspx

Johnson BM, Webber PB (2005) *An introduction to theory and reasoning in nursing.* Lippincott, Williams & Wilkins, Philadelphia

Lessing M (2004) Up close and personal. Interview with Rear

Admiral Faye Glenn Abdellah. *Military Medicine* **169**: iii–xi

McAuliffe MS (1998) Interview with Faye G Abdellah on Nursing Research and Health Policy. *Image – The Journal of Nursing Scholarship* **30**(3): 215–9

Meleis AI (1997) *Theoretical nursing: Development and progress.* Lippincott, Philadelphia

Parse ME (2006) *Nursing theories and nursing practice.* 2nd edn. FA Davis Company, Philadelphia

Rodin J (1984) Interview with Faye Abdellah. *American Psychologist* **39**(1): 67–70

Schmeiding JM (2006) Orlando's Nursing Process Theory in nursing practice. In Tomey AM, Allgood MR (eds) *Nursing theorists and their work*. Mosby Elseiver, St Louis

Tomey AM (2006) Nursing theorists of historical significance. In Marriner-Tomey A, Raile Alligood M (eds) *Nursing theorists and their work*. 6th edn. Mosby Elsevier, Missouri

Wills E (2007) Overview of Grand Nursing Theories. In McEwen M, Wills E (eds) *Theoretical basis for nursing*. 2nd edn. Lippincott, Williams & Wilkins, Philadelphia

Where to find out more

The reference list contains journal articles and books that discuss in some depth the work of Faye Glenn Abdellah, some further information can also be found at the following websites.

- http://www.greatwomen.org
- Uniform Services University of the Health Sciences: http://www.usuhs.mil/vpe/profiles/abdellah.pdf
- National Library of Medicine:http://www.nlm.nih.gov

to medical guidance but not dependent on it, was, of its time, a revolutionary way of conceptualising the profession. The core activity associated with the framework is that of problem solving which has a process and structure similarity with Orlando's later described nursing process (Schmieding, 2006). The framework acknowledged the individual as a whole, comprising psychological, physiological and sociological aspects (Fortin, 2006). The problem or need faced by the patient that could be met by the nurse could be overt or covert, and the application of problem solving aided the nurse in the identification of these needs. Abdellah proposed that sometimes the identification of covert needs would aid in the resolving of overt needs, so the nurse was encouraged to be aware of the individual beyond the parameters created by the diagnosis. This is a relatively complex framework (Wills, 2007) that encompasses the potential for a full and detailed assessment of individual need when used to structure nursing care.

Influence

When one considers the influence of Abdellah's theory of patient-centred approaches to nursing it is difficult to separate the theory from the impact of her professional roles and drives. Possibly more influential than the theory itself, is the influence of Abdellah's perspective of nursing as a profession in its own right that should be practised within a context of evidence and scientific premise.

Wills (2007) notes that Abdellah's influence can be found in the structure and organisation that her model helped bring to nurse education and in her identification of characteristics that helped differentiate nursing within the allied professions of health. Gordon (1998) comments on the influence of Abdellah's classification of nursing goals as drivers in the organisation of curricula and practice nationally. Falco (2002) remarks on the paucity of research that explores the impact of the framework on patient outcomes but given the initial focus on the educational curricula for nurses this is perhaps unsurprising. Fortin (2006) proposes that the influence of Abdellah lies most importantly in how the success of her activities in education, research and practice laid the groundwork for future nurses. In her interview with Rodin (1984) Abdellah speaks of the importance of the work of the Chief Nursing Officer to public health promotion. She personally placed real value on her influence of the policymakers through the production of research evidence that recognised the factors which would have an impact on the provision of health care. Faye Abdellah perhaps learned to adapt to meet the needs of her audience and cites the change of title of a patient assessment project, that she was struggling to gain financial support for due to cost implications, to 'patient management', a simple name change that allowed this project to be funded due to a more acceptable title (Rodin, 1984).

In a later interview Abdellah speaks of her sense of accomplishment in being able to be part of the development of the groundwork for nursing research as a science (Lessing, 2004). When one reads of Abdellah's endeavours, an image comes to mind of a focused and driven individual who was unwilling to accept the status quo and who was willing to work hard to achieve change. She was and is a visionary for nursing as a profession, with the grand ambition that nursing should not be static or unscientific in progression.

Section Two

How do I do the job?

Development of the knowledge and skills required in nursing

Overview

Traditionally, nurses learned how to nurse from other experienced nurses. By learning the tasks involved and completing their skills books they proved they were able to do the job. This apprenticeship model has a long history and indeed has some merit, but ultimately it cannot answer the question, 'What is the unique nature of nursing knowledge that defines the professional nurse?'

The theorists in this section grapple with the notion that nursing is at once a science and an art. The scientific element of nursing may allow us to classify and measure our nursing but nursing without art is like painting by numbers – a rough approximation of the scene, lacking depth and a sense of the personal. The knowledge and skills required for nursing are complex and human – the theorists in this section are still attempting to unravel them.

It will be clear from reading about the theorists discussed in this section that they all see skills and knowledge as something intimately related to a wider concept of care. Nevertheless it is a convenient way to introduce some of the most important theories of nursing. To put it the other way round, it is not possible to imagine caring effectively for somebody without some idea of what to do.

Lydia Hall

The section begins with Lydia Hall, a remarkable woman brought to life here by Elaine Stevens. Setevens shows how Hall challenged the medical model and the idea that nurses were doctors' assistants. Hall's innovative notion that nurses were in charge of the patient's care with all other services secondary, aimed to show that, after the initial medical crisis, nurses were key to the recovery of patients.

Hall argues that nursing cannot be reduced to a series of tasks and she reminds us that nursing is a complex and human activity requiring empathy and well-honed relationship-building skills.

Barbara Carper

Our next theorist, Barbara Carper, attempted to discover the unique quality of the knowledge necessary for the complex activity of nursing. Carper's work has been influential in the development of reflection as a crucial skill of the modern nurse. Reflecting on nursing practice involves relating the facts, the science of the situation, to the nurse's unique personal experience to provide a new and deeper understanding of the meaning of nursing. As Maria Pollard writes, 'Carper cleared the path for nursing practice to move away from the medical model to a holistic and therapeutic one'.

Josephine Paterson and Loretta Zderad

Paterson and Zderad continue this vein of humanistic nursing and Anne Kay illuminates their contribution in this chapter. Their philosophical notions of the unique transformational power of the nurse–patient relationship may seem at odds with the practical sounding title of this section. It is however fundamental, literally essential, to the understanding of the nature of the knowing necessary for the job of the modern nurse.

Catherine Kolcaba

Catherine Kolcaba worked in a dementia unit and there, according to Atkinson and Christley, she 'transformed woolly ideas about comfort into a measurable, curative and moral component of nursing practice'. In a very practical way, Kolcaba utilised the work of other theorists, notably Orlando, Henderson and Watson, and proposed an answer to the question, 'How do I provide comfort for my patients?' Surely this is a question most nurses will want answered.

Ramona Thieme Mercer

Like Kolcaba, Mercer is classed as a middle range theorist. Lesley Storrie describes how Mercer's Maternal Role Attainment Theory has developed over time and provides insight into the context of this development. By skilfully integrating the theoretical work of a wide range of scholars Mercer achieves a coherent explanation of the process of maternal role attainment. In doing so she formulates a framework for nurses to support mothers in achieving a strong maternal identity. Knowledge of this theory allows nurses to plan care and make appropriate referrals. Storrie concludes with an interesting contrast between maternity services in UK and USA, using the influence of Mercer as illustration.

Patricia Benner

Patricia Benner also examined the nature of nursing knowledge. She wanted answers to the question, 'What makes an expert nurse?' To answer this she gathered stories from expert nurses and through examining these narratives attempted to construct a theory about how we develop our nursing knowledge and skills. Benner is a prime example of how reflection can be used to explore and understand nursing practice. Her 'grounded theory' approach to research has also been influential in persuading nurses to examine practice as a means of developing theory.

The theorists in this section have all tried to find answers to the question, 'What knowledge and skills are required to be a nurse?' Educationalists continue to debate this and, by reading this section, we hope we can encourage you to see that nursing cannot be reduced to a finite series of tasks and yet proficiency must be able to be measured in some way that ensures patient safety. If we cannot answer this question as a profession, it is likely to be answered for us.

CHAPTER 5

Lydia Hall
Elaine Stevens

Biography

Lydia Eloise Hall was born on 21st of September 1906 in New York City (Hutchison, 2006). Hall's parents were Louis and Anna Williams and she was the elder of their two children. Despite being born in New York, Hall grew up and completed her nursing training in York, Pennsylvania where her father practised as a surgeon (Loose, 1994).

Hall graduated with a diploma in nursing from the York Hospital School of Nursing in Pennsylvania in 1927 where she spent much of her early career in a variety of nursing posts (Touhy and Birnbach, 2006). By the mid-1930s Hall had returned to New York, graduating from the Teachers College of Columbia University with a BSc in 1937. This was soon followed by the successful completion of an MA in 1942. It is also known that Hall completed her doctoral research but did not submit the final dissertation (Hutchison, 2006).

From writings on Hall's career it is known that she worked for the New York Heart Association as a researcher whilst continuing with her academic studies (Grandstaff et al., 1994). During her time at the New York Heart Foundation she met her future husband, Reginald, who worked for the Hallmark Card Company (Loose, 1994) and they were married in 1945.

For a short time in the late 1940s Hall returned to nurse teaching, working in the nursing faculty of Fordham Hospital. However in 1950 she returned to the New York Heart Association where she was employed in a number of roles including a joint position as teacher and researcher with Teachers College at Columbia University.

The development of Hall's main interests, the provision of high quality rehabilitative care for people with chronic illness by professional nurses (now referred to as Registered Nurses), began in earnest when she met Dr Martin Cherkasky in 1947. Cherkasky became the Director of the home care division of the Montefiore Medical Centre in The Bronx, New York, where he had frequent contact with Hall in her professional capacity at the New York Heart Foundation (Touhy and Birnbach, 2006). In 1957 the Board of Trustees at Montefiore utilised funds made available from the Solomon and Betty Loeb Trust to construct a new facility to provide a better standard of care for sick people in the community (Hutchison, 2006). So, in 1957, some 10 years after their first meeting, Hall was invited by Cherkasky to take a major role in the development of this centre of excellence. This was Hall's greatest professional challenge which led to the provision of a fully nurse-led rehabilitative care system within the Loeb Centre in New York.

Hall became the centre's first Administrative Director working not only on the development of the physical environment but also on the underpinning philosophies that would support her emerging nursing model. She used her authority well to ensure that professional nursing care was high on the agenda when developing the philosophy of the new facility (Hutchison, 2006). The Loeb Centre opened its doors to its first patients on the 10th of January 1963 following a dedication address by Lucile Petry Leone, Chief Nursing Officer for the Public Health Service in the Department of Health and Welfare (Hutchison, 2006). Hall continued to develop and put into practice her theories and model of care, writing regularly for nursing and healthcare

Profile

We have seen that Hall's pioneering philosophy of nursing and model of care were only really utilised in one care setting during her lifetime. However we have also seen that the principles that Hall developed some 40 years ago are still being used in contemporary nursing practice. Although her ideas have been modified and adapted to meet the needs of a modern day health care system Hall's work continues to influence nurses and nursing.

Key dates

1927	Graduates from York Hospital School of Nursing Pennsylvania
1937	Awarded BSc degree from Teachers College, Columbia University
1942	Awarded MA degree from Teachers College, Columbia University
1945	Marries Reginald Hall
1957	Invited by Cherkasky to take lead role in set up of Loeb Centre in New York where she later became Administrative Director
1963	Loeb Centre opens
1967	Receives Teachers College Alumni Award for Distinguished Achievement in Nursing Practice
1969	Dies of heart disease in Queen's Hospital, New York
1984	Posthumously inducted into the ANA Hall for Fame

journals. So innovative and forward thinking were her ideas she received the Teachers College Alumni Award for Distinguished Achievement in Nursing Practice in 1967 (Loose, 1994).

Hall continued as the Director of the Loeb Centre until her death on the 27th of February 1969. She died in Queens Hospital, New York from heart disease at 63 years of age. However her theory and practices lived on within Loeb until 1984 under the direction of Hall's assistant director and close friend Genrose Alfano (Hutchison, 2006). In 1984 the Loeb Centre changed direction to meet the needs of a modern healthcare system and is now a nursing home called the Loeb Centre for Nursing Rehab (Hospital Data.com, 2009).

Special interests

Throughout her career Hall had a keen interest in people of all ages who experienced chronic illness. For instance Hall worked as a visiting nurse for the New York Heart Association where she researched the effects of heart disease as a chronic condition in children (Hall et al., 1949; Hall, 1951). Hall was a prominent proponent of public health nursing and her interests relating to the rehabilitation of those experiencing chronic disease included the provision of holistic, person-centred care (Hutchison, 2006).

As Hall's interest in chronic disease rehabilitation grew so did her ideas about the quality of care that was provided by professionals who came into contact with people with chronic disease in the acute phase of their illness as well as in their rehabilitation. This led Hall to investigate the way nursing was being practised in the American healthcare system. From this she noted that nursing seemed to have evolved into a task-orientated vocation rather than a professional occupation which was concerned with the management of complex, patient-centred care. It was, however the invitation to have a major role in the development of a new rehabilitation facility, in the late 1950s, that allowed Hall to further develop and put into practice her innovative nurse-centred model of rehabilitation (Touhy and Birnbach, 2006). Indeed it was Hall's fortitude and high standing as a nurse leader which ensured that her emerging philosophy of nurse-led rehabilitation was accepted as the sole model of care when the services at the Loeb Centre for Nursing and Rehabilitation were developed (Hutchison, 2006).

The Loeb Centre was part of the Montefiore Hospital in New York although it had its own funding and administration system that allowed for the implementation of Hall's pioneering model of care (Touhy and Birnbach, 2006). The centre had 80 beds and catered for the rehabilitative needs of people over 16 years of age (Hall, 1963). Hall firmly believed that the only way to successfully rehabilitate patients who were recovering from the acute phase of an illness was through the application of skilled care provided exclusively by the professional nurse. She remarked,

The public deserves and can profit from professional nursing care.

(Hall, 1963: 806)

As such, patients were selected for admission to Loeb based on Hall's assessment of their ability to be rehabilitated within a total care programme applied by the professional nurse.

Hall's vision was that each professional nurse would

...work with patients through integration of the social, biological, pathological and therapeutic sciences in the art of nursing.

(Hall, 1963: 806)

This patient-centred approach was the foundation of the care at Loeb, the nurse being the teacher and nurturing patients until they understood all about themselves and what they wanted to achieve within their rehabilitation programme (Hall, 1964). Other health professionals, including doctors, were viewed by Hall as secondary therapists at this stage of the individual's illness, attending only when the professional nurse felt it applicable to do so (Hall, 1964). This idea originated from Hall's premise that there were two distinct phases of medical care provided in the hospital setting. The first stage she suggested is the biological crisis in which medicine has a primary role to diagnose the cause of the illness while the second is to instigate treatments to cure the illness (Hall, 1969). However, once the biological crisis subsides, Hall's proposition was that the role of medicine then decreased while the role of the professional nurse increased to provide a whole person approach to rehabilitation which Hall (1963: 806) defined as 'progressive patient care'. However, it should be noted that the Loeb was heavily staffed by nursing aides and administrative assistants, carefully selected by Hall, to support the professional nurses in their provision of holistic care to the patients; however, under no circumstances were any of these employees allowed to provide hands on nursing care; this was solely the domain of the professional nurse (Hall, 1963).

As part of Hall's philosophy the professional nurse was encouraged to make use of the therapeutic self; and the use of reflection as a way of engaging with the patient was integral (Hall, 1965a). Hall (1958) acknowledged that her ideas for this type of 'nurturing' care came from disciplines such as sociology, psychology and psychiatry and that this allowed patients to express their feelings to their nurse which then acknowledged that patients were a central component in their individual rehabilitation process.

Hall saw Loeb as 'a halfway house on the road home' and was instrumental in ensuring that the centre was not only fit for its rehabilitative purposes but was also decorated to provide a homely environment with an atmosphere that stimulated the patient to learn how to progress within their recovery programme (Hall, 1963). Another of Hall's proposals was that the patients' concerns and ideas were central to their recovery. As such Hall proposed that all patients should receive as much information as they required to develop their own goals of care in partnership with their allocated professional nurse. This ethos was very different from the medical establishments of the 1960s where the doctor decided on the goals of care and the patient (and nurse) obeyed. To ensure the success of this part of Hall's ethos she implemented 'patient progress notes' in which all disciplines recorded how the patient's own goals were being addressed and met (Hall, 1969). This was a radical move away from the usual, separate, doctor's and nurses' notes and perpetuated a more patient-centred approach to care.

Underpinning Hall's ethos of care was that of learning and as a seasoned nurse teacher Hall understood the importance of education. So at Loeb regular seminars took place to ensure all professional nurses were able to reflect on their practice, thus continually improving the quality of care provision. However, not all the seminars were uni-disciplinary and the cross-fertilisation of ideas between doctors and nurses led to a more cohesive approach to care which was then implemented under Hall's direction (Hall, 1969).

Over a remarkably short period of time Loeb became a centre of excellence and well known for its cost-effective, highly professional, nursing model of rehabilitation (Hall, 1969). After Hall's death her successor Genrose Alfano continued to support the use of Hall's pioneering philosophy of patient-centred rehabilitation for approximately another 20 years. Indeed Touhy and Birnbach (2006) note that the ongoing effectiveness of the nursing model at Loeb was primarily due to the significant influence that the professional nurse had in determining care packages within an ethos of expert care and autonomy. Such was its success that it became the basis for work in the 1980s on nursing development units in the UK (Pearson, 2007): an influence which will be reviewed in more detail later in this chapter.

Summary of writings

Hall's writings primarily focused on the model of care adopted at the Loeb Centre and in the main were published in the final decade before her untimely death. A brief mention of Hall's early writings is made here before focusing on her later pioneering ideas by reviewing both published and unpublished materials. It has to be noted that Hall constantly reviewed and revised her ideas, updating her writings as her theories and ideas progressed. As such a number of Hall's published writings reconsider the same principles and ethos, albeit in a modified format. As well as this, some of Hall's published papers had previously been presented as speeches to prominent nursing groups of the day and again these were modified for publication. An example is Hall's unpublished paper of 1958 entitled, *Nursing: What is it?* This was revised and published by the Virginia State Nurses Association in 1959, presented as a speech in Toronto in 1963, published in the journal *Canadian Nurse* in 1964 and formed a section Baumgarten's book on nursing home administration in 1965 (Hall, 1965b).

One of Hall's first papers, possibly related to her academic studies and her work at the New York Heart Association, focused on the continuing care of the child with a cardiac condition (Hall et al., 1949). Another early publication which focused on cardiac care of the child was entitled, *What the classroom teacher should know and do about children with heart disease* (Hall, 1951). This leaflet gave advice to schoolteachers on the care and support required by pupils with heart conditions. However, it was not until the mid 1950s that Hall began to present publicly her views on the quality of nursing care.

In 1955 Hall presented her first thoughts on nursing care to members of the nursing faculty at Seaton Hall University. This was entitled the 'Quality of Nursing Care'. In this speech Hall spoke of the changes in modern day healthcare including the promotion of scientific care and the influence this had on nursing practice. Here Hall made her first reference to professional nurses having an exclusive role in the provision of intimate bodily care; a role no other professional group could perform. Indeed it is this role that would become integral to Hall's philosophy of nursing care in later writings. Hall also spoke of the current trend of task-orientated nursing and how this prevented the nurse from fully engaging with the patient in a therapeutic relationship. Indeed Hall noted that instead of nursing interventions being offered 'at' patients, 'to' patients or 'for' patients, they should be provided 'with' patients. Hall stated that in this partnership of care the nurse had needed to make judgements about the patient's care using knowledge and understanding rather than just doing a task that required little thinking. Hall suggested that this care partnership allowed the nurse to provide care that addressed the patient's social, emotional, spiritual and intellectual needs which were set against a backdrop of their own family and community as well the institution in which they were being cared for. In this speech Hall also described nursing as a complex process that needed to be evaluated from a number of viewpoints in order to improve practice over time. This proposal is credited as being one of the first descriptions of what would become known as the nursing process (Slevin, 2003).

From 1958 onwards Hall's writings focused on the development of the Loeb model of care which had two components. In the first element of this model the patient was depicted as three overlapping circles (the body, the person and the disease). Hall suggested that a combination of professionals attended to the patients' needs at different stages in their illness and to illustrate this Hall (1958) assigned the word 'core' to the person circle to depict whole person care (provided by many professionals), 'care' to the body circle to depict intimate bodily care (provided by the nurse) and 'cure' to the disease circle to depict medical care (overseen by the doctor but often designated to the nurse). Hall (1958, 1963, 1965a) indicated that nursing care, provided within this model, should integrate the social, biological, pathological and therapeutic sciences as these theories underpinned the quality of care provided within each of the three circles.

The second component of the Loeb model focused on Hall's philosophy of nursing care. Hall's philosophy was that all nursing care should be provided by the professional nurse as they were providing complex care that was part of an ongoing relationship between the nurse and the ill person (Hall, 1963). In this partnership Hall (1958) believed that professional nurses used their nursing art within their specific sphere of care; namely the provision of intimate bodily care. Hall surmised that having intimate contact with patients for prolonged periods of the day helped to build and maintain a high quality therapeutic relationship which allowed patients to become equal partners in their care (Hall, 1963). Although her model was not based on formal research Hall demonstrated that she drew on theories from psychology, psychiatry and social sciences to ensure that the professional nurse had the knowledge and expertise to provide the quality of care she envisaged (Hall, 1958, 1965b, 1969). These theories were utilised by Hall to link the use of the therapeutic self to whole person care which allowed the nurse to explore the patients' thoughts and feelings in depth and to nurture them through the recuperative stage of their illness with less fear and anxiety (Hall, 1963).

It would seem that the majority of Hall's writings focused on the development of the Loeb model of care and it was not until just before her death that her writings returned to the evaluative processes of nursing care she mentioned in 1958. In a presentation to the New York State Nurses Association in 1968 (subsequently published 1969) Hall, as well as discussing her model of care, went on to discuss the effectiveness of the care at Loeb. Hall (1969) intimated that the cost of care at Loeb was half that of traditional hospital care and in addition patients at Loeb recuperated much quicker and were often discharged in half the amount of time. Blue Cross Insurance noted that only 3.6% of Loeb patients were re-admitted to hospital care in the year following discharge from Loeb, in contrast to the usual 18% who had received traditional hospital care (Hall, 1969).

Further evidence of the success of Loeb was presented as nursing satisfaction, with Hall reporting that nurses felt that they could practise as professional nurses at Loeb, using their skill and judgement to provide high quality nursing care. At the end of this final speech of Hall's career she presented a case to show how the programme practised at Loeb could enable patients to make the most of their rehabilitation programme and allow them to return home with quality of life rather than being sent to a nursing home as the medical team suggested.

Further writings about the Loeb model and evaluations of its effectiveness continued after Hall's death. Indeed Genrose Alfano continued to write about its successes for nearly 20 years (Alfano, 1969, 1971, 1987) while other published writings by members of the Loeb nursing team provided evidence of its success in providing a nurse-led, person-centred rehabilitation programme (Englert, 1971; Bowar-Ferres, 1975).

Theory

We now focus more fully on the nursing philosophy and the model of care Hall developed doing her time as the Administrative Director at the Loeb Centre.

As previously noted the model of care at Loeb had two distinct arms. The first was the therapeutic use of only qualified nurses in the holistic care of patients, while the second was the use of a rehabilitative paradigm known as the Care, Core and Cure Model (Hall, 1964). Both elements of Hall's theory that she utilised to underpin the model of care practised at Loeb are reviewed here.

Professional nursing care

Hall openly renounced task-orientated nursing which was becoming favourable in the US in the 1960s, suggesting that it epitomised nursing as a trade or vocation rather than a professional occupation in which the professional nurse was part of a 'complex helping relationship' (Hall, 1964). Indeed she suggested that nursing could be seen as a wedge – ranging from simple tasks at the thin edge of the wedge to complex tasks at the other (*Figure 5.1*). Furthermore, she suggested that the tasks at the thin end required little in the way of judgement and were the domain of less qualified nurses while those at the other end required complex thinking and judgements and thus should only be the province of the professional nurse (Hall, 1958).

So Hall's theory of successful rehabilitation was the use of the qualified nurse acting as a therapeutic agent, supporting and teaching people who were recovering from the acute phase of an illness (Hall, 1969). Indeed in her 'care, cure, core' model of care patients were in charge of their recovery, with the nurse acting as an advocate, ensuring the highest possible care was provided to aid a speedy recovery (Hall, 1969).

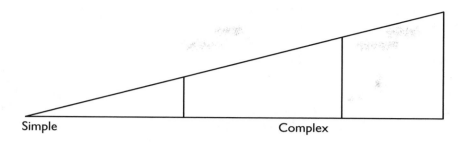

Figure 5.1. The functions of nursing (Hall, 1958: 5).

The Care, Core, Cure Model

Hall described each individual patient as having three main elements; the person, the body and the disease (*Figure 5.2*). It was quite clear in Hall's mind that each facet of the patient was interlinked and issues in one circle could affect the others and thus influence the progression of their rehabilitation positively or negatively (Hall, 1964). In 1965 Hall (1965a) commented that professional groups may work with or indeed neglect one or more of the domains depending on their own professional expertise, but each professional group must have its own expertise in one of the domains. For example in acute illness it is the disease that requires the professional expertise of the doctor (Hall, 1969), while the exclusive expertise of nursing lies in the provision of 'intimate bodily care' (Hall, 1964: 150).

From her supposition that the patient had three main areas of concern Hall (1964) suggested that nursing care could be divided into three discrete circles to ensure all the patient's concerns were addressed. These are the Care circle, the Core circle and the Cure circle (*Figure 5.2*); each of which may assume a higher importance than the others depending on the phase of illness the patient is experiencing (Hall, 1969).

Care is the domain of Hall's model that is concerned with the care of the body and intimate bodily care (Hall, 1964). Hall considered this domain to belong entirely to the nursing profession (Touhy and Birnbach, 2006)

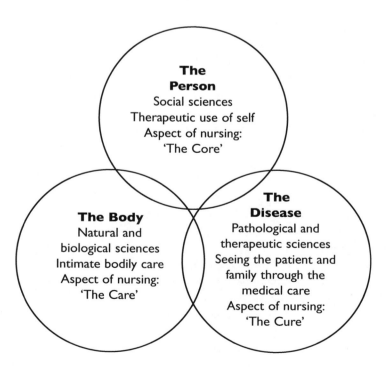

Figure 5.2. The Care, Core, Cure Model (Hall, 1964: 151).

Links to other nursing theorists

Lydia Hall was a contemporary of Ida Orlando (*see Chapter 22*) and had similar ideas about the role of nurses in patient-centred care.

Allan Pearson used Hall's work to develop the Burford Model of Care which was utilised by nursing.

References

Alfano G (1969) The Loeb Center for Nursing and Rehabilitation. *Nursing Clinics of North America* **4**: 487–3

Alfano GJ (1971) Healing or Caretaking – Which will it Be? *Nursing Clinics of North America* **6**: 273–80.

Alfano G (1983) Whom do you care for? *Nursing Practice* **1**: 1–3

Alfano G (1987) The Loeb Center for Nursing and Rehabilitation. In Vladeck BC, Alfano G (Eds). *Medicare and extended care: Issues, problems and prospects*. Rynd Communications, Maryland

Bernardin E (1964) Loeb Center – As the Staff Nurse sees it. *American Journal of Nursing* **64**(6) 85–6

Bowar-Ferres S (1975) Loeb Center and its philosophy of nursing. *American Journal of Nursing* **75**: 810–15

Davies B, Oberle K (1990) Dimensions of the supportive role of the nurse in palliative care. *Oncology NursingForum* **17**(1): 87–94

Endacott R, Chaboyer W (2006) Practice development. In Elliott D, Aitken L, Chaboyer W (Eds). *AACNS Critical Care Nursing*. Mosby Elsevier.

Englert B (1971) How a staff nurse perceives her tole at Loeb Centre. *Nursing Clinics of North America* **6**(2): 281–92

Gesse T, Dombro M, Gordon SC, Rittman MR (2006) Wiedenbach, Henderson, and Orlando's theories and their application. In Parker M (ed) *Nursing theories and nursing practice* (2nd edn). FA Davis, Philadelphia

Grandstaff M, Gumm B, Marriner-Tomey A, Peskoe KT (1994) *Lydia E Hall: Core, Care and Cure Model*. St. Louis, Mosby

Hall LE (1951) *What the classroom teacher should know and do about children with heart disease*. American Heart Association, New York

Hall LE (1955) *Quality of nursing care*. Address to a meeting of the Department of Baccalaureates and Higher Degree Programs of the New Jersey League of Nursing. Held of Feb 7 1955, Seaton Hall University, New Jersey. New York, Loeb Centre for Nursing Records.

Hall LE (1958) *Nursing: What is it?* Unpublished Report. New York, Loeb Centre for Nursing Records.

Hall LE (1963) A centre for nursing. *Nursing Outlook* **11**(11): 805–6

Hall LE (1964) Nursing: What is it? *Canadian Nurse* **Feb**: 150–4

Hall LE (1965a) *Another view of nursing care and quality*. Address Delivered to Catholic University, Washington DC. New York, Loeb Centre for Nursing Records.

Hall LE (1965b) Nursing: What is it? In Baumgarten H (ed) *Concepts of nursing home administration; A manual for executives of prolonged-illness institutions*. Macmillan, New York

Hall LE (1969) The Loeb Center for Nursing and Rehabilitation, Montefiore Hospital and Medical Center, Bronx, New York. *International Journal of Nursing Studies* **6**: 81–97

and firmly believed that the provision of all 'intimate bodily care' by a professional nurse allowed the nurse to be in close proximity to the patient for much of the day. Hall (1964) suggested that this closeness was akin to the role of a mother and teacher which comforted patients in a professional manner. This promoted a therapeutic relationship which helped each patient to understand that their own dedicated, professional nurse was empathetic and able to address their concerns in a restorative way.

The core domain focuses on individual patients in a holistic way seeing them as an integrated whole in which the nurses use themselves as a therapeutic agent in the development and maintenance of a therapeutic relationship. This therapeutic relationship was again the mainstay of the professional nurse's role in order to comfort patients and enable them to navigate their rehabilitation programme as a team in order to optimise their health and wellbeing (Hall, 1969).

In the cure domain Hall (1958) suggested that the nurse has two distinct roles. The first of these was to assist the doctor in ensuring an accurate diagnosis is made and the correct treatments are provided to the patient. This role, Hall (1969) suggested, encompassed little in the way of professional nursing, since the tasks were merely devolved by the doctor with little discussion. Indeed Hall (1969) suggested that the increasing medical role of nurses detracted from their professionalism suggesting that nurses could easily be renamed as doctor's aides rather than professional nurses with their own exclusive role. The second role of the nurse in the cure circle is a more active helping role that Hall (1964) believed encouraged and reassured the patient throughout the journey of illness and into rehabilitation.

In conclusion Hall was quite clear that, at Loeb, rehabilitation focused on the core and care elements with a reduced, although still relevant, cure element and as such the professional nurse was in the best position to help patients on the road to recovery by utilising a holistic person-centred approach to their care.

Hall's theory in practice and its influence in contemporary nursing

Hall's ideology for rehabilitative care was in the main practised at Loeb although some of the elements of her work can still be found in contemporary nursing practices. Here we summarise how Hall's model of care developed during her lifetime before reviewing the influence Hall's nursing theories and model of care have on contemporary nursing practice.

The development of theory into practice

As this chapter has shown Hall was well known for her development of innovative theories relating to rehabilitation nursing during the 1950s. However, the introduction of a nurse-led rehabilitation programme into the healthcare system in the United States in the late 1950s was an onerous task as the biomedical model was the predominant model of care, especially within institutional settings. In this model the doctor was firmly in charge of the patient's care, and elimination of disease was the primary outcome. It therefore took strong determination and imaginative leadership to ensure the rehabilitation programme at the Loeb was developed and practised with the utmost professionalism. Indeed there was much opposition to Hall's ideology from the medical establishment of the day and it was only her standing as an expert, visionary nurse that persuaded the Board at Montefiore to allow her model of care to be practised at Loeb. As Hall's model of care advanced at Loeb it was evaluated by Hall and other members of her team and found to be of extreme value by the patients as well as being more cost-effective than the traditional method of hospital rehabilitation (Bernardin, 1964; Hall, 1969; Alfano, 1983).

Such was the impact of Hall's visionary rehabilitation programme on nursing in the USA she was posthumously inducted into the American Nurses Hall of Fame in 1984 (Montefiore Network News, 1984).

Influence on contemporary nursing practice

Nurse-led clinical services

The use of only professional nurses to provide patient-centred care, although proven to be both cost-effective and to improve patient outcomes by Hall and her team (Hall, 1969; Alfano, 1983), did not really move into mainstream nursing practice (Henderson, 1964), although there do not seem be any concrete reasons for this. However, there are some suggestions that nurse-led units, developed in the United Kingdom in the 1980s as a direct result from visiting the Loeb Centre and reviewing Hall's work, may have overtly challenged the existing medical model of care (Pearson, 2003) or did not fully integrate themselves with other services (Pembrey and Punto, 1990). Indeed studies into the outcomes of the first two Nursing Development Units (NDUs) in the UK, at Burford and Oxford, showed quite clearly that nurse-led services such as those practised at Loeb were cost-effective, provided high quality care and had a positive effect on the recovery of patients (Pearson, 2003). This evidence led directly to a King's Fund Project which enabled the development of a number of nurse-led clinical units across the UK (Salvage, 1989).

However, Pearson (1997) noted in his evaluation of the development of such units that the lack of adequate funding to set up an NDU, combined with the introduction of a new model of care and the bureaucracy in the healthcare service, led to a lack of motivation in staff and as such may partially explain why the concept did not come to full fruition in the UK. However Endacott and Chaboyer (2006) noted that NDUs were instrumental in recognising and extending the role of the nurse within the healthcare arena as well as promoting nursing autonomy. However, they went on to suggest that as healthcare has evolved over time there has been more importance put on multi-professional working and as such the term NDU has been subsumed by PDU (Professional Development Unit) to reflect this (Endacott and Chaboyer, 2006). So perhaps Hall's use of the professional nurse in the expert care of patients and families is still alive and well albeit in a modified form that reflects a 21st century healthcare system. Indeed development of specialist nursing roles within the modern healthcare arena that use the principles of case management may also be related to Hall's ideas of using nursing expertise to engage with the patient to allow partnership working and improvement in health outcomes.

The use of the nurse as a therapeutic agent

Although Hall did not have a formal research base for her model of care many of her ideas were generated from the influential works of her contemporaries working in the fields of psychology and psychiatry (Grandstaff et al., 1994). Indeed Hall's use of the nurse as a therapeutic agent to support patients in helping themselves through the rehabilitation phase of their illness is based on theories from humanistic psychology. In humanistic psychology people are viewed as individuals who are able to take responsibility for their own circumstances in order to grow and become 'self-actualising' (Van Wagner, 2009). One of the major proponents of humanistic psychology was Carl Rogers who is now regarded as one of the most influential person-centred therapists of the 20th century. Hall herself noted that Rogerian ideas

Hall LE, Hauck M, Rosenson L (1949). *The cardiac child in school and community*. New York Heart Association, New York

Henderson C (1964) Can nursing care hasten recovery? *American Journal of Nursing* **64**: 81–95

Hospital Data (2009) *Loeb Center for Nursing Rehab*. Available from: http://www.hospital-data.com/hospitals/LOEB-CENTER-FOR-NURSING--REHAB-BRONX.html [accessed 21-07-09].

Hutchison G (2006) *Loeb Center for Nursing and Rehabilitation Records: 1963–1984*. Available from: 198.66.139.217/collections/MC39fa.htm [accessed 21-07-09]

Loose V (1994) Lydia E Hall: Rehabilitation nurse pioneer in the ANA Hall of Fame. *Rehabilitation Nursing* **19**(3): 174–6

McCoy ML (2007) *Care of the Congestive Heart Failure Patients: The Care, Cure, and Core Model. National Association for Practical Nurse Education and Service*. Available from: http://www. napnes.org/practice/news/clinical_articles/care_of_the_congestive_heart_failure_patient. html accessed 01-11-09.

Orlando IJ (1961) *The dynamic nurse–patient relationship. Function, process and principles*. Putnam, New York

Pearson A (1997) Evaluation of the King's Fund Centre NDU. *Journal of Clinical Nursing* **6**: 25–33

Pearson A (2003) A blast from the past: Whatever happened to "new nursing" and "nursing beds"? *International Journal of Nursing Practice* **9**: 67–9

Pearson A (2007) Dead poets, Nursing theorists' contemporary nursing practice 2. *International Journal of Nursing Practice* **13**: 321–3

Pembrey S, Punto S (1990) The lessons of nursing beds. *Nursing Times* **86**: 44–5

Quan K (2007) *The Nursing Process*. Available from: http://www.thenursingsite.com/Articles/the%20nursing%20process.htm [accessed 31-10-09]

Rogers C (1951) *Client centred therapy*. Constable & Co, London

Salvage J (1989) Nursing developments. *Nursing Standard* **3**(22) 25–8

Slevin O (2003) An Epistemology of Nursing Ways of Knowing and Being. In Basford L, Slevin O (Eds). *Theory and practice of nursing: An integrated approach to caring practice*. Nelson Thornes. Cheltenham

Snowden A (2009) Assessment and care planning. In Kydd A, Duffy T, Duffy FJR (Eds) *The care and wellbeing of older people*. Reflect Press, Exeter

Stevens E, Sutherland N (2008) Essential concepts. In Stevens E, Edwards J (Eds) *Palliative care: Learning in practice*. Reflect Press, Exeter

Touhy TA, Birnbach N (2006) Lydia Hall. In Parker M (Ed). *Nursing theories and nursing practice* (2nd Edn). FA Davis, Philadelphia

Van Wagner K (2009) *Humanistic Psychology: The Third Force in Psychology*. Available from: http://psychology.about.com/od/historyofpsychology/a/hist_humanistic.htm [accessed 31-07-09]

influenced the care at Loeb and this can be clearly seen in the core circle of Hall's model in which the nurse attends to each individual patient as an integrated whole (Hall, 1964). To ensure a true person-centred approach that enables individuals to learn, grow and find the answer to their issues Rogers (1951) suggested that the practitioner required three important attributes: empathy, unconditional positive regard and sincerity. Empathy is integral to nursing practice and helps patients to determine how well the nurse understands them. This in turn promotes the development of a therapeutic relationship, an important aspect of all three domains of Hall's model, since, without empathy, little of the professional nurse's work would have been achieved. Unconditional positive regard or acceptance of the patient as a human being, without being judgemental, is also central to the therapeutic use of self, while sincerity is a key to good nursing care. Both of these have the ability to deepen the nurse–patient relationship and it is only once trust and rapport occur that the nurse can provide truly empathetic nursing care. In Hall's model the expertise of the professional nurse is found in the domain of care where empathy, positive unconditional regard and sincerity are utilised to provide the nurture individuals need to find their way through the rehabilitative maze.

In contemporary nursing the therapeutic use of self continues to be an important role allowing the nurse to explore issues with patients across many settings. In cancer care Davies and Oberle (1990) developed the supportive role of the nurse in which the therapeutic use of nursing expertise was utilised to provide whole person care in the face of serious illness. Meanwhile one of the central tenets of palliative nursing is 'being with' in which the development of and maintenance of the therapeutic relationship is central to the care and support of people in the last stages of life (Stevens and Sutherland, 2008). Finally, and most recently, Hall's own Care, Cure, Core model has been revived for use in the care of congestive cardiac patients (McCoy, 2007). In her article, McCoy (2007) uses Hall's model to develop a framework for the care of people with heart failure to encourage communication between the nurse and patient. McCoy (2007) illustrates how expert cardiac nursing care can be provided within Hall's three circles of care to assess and diagnose patient problems, to implement a mutually agreeable care plan and to evaluate the outcomes of care. This paper eloquently shows how Hall's 40-year-old model of care is still relevant to nursing today and that it can be utilised in a modern healthcare system with a little adaptation to ensure it is fit for purpose.

The nursing process

In her 1955 paper Hall made direct reference to the process of nursing in relation to professional nurses using their skill and judgement to address and manage patients' issues. Slevin (2003) indicates that this is one of the earliest mentions of such a phrase within nursing literature. Hall (1955) also suggested that the process of nursing should include working with the other helping professionals to ensure a consistent and jointly formulated approach to solving the patient's problems. Another integral part of the process of nursing is identified by Hall (1955) as evaluation; in that, care should be evaluated using a number of different methods of enquiry such as examining the patient's level of recovery on discharge, how they experienced the quality of care received as well as observing the quality of nursing care itself. These insights were published some five years before Orlando's (1961) seminal publication which is identified as the origin of the modern-day nursing process. In her work Orlando recognised nursing as a cyclical process that involved the nurse identifying patient needs as well as taking action based on these needs to improve patient well-being

(Gesse et al., 2006). However, it is interesting to note that both Hall and Orlando were associated with Teachers College at Columbia University and worked in New York around the same time and as such the exchange of professional ideas may have occurred with each making use of new ideas to further the process of professional nursing. Indeed the other major constituents of Orlando's (1961) theory included the influence of nurses on patient outcomes and their role as independent practitioners that are actively engaged in complex patient interactions. This is very similar to Hall's own philosophy of nursing. However, the nursing process has become a central tenet of good practice in contemporary nursing although it tends to be presented as a linear model to aid nursing assessment and care planning rather than the cyclical process identified by Orlando. The main components of the nursing process are shown below and should be used in a systematic way to enable the nurse mutually to agree a care plan with the patient that is based on a full and comprehensive assessment (Snowden, 2009).

- Assessment: Collecting the data
- Diagnosis: Formulating nursing diagnoses
- Planning: Setting the goals of care
- Implementation: Setting the plan into action
- Evaluation: Analysing successes and failures.

(adapted from Quan, 2007)

So it can be seen that Hall's idea of a systematic process of professional nursing that allowed the nurse to engage with the patient to formulate an agreeable programme of care is alive and well and continues to act as a base for the provision of high quality, patient-centred nursing care.

Where to find out more

American Nurses Association Hall of Fame

- http://www.nursingworld.org/ FunctionalMenuCategories/ AboutANA/ WhereWeComeFrom/ HallofFame.aspx

Lydia Hall was posthumously inducted into the ANA Hall for Fame in 1984 for her services to rehabilitation nursing.

Loeb Centre for Nursing and Rehabilitation Records

- http://foundationnysnurses. org/bellevue/ guidetoarchivalrecords/ collections/MC39fa. php#history

This website includes a specific archive which contains many of Hall's writings as well as other information about the Loeb Centre.

Information and resources for nurses worldwide

- http://www.nurses.info/ nursing_theory_person_hall_ lydia.htm Nurses.info

This website is dedicated to the provision of quality healthcare information for the professional development of nurses and health professionals. Links to a range of educational and vocational information that will meet this outcome are provided.

Barbara A Carper
Birthdate:
Not known

Key dates

1962   Received Clinical Certificate in Anaesthesia

1976   Awarded EdD, Teachers College, Columbia University

1978   First published *Fundamental patterns of knowing in nursing*

Barbara Carper
Maria Pollard

Biography

Barbara Carper is a Registered General Nurse who received her degree in nursing from Texas Woman's University and was awarded her Master of Education and Education Doctorate from Columbia Teacher's College. She also received a Clinical Certificate in Anaesthesia in 1962 from the University of Michigan.

At the time of publishing her seminal work *Fundamental patterns of knowing in nursing* in 1978 she was Associate Professor and Chairman at Texas Woman's University, and between 1981 and 1982 she was visiting Scholar in Medical Ethics at Harvard University. Before retirement she was Associate Dean for Academic Affairs, College of Nursing, University of North Carolina, Charlotte where she is currently Professor Emeritus.

Summary of writings

Barbara Carper wrote the *Fundamental patterns of knowing in nursing* in 1976 as part of her Education Doctorate. It was written with the aim of clarifying what she saw as the confusion over what should be taught in a nursing curriculum. In her own words she 'never anticipated how popular the article would become' (Carper, 2009: 384).

The paper was published in 1978, in the first edition of the journal *Advances in Nursing Science*. It was written at a time of great change in nursing and midwifery practice and education, when knowledge was moving from description and classification towards being more analytical, seeking to explain phenomena from a holistic point of view as opposed to a one dimensional perspective of ill health.

Carper believed the concept of health to be more than the absence of illness and referred to it as a 'dynamic state or process which changes over a given period of time and varies according to circumstances' (1978: 14). She went on to develop a conceptual framework to explain what it means to know and what kinds of knowledge are most valuable to ensure effective and satisfying nursing practice. This framework identified the fundamental patterns of knowing as:

- Empirics – the science of nursing
- Aesthetics – the art of nursing
- Personal knowing
- Ethics – moral knowing.

Carper explained that although each area is essential to practice none can stand alone or be taught exclusively as each is dependent on the other to develop the skills to resolve dilemmas in practice.

The theory

The fundamental patterns of knowing

Carper (1978: 13) believed that in order to successfully teach and learn about nursing it was necessary to understand the 'patterns, forms and structure' of the body of knowledge that informs nursing practice. She described four fundamental patterns of knowing, which, when applied collectively, would ensure nurses were equipped to provide appropriate, acceptable and holistic care for their clients, emphasising that each of the components was inter-related and interdependent.

Empirics – the science of nursing

Acknowledging science in nursing was not as rigorous in 1978 as in other medical disciplines. Carper expressed the desire for the profession to develop systematic inquiry that would 'describe, explain and predict phenomena of special concern to the discipline of nursing' (1978: 14) in an objective and systematic way. She described this as the first fundamental pattern of knowing in nursing and conceptualised this component as being

> *...empirical, factual, descriptive and ultimately aimed at developing abstract and theoretical explanations.*
> (Carper, 1978: 15)

At the time this paper was written it was acknowledged there was an 'urgency' for the development of empirical knowledge that was specific to nursing and midwifery practice to improve the status of the profession. What was required was theory that was objective, research-based and could be verified.

Aesthetics – the art of nursing

The need to develop a specific body of empirical knowledge for nursing practice led to a dissociation with the concept of nursing as an 'art'. Carper highlighted the reluctance in nursing literature at the time to consider patterns of knowing other than those that were empirical and suggested this was partly due to the shift from the apprenticeship-style of nursing education to a more scientific approach. She did acknowledge that some reference was made to the 'art' of nursing; however, this aspect was not explored in any detail other than to describe it as the skills of practice.

In contrast to empirical knowing, aesthetic knowing refers to knowing that is subjective and unique. Carper believed that the aesthetic meaning broadened the boundaries of the definition of the art of nursing practice to include the expressive and 'creative process of discovery' rather than relying on knowledge acquired through reason. She described it as

> *...the creation and/or appreciation of a singular, particular, subjective expression of imagined possibilities or equivalent realities which resists projection into the discursive form of language.*
> (Carper, 1978: 16)

Aesthetic knowing refers to the nurse or midwife considering clients as a whole rather than as an accumulation of separate parts, and being able to interpret and respond appropriately to their behaviour in a particular situation rather than according to rules, guidelines or protocol. Clements and Averill (2006: 270) describe it as experiential, non-verbal and shared by the nurse and client.

Carper referred to Dewey and Wiedenbach when she discussed the aesthetic process as the difference between recognition and perception. Recognition enables the nurse to classify and label, whereas perception involves pulling all the information together to form a whole. She described empathy as an example of an aesthetic pattern of knowing where one experiences another's feelings vicariously, identifying what the person's 'goal' is and what he or she wants from the situation or experience. Carper suggested that the more adept in perception and empathy a nurse is the more she or he has to gain in knowledge and understanding by being given a 'larger repertoire' in providing care that is 'effective and satisfying'. She stated that the aesthetic pattern of knowing is the 'knowing of a unique particular rather than an exemplary class' (Carper, 1978: 17–18).

The component of personal knowledge

Carper described personal knowledge as the most essential pattern of knowing whilst being the most difficult to teach. Similar to aesthetic knowing personal knowing is subjective and is about learning to know ourselves, and utilising personal meaning gained from experience to develop effective interpersonal skills. Although it is sometimes confused with factual knowledge used in practice it actually involves understanding ourselves and how we relate to others.

Nursing and midwifery practice relies on personal interaction and the development of a therapeutic relationship which in turn is influenced by how individual nurses or midwives see themselves, and how they perceive their client. Carper described personal knowledge as

> *...concerned with the knowing, encountering and actualisation of the concrete, the individual self.*
> (Carper, 1978: 18)

Carper continued,

> *...an authentic personal relation requires the acceptance of others in their freedom to create themselves and the recognition that each person is not a fixed entity, but constantly engaged in the process of becoming.*
> (Carper, 1978: 19)

With this in mind Carper went on to question how nurses can rationalise care that is routine or based on empirical generalisations when on an individual basis people are not always predictable and will have their own unique patterns of behaviours and preferences, some of which the nurse may not agree with or understand, and which may not conform to expected norms.

Carper ultimately believed that personal knowing was

...concerned with kind of knowing that promotes wholeness and integrity in the personal encounter, the achievement of engagement rather than detachment; and it denies the manipulative, impersonal orientation.

(Carper, 1978: 20)

Ethics, moral knowledge

The context of nursing and midwifery care is complex and as a consequence can make decision making difficult. Whilst Carper acknowledged the importance of professional codes and standards in helping nurses understand what is morally right and guiding them in the moral choices they make, she highlighted the difficult nature of decision making in unique, individual clinical situations which are often ambiguous.

Carper suggested this fundamental pattern of knowing goes beyond familiarity with, and understanding of, nursing codes and guidelines, believing it to include other forms of moral knowing; knowing what is right and wrong in the provision of care. Carper believed ethics to go beyond obligation and that moral knowledge

...goes beyond simply knowing the norms and ethical codes of the discipline. It includes all voluntary actions that are deliberate and subject to the judgement of right and wrong – including judgements of moral values in relation to motives, intentions and character traits.

(Carper, 1978: 20)

Putting theory into practice

Carper's fundamental patterns of knowing in nursing are still used in curriculum development today but are more commonly expressed in the literature as the foundation of reflective practice tools in nursing and midwifery as well as other disciplines related to health.

Johns (1995) compiled a set of questions based around the four patterns which aim to encourage the practitioner to be reflexive about their practice and adaptable to new situations. He used Carper's work to demonstrate that his model is a framework designed to challenge practice and in particular to interpret subjective experiences and explore nursing actions – how they are carried out and by what sort of person.

Johns (1995: 226) points out that becoming an effective practitioner is not only about developing technical skills but also involves personal deconstruction and reconstruction, stating that learning through reflection is a process of enlightenment (understand who I am), empowerment (change who I am), and emancipation (liberate who I need to be).

Reflective practice is where practitioners learn through experience and, through the process of reflection, identify how they feel about the situation in light of current knowledge and how to plan for future action. Johns' (1995) model of structured reflection uses Carper's four patterns of knowing to develop cue questions to aid practitioners to make sense of their experiences. These cue questions also take cognisance of the critical questions developed by Jacobs-Kramer and Chinn (1988) who extended Carper's patterns of knowing, developing a model that aimed to conceptualise how the four patterns could be put into practice in a more effective manner (See *Table 6.1*). Both models highlight that the patterns of knowing cannot be considered in isolation and accordingly provide questions that the practitioner can use to reflect on practice and identify

Table 6.1. A framework for reflection		
Carper's four patterns of knowing in nursing	*Jacobs-Kramer and Chinn (1988) critical questions*	*Johns' cue questions (1995) for reflection*
Empirics	What does this represent? How is this representative?	What knowledge did or should have informed me?
Aesthetics	What does this mean?	What was I trying to achieve? Why did I respond as I did? What were the consequences for the client, others, myself? How did the client feel? How did I know this?
Personal knowing	Do I know what I do? Do I do what I know?	How did I feel in this situation? What internal factors were influencing me?
Ethics	Is this right? Is this just?	How did my actions match with my beliefs? What factors made me act in incongruent ways?
Source: Carper, 1978; Jacobs-Kramer and Chinn, 1988; Johns, 1995		

the areas of knowing that are required to provide effective, safe and satisfying care for clients.

Carper stated:

One is almost led to believe that the only valid and reliable knowledge is that which is empirical, factual, objectively descriptive and generalisable.

(Carper, 1978: 16)

This could be a quote from a contemporary paper given the emphasis on evidence-based research in current nursing and midwifery practice. The focus on objective, empirical evidence where randomised controlled trials are seen as the gold standard has led to concerns that nurses and midwives may not be able to fully respond to the complex and diverse nature of the clinical situations with which they are faced. However, as acknowledged in Carper's taxonomy, for care to be meaningful and effective objective empirical knowledge cannot be exclusive as it cannot provide the answers to all practice questions and needs to be considered alongside other forms of qualitative evidence as well as the other patterns of knowing (White, 1995).

In contrast to Carper, Johns (1995) believes aesthetics to be at the root of knowing and that empirical, personal and ethical knowing all inform this, the holistic response to a clinical situation. He suggests that in order to provide individualised care the nurse must interpret the empirical evidence to suit the clinical situation rather than the other way around.

The aesthetic pattern is subjective and involves the nurse or midwife interpreting unique situations to understand what they mean to others. It is sometimes confused with the skills of practice rather than the broader concept of the expression of creativity in providing care. Jacobs-Kramer and Chinn (1988) summarise it as the ability to engage, interpret and envision through action. In practice the nurse or midwife develops a reciprocal relationship with the client rather than just providing prescribed care. In the case of midwifery it means truly 'being with woman' as in the literal meaning of midwife.

As Carper stated, personal knowing is about being self-aware, knowing oneself in order to understand and know others. Personal knowing cannot be articulated in words but is expressed through existence and is often explained as intuition. Reflection is a tool that can help nurses and midwives to do this. Johns' (1995: 229) states that personal knowing involves:

- The perception of the self's feelings and prejudices within a situation.
- The management of these feelings and prejudices in order to respond appropriately.
- Managing anxiety and sustaining the self.

Before engaging in a therapeutic relationship nurses and midwives need to know who they are before they can truly provide non-judgemental care. Johns believes this to be particularly important when the nurse or midwife has a negative feeling towards a client which may affect the therapeutic relationship. Where empirical knowing promotes detachment personal knowing encourages nurses and midwives not to hide their feelings when dealing with intimate or complex situations, instead they should be able to reflect and identify their feelings and recognise how they may contribute positively to the therapeutic relationship or negatively affect it.

Ethical decision making can be difficult, however nurses and midwives are accountable for their practice and therefore must be able to justify their actions or omissions. As Johns states (1995: 229), as with empirical

Links with other nursing theorists

Barbara Carper's theory links with Donald Schön's work on the practice of reflective learning; Michael Polanyi's tacit knowing; the work of the German philosoper Jürgen Habermas; John Dewey's philosophy of education, and Patricia Benner's Theory of Skill Acquisition (*see Chapter 10*).

References

Carper BA (1978) Fundamental patterns of knowing in nursing. *Advances in Nursing Science* **1**(1): 13–23

Carper BA (1988) Response to "Perspectives of knowing: A model of nursing knowledge" *Scholarly Inquiry for Nursing Practice* **2**(2): 141–3

Carper BA (2009) Fundamental patterns of knowing in nursing. In: Reed PG, Crawford Sheerer NB (eds) *Perspectives on nursing theory* (5th edn) Wolters Kluwer/ Lippincott Williams & Wilkins, Philadelphia

Clements P, Averill J (2006) Finding patterns of knowing in the work of Florence Nightingale. *Nursing Outlook* **54**(5): 268–74

Jacobs-Kramer M, Chinn P (1988) Perspectives on knowing: A model of nursing knowledge. Scholarly *Inquiry for Nursing Practice* **2**(2): 129–39

Johns C (1995) Framing learning through reflection within Carper's fundmental ways of knowing in nursing. *Journal of Advanced Nursing* **22**: 226–34

Munhall P (2001) Epistemology in Nursing. In: Munhall P (ed.) *Nursing research: A qualitative perspective* (3rd edn). Jones and Bartlett, London

White J (1995) Patterns of knowing: Review, critique, and update. *Advances in Nursing Science* **17**(4): 73–86

knowing, ethics only informs practice, and the challenge to practitioners is to be clear about what is right and what is wrong in a particular situation as this will affect the aesthetic response.

As Carper (1978) highlighted, none of the patterns of knowing can be isolated in the provision of skilled nursing and midwifery practice. Empirical research is crucial to provide the basis of sound evidence-based practice; however, it is also essential that care is creative and meaningful, whilst also being morally right, in order to provide choice for individuals in unique situations. To achieve this, the practitioner must be able to engage with clients, interpret their experiences and respond appropriately to their needs. In reality, nurses and midwives often have difficulty expressing how Carper's patterns of knowing shape their practice; a reflective tool such as Johns' is valuable in enabling them to disassemble the components of their practice so as to inform future actions.

Carper's influence

Over recent years there have been numerous changes in the provision of healthcare, from changing client demographics and expectations to the increasing use of technology. Despite these changes, Carper's *Fundamental patterns of knowing in nursing* has continued to be influential in the development of nursing and midwifery education, where the patterns have ensured that the wide spectrum of knowledge and skills required are included in education programmes both at pre- and post-registration level. Furthermore, they have enabled practitioners to provide care in a dynamic social context and for clients with complex individual needs.

Not only has this taxonomy been fundamental in the development of learning theory, it has also provided the foundation for other theorists to develop innovative models and theories for nursing and midwifery practice. In an attempt to integrate Carper's framework more effectively into clinical practice Jacobs-Kramer and Chinn (1988) developed it further, a decade after the original publication, and produced a model that clarified the expression, processes and assessment of each of the four patterns so that they could be integrated more effectively into practice (see *Table 6.1*). Carper responded to this model in 1988 commending it as necessary in the discussion surrounding nursing epistemology in an era dominated by scientific inquiry.

In 1993, Munhall (2001) also added a fifth pattern to Carper's taxonomy, which she labelled 'unknowing'. She proposed that unknowing was related to developing an openness to other ways of doing things and believed that nurses can unwittingly become limited by their own beliefs and stop looking for further explanation in their practice. Munhall explained this pattern citing the poet James Russell Lowell 'only by unlearning wisdom comes' (Munhall, 2001: 42).

White (1995) however believed the context of learning was missing from these patterns and models and added yet another pattern – 'socio-political' knowing, which she believed to be fundamental to all the other patterns. This pattern shifts the focus from the nurse–client relationship and situates it in a wider context, thus encouraging the nurse to examine professional practice and the politics of service provision. White (1995: 84) relates socio-political knowing with cultural identity and suggests that in order to understand concepts of health, as they pertain to both the nurse and client, the nurse must have a wider knowledge of the social, political and economic influences on service provision.

Carper has played a crucial role in laying the foundations of nursing theory by identifying the fundamental patterns of knowing for nursing and midwifery education and practice. These patterns of knowing have since been critically examined and developed by others. Despite the more recent focus on evidence-based practice there is general consensus with Barbara Carper in the literature that both scientific and non-scientific forms of knowledge have equal standing, and are necessary in nursing and midwifery practice. Care cannot be based on empirical evidence alone because human beings are complex and must be considered in context. Care must also be informed by other patterns of knowing, such as ethical and personal knowing, to enable practitioners to be creative in the delivery of appropriate and effective care.

Where to find out more

Carper BA (1992) Philosophical inquiry in nursing: An application In: Kikuchi F, Simmons H (eds) *Philosophic inquiry in nursing*. Sage, London

McKenna H, Slevin O (2008) *Nursing models, theories and practice*. Blackwell Publishing, Oxford

Reed P, Crawford Shearer N (eds) (2009) *Perspectives on nursing theory* (5th edn) Wolters Kluwer/Lippincott, Williams and Wilkins, London

Profile

Paterson and Zderad were champions and pioneers of nursing in that they attempted to move on from the positivist approach, common in nursing at the time, and became more focused on the people involved in nursing and the development of relationships between nurses and patients. However, they recognised that both science and art should be valued for their contribution to the continuing development of human potential (Paterson and Zderad, 2007).

Key dates

Paterson

1945	Nursing diploma
1954	BSc in nurse education
1955	MA in public health
1968	Doctorate in Nursing

Zderad

1947	Nursing diploma
	BSc in nurse education
1950	MA in philosophy
1952	MSc in nurse education
1968	PhD

Paterson and Zderad

Mid-50s	Teaching with graduate nursing programme
1972	Invited to develop course for qualified nurses
1976	Publication of *Humanistic Nursing*
1978	Teaching on humanistic nursing course
1985	Retire

CHAPTER 7

Josephine Paterson and Loretta Zderad

Anne Kay

Biography

Josephine Paterson was born in Freeport, New York on 1st September 1924. She graduated, with a diploma, from Lenox Hill School of Nursing (New York) in 1945. In 1954, she graduated from St John's University (Brooklyn, New York) obtaining a Bachelor of Science in Nursing Education and, in 1955, she completed a Master of Public Health from the John Hopkins School of Hygiene and Public Health in Baltimore, Maryland. She specialised in public and mental health nursing. In 1969, Paterson received a Doctorate in Nursing from Boston University within the specialty of psychiatric mental health. The subject of her doctoral dissertation was comfort.

Loretta Zderad was born in Chicago, Illinois on 7th June 1925. In 1947, she received a diploma from St Bernard's School of Nursing (Chicago) and, at the same time, gained a Bachelor of Science in Nursing Education from the Loyola University of Chicago. Five years later, she gained a Master of Science in Nursing Education (Catholic University of America) where she specialised in psychiatric nursing with a bent towards philosophy. In 1950, she completed a Master of Arts in philosophy and, subsequently, completed her PhD in philosophy in 1968 (both at Georgetown University). The subject of her doctoral dissertation was empathy.

During the 1950s and 1960s, Paterson and Zderad gained the nursing experience that would help them formulate their theory of nursing. From the mid-1950s, as well as being doctoral students themselves, they taught in a graduate nursing programme in the Catholic University where they were involved in developing a course that would integrate community health and psychiatric nursing elements of the nursing programme. They have worked together and been friends since that time.

During the period when they worked together in the 1960s, they began to struggle with the meanings of concepts and with the issues faced by nurses, both professionally and clinically. Through an attempt to clarify their thoughts, through open and honest argument and through the process of dialogue with their students, patients and other professionals, they became aware that their struggle was 'with' and not 'against' the ideas of others. Both theorists valued the opportunity to engage in dialogue with others as this dialogue helped clarify meaning and expand experience. This approach permeates humanistic nursing theory (Paterson and Zderad, 2007).

In 1972, Marguerite L Burt, then Chief of Nursing Service of the Veterans Administration Hospital (Northport, New York) asked Paterson and Zderad to develop a course for the professional nursing staff at the hospital. This resulted in the Humanistic Nursing Course, which they taught in New York until 1978. Subsequently, they were encouraged to put their concepts into writing by Miss Burt. In *Humanistic nursing*, first published in 1976, they describe the experience of developing their theory with the assistance of the students who completed their course through the linked processes of learning, clarification and revision (Paterson and Zderad, 2007).

Both nurse theorists held the position of 'nursologist' at the Northport Veterans Administration Hospital in Northport, New York, which focused on improving patient care through the elements of clinical practice, education and research. In 1978, following reorganisation of the service of the hospital, Paterson worked as a psychotherapist and Zderad as the associate chief of the Nursing Service for Education. Both nurse theorists retired to Shallotte, North Carolina in 1985.

Summary of writings

Most of Paterson and Zderad's publications date from the 1960s and 1970s and may be difficult to track down. Their magnum opus, *Humanistic nursing* (1976), in which they describe their theory of nursing, was reissued in 1988. According to Kleiman (Paterson and Zderad, 2007), the book's original intent was to define Humanistic Nursing Theory and to stimulate nurses to become more. 'Becoming more' involves the nurse in gaining experience, followed by questioning and reflection on that experience to allow development of self-awareness, learning and the realisation of potential through openness to the endless possibilities of a situation.

Humanistic nursing is divided into two sections (Theoretical roots; and Methodology: a process of being) and details the theory, its roots (phenomenology and existentialism) and how it was developed over a number of years, based on reflection and discussion between the two nurse theorists and their students. Practice, research and education are viewed as equal and inseparable components of the theory and their interests in continuing the development of the concepts of comfort and empathy, the foci of their separate doctoral theses, is evidenced throughout this work.

Nursing is identified as a specific form of human dialogue. Indeed, the concept of dialogue is inherent in the theory and is advocated as a key way to continue its development. However, dialogue does not merely entail speech but includes all that goes on between nurse and patient and culminates in the process of 'call and response' that is nursing.

Interestingly, a focus of Humanistic Nursing Theory is the concept of 'becoming more'. This term could equally apply to the language of the theory. Everyday words are used (Paterson and Zderad, 2007), but their meaning within the theory often extends beyond common usage and, thus entails a form of 'becoming more' than the day-to-day use of these words. For example, the word 'between', in everyday use, means 'at a point or in a region intermediate to two other points in space, times, degrees, etc.' (Collins Dictionary, 2007). Paterson and Zderad (2007) use the words 'the between' to describe the point where nurses and the nursed meet and interact. The nurse is aware of the experience of caring for someone, the nursed is aware of the experience of being cared for, but each is also aware of the experience of interaction that has occurred and the inter-human process experienced.

Other key concepts, which inform the theory, are community and noetic locus. Community means the family, the place where the person lives (town or country) and how these impact on the person. Noetic locus is used to describe the nurse as a 'knowing place', the source of experience and knowledge. Nursing is described as a multi-faceted concept with the acknowledgement of a range of factors, which must be taken into account when carrying out the act of nursing. These include age, health problem, help needed (including duration, location, and potential for obtaining and using the help), the nurse's perception of what is going on and her capacity to help the other person. Paterson and Zderad (2007) note that all of these issues exist regardless of nurses' specialist areas and recommend that, in order to be able to focus on the phenomenon of nursing, nurses should attempt to 'bracket' (hold in abeyance) their specialist knowledge. This is in order to see nursing in a more focused way, in order to see the thing itself – nursing, because the act of nursing applies to a wide range of

Links with other nursing theorists

Josephine Paterson and Loretta Zderad's work links with Katherine Kolcaba's Theory of Comfort (*see Chapter 8*), Anne Boykin and Savina Schoenhofer's Nursing as Caring and Susan Kleiman's Human-Centred Nursing

References and further reading

AraÃjo MAL, de Farias FLR, Rodrigues AVB (2006) Anti-HIV after-test counselling: analysis at a light of a nursing humanistic theory [sic] [Portuguese]. *Escola Anna Nery Revista de Enfermagem* **10**(3): 425–31

Boykin A, Schoenhofer S (1993) *Nursing as Caring: A model for transforming practice.* National League for Nursing Press, New York

Boykin A, Schoenhofer S (2001) *Nursing as Caring: A model for transforming practice.* National League for Nursing Press, New York

Collins Dictionary (2007) *Collins Dictionary.* Harper Collins Publishers, Glasgow

da Silva LMP, GalvÃo MTG, de AraÃjo TL, Cardoso MVL (2007) Taking care of children's family on sexual abuse situation considering the humanistic theory [in Portuguese]. *Brazilian Journal of Nursing* **6**(1) [online]

Decker-Brown K (2009) *Paterson and Zderad's Humanistic Nursing Theory.* Available from: http://www.humanistic-nursing theory.com [accessed 19 May 2009]

Dowd T (2006) Theory of comfort. In Tomey MA, Alligood MR (eds) *Nursing theorists and their work.* (6th edn) Mosby Elsevier, St. Louis

Fredriksson L (1999) Modes of relating in a caring conversation: A research synthesis on presence, touch and listening. *Journal of Advanced Nursing* **30**(5): 1167–76

Holmes CA (1990) Alternatives to natural science foundations for nursing. *International Journal of Nursing Studies* **27**(3): 187–98

Kleiman S (2006) Josephine

situations and the things that matter most, the foundational principles, are the same, regardless of age, problems faced, etc.

Humanistic Nursing Theory

Kleiman (2006) describes Humanistic Nursing Theory as multi-dimensional and notes that it is focused on the essences of nursing and the dynamics of being, becoming and changing. Meleis (1997) describes Humanistic Nursing Theory as an interaction theory. He notes that earlier nurse theorists (Abdellah, Henderson, Orem) focused on a needs approach and their theories were developed in order to answer questions about what nurses do, what their functions are and what roles they play. While later theorists (King, Orlando, Paterson and Zderad, Peplau, Travelbee and Wiedenbach) were still concerned with these questions, they were more interested in discovering/describing how nurses do what they do and they developed a focus on interactions. Some of the factors leading to the development of interaction theories included: the social change in relationships between people, where there was a greater awareness of the human need for intimacy and a moving away from the mechanism and dehumanisation of technology in nursing; and the integration of curricula, which allowed psychiatric nurses to focus on fundamental concepts through observation and reflection, which could be integrated into all nursing subspecialties. Interaction theories focus on the process of care and on the interaction between participants in care.

Paterson and Zderad were pioneers of nursing in that they attempted to move on (rather than away) from the positivist approach described by Holmes (1990: 187) as 'mechanistic, analytic and reactive', towards a focus on the people involved in nursing – the nurse and the nursed – and the process of interaction which focused on the development of relationships between nurses and patients. However, Paterson and Zderad did not reject the scientific, recognising that both science and art are responses to the human situation and as such should be valued for their contribution to the continuing development of human potential (Paterson and Zderad, 2007).

Humanistic Nursing Theory combines elements of phenomenology and existentialism. The focus of phenomenology is the 'here and now', defined by Paterson and Zderad (2007) as the person's unique experience, involving temporal and spatial awareness of his or her past and hopes for the future, and entails the study of the entirety of a phenomenon (Meleis, 1997). It is also a methodology, which opens phenomena up to scrutiny as they occur in the world so that they can be described and appreciated from the perspective of the subject of the phenomena rather than from an objective viewpoint (Pearson et al., 2005). The phenomenon of study in Paterson and Zderad's theory is the rich experience of nursing and they have used phenomenology to describe the 'angular views' of nurses and to clarify nursing phenomena. In the theory, 'angular view' refers to individuals' unique vision of the reality in which they find themselves but which may be restricted because of the angle of the current here and now of the situation.

Existentialism views the person as unique and focuses on describing what 'is' rather than attempting to understand 'why' things happen. Freedom of choice and personal responsibility are underlying tenets of existentialism and there is an emphasis on the lack of a fixed nature and the possibility of becoming something else (Meleis, 1997). Pearson et al. (2005) note that

...people are in an enduring state of development, the hopes and strategies for their future impinge on individuals as they are now and have been. A person's essence (what the person is) is a product of their existence and

therefore existence (the becoming) precedes and shapes the person's ever-developing essence.

(Pearson et al., 2005: 194)

Paterson and Zderad (2007) describe the existential experience as an awareness of self and others, which calls for recognition of the uniqueness of the individual and his or her struggle to survive and become more. They also note that

...nurses consciously and deliberately approach nursing as an existential experience.

(Paterson and Zderad, 2007)

Paterson and Zderad (2007) define nursing as a form of lived, human dialogue, which offers nurturing and intersubjective relating to the participants of the dialogue. The concept of dialogue is not simply defined as sending and receiving messages but includes full engagement of the people involved, referred to as a purposeful 'call and response'. The person who has a problem (the nursed) sends out a call and the helper (the nurse or other professional) responds. Humanistic nursing is undertaken as a deliberate act, not a lucky happenstance, and is ai`zmed at nurturing all of those involved to a state of well-being or more-being (the potential for human development). The dialogue of nursing takes place in the 'community' where two or more people work together to understand one another as unique individuals (Praeger, 2002).

Nursing involves nurses in being and doing. The things that nurses do are very familiar and relatively easy to describe, but 'being' with someone is often more important than what is done. The idea of 'presence' is key to the theory but there must be the belief that presence is of value and will make a difference to the experience (Paterson and Zderad, 2007). O'Connor (1993, 1995) notes that Paterson and Zderad were among the first nurse theorists to attempt to articulate the concept of presence. Individuals in the nursing experience may be changed by what happens and may be aware of the nature of the change. However, they may also be aware of an extra element, 'the between' which may be described as happening in the 'space between' the process of being and doing. While nurses may find it easy to describe what they mean by 'nursing' by answering the question, 'What did you do?' in a situation, the response will not always articulate all that happened. Paterson and Zderad suggest that in trying to elucidate the concept of nursing, it might be more pertinent to answer the question, 'What happened between you?'

Humanistic Nursing Theory is clearly focused on explaining what nursing is and gives an opportunity to explore the multiplicity of concepts, which make up the whole. As such, it may offer an opportunity to bridge the theory–practice gap, through the elucidation of both via research. Rolfe (1996) describes this 'gap' as the difference between what theory and research suggest ought to happen and what actually does happen in practice.

Putting theory into practice

Kleiman (2006) offers an insight into the practical applications of Humanistic Nursing Theory from her own experience by describing three separate situations where she has found it beneficial. She has found it useful in the process of clinical supervision, which she likens to 'call and response'. She outlines the story of a nurse with whom she had been working who felt that medical staff were not responding to the needs of a young woman who had been diagnosed as HIV positive. Through exploration, they reached the

Paterson and Loretta Zderad's Humanistic Nursing Theory and its applications. In Parker ME (ed) *Nursing theories and nursing practice* (2nd edn) FA Davis Company, Philadelphia

Kleiman S (2009a) *Humanistic Nursing*. Available from: http://www.humanistic-nursing.com [accessed 19 May 2009]

Kleiman S (2009b) *Human Centered Nursing*. FA Davis Company, Philadelphia

Kolcaba KY, Kolcaba RJ (1991) An analysis of the concept of comfort. *Journal of Advanced Nursing* **16**: 1301–10

LÃcio IML, Pagliuca LMF, Cardoso MVL (2008) Dialogue as a presupposition [sic] in the humanistic nursing theory: Relationship mother-nurse-newborn [in Portuguese]. *Revista da Escola de Enfermagem da USP* **42**(1): 173–80

McQuiston CM, Webb AA (eds) (1995) *Foundations of nursing theory*. Sage Publications, Thousand Oaks

Medeiros HMF, da Motta MGC (2008) HIV/AIDS children living in shelters under the perspective of humanistic nursing [in Portuguese]. *Revista Gaucha de Enfermagem* **29**(3): 400–7

Meleis AI (1997) *Theoretical nursing: Development and progress* (3rd edn) Lippincott, Philadelphia

Mitchell GJ, Cody WK (1999) Nursing knowledge and human science: Ontological and epistemological considerations. In Polifroni EC, Welch M (eds) *Perspectives on philosophy of science in nursing*. Lippincott, Philadelphia

O'Connor N (1993) *Paterson and Zderad: Humanistic Nursing Theory*. Sage Publications, Newbury Park, Ca

O'Connor N (1995) Paterson and Zderad: Humanistic Nursing

Theory. In McQuiston CM, Webb AA (eds) *Foundations of nursing theory*. Sage Publications, Thousand Oaks

Ordahi LFB, Padilha MIC, Souza LNA (2007) Communication between nursing staff and clients unable to communicate verbally. *Revista Latino-Americana de Enfermagen* **15**(5): 965–72

Paterson J, Zderad L (2007) *Humanistic Nursing*. Available from: http://The Project Gutenberg eBook Humanistic nursing.com [accessed 17 June 2009]

Pearson A, Vaughan B, Fitzgerald M (2005) *Nursing models for Practice* (3rd edn) Butterworth Heinemann, Edinburgh

Persegona KR, Zagonel IPS (2008) The intersubjective relationship between nurse and child with pain in post-surgical fase [sic] in the caring act [in Portuguese].*Escola Anna Nery Revista de Enfermagem* **12**(3): 430–6

Polifroni EC, Packard S (1999) Psychological determinism and the evolving nurse paradigm. In Polifroni EC, Welch M (eds) *Perspectives on philosophy of science in nursing*. Lippincott, Philadelphia

Polifroni EC, Welch M (eds) (1999) *Perspectives on philosophy of science in nursing*. Lippincott, Philadelphia

Praeger SG (2002) Humanistic Nursing Josephine G. Paterson and Loretta T Zderad. In George JB (ed) *Nursing theories. The base for professional nursing practice* (5th edn) Prentice Hall, Upper Saddle River, NJ

Purnell MJ (2006) Nursing as Caring: A model for transforming practice. In Tomey MA, Alligood MR (eds) *Nursing theorists and their work* (6th edn) Mosby Elsevier, St. Louis

Reed PG (1999) A treatise on nurs-

conclusion that it was not medical support that the woman required, but nursing. Part of the problem faced by the nurse was her personal experience of losing a friend who was similar in appearance. Thus was revealed her 'angular view' of the situation. Further exploration uncovered the difficulty that the nurse was having in understanding the relationship the young woman had with the boyfriend who had infected her. By using the process of bracketing, the nurse was able to put aside, or hold in abeyance, her own thoughts leading her to an appreciation of the right to choices, which are fundamental in humanistic nursing. The nurse was able to develop her own awareness of herself as a noetic locus or knowing place. Kleiman concludes that Humanistic Nursing Theory benefits nurses (supervisors and supervisees) as well as the nursed to become more.

Kleiman goes on to describe the usefulness of Humanistic Nursing Theory in research. She helped prepare some nursing colleagues to undertake phenomenological research into non-concordance with psychiatric day hospital treatment. Firstly, she helped expand their angular view by educating them about phenomenology and how to conduct unstructured interviews. In order to make themselves open to what they would uncover, the nurses learned to bracket their own experiences. The nurses discovered that, for the nursed, entering the day hospital for the first time was, not surprisingly, fraught with anxiety. However, the nurses had not appreciated that there were no anxiety reducing aspects in place. The study resulted in changes being made which helped people settle in (Kleiman, 2006).

Finally, Kleiman discusses using Humanistic Nursing Theory to assist a group of staff to respond to a policy change, which led to alterations in their nursing roles. The community of nurses worked together to find solutions to their problems, leading to a sharing of experience and a broadening of their angular views. Through reflection, they learned to appreciate their own uniqueness and strengths and were able to understand that their image as competent individuals was theirs to control and led to the growth of empowerment within the community (Kleiman, 2006).

Tyler-Ball (2007) describes the experience of 'entering the between' in relation to her work. She tells the story of 'James' a young man admitted to her care who had been left paralysed from the neck down. She and her colleagues knew that James would be committed to a wheelchair and the use of a ventilator for the rest of his life. Initially, she hoped to avoid having to answer questions from his mother about his prognosis because she dreaded the mother's reaction to the reality of the situation. However, Tyler-Ball realised that waiting for the mother to ask the specific question about James' recovery was worse than facing the truth of the situation with her. Eventually, she realised the need to 'enter the between' and led James's mother into a discussion about his future. James was fully aware of the lack of hope for his future and decided that he wanted to have life-sustaining support withdrawn. He called on Tyler-Ball and his mother to help him and they responded by becoming his advocates. By answering James's call, Tyler-Ball entered the dialogue of nursing with him and his mother to help both to adapt and cope with his situation. Tyler-Ball notes that

Nursing is inadequately represented by a singular scientific focus. Through commitment and courage, I have been honoured…to answer the call of nursing. The 'between' of these nursing experiences have allowed me to share experiences of honesty, humility, knowing and alternating rhythms.

(Tyler-Ball, 2007: 83)

Vassallo (2001) demonstrates how Humanistic Nursing Theory can be applied to care of the dying and their families. In a full account of the work of hospice nurses, she focuses on demonstrating the application of the elements of angular view, bracketing and noetic locus. The angular view of hospice nurses includes an awareness of their own mortality, spirituality and uniqueness as individuals. As a result, they can support the dying person and family to come to terms with their situation. By bracketing judgements and biases, nurses can fully focus on the needs of the nursed so that, ultimately, they can die in their own way. She indicates that hospice nurses become the noetic focus or knowing place by bringing the fullness of their personal experiences and intuition, as well as their professional knowledge, to the spiritual care of the dying. Other aspects of the theory, which can be applied to the care of the dying, are 'presence' and 'call and response'. Vassallo (2001:27) notes that '…presence is a priceless source of comfort to the dying person' and indicates the frequency of the request '…for someone to be there'. Nursing requires the nurse to respond to the call of the nursed; Vassallo describes the response to this ultimate call and tells us that the hospice nurse will remain connected to the dying person and his or her family for as long as required by a common bond of caring (Vassallo, 2001).

In searching for recent literature, it became evident that there is considerable recent interest in the application of Paterson and Zderad's work amongst Spanish and Portuguese speaking nurses. Unfortunately, these are published in the language of the authors, but available abstracts give some idea of the range of work being undertaken. For example, Santos et al. (2007a) describe the care of patients who have no hope of recovery. The authors aimed to increase the quality of the lives of those in their care by using Humanistic Nursing Theory to acknowledge the person's unique experience and give the nurse the opportunity to understand the person's meaning in the process of the disease. Ordahi et al (2007) applied the theory to help them reflect on caring for clients who could not communicate. Other works suggest the use of the theory in HIV-counselling, family care in child sexual abuse, defining the concept of health, paediatric post-operative care, working with children who are HIV positive, and neonatal nursing (AraÃjo et al., 2006; da Silva et al., 2007; Santos et al., 2007b, Persegona and Zagonel, 2008; Medeiros et al., 2008; Rolim, 2008).

In exploring the concept of comfort, Tutton and Seers (2003) suggest that Humanistic Nursing Theory may have limitations because of a lack of consideration of physical needs. The range of applications discussed might suggest that other authors have not found this to be a drawback.

Influence

One of the main authors influenced by Paterson and Zderad is Kleiman (2006; 2009a, b), a former student whom Paterson supervised in her PhD work. Kleiman has continued to develop Humanistic Nursing Theory, in line with the expressed wishes of Paterson and Zderad, and she has had the opportunity for discussion with them over a number of years. She has contributed a variety of writings to journals and books, as well as maintaining a website devoted to Humanistic Nursing Theory. However, she is not a mere acolyte and continues to develop the theory as evidenced in her book, *Human centered nursing* (2009b). Kleiman defines human-centred nursing as

> *…a lived dialogue, a call and response event that occurs between a nurse and a person who come together in a nursing occasion.*
>
> (Kleiman, 2009b: 5)

While this may sound very similar to the work of Paterson and Zderad, Kleiman has conducted her own research, which has allowed her to expand

ing knowledge development for the 21st century: Beyond postmodernism. In Polifroni EC, Welch M (eds) *Perspectives on philosophy of science in nursing*. Lippincott, Philadelphia

Rolfe G (1996) *Closing the theory–practice gap*. Butterworth-Heinemann, Oxford

Rolim KMC (2008) Humanistic nursing: Contribute for development of the nurse in neonatal unit [in Portuguese]. *Revista Eletronica de Enfermage* **10**(1): 251–3

Santos MCL, Pagliuca LMF, Fernandes AFC (2007a) Palliative care to the cancer patient: Reflections according to Paterson and Zderad's view. *Revista Latino-Americana de Enfermagen* **15**(2): 350–4

Santos MCL, Pagliuca LMF, Fernandes AFC (2007b) Humanistic theory: Dimensional analysis of the concept of health [in Spanish]. *Metas de EnfermerÃa.* **10**(4): 56–60

Tutton E, Seers K (2003) An exploration of the concept of comfort. *Journal of Clinical Nursing* **12**(5): 689–96

Tyler-Ball S (2007) Entering the between: Courage to attend to suffering. *International Journal for Human Caring* **11**(2): 81–3

Vassallo BM (2001) The spiritual aspects of dying at home. *Holistic Nursing Practice* **15**(2): 17–29

Where to find out more

- http://The Project Gutenberg eBook Humanistic nursing.com
Humanistic nursing has been re-issued as an e-book (currently available as a free download via the Gutenberg Press at the above website).

- Kleiman (2006, 2009a, b) Susan Kleiman is currently the main champion of the work of Paterson and Zderad and her body of work is a rich source for those who wish to know more about the theory.

- http://www.humanisticnursing theory.com
Karen Decker-Brown maintains this website devoted to humanistic nursing theory, which includes outline biographies of Paterson and Zderad in their historical context; a glossary of terms; an outline of the content of Humanistic Nursing and a resource list.

- Nancy O'Connor has contributed a monograph on the theory to the *Notes on nursing theories* series, published by Sage (1993) and replicated in McQuiston and Webb (1995). This document is a fairly complex critique of the theory and may be more appropriate as a source for students following some general reading.

A range of other readings can be found in the reference and further reading list for this chapter.

the original constructs of Humanistic Nursing and give them an immediacy suited to current events in the world of nursing.

Purnell (2006) discusses the various works that influenced Boykin and Schoenhofer in developing their theory: Nursing as Caring. One of these was Paterson and Zderad's theory, which they credit as the '...historical antecedent of Nursing as Caring' (Purnell, 2006: 407). In addition, the theory spawned the development of Boykin and Schoenhofer's ideas on 'the between', 'the call for nursing', 'the nursing response' and 'personhood'. Boykin and Schoenhofer (2001) discuss 'caring between', which they describe as the development of caring when the nurse enters the world of the patient with the intention of helping, learning about the other person and nurturing personhood in them; without this element, they believe, nursing in its fullest sense will not happen. The 'call for nursing', which is described as a call for nurturance, and the 'nursing response' where the nurse transforms her knowledge from the general to the specific needs of the individual (Boykin and Schoenhofer, 1993) relate very closely to the concept of 'call and response' in Humanistic Nursing Theory. In discussing 'personhood', Boykin and Schoenhofer (2001) note that it describes the unique experience of each individual and requires authenticity of response from nurses; these ideas appear to have their base in the work of Paterson and Zderad.

Dowd (2006) indicates that, in developing her Theory of Comfort, Kolcaba derived the term transcendence from the work of Paterson and Zderad who believed that nurses helped patients to rise above their difficulties. Kolcaba's definition of transcendence includes the idea that the individual will rise above pain or problems, which have resulted in the need for nursing. In developing her own theory, Kolcaba attempted to analyse the meanings of 'comfort' and indicated that Paterson saw comfort as fundamental to the nature of nursing. Paterson's perception '...conforms well to a patient being strengthened, encouraged, supported, physically refreshed and/or invigorated...' (Kolcaba and Kolcaba, 1991: 1305) and links to the properties of transcendence including renewal, increased power, positive ways of thinking and readiness for action as described by Kolcaba and Kolcaba.

CHAPTER 8

Katharine Kolcaba

John Atkinson and Yvonne Christley

Biography

Katharine Kolcaba was born on the 28th December 1944 in Cleveland, Ohio in the United States. She commenced her nurse training in 1962 and graduated with a diploma in nursing studies from St Luke's Hospital School of Nursing, Cleveland in 1965. Between 1965 and 1985 Kolcaba combined practising as a clinical nurse with bringing up her three daughters; during this time she gained considerable experience in medical, surgical, community and continuing care nursing. The experiences she gained during this time, and in particular while nursing people with dementia, contributed significantly to the later development of her theory. By 1985 her children were becoming more independent and this enabled her to focus more fully on her career aspirations (Tomey and Alligood, 2006).

To progress her career Kolcaba realised that she would need to augment her clinical experience with an academic degree. As such, she enrolled in a Masters in Nursing Studies at the Frances Payne Bolton School of Nursing, Case Western Reserve University, Ohio. Throughout the duration of her masters degree Kolcaba continued to practice as a senior nurse in a dementia unit. It was this blending of clinical and academic experiences that allowed her to start to explore, think and theorise about the concept of comfort in nursing practice. Kolcaba completed her masters studies in 1987.

Shortly after the completion her masters Kolcaba was appointed to the position of lecturer at the University of Akron College of Nursing, Ohio. This appointment required her to undertake a PhD, which she completed on a part-time basis at Case Western Reserve University, Ohio in 1997. In the same year she received the Marie Haug Student Award for excellence in aging studies. In 2003 she was granted the Advancement of Science Award from Midwest Nursing Research Society (Kolcaba, 2003).

Kolcaba has spent the last two decades of her academic career at the University of Akron College of Nursing where she is currently Associate Professor Emeritus. Throughout this time she has contributed significantly to nurse teaching, theory and research and is an internationally renowned scholar, leader, educator and researcher.

Special interest

The beginnings of Comfort Theory are firmly rooted in and originate from Kolcaba's reflections on her experience as a clinical nurse caring for older people. Kolcaba was a senior nurse in a dementia unit when she began to think about the importance of comfort in nursing care. She formalised this insight by developing and publishing a framework for dementia care nursing (Kolcaba, 1988). This piece of work introduced and articulated the initial stages of Comfort Theory which were further refined and expanded upon by the completion of a comprehensive concept analysis of comfort. The concept analysis of comfort required the completion of a wide ranging review of the literature, which included not only nursing but other professional disciplines such as medicine, ergonomics and psychology (Kolcaba and Kolcaba, 1991).

Kolcaba also examined the historical significance of comfort to nursing practice. She found that comfort featured extensively in the nursing literature

Katharine Kolcaba
Born 1944

Profile

Katharine Kolcaba developed and pioneered the theory of comfort. She is an internationally distinguished scholar and has published extensively on the concept of comfort and its importance to nursing practice, education and research. Kolcaba's vision, leadership and ingenuity has resulted in a nursing theory that recognises, focuses and provides a means of systematically evaluating the importance of comfort to the meaningful and therapeutic nursing care of patients.

Key dates

1965	Graduated with a diploma in nursing from St. Luke's Hospital School of Nursing
1987	Graduated with a MSc in nursing from the Frances Payne Bolton School of Nursing, Case Western Reserve University
1991	Published an analysis of the concept of comfort
1991	Published the taxonomic structure of comfort
1994	Published a theory of holistic comfort for nursing
1997	PhD in nursing from the Case Western Reserve University. Awarded the Marie Haug Student Award for excellence in aging studies
2003	Awarded the Advancement of Science Award from Midwest Nursing Research Society
2003	Published *Comfort Theory and practice: A vision for holistic healthcare and research*

from as early as Florence Nightingale in the 1850s; the original Nightingale nurses were duty bound to create therapeutic caring environments, aimed at ensuring patients received the highest standards of personal care and comfort (Kolcaba and Kolcaba, 1991). Kolcaba's concept analysis demonstrated that comfort was not new to nursing; however what was new was the articulation and identification of the essential supporting features of comfort to therapeutic and holistic nursing care. In essence Kolcaba transformed comfort from a woolly, difficult-to-define concept into an essential, measurable, empirical, curative, palliative and moral component of nursing practice.

The knowledge derived from the concept analysis was used in conjunction with key aspects of other nursing theories to construct the three types of comfort (relief, ease and transcendence) identified within Comfort Theory.

- *Relief* was developed from Orlando's (1961) Nursing Process Theory, which asserts that an essential function of the nurse is to relieve patients' care needs.
- *Ease* was developed from the work of Henderson (1966) who explained the essential functions required to maintain homeostasis.
- *Transcendence* was deduced from the work of Paterson and Zderad (1975) who asserted that nursing care could assist patients to rise above their problems.

The comfort types of relief, ease and transcendence, in conjunction with the four contexts within which comfort occurs, provide a guiding structure from which nurses can design and deliver holistic comfort care for patients.

Comfort Theory clearly places the care needs of the patients at the centre of the nursing role and function, and this message has important considerations for both nurses and care providers. In the current healthcare climate, where evidence-based practice and value for money are of paramount importance, distinctions are often made between what is 'nice if you have the time' and what is absolutely necessary to assist patients on their healthcare journey. Prior to the development of Comfort Theory the provision of comfort was in danger of being perceived as a woolly 'nice if you have the time' concept rather than essential evidence-based nursing intervention (Kolcaba, 2003).

The Comfort Theory has highlighted the significance and meaning of comfort to therapeutic and effective nursing care. In developing and refining the theory Kolcaba made use of quantitative and qualitative research methods, which has allowed her systematically to measure the importance of comfort to clinical practice, research and education. This has enabled Kolcaba to refine Comfort Theory into a clearly structured and straightforward theory that can be used in almost any practice, educational or research environment. Kolcaba

continues to improve and develop the theory of comfort thereby addressing some of the core issues of how nursing and nursing care is defined, developed and understood (Kolcaba, 2000).

Summary of writings

Kolcaba has written numerous journal articles and book chapters and a book on the concept of comfort and its relationship to nursing practice and care. Some of her most important writings are contained within the following four groundbreaking works.

An analysis of the concept of comfort (Kolcaba and Kolcaba, 1991) introduced to the nursing literature the early beginnings of Comfort Theory. This paper pioneered the identification and development of the three types of comfort: relief, ease and transcendence. This initial introductory paper was followed shortly after with the publication of *A taxonomic structure for the concept comfort* (Kolcaba, 1991). This important paper developed, refined and expanded Kolcaba's previous work on the three types of comfort into a holistic taxonomy (*Table 8.1*). The taxonomy continued to include the three types of comfort identified in the previous paper, however it also expanded Comfort Theory to included four contexts of experience within which comfort occurs; these contexts are identified as physical, environmental, psychospiritual and sociocultural. In 1994 Kolcaba published a paper entitled *A theory of holistic comfort for nursing* (Kolcaba, 1994). This paper conceptualised comfort within a theory of nursing and articulates the importance of understanding patients' comfort needs to guide the delivery of effective nursing care. In 2003 Kolcaba authored her definitive work in a book entitled *Comfort Theory and practice: A vision for holistic healthcare and research* (Kolcaba, 2003). The book contains the theoretical, philosophical and conceptual underpinnings of Comfort Theory and its application to clinical nursing practice, education and research. It remains the most authoritative source of knowledge on comfort, Comfort Theory and its importance to nursing. The book outlines the theory and provides a simple structure by which nurses can unravel, understand and attend to the comfort needs of patients.

Kolcaba's many published works have not been limited to the theoretical development of Comfort Theory. Comfort Theory has always been about providing holistic and effective nursing care to patients, and, as such, Kolcaba has published extensively on

Table 8.1. Taxonomy of comfort needs			
	Relief	Ease	Transcendence
Physical			
Psychospiritual			
Sociocultural			
Environmental			

the application of Comfort Theory to the care of patients at the end of life (Vendlinski and Kolcaba, 1997), in pre- and post-operative patients (Kolcaba et al., 2000), in the care of older people (Kolcaba et al., 2006), and in the care of critically ill patients and children (Kolcaba and DiMarco, 2005).

The Comfort Theory

The Comfort Theory is described as a middle-range nursing theory. Middle-range theories aim to integrate theory with practice and are designed to include only a small number of key concepts which should be easy to recognise and apply to everyday nursing practice. The emergence of middle-range theories came as a response to criticisms of grand theories which were often structured around broad abstract concepts associated with nursing. Thus Comfort Theory is a middle-range theory as it is fundamentally concerned with enabling nurses to provide care that enhances patient comfort (Kolcaba, 2001).

Comfort Theory asserts that an essential feature of professional nursing practice is the delivery of care that promotes patient comfort. In order to fully appreciate the theory it is important to understand how comfort is defined within the theory. Kolcaba developed a definition of holistic comfort for nursing, which she defines as the attentive and timely provision of relief, ease and transcendence (Kolcaba and Wilson, 2002). Relief, ease and transcendence are referred to as the three types of comfort:

- *Relief:* the experience of having a comfort need met.
- *Ease*: the experience of care that promotes calm and/or contentment.
- *Transcendence*: the experience in which care enables a patient to rise above problems or pain.

In addition to the three types of comfort described the theory identifies and explains four contexts within which individuals experience the three types of comfort (Kolcaba et al, 2006). These contexts of experience are:

- *Physical*: the physiological and homeostatic components of a person's health and wellbeing.
- *Psychospiritual*: the person's sense of self and includes self-esteem, sexuality and spirituality.
- *Sociocultural*: the person's social relationships and includes family, friends, community and societal interactions (finances, healthcare personnel, family customs and religious practices).
- *Environmental*: the person's physical surroundings.

Both the three types and four contexts of comfort described by Kolcaba were developed following an extensive literature review on the concept of comfort as described in the nursing, medical, psychological, theological and ergonomic literature (Kolcaba and Kolcaba, 1991).

The theory presents the three types of comfort and the four contexts of experience in a taxonomy (or table); referred to as the taxonomic structure of comfort needs (see *Table 8.1*).

The taxonomy presented in *Table 8.1* permits the comprehensive identification of patient comfort needs and provides the space and flexibility for all comfort needs to be positioned somewhere on the table. Kolcaba also points out that considerable overlap can occur between individual components of the taxonomy and that no one part is considered mutually exclusive (Kolcaba, 1991). Kolcaba intended that the taxonomy be used as a brief guide to assist in the initial identification and assessment of patient comfort needs.

Links with other nursing theorists

Katharine Kolcaba utilised the work of a number of nurse theorists in the initial development and refinement of comfort theory. The identification of the three types and contexts of comfort were influenced by Ida Orlando's Nursing Process Theory (*see Chapter 22*), Virginia Henderson's 13 Basic Functions of Human Beings (*see Chapter 11*), and Jean Watson's (1979) Theory of Caring. She was also influenced by Josephine Paterson and Loretta Zderad's work on humanistic nursing (*see Chapter 7*).

References

Apostolo JL, Kolcaba K (2009) The effects of guided imagery on comfort, depression, anxiety, and stress of psychiatric inpatients with depressive disorders. *Archives of Psychiatric Nursing* **23**(6): 403–11

Bortolusso V, Boscolo A, Zampieron A (2007) Survey about the comfort level according to Kolcaba on a sample of oncologic patients. *Professioni infermieristiche* **60**(3): 166–9

Bredemeyer S, Reid S, Polverino J, Wocadlo C (2008) Implementation and evaluation of an individualized developmental care program in a neonatal intensive care unit. *Journal of Specialisit Pediatric nursing* **13**(4): 281–9

Bredemeyer S, Reid S, Wallace M (2005) Thermal management for premature births. *Journal of Advanced Nursing* **52**(5): 482–9

Dowd T, Kolcaba K (2007) Two interventions to relieve stress in college students. *Beginnings (American Holistic Nurses' Association)* **27**(1): 10–11

Dowd T, Kolcaba K, Steiner R (2000) Using cognitive strategies to enhance bladder control and comfort. *Holistic Nursing Practice* **14**(2): 91–103

Fitzpatrick J (1998) *Encyclopedia of nursing research*. Springer, New York

Henderson V (1966) *The Nature of Nursing*. Macmillan Publishing, New York

Kolcaba K (1988) A framework for the nursing care of dementia patients. *Mainlines* **9**(6): 12–13

Kolcaba KY (1991) A taxonomic structure for the concept comfort. *Journal of Nursing Scholarship* **23**(4): 237–40

Kolcaba K (1992a) Holistic comfort: Operationalizing the construct as a nurse-sensitive outcome. *Advances in Nursing Science* **15**(1): 1–10

Kolcaba K (1992b) Gerontological nursing. The concept of comfort in an environmental framework. *Journal of Gerontological Nursing* **18**(6): 33–40

Kolcaba K (1994) A theory of holistic comfort for nursing. *Journal of Advanced Nursing* **19**(6): 1178–84

Kolcaba K (2000) Holistic care. Is it feasible in today's health care environment? *Counterpoint. Nursing Leadership Forum* **4**(4): 105–7

Kolcaba K (2001) Evolution of the mid range theory of comfort for outcomes research. *Nursing Outlook* **49**(2): 86–92

Kolcaba K (2003) *Comfort Theory and practice: A vision for holis-*

Comfort interventions

Once the nurse has used the taxonomy to identify the patient's comfort needs the information contained within it can then be used to design comfort interventions for the patient. The theory of comfort groups comfort interventions into three categories (Kolcaba, 2003), namely: standard comfort interventions, coaching, and comfort food for the soul.

- *Standard comfort interventions* involve assisting the patient maintain or regain former levels of physical ability and preventing and detecting patient deterioration and/or complications. Some examples of how the nurse might deliver these interventions include monitoring and responding to changes in the patient's vital signs, ensuring that the patient receives adequate levels of analgesia, and maintaining fluid and electrolyte balance, etc.
- *Coaching* involves interventions that will assist the patient to cope effectively with ill health, prepare for recovery and or embrace a peaceful death. These activities require that nurses actively listen, respond and reassure patients regarding their concerns, etc.
- *Comfort food for the soul* involves interventions that include the therapeutic use of touch, promoting a calm and peaceful environment, guided imagery, etc. Kolcaba argues that these areas of nursing care are often neglected in contemporary practice and are in fact very important in assisting patients to transcend the many unpleasant experiences they may encounter in the healthcare environment.

A sensitive and caring approach by the nurse to the delivery of the three comfort interventions is essential if they are to contribute to patient comfort. This type of comfort care is intended to be positive, proactive, nurturing and desired by patients and their families. The nurse's contribution to comfort care is seen as more than the physical or emotional alleviation of patient distress and embraces a wider, more holistic, view of comfort (Kolcaba, 1992a).

Metaparadigms

In addition to the types of comfort, contexts of comfort and comfort interventions, Comfort Theory also includes a number of important metaparadigms. Metaparadigms are the essential components of a theory that must be present for it to be considered a legitimate nursing theory. In nursing these components or metaparadigms are nursing, health, the person and the environment (McKenna and Slevin, 2008). Although they are the same for all nursing theories, the way in which the four metaparadigms are interpreted varies between theories. Kolcaba's (2003) interpretation of the four metaparadigms in the theory of comfort is as follows:

- *Nursing*: the intentional assessment of comfort needs, the design of comfort measures to address those needs, and the reassessment of comfort levels after implementation. Assessment can be subjective or objective. Subjective assessment relates to instances where nurses, for example, enquire as to the patient's perceived level of comfort and where objective assessments relate to, for example, estimations of wound healing/ deterioration or changes in the patient's clinical condition.
- *Health*: considered to be the highest attainable level of function as defined by the patient, family or community.
- *Person*: an individual, family, organisation or community requiring healthcare.

Table 8.2. Comfort needs table for baby Muirin Stuart

	Relief	Ease	Transcendence
Physical	Vital signs Fluids and electrolytes Mechanical ventilation	Limit distressing procedures Infant positioning	Non-nutritive sucking to promote self-calm
Psychospiritual	Organisation of infant care provision	Gentle touch	Physical contact with parents
Sociocultural	Parents not present	Communication difficulties	Need for support from parents
Environmental	Noise Light Temperature	Attention to noise Subdued light Quite time and rest periods	Calm, safe and familiar environment

- *Environment*: the patient, family or organisational background that can be influenced by the nurse or carers to improve comfort.

In summary, the theory of comfort provides nurses with a simple yet holistic mechanism for identifying, assessing and providing care interventions that are focused on the comfort needs of the patient.

Putting theory into practice

The following clinical example illustrates the potential application of Comfort Theory to the nursing care of a premature infant in the neonatal intensive care (NICU). In particular, the example highlights the centrality and value of comfort to therapeutic and effective care of infants in the NICU, an environment which, by its very nature, exposes infants to varying levels of discomfort.

Case study

Baby Muirin Stuart is a newborn premature infant with a gestational age of 28 weeks. She was admitted to the neonatal intensive care unit following delivery by emergency caesarean section. Early delivery was consequent to placental insufficiency and foetal growth retardation. In light of the infant's prematurity she required numerous invasive life-sustaining treatments including assisted mechanical ventilation.

The application of Comfort Theory to the care of baby Muirin requires that the nurse systematically identify and assess her comfort care needs. This is achieved using the three types (relief, ease and transcendence) and the four contexts (physical, psychospiritual, environmental and sociocultural) of comfort. Kolcaba produced and developed a table or taxonomy of the three types and four contexts of comfort to guide in the holistic identification of patient comfort needs (Kolcaba, 1991). The table was designed to be used as a method of developing a brief baseline assessment of comfort needs. The table, once completed, can be used to guide the nurse in the identification and organisation of individualised and holistic comfort care interventions. *Table 8.2* illustrates some of the comfort needs that the nurse might want to consider when caring for baby Muirin.

The table provides a comprehensive overview of the comfort needs of this preterm infant. All of the infant's comfort needs can be located somewhere on the table, furthermore the comfort needs placed in the individual boxes of the table can overlap. The nurse, having completed the comfort needs table, can then use the information to guide the design of suitable and therapeutic comfort interventions.

tic health care and research. Springer Publishing, London

Kolcaba K, DiMarco MA (2005) Comfort Theory and its application to pediatric nursing. *Pediatric Nursing* **31**(3): 187–94

Kolcaba K, Kolcaba RJ (1991) An analysis of the concept of comfort. *Journal of Advanced Nursing* **16**(11): 1301–10

Kolcaba K, Miller CA (1989) Geropharmacology treatment: Behavioral problems extend nursing responsibility. *Journal of Gerontological Nursing* **15**(5): 29–35

Kolcaba K, Panno J, Holder C (2000) Acute care for elders: A holistic model for geriatric orthopaedic nursing care. *Journal of Orthopaedic Nursing* **19**(6): 53–60

Kolcaba K, Schirm V, Steiner R (2006) Effects of hand massage on comfort of nursing home residents. *Geriatric nursing (New York)* **27**(2): 85–91

Kolcaba K, Tilton C, Drouin C (2006) Comfort Theory: A unifying framework to enhance the practice environment. *Journal of Nursing Administration* **36**(11): 538–44

Kolcaba K, Wilson L (2002) Comfort care: A framework for perianesthesia nursing. *Journal of Perianesthesia Nursing - American Society of PeriAnesthesia Nurses* **17**(2): 102–11

McKenna HP, Slevin O (2008) *Nursing models, theories and practice.* Blackwell, Oxford

Novak B, Kolcaba K, Steiner R, Dowd T (2001) Measuring comfort in caregivers and patients during late end-of-life care. *American Journal of Hospice & Palliative Care* **18**(3): 170–80

Orlando IJ (1961) *The dynamic nurse–patient relationship, function, process and principles.* GP Putnam, New York

Panno JM, Kolcaba K, Holder C (2000) Acute care for elders (ACE): A holistic model for geriatric orthopaedic nursing care. *Orthopaedic Nursing/ National Association of Orthopaedic Nurses* **19**(6): 53–60

Patterson J, Zderad L (1975) *Humanistic Nursing.* National League for Nursing, New York

Penticuff JH, Walden M (2000) Influence of practice environment and nurse characteristics on perinatal nurses' responses to ethical dilemmas. *Nursing Research* **49**(2): 64–72

Sitzman K (2004) *Understanding the work of nurse theorists: A creative beginning.* Jones and Bartlett Publishers, Sudbury, Mass, London

Tomey AM, Alligood MR (2006) *Nursing theorists and their work.* (6th edn) Mosby, London

Vendlinski S, Kolcaba KY (1997) Comfort care: A framework for hospice nursing. *American Journal of Hospice & Palliative Care* **14**(6): 271–6

Walden M, Robinson T, Turnage Carrier C (2001) Comfort care for infants in the neonatal intensive care unit at end of life. *Newborn and Infant Nursing Reviews* **1**(2): 97–105

Watson J (1979) *Nursing; the philosophy and science of caring.* Associated University Press; New York

Comfort interventions

Comfort Theory organises comfort interventions into three categories: standard comfort interventions, coaching, and comfort food for the soul (Kolcaba, 2003).

Standard comfort interventions

Standard comfort interventions are primarily concerned with assisting the patient to maintain a homeostatic balance and are used in this example to address the infant's need for physical relief, ease and transcendence as identified in the *Table 8.2*. In order to provide baby Muirin with physical relief the nurse will monitor and respond to changes in her vital signs, maintain adequate fluid and electrolyte balance and provide and monitor the infant's requirements for assisted mechanical ventilation. The infant's need for physical ease is facilitated by limiting the number of painful or distressing procedures and providing her with developmentally supportive positioning. Developmentally supportive positioning encourages neuromuscular maturity and assists the infant to develop hand to mouth co-ordination, which helps the infant to address the need for physical transcendence. Hand sucking provides baby Muirin with a mechanism to independently calm and soothe herself (Bredemeyer et al, 2008).

Coaching

The comfort needs identified in the psychospiritual and sociocultural domains of *Table 8.2* will be addressed for this infant by coaching. Interventions related to coaching involve supporting the patient to successfully cope with ill health, get ready for recovery or embrace a peaceful death. In order to use coaching to attend to the psychospiritual and sociocultural relief needs of this infant the nurse will ensure that baby Muirin's care is organised to provide periods of undisturbed rest, and physical touch and contact with parents (Penticuff and Walden, 2000). Furthermore, within the psychospiritual and sociocultural ease and transcendence domains touch will be used to promote and enhance emotional attachment between the infant and her parents. Opportunities for physical skin-to-skin contact between the infant and her parents will be provided. The nurse will also monitor the infant for signs of physiological or emotional distress as touch can be stressful to the pre-term infant and must be delivered according to the infant's individual level of tolerance.

Comfort food for the soul

Comfort food for the soul involves interventions that require the provision of a calm and peaceful environment. The infant's comfort needs for the soul involve providing relief, ease and transcendence for the care needs identified under environment in *Table 8.2*. Environmental relief, ease and transcendence are important care considerations for the premature infant as the nervous system is immature and unable to tolerate excessive stimulation. The nurse will provide care that reduces baby Muirin's exposure to auditory and visual stimuli, by ensuring the ambient noise in the NICU is kept to a minimum. The nurse will also encourage the parents to talk to their baby, as infants find these familiar voices to be soothing. The nurse will also address the visual effects of the NICU lights, which can be minimised by ensuring the infant's incubator is covered when the infant is at rest and by using subdued lighting if possible when providing care. In addition to lighting and sound the nurse must ensure that the infant's body temperature is maintained. This is achieved by the provision of an incubator that assists the infant maintain the optimum body temperature. Heat loss can also be addressed by keeping the infant's head covered with a hat and replacing wet blankets immediately with dry warmed blankets (Bredemeyer et al., 2005).

Summary

In summary, Comfort Theory is easily applied to the holistic care of a pre-term infant. The comfort needs taxonomy acted as a simple and effective resource for identifying and assessing the complex care needs of baby Muirin and permitted the development of comfort interventions. The nurse, by delivering comfort interventions, provided holistic comfort care to the infant and her parents that addressed not only the infant's physical comfort needs but also her psychospiritual, sociocultural and environmental requirements.

Influence

Comfort Theory has made a profound contribution to nursing practice, education and research. The significance of the theory was recognised in 1998 when it was entered into the *Encyclopaedia of nursing research* (Fitzpatrick, 1998). Kolcaba's work has highlighted the historical importance of comfort to nursing and reignited interest in comfort as an essential aspect of nursing practice (Tomey and Alligood, 2006). The careful attention invested by Kolcaba in the development of Comfort Theory has resulted in an elegant, logically expressed model that can be applied to any nursing practice, education or research environment.

Despite all of her many achievements perhaps Kolcaba's greatest contribution to nursing has been her commitment to providing a mechanism whereby comfort care can be structured and evaluated and be seen to make a measurable difference to patient outcome. Comfort Theory challenges those who are critical of the importance of the softer 'fluffing up the pillows' activities which are so essential to therapeutic nursing care (Sitzman, 2004).

Comfort Theory has also impacted upon nurse education and research. In education the theory of comfort has been used by educators to assist students to gain a better understanding of the holistic comfort needs of patients in acute and non-acute care environments (Dowd and Kolcaba, 2007). The simplicity of the theory makes it a valuable structure to guide students in their learning on comfort and on the important role of the nurse in the consistent delivery and evaluation of comfort care to patients. In research Comfort Theory has been used to provide systematic evidence of the value of holistic nursing care to successful patient outcomes (Bortolusso et al., 2007; Dowd et al., 2000; Apostolo et al., 2009). Kolcaba's three types and contexts of comfort present researchers with a comprehensive diagram of the core attributes of comfort which can been used to guide in the design of comfort measures and instruments (Novak et al., 2001). Kolcaba's website (www.thecomfortline.com) offers researchers advice and suggestions for adapting Comfort Theory and provides questionnaires specific to the diverse array of nursing research environments.

In summary, Comfort Theory has had a major impact on nursing practice, education and research. It focuses on the centrality and value of comfort to the delivery of holistic nursing care. Its simplicity and ease of application permit its use in any care setting and enable nurses to provide care that is individualised, competent and focused on the needs of the patient.

Where to find out more

Website
- www.thecomfortline.com
This website is devoted to the concept of comfort in nursing and the work of the nurse theorist Katharine Kolcaba.

Journal articles
Kolcaba K (1991) A taxonomic structure for the concept comfort. *Image: Journal of Nursing Scholarship* **23**(4): 237–40

Kolcaba K (1994) A theory of holistic comfort for nursing. *Journal of Advanced Nursing* **19**: 1178–84

Kolcaba K (1995) Comfort as process and product, merged in holistic nursing art. *Journal of Holistic Nursing* **13**(2): 117–31

Kolcaba K, Kolcaba R (1991) An analysis of the concept of comfort. *Journal of Advanced Nursing* **16**: 1301–10

Books and book chapters
Kolcaba K (2003) *Comfort Theory and practice: A vision for holistic health care and research.* Springer Publishing, London.

Kolcaba K (2004) *The Theory of Comfort. Middle range theories: Application to nursing research.* Lippincott, Williams, & Wilkins. London

Tomey AM, Alligood MR (2006) *Nursing theorists and their work* (6th edn) Mosby, London

Key dates

1950	Registered as a nurse
1962	BSc in nursing from University of New Mexico
1964	MSc from Emory University
1973	Completed PhD studies
1980–	Developed her maternal role attainment/Becoming a mother theory
1987	ASPO/Lameze National Research Award
1988	Awarded the Distinguished Research Lectureship Award
1990	Received the American Nurses Foundation's Distinguished Contribution to Nursing Science Award
2003	Named living legend by the American Academy of Nursing
2004	Received the first University of New Mexico College of Nursing Distinguished Alumni Award

CHAPTER 9

Ramona Thieme Mercer

Lesley Storrie

Biography

Ramona Thieme Mercer was born in 1929. She started her nursing career in 1950, exiting with a Diploma in nursing from St Margaret's School of Nursing, Montgomery, Alabama. During her clinical career she had a special interest in maternity nursing, and held positions as staff nurse in intrapartum, postpartum and newborn nursery units and as head nurse in paediatrics.

In 1962 she completed a BSc in nursing, with distinction, from the University of New Mexico, Albuquerque. In 1964 she completed an MSc in maternal–child nursing from Emory University, and completed a PhD in the maternity nursing field at the University of Pittsburg in 1973. Mercer then took up posts as assistant professor and subsequently associate professor in the Department of Family Health Care Nursing at the University of California, San Francisco, retiring as Professor Emeritus in 1988.

Mercer has been a lecturer in maternity nursing, consultant on matters related to maternity care, writer and visiting professor. Her professional activities have included service on national and State committees. She has served on several editorial and review boards for journals as a content expert, and as an invited speaker on many panels and roundtables.

As noted by Meighan (2006), Mercer has received many awards. In 1987 she was awarded the American Society for Psychoprophylaxis in Obstetrics (ASPO)/Lamaze National Research Award. In 1988 she was awarded the Distinguished Research Lectureship Award by the Western Society for Research in Nursing in recognition of her substantial and sustained contribution to nursing. In 1990 she received the American Nurses Foundation's Distinguished Contribution to Nursing Science Award. She was named a living legend by the American Academy of Nursing in 2003. In 2004 she received the first University of New Mexico College of Nursing Distinguished Alumni Award.

Special interest

Mercer is best known for her pioneering work in the transition to the maternal role and the development of a maternal role identity. Her research interest in early mothering began while at the faculty at Emory where she studied maternal adaptation to breastfeeding and mothers with postnatal illness. She began with a study of mothers who had an infant with a birth defect (1971–1973). She focused next on teenage mothers during their first year of motherhood, and collaborated in a cross-cultural comparison of mothers' responses to caesarean and vaginal births. Mercer is classed as a middle-range theorist. Middle-range theory, developed by Robert K Merton (1968), follows a traditional social science approach to theory development through research. The theory generated focuses on a limited number of concepts.

An original paper on maternal role attainment served as the beginning of Mercer's middle-range theory development, and provided the framework for her research comparing three age groups of mothers (15–19, 20–29, and 30–42 years) over their first year of motherhood (1979–1982). In collaborative investigations, she examined transitions in the lives of mothers and non-mothers aged 60 to 95, and the impact of maternal hospitalisation during pregnancy on mothers' and fathers' transitions to parenthood and their family functioning during their first eight months following birth.

Summary of writings

Mercer has been a prolific writer. Her publications include over 90 journal articles, six books and several book chapters, and her research results have also been reported in several lay magazines. In addition she has produced several online continuing professional development education programmes.

Her early writing from 1973 is related to her doctoral dissertation work on the responses of mothers to the birth of a child with a defect. From 1976 she wrote about teenage pregnancy and motherhood, a topic she became interested in when studying for her dissertation, when she noticed that teenage mothers responded and coped differently from older mothers to the birth of an infant with a defect. As noted by Meighan (1996), Mercer has been awarded the *American Journal of Nursing* Book Award on three occasions with the following titles:

- *Nursing care for patients at risk* (1977)
- *Perspectives on adolescent health care* (1979)
- *Parents at risk* (1990)

From 1980 onwards her writing has focused on her theory of maternal role attainment and becoming a mother. From the development of the initial theoretical framework Mercer investigated the variables that have been shown to have an impact on maternal role attainment. Many of these studies have been undertaken in conjunction with Sandra L Ferketich, Professor and Director of the Division of Family and Community Health Nursing, University of Arizona and previously at the faculty of the School of Nursing, University of California.

Maternal Role Attainment Theory

The Maternal Role Attainment Theory of Mercer has developed over time to explain the factors which may impact on the maternal role. The complex theory is based on the earlier work of Reva Rubin (1967), the professor and mentor of Mercer, who introduced the concept of maternal role attainment as a process leading to the achievement of maternal role identity. The work of Rubin concentrated on the prenatal and postnatal phases and not on labour and delivery. She described the maternal role as a complex cognitive and social process which is learned, reciprocal, and interactive. Maternal identity is considered the culmination or end-point of maternal role attainment, characterised by the woman's comfort in her role. The work of Rubin focused on

traditional mothers (mothers in their 20s), and dealt with maternal role attainment from the point of acceptance of the pregnancy to six weeks postpartum.

Building on the work of Rubin, Mercer began a series of studies investigating the factors occurring during the first year of motherhood that may have had the greatest impact on maternal role attainment. To aid theory development Mercer extended the timescale from the six week period investigated by Rubin to 12 months. She studied mothers of all age groups and experiences and created the practice-oriented theory of maternal role attainment (Mercer, 1981, 1985, 1986).

In 1981 Mercer published her theoretical framework for studying the factors that impact on the maternal role. This framework provided direction for the research that underpinned the development and expansion of her theory.

Based on the work of Rubin, Meighan (2006) notes that Mercer adopted the interactionist approach to role theory using both the Role Enactment Theory of Mead (1934) and the Core Self Theory of Turner (1978). In addition, the theory is shaped by the work of other interactionist and developmental theorists and the Role Acquisition Theory of Thornton and Nardi (1975), adapted to describe the process of transition to the maternal role. The model of maternal role attainment uses the Bronfenbrenner's (1979) concept of nested circles to portray the environmental influences. The inner circle represents the microsystem and influence of family and friends, the mesosystem represents the community, which includes healthcare, employment and recreation, and the macrosystem represents the influence of the wider society with its effect on legislation, school and work settings, and healthcare programmes (see *Figure 9.1*) (Meighan, 2006; Mercer, 2006).

In developing the theoretical framework Mercer

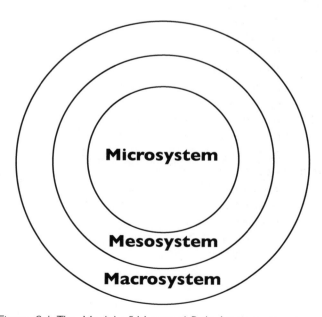

Figure 9.1. The Model of Maternal Role Attainment using Bonfenbrenner's concept of nested circles.

noted that the literature reported certain key variables as having an impact on the maternal role.

- Age
- Perceptions of the birth experience
- Early maternal–infant separation
- Support systems
- Self-concept and personality traits
- Maternal illness
- Child rearing attitudes
- Infant temperament
- Infant illness
- Other factors, e.g. socioeconomic status.

Mercer studied the influence of these factors over several intervals: one month, four months, eight months and 12 months after birth. She studied teenagers, older mothers, mothers of babies with defects, high risk families, mothers who had had a caesarian section and the role of the father. She found them to be associated with maternal role attainment and the woman's sense of competency in the maternal role. In addition to those variables listed, maternal role attainment is affected by maternal role strain and the mother's perception of the infant. Additional infant variables include appearance and responsiveness.

According to Mercer (2004), maternal role attainment is based on the following concepts:

- *Primary concept*: Developmental and interactional process which occurs over a period of time
- *Mother bonds with infant*: Mother acquires competence in caretaking tasks, enjoys and expresses joy and pleasure in the role
- *Maternal identity*: A personal state of harmony, confidence and competence. The end point of maternal role attainment.

The process follows four stages

- *Anticipatory stage*: Begins in pregnancy with social and psychological adaptation to role; the woman learns the expectations of the motherhood role. The mother visualises herself in the role.
- *Formal stage*: Assumes the role at birth; behaviours are guided by professionals and others in social system.
- *Informal stage*: The mother develops her own ways of mothering; develops her own style of dealing with the role.
- *Personal stage*: The mother is secure in her role as a mother; she displays harmony, confidence, and competence in maternal role.

In the anticipatory stage the woman prepares for her role as a mother. The formal stage begins with the birth of the baby. During this stage the mother begins to bond with her infant, and begins caretaking tasks under the guidance of the professional. During the informal stage the mother is using her own judgement about how to care for her infant. The personal stage is characterised by the mother's sense of harmony, of confidence, competence and satisfaction in the role.

Using Bronfenbrenner's concept of nested circles, Mercer found the intimate environment or microsystem of family and friends to be the most influential in maternal role attainment with the interaction between the father, mother and infant to be the most important factor. The father is seen as key in providing support and guidance. Individual mother and infant characteristics interact and influence one another as the maternal role identity develops through the four stages. Maternal role attainment can be affected by how sensitive the mother is to the infant cues, her maturity and the developmental responses from the infant. Maternal competence was significantly related to self-esteem and the mother's concept of the self and is a major predictor of maternal–infant attachment (Mercer and Ferketich, 1990). Infant traits have an impact on maternal role attainment. The developmental responses of eye contact, smile and interactive behaviour and the response of the mother all play a part, as do health and temperament.

It is worthy of note that family and friends can act as stressors during this stage of transition. Mercer (2004) concluded that maternal role attainment encompassed multiple processes, including how the new mother replicates her own mother's style of mothering, how she role plays to become comfortable with the new role, how she fantasizes about mothering, how she gathers information and seeks new expert models, and how she must grieve for the parts of her life she will have to give up to become a mother.

Maternal role attainment is achieved by the majority of mothers by four months, decreasing significantly at eight and 12 months. Gratification with mothering increases for teenage mothers at four months and decreases between eight and 12 months. With older mothers, gratification with mothering continues to increase from four, eight and 12 months. At eight months there is a clash between the increasing demands of the baby and the regaining of a sense of self, of being a wife and being in employment. Difficulty with balancing the demands could result in feelings of incompetence and role strain.

In a study undertaken by Mercer and Ferketich (1990) comparing high risk mothers who had been hospitalised in the third trimester and women with low risk demonstrated no difference in attachment to their infant at eight months. Anxiety and lack of support from the partner had negative effects in the early postpartum period for low risk women. Family functioning, support and relationships with their own mothers as children were also variables which affected attachment with their infants. A further study undertaken by Mercer and Ferketich (1994) demonstrated no difference in parental competence at eight months. Anxiety and depression were significant predictors of feelings of competence in both groups.

Women who have other children have more positive attitudes and self-confidence than first time mothers. Their lives are, however, more complex and tiring. There are concerns about the changing relationship with an older child or children and integrating the baby into the family (Mercer, 1995). Mercer and Ferketich (1995) provided some inconclusive evidence on the mother's perception of her increasing competence in her mothering role with subsequent children. They suggested that this was possibly due to the greater challenge of caring for two or more children.

Ferketich and Mercer studied the role of the father in the transition process. In 1990 their study revealed that stressful situations related to the birth experience can result in the father showing greater attachment to the infant. In 1995 they also studied the infant attachment behaviour of fathers and found that the best predictor of early postnatal attachment was fetal attachment. It is noted that the mother controls access to the fetus during pregnancy and fetal attachment for fathers depends on the quality of the relationship. They concluded that further research in this area is required.

In 2004 Mercer reviewed the development of the Maternal Role Attainment Theory. She re-examined the theory and reviewed the research which had been undertaken in the field since her initial publication. This review included a large number of qualitative studies, which had focused on preparation for becoming a mother, prenatal attachment, women's relationship with their own mother, women with postnatal depression and the transition to motherhood. Mercer noted that her maternal role attainment theory did not take account of the life-changing and transformational experience of motherhood. In particular she noted that the affective and behavioural dimensions of maternal role attainment were not addressed. The theory was no longer conveyed by the terminology. There was recognition that women continue to grow as mothers throughout their lives and that becoming a mother was not a static process. Attaining the role was not becoming the role.

She made the argument to replace the term maternal role attainment with the term becoming a mother. New names for the stages in becoming a mother were proposed, noting that the final three were overlapping and variable in timescale. They are also affected by maternal and infant factors and by the social environment.

- Commitment, attachment, and preparation
- Acquaintance, learning and physical recovery
- Moving towards a new normal
- Achievement of the maternal identity.

There are similarities between the stages of becoming a mother and maternal role attainment but they are now approached from a more qualitative perspective. The commitment, attachment and preparation stage begins during pregnancy and Mercer (2004) suggests that the more involved the woman is at this stage, the more positive the adaptation to motherhood. The acquaintance, learning and physical recovery stage occurs between two and six weeks following birth. During this stage the mother learns about her new infant and how it responds to her and to others. She learns to care for and comfort her infant. Moving to a new normal stage takes from two weeks to four months. During this stage the mother adjusts to the new changed relationship with her partner, family and friends. She adjusts to the reality of her new status. Achievement of the maternal identity, the final stage, occurs at around four months for the majority of women. The mother is competent

Links to other nursing theorists

Ramona Mercer's work has links with other middle-range theorists including Phil Barker's Tidal Model of Mental Health Recovery (*see Chapter 27*) and Katharine Kolcaba's Theory of Comfort (*see Chapter 8*).

References

Bronfenbrenner U (1979) *The ecology of human development: Experiment by nature and design*. Harvard University Press, Cambridge MA

Mead GH (1934) *Mind, self and society*. University of Chicago Press, Chicago

Meighan M (2006) Ramona T Mercer: Maternal role attainment - becoming a mother. In Tomey AM, Alligood MR (eds) *Nursing theorists and their work* (6th edn) Mosby Elsevier, St Louis,

Mercer RT (1977) *Nursing care for parents at risk*. Thorofare, NJ

Mercer RT (1979) *Perspectives on adolescent health care*. Lippincott, Philadelphia

Mercer RT (1981) A theoretical framework for studying factors that impact on the maternal role. *Nursing Research* **30**(2): 73–7

Mercer RT (1985) The process of maternal role attainment over the first year. *Nursing Research* **34**(4): 198–204

Mercer RT (1986) The relationship of developmental variables to maternal behaviour. *Research in Nursing and Health* **9**(1): 25–33

Mercer RT (1990) *Parents at risk*. Springer, New York

Mercer RT (1995) *Becoming a mother: Research on maternal identity from Rubin to the present*. Springer, New York

Mercer RT (2004) Becoming a

mother versus maternal role attainment. *Journal of Nursing Scholarship* **36**(3): 226–32

Mercer RT (2006) Nursing support of the process of becoming a mother. *Journal of Obstetric, Gynecologic and Neonatal Nursing* **35**(5): 649–51

Mercer RT, Ferketich S (1990) Predictors of parental attachment during early parenthood. *Journal of Advanced Nursing* **15**: 268–80

Mercer RT, Ferketich S (1994) Maternal–infant attachment of experienced and inexperienced mothers during infancy. *Nursing Research* **43**(6): 344–51

Mercer RT, Ferketich S (1995) Experienced and inexperienced mothers' maternal competence during infancy. *Research in Nursing and Health* **18**(4): 333–43

Mercer RT, Walker LO (2006) A review of nursing interventions to foster becoming a mother. Journal of Obstetric, *Gynecologic and Neonatal Nursing* **35**(5): 568–82

Merton RK (1968) *Social theory and social structure*. Free Press, NY

Rubin R (1967) Attainment of the maternal role: Part 1. Processes. *Nursing Research* 16: 237–45

Turner JH (1978) *The structure of sociological theory*. Dorsey Press, Illinois

Where to find out more

Further information about Ramona Mercer can be found in the following publications:

Meighan M (2006)
Mercer RT (1981, 1995, 2004)

and confident in her role. She has an intimate knowledge of and love for her infant and her family life has adjusted to her new identity as a mother. When a woman has other children she builds on her existing knowledge and competence in the role, adapting to the more challenging and complex aspects of integrating the new infant within the existing family.

Theory to practice

The maternal role attainment/becoming a mother theory was formulated to serve as a framework for nurses, to enable them to provide healthcare interventions which supported mothers in achieving a strong maternal identity. Mercer (2006), notes that nurses are in a strong and unique position to support the transition to motherhood but that empathetic listening and interactive dialogue were more important than educational materials. Infancy is a time when nurses and other healthcare workers are in frequent contact with mothers and their infants, with the opportunity of identifying potential problems. Knowledge of the theory would allow nurses to plan care and make appropriate referrals. In 2006, Mercer and Walker reviewed current nursing knowledge about interventions which would foster the process of becoming a mother. They concluded that interactive and reciprocal nursing interventions were most effective when they were directly related to child care. They found that there was limited evidence available which directly supported the development of maternal confidence and competence.

Influence

Mercer's theory has had a strong impact on researchers in the parent–child arena and is the chief theoretical framework upon which many studies in this field are based. She is well known and well respected as an academic and researcher, receiving many awards for her contribution to nursing, and being honoured as a living legend by the American Academy of Nursing in 2003.

Her theory has been used by researchers investigating postnatal depression, maternal–child attachment, adolescence and the transition to motherhood. In addition Mercer has produced online continuing education programmes and written for lay readers.

Her influence on clinical practice has been in the USA, but the practising nurse, the nurse researcher and other healthcare professionals will find Mercer's research findings of particular interest. Her research has provided information that clinicians can use to make a positive difference for new parents and their infants.

The differences in the way in which maternity care is delivered may account for the limited influence Mercer's work has had in the UK. There is a long history of midwifery as a profession in the UK which has been in statute since 1902. In the USA maternity care nurses have traditionally supported obstetricians in the delivery of the maternity service. Their involvement in care often terminates when the mother is transferred home. In the UK, midwives provide care during the prenatal, intranatal and postnatal period and all women have access to a midwife. This puts the midwife in the UK in a unique position to educate and empower women from the pre-conception to the postnatal period. There is a wealth of midwifery research which underpins practice.

CHAPTER 10

Patricia Benner

Mary Milligan

Patricia Benner
Birthdate:
Not known

Profile

Patricia Benner's theory of skill acquisition, first published in her 1984 book *From novice to expert*, has had an enormous impact on professional nurse education world-wide. It highlights the importance of experience in practice on the development of nursing expertise and it continues to influence theory and skill development within nursing.

Biography

Patricia E Benner is Professor Emeritus at the Department of Social and Behavioural Sciences, University of California, San Francisco. Benner graduated with a bachelor's degree in nursing from Pasadena College in 1964. She received a master's degree in medical and surgical nursing in 1970 from the University of California, San Francisco and a PhD in Stress and Coping and Health in 1982 from the University of California, Berkeley under the direction of Hubert Dreyfus and Richard Lazarus. Clinical nursing experience from 1966 to 1969 included staff nurse in medical-surgical, emergency room, coronary care, intensive care and home care. Patricia Benner was research associate at the School of Nursing, University of California from 1970 to 1975 and research assistant to Richard Lazarus from 1976 to 1978. She was Project Director for Achieving Methods of Intraprofessional Consensus, Assessment and Evaluation (AMICAE), University of California from 1979 to 1981. From 1982 to 1989 Benner was Associate Professor, Department of Physiological Nursing, University of California and Professor from 1989. Benner is the author and co-author of a number of books that have international acclaim.

Benner is an internationally noted researcher and lecturer on health, stress and coping, skill acquisition and ethics. Her work has influenced nursing nationally and internationally. She is a Fellow of the American Academy of Nursing and was elected an Honorary Fellow of the Royal College of Nursing. Benner formerly held the Thelma Shobe Endowed Chair in Ethics and Spirituality.

Currently Benner is the Director of a National Nursing Education Research project within the Carnegie Foundation for the Advancement of Teaching. This two-phase study of nursing education aims to understand how teachers might improve their practice and is the first national study of nurse education in the US for the past 30 years. The findings of this project are the subject of a forthcoming book (Benner et al., 2009b).

Special interest

For more than 30 years Patricia Benner has studied expertise and clinical judgement in nursing practice. In a three-staged inquiry she has developed and refined a theory of skill acquisition and identified domains of practice relevant to specific clinical areas. Her work has challenged predominant thinking about learning in practice within nurse education, in particular, the assumed supremacy of theoretical knowledge and a technical-rational approach to clinical problem solving. Benner's inquiry is grounded in observation of real practice from which theory is derived using a rigorous interpretive phenomenological approach. Her commitment to examining the importance of experiential learning in clinical judgement and individual development has meant that her stance continues to challenge assumptions about knowledge use in practice.

Three studies have contributed to the investigation of skill acquisition and knowledge use in expert practice in nursing (Benner et al., 2009a). In the first stage of the investigation differences in levels of skilled performance

Key dates

1964   BSc in nursing from Pasadena College

1970   MSc in medical and surgical nursing from University of California, San Francisco

1982   Received PhD in stress and coping and health, University of California

1979   Appointed Project Director for AMICAE, University of California.

1984   *From novice to expert: Excellence and power in clinical nursing practice* first published.

2004   Appointed Project Director for National Study of Nurse Education Research, Carnegie Foundation for the Advancement of Teaching

2009   *Educating nurses: A call for radical transformation* published

between newly qualified and experienced nurses were studied and reported (Benner, 1984, 2001). Using critical incident descriptions of real situations, this study provided an accessible view of clinical decision making based on individual nurses' theories in use within nursing practice. The study described the characteristics of practice denoting five levels of ability: novice, advanced beginner, competent, proficient and expert (for summary see *Table 10.1*). Assumptions about the development of skilled, context-dependent judgement were demonstrated in relation to nursing practice. The assumptions are that:

- In the development of skilled clinical judgement, individuals move from reliance on abstract principles and rules towards using their own past experience of particular cases. An expert's fluency occurs only when he or she no longer relies on or adheres to rules.
- At the expert level of practice individuals perceive situations as a whole rather than as a compilation of relevant aspects. This ability marks the difference between competent and proficient/expert levels of skilled judgement.

Expert judgement involves an initial intuitive grasp of a contextualised problem, which is dependent on complete involvement in the situation. This compares to the more detached observation of an event evident in less experienced nurses.

The meaning of nursing expertise that emerged from the narratives contributed to the formation of 31 competencies which were categorised into seven domains of practice according to similarities in function and intent (for list see *Table 10.2*). Benner points out that the list is not exhaustive and encourages individual enhancement of experiential learning through use of critical reflection on the nature of nursing practice and engagement (Benner, 1984).

Studies in the second and third stages of the investigation extended and refined the original theory (Benner et al., 1996, 2009a) reaffirming the difference in perception and response of experts and also their level of involvement with patients and families. Expert nurses demonstrated a greater degree of agency in relation to their practice and, as a result, were more able and driven to positively influence care. By comparison, advanced

Table 10.1. Stages of skill acquisition

Stage	Experience	Perception	Judgement and decision making	Facilitative strategies
Novice	No experience of real situations Learns about practice out of context	Guided by rules	Actions limited and inflexible Needs help determining the relevance of tasks to be performed	Benefits from simulation
Advanced beginner	Has experienced sufficient real situations	Identifies meaningful aspects	Cannot differentiate between importance of different aspects	Needs help to prioritise between aspects
Ccmpetent	2–3 years in the same or a similar environment	Consciously aware of actions as long-term goals Feeling of mastery within situations	Engages in conscious deliberate planning to elicit actions Lacks speed and flexibility	Benefits from practice in planning multiple, complex, patient care demands
Proficient	3–5 years in situations involving similar patient populations	Perceives situation as a whole rather than separate aspects	Performance guided by nuances of situation – maxims Perspective of situation presents itself without conscious deliberation Uses experience and exemplars	Benefits from case studies which develop ability to grasp situations
Expert	Sufficient experience to have an intuitive grasp of each situation	Deep understanding of the whole situation	No longer uses rules or guidelines Automatically focuses on problem (perceptual acuity) Performance is fluent and flexible	Interpretive reflection on narratives can make visible experiential knowledge

Adapted from Benner (1984)

Table 10.2. Seven domains of nursing practice

- The helping role
- The teaching–coaching function
- The diagnostic and monitoring function
- Effective management of rapidly changing situations
- Administering and monitoring therapeutic interventions
- Monitoring and assuring the quality of healthcare practices
- Organisational and work–role competencies

Source: Benner (1984)

Table 10.3. Habits of thought and action and domains of critical care practice

Habits of thought and action
- Clinical grasp and clinical inquiry: problem identification and clinical problem-solving
- Clinical forethought: anticipating and preventing potential problems

Nine domains of critical care practice
- Diagnosing and managing life sustaining physiological functions in unstable patients
- The skilled know-how of managing a crisis
- Providing comfort measures for the critically ill
- Caring for patients' families
- Preventing hazards in a technological environment
- Facing death: end of life care and decision-making
- Communicating and negotiating multiple perspectives
- Monitoring quality and managing breakdown
- The skilled know-how of clinical leadership and the coaching and mentoring of others

Source: Benner et al. (1999)

beginners were more detached and their reasoning less engaged. With a sense of agency developed with experience of practice, however, the actions of proficient nurses were found to be less tacit than those of experts.

The third and final study further extends the investigation into skilled judgement in nursing practice specifically within critical care settings (Benner et al., 1999). In particular it articulates the situated nature of experiential learning that is central to the development of clinical expertise and judgement. Two habits of thought and action related to the anticipation, prevention, identification and solution of problems emerged from interpretive analysis. In addition, nine domains of practice were identified that can act as a guide to experiential learning specifically within critical care nursing (for list see *Table 10.3*).

In summary, tacit, experiential knowledge is an important aspect in the development of expertise in clinical judgement. In order to make the transition from proficient to expert levels an individual must go beyond reliance on rules and regulations. Practice is guided by perceptual acuity derived from recognition of issues from previous experience of similar cases (paradigm cases) that influence judgement. Expertise involves an initial intuitive response that appears to be automatic. The nature of tacit wisdom is not easily expressed. However, Benner believes that it could be made accessible to individuals and others through interpretive reflection of practice narratives.

Summary of writings

From Novice to Expert: Excellence and power in clinical nursing practice (Benner, 1984) reports on the first stage in Benner's inquiry, a study that was conducted from 1978 to 1981 into experiential learning and the development of nursing expertise. Differences in judgement and performance between novice nurses and experienced nurses recognised for their expertise are described and a detailed account of the methodology and underlying philosophy is provided. Findings are

linked to the framework of the Dreyfus Theory of Skill Acquisition (Dreyfus and Dreyfus, 1986).

The second part of Benner's three-staged study is reported in *Expertise in nursing practice: Caring, clinical judgement and ethics* (Benner et al., 1996, 2009a). This interpretive study of nursing practice, undertaken between 1988 and 1994, considers the nature of skill acquisition in critical care units and is based on the assumption that practical knowledge is embedded in expert practice.

The third stage undertaken from 1996 to 1997 and reported in *Clinical wisdom and interventions in critical care: A thinking-in-action approach* (Benner et al., 1999) is an extension of the previous studies that includes other specialised units and increases the participant sample. The main aim of the study was the articulation of knowledge underpinning critical care nursing. All three studies used inter-related methods including paradigm cases, exemplars and thematic analyses. An interpretive phenomenological approach was used to understand meaning within the context of a situation and its relation to action.

In *The primacy of caring: Stress and coping in health and illness* (Benner and Wrubel, 1989), the view that knowledge derives from and is developed within practice is further endorsed. According to the interpretive theory portrayed, nursing practice is concerned with helping people to cope with the stress of illness, and the primacy of caring is viewed as 'the enabling condition of nursing practice'.

Interpretive phenomenology: Embodiment, caring and ethics in health and illness (Benner, 1994) is an edited collection of writings that aims to provide an introduction to the philosophical underpinning of this methodology and also to consider its potential influence on nursing science. It emphasises the importance of human understanding, experience and practical wisdom over scientific theories that are considered reductionist and decontextualised.

Educating nurses: A call for radical transformation (Benner et al., 2009b) contains the results of a National Nursing Education Research project of which Benner is Director. The aim of the two-phase project is to understand how the practice of teaching can be improved.

Theory

Benner's construction of a theory of skilled judgement in practice that derives from nurses' accounts of what they do in specific situations challenges the assumptions that objective theory is taught and then applied to practice with a detached rationality (Rolfe et al., 2001). In Benner's theory tacit, experiential knowledge takes precedence over theoretical knowledge in expert clinical judgement. From an interpretive, phenomenological perspective, theory of practice derives from an individual's perception and understanding of meaning within the context of a situation. Furthermore, multiple meanings are possible and expert nurses require to remain open and receptive to possible interpretations. The potential exists for experiential learning to be made explicit in order to facilitate the development of skilled clinical judgement.

Benner acknowledges the complexity of decision-making within nursing and medicine where the exigencies of clinical practice are unpredictable. A technical rational approach to problem-solving assumes that strategies can be learned for application within practice. However, Benner's theory focuses on learning from reflection on thinking and action within the context of actual situations of practice and the development of individual theories in use (Schon, 1987) within skilled practice. Reflecting interpretively on narrative accounts can disclose knowledge and skills derived from experience, and illuminate intentions and influences on effectiveness (Benner, 1984). Furthermore, Benner claims that learning about skilled practice from narratives is transferable and generalisable. Because of shared meanings about common issues of practice, individuals can learn from others' narratives enabling comparison of their own perspective with that of others (Benner et al., 2009a). Emphasis on pre-determined outcomes can reduce practice to decontextualised elements and fails to consider the influence of tacit, experiential knowledge on skilled clinical judgement. The importance of theoretical knowledge and evidence-based practice is acknowledged. However, consideration is given to how and when that knowledge is used. Benner emphasises the significance of the development of perceptual acuity in problem identification that is contextualised. Recognition of the importance of experiential learning in skilled clinical judgement and the promotion of its development can enable individuals to make the transition to expertise in terms of agency and involvement (Benner et al., 2009a).

The assumptions underlying Benner's theory and influencing the methodology of her study derive from an existential phenomenology influenced mainly by Heidegger (1962). In nursing it is important to recognise the other as a unique human being. In skilled practice it is possible, from experience of involvement, to perceive an individual's concerns and to discern possibilities for caring. Nurses convey respect for the uniqueness of the other person through the way that they behave; they identify concerns of the other and reach an understanding of the shared meaning of the possibilities open to them; both the nurse and the other are active participants in this dialogue. With reference to paradigm cases the nurse derives knowledge from experience of another's sense of being in a situation and any concerns and possibilities open to both for caring. Perceptual acuity, derived from experience, enables the nurse to recognise within situations, influences on others and the potential possibilities for caring.

Skilled ethical comportment is a key attribute of the expert nurse. It involves what has been learned from experience and the development of perceptual acuity that influences situated cognition and the ability to recognise what is appropriate through participation and being involved with the other. It enables the nurse to attune to any concerns of the other and to clarify possibilities for caring. Comportment concerns the way that nurses present themselves to the other that facilitates dialogue. Involvement of the nurse with the other is essential if the nurse is to understand the other's concerns and to open up possibilities for caring. However, it is important that nurses are aware of not imposing their will on the other. Ethically, nursing embodies a sense of acting well and doing good for another. This involves constantly seeking to understand the concerns of the other, to discern possibilities for caring and to convey these to the other through dialogue.

Embodiment in caring as a way of being involves recognising the uniqueness of the way that individuals make sense of the world and searching for shared meanings that enable understanding of another's way of seeing. This is essential if nurses are to enable others to understand what is happening and to help them to realise future possibilities. Embodied care involves caring for the other as a unique and whole person whose experience is influenced by 'culture, families and individual structure of their world' (Dreyfus, 1994) rather than carrying out caring tasks on another's physical body. In the latter, caring does not necessitate the same level of involvement of the nurse, however, it is more likely that the nurse will assume control of decisions about the care being given to the other person.

From an interpretive phenomenological perspective, Benner acknowledges the primacy of caring as the source of knowledge in nursing expertise. From this viewpoint knowledge of appropriate possibilities come from within the situation. A skilled nurse knows intuitively, from experience, how to relate to another to discern concerns and clarify possibilities. This tacit knowing is more than technical knowledge of how to do something and is an essential quality in being able to respond instinctively and automatically according to one's perception of a situation (Polanyi, 1966). This perspective opposes the positivistic objectivity of naturalistic scientific enquiry where knowledge is hypothetically deduced from the observation of objects in isolation from the context in which they exist in order to determine causative relations and to predict behaviour. In existential phenomenology individuals are unique human beings rather than predictable objects. Benner's theory of caring aims to clarify what skilled nursing is by examining what nurses do in practice and to make explicit the knowledge embedded within practice that nurses use to inform skilled practice. From this it is possible to identify the essential attributes for nursing expertise that will enable improvement in practice (Fjelland and Gjengedal, 1994).

Caring as an existential skill involves a practical wisdom that influences one's 'ability to perceive and respond to the particular needs of another' (Benner, 1994). With reference to the Aristotelian distinction between '*techne*' or practical know how that is dependent on objective fact, and '*phronesis*' which is practical wisdom derived from experience, Benner believes that both aspects are necessary for skilled professional practice.

> *Those engaged in caring must be able to take on the perspective of the patient and make his or her peace with the situation and its suffering in order to be touched by the situation of a fellow human being. They must have the tact to enable that person to face, surmount or weather his or her illness. Only by combining both technological and existential skills can we approach healing the embodied person.*
>
> (Dreyfus, 1994: x).

Skilled practice requires involvement and an ability to relate to the needs of the other, which cannot be predicted. The discrimination of what is more or less effective within a given situation is informed by paradigm cases that derive from experience. Ethical comportment involves a perceptual ability to recognise and understand the concerns of another and to discern shared meanings and future caring possibilities.

Putting theory into practice

The following examples drawn from nursing literature illustrate the application of Benner's theory within clinical practice, nurse education and nursing research.

Clinical practice

Articles have been selected to illustrate the potential benefit of the use of aspects of Benner's theory to patients and their families.

The first supports the claim that experience contributes to skilled clinical judgement. Fuller and Conner (1997) examined differences in the accuracy of nurses' assessment of infant pain and found that the degree of experience influenced the cues used in the assessment of pain with least and most

Links with other nursing theorists

Benner shares with Virginia Henderson (*see Chapter 11*) the view that knowledge essential to the development of nursing expertise derives from practice as opposed to the application of mechanistic theoretical models.

Like Florence Nightingale (*see Chapter 1*) Benner challenges the limitations of a medical view of health in which it is perceived as an absence of disease.

In common with Simone Roach's work on caring, Madeleine Leininger's Culture Care Diversity and Universality Nursing Theory (*see Chapter 12*) and Jean Watson's Theory of Caring, Benner perceives caring as a way of being in the world.

References

Benner P (1984) *From novice to expert: Excellence and power in clinical nursing practice.* Addison-Wesley, California

Benner P (ed) (1994) *Interpretive phenomenology: Embodiment, caring and ethics in health and illness.* Sage, Newbury Park, California

Benner P (2001) *From novice to expert: Excellence and power in clinical nursing practice.* Commemorative Edition. Addison-Wesley, California

Benner P, Tanner C, Chesla C (1996) *Expertise in nursing practice: Caring, clinical judgement and ethics.* Springer, New York

Benner P, Hooper-Kyriakidis P, Stannard D (1999) *Clinical wisdom and interventions in critical care: A thinking-in-action approach.* W.B. Saunders, Philadelphia

Benner P, Wrubel J (1989) *The primacy of caring: Stress and coping in health and illness.* Addison Wesley, California

Benner P, Tanner C, Chesla C (2009a) *Expertise in nursing practice: Caring, clinical judgement and ethics* (2nd edn) Springer, New York

Benner P, Sutphen M, Leonard V, Day L (2009b) *Educating nurses: A call for radical transformation.* Josey Bass, California/Carnegie Foundation for the Advancement of Teaching

Dreyfus HL, Dreyfus SE (1986) *Mind over machine: The power of human intuition and expertise in the era of the computer.* Free Press, New York

Dreyfus HL (1994) Preface. In Benner P (ed) *Interpretive phenomenology: Embodiment, caring and ethics in health and illness.* Sage, Newbury Park, California

Edwards SD (2001) Benner and

experienced nurses not always using the same cues or reaching the same decision. Furthermore the least experienced nurses did not always reach a decision that matched that of the expert panel's judgement. Fuller and Conner concluded that there is a need to improve pain assessment through education and support of inexperienced nurses. The use of narratives to articulate experienced nurses' judgements and cue selection is a valuable learning tool.

In a study of the lived experience of women undergoing breast biopsy, O'Mahony (2001) used participants' narratives to explore and understand the meaning of their experiences. Using Benner's (1994) framework to study the experiences of eight women with benign diagnoses, insight into the anxieties felt and influences on their feelings were highlighted. As a result nurses in this field of care can use the findings to examine, inform and improve their involvement with patients and families.

Reynolds' (2002) use of reflection on exemplars of practice within paediatric oncology enabled the examination of care in relation to Benner's (1984) helping role (see *Table 10.4*). Analysis focused specifically on the skilled use of touch and active listening as a means of enabling deeper involvement with patients and relatives, particularly in relation to enabling grieving. The exemplars allowed the articulation and evaluation of skilled judgement, for instance in the use of verbal and non-verbal cues in the assessment and appropriate use of touch. Reflection raised awareness of social and gendered influences on judgement and the importance of non-imposition of the will of the nurse on the other (Reynolds, 2002).

Nurse education

Most studies from nurse education focus on the assessment of clinical competence in practice for pre- and post-registration nursing students.

Neary (2001) considered problems with the assessment of the clinical practice of student nurses. The study highlighted that a gap existed between the reality of practice and the ideals of the College which led assessors and students to develop their own strategies for assessment within the reality of practice and to 'tick boxes' to satisfy the requirements of the College. Although students preferred criterion-referenced assessment they wanted

---

Table 10.4. The helping role domain

The helping role
- The healing relationship: creating a climate for establishing a commitment to healing.
- Providing comfort measures and preserving personhood in the face of pain and extreme breakdown.
- Presencing: being with a patient.
- Maximising the patients' participation and control in his or her own recovery.
- Interpreting types of pain and selecting appropriate strategies for pain management and control.
- Providing comfort znd communication through touch.
- Providing emotional and informational support to patients' families.
- Guiding a patient through emotional and developmental change: providing new options, closing off old ones: channelling, teaching, mediating
  - Acting as a psychological and cultural mediator.
  - Using goals therapeutically.
  - Working to build and maintain a therapeutic community.

Source: Benner (1984: 50)

greater flexibility. Assessors also felt that assessment was constrained by predetermined outcomes and preferred to assess performance in relation to the context of actual care. As a result of these findings Neary (2001) suggested the development of a 'Responsive Assessment' that could adapt to the events encountered with greater emphasis on the demonstration of learning through reflection and formative, constructive feedback. Within this framework learning outcomes could be used to facilitate the process of learning and enable growth rather than highlight deficiencies or weaknesses. Neary's conceptual framework uses Benner's (1984) notion of knowledge embedded within practice as a source of learning and development. Students reflect on actions and thinking within the context of a specific situation in order to develop insight into their practice and the assumptions on which it rests. This enables students to acquire a holistic perspective of practice.

Similarly, Benner's (1984) skill acquisition levels formed the basis of a generic assessment grid developed by Lemmer and O'Riordan (1997) following a study that evaluated educational assessment in clinical practice. The study focused on the assessment of resuscitation competence using a process-oriented assessment based on supervisor feedback. Findings suggested that the assessment procedure positively influenced critical thinking. It involved initial assessment by students of their current level of competence against a profile of skills at different levels following which specific learning needs were identified and a learning contract negotiated with the clinical supervisor. Critical incident descriptions were utilised to demonstrate evidence of acquisition of a competent level of practice. The grid shows clearly how performance in relation to a specific aspect of care, for example resuscitation, would differ at each level of skill acquisition.

Nursing research

Benner's (1984) use of phenomenology and interpretive analysis to study meaning provided an opening for the use of qualitative studies, the results of which could positively impact on nurse involvement to the benefit of patients and their families. Taylor (2001) aimed to raise awareness of what it means to be a patient diagnosed with colorectal cancer, enabling healthcare professionals to gain greater insight into personal experience, thus informing and improving care. For example, insight into the needs of the patient and family for the provision of adequate and timely information can guide practice. It can also enable healthcare professionals to develop a deeper level of involvement with patients and families and to offer counselling and an opportunity to facilitate the patient's insight and ability to make sense of and cope with the experience. Taylor uses a hermeneutic phenomenological approach to focus on the meaning of the experience to the individual.

King and Macleod Clark (2002) examined the influence of intuition in judgement and decision-making in clinical practice and, in particular, the use of intuition by non-expert nurses. Acknowledging Benner's (1984) link between intuition and clinical expertise, the understanding and use of intuition by nurses in the post-operative assessment of patients was explored. Participants reflected on their actions and judgement within the situation and were also asked to discuss their understanding of the development of their decision-making skills. Differences in decision-making skill emerged at four different levels that accord with Benner's (1984) skill acquisition levels from advanced beginner to expert. In addition, two processes involved in decision making were identified, 'analytical thinking' and 'intuitive awareness'. Intuitive awareness was present at every level of skill acquisition but was most refined in clinical experts. Decision-making skill and effective use of intuition progressively increased from advanced beginner to expert. However, experts demonstrated the greatest ability due to the depth of acquired knowledge, skill and confidence. King and Macleod

Wrubel on caring in nursing. *Journal of Advanced Nursing* **33**: 161–71

English I (1993) Intuition as a function of the expert nurse: A critique of Benner's novice to expert model. *Journal of Advanced Nursing* **18**: 387-393

Fjelland R, Gjengedal E (1994) A theoretical foundation for nursing as a science. In Benner P (ed) *Interpretive phenomenology: Embodiment, caring and ethics in health and illness.* Sage, Newbury Park, California

Fuller BF, Conner DA (1997) The influence of pediatric nursing experience on key cues used to assess infant pain. *Journal of Pediatric Nursing* **12**(3): 155–68

Green AJ, Holloway DG (1997) Using a phenomenological research tachnique to examine student nurses' understandings of experiential teaching and learning: A critical review of methodological issues. *Journal of Advanced Nursing* **26**: 1013–19

Heidegger M (1962) *Being and time.* Harper Row, New York

Horrocks S (2002) Edwards, Benner and Wrubel on caring. *Journal of Advanced Nursing* **40**: 36–41

Horrocks S (2004) Saving Heidegger from Benner and Wrubel. *Nursing Philosophy* **5**: 175–81

King L, Macleod Clark J (2002) Intuition and the development of expertise in surgical ward and intensive care nurses. *Journal of Advanced Nursing* **37**: 322–9

Lemmer B, O'Riordan B (1997) Using research to find the effects of process-oriented educational assessment in critical care in nursing practice. *Intensive and Critical Care Nursing* **13**: 273–81

Neary M (2001) Responsive assessment: Assessing student

nurses' clinical competence. *Nurse Education Today* **21**: 3–17

Nelson S (2004) The search for the good in nursing? The burden of ethical expertise. *Nursing Philosophy* **5**: 12–22

Nelson S, McGillion M (2004) Expertise or performance? Questioning the rhetoric of contemporary narrative use in nursing. *Journal of Advanced Nursing* **47**: 631–8

O'Mahony M (2001) Women's lived experience of breast biopsy: A phenomenological study. *Journal of Clinical Nursing* **10**: 512–20

Paley J (1996) Intuition and expertise: Comments on the Benner debate. *Journal of Advanced Nursing* **23**: 665–71

Paley J (2004) Clinical cognition and embodiment. *International Journal of Nursing Studies* **41**: 1–31

Paley J (2002) Virtues of autonomy: The Kantian ethics of care. *Nursing Philosophy* **3**: 133–43

Polanyi M (1966) *The tacit dimension.* Routledge and Kegan Paul, London

Reynolds M (2002) Reflecting on paediatric oncology: Nursing practice using Benner's Helping Role as a framework to examine aspects of caring. *European Journal of Oncology Nursing* **6**(1): 30–6

Rolfe G, Freshwater D, Jasper M (2001) *Critical reflection for nursing and the helping professions: A user's guide.* Palgrave Macmillan, Basingstoke

Schon D (1987) *Educating the reflective practitioner.* Jossey-Bass, San Francisco

Taylor C (2001) Patients' experiences of 'feeling on their own' following a diagnosis of colorectal cancer: A phenomenological approach. *International Journal of Nursing Studies* **38**: 651–61

Clark (2002) highlight the need to acknowledge the importance of both the analytical and intuitive components of decision-making in clinical practice and the need for education to facilitate the full development of nurses' decision-making skills.

Since the publication of *Novice to Expert* (Benner, 1984), Benner's theory has influenced nursing practice, education and research. Her work continues to have an impact on development within the profession and has contributed to the promotion of critical debate and the need to challenge assumptions.

Influence

The impact of Benner's work on contemporary nursing is wide and has influenced development within clinical practice, nurse education and nursing research. The need of less experienced nurses for education and support has been highlighted. Theory development from the articulation of experienced nurses' tacit knowledge could be used to inform patient assessment and stimulate further investigation into the relationship between salience and physiological changes. A hermeneutic phenomenological approach that enables individual meaning to be understood can inform practice and allow greater involvement with patients and families. Use of narrative techniques such as critical incident analysis and reflective journal writing can facilitate reflective practice and enable the articulation of skilled judgement and expertise. Critical insight by practitioners into their own assumptions and actions can enhance learning, increase confidence in practice, reinforce good practice and enable doubts and concerns to be addressed. Use of a framework such as the seven domains (Benner, 1984) can facilitate reflection and use of exemplars.

In nurse education a common process is evident involving the use of descriptions of practice from which strengths and needs for development are identified and a learning contract negotiated. The situated nature of learning in practice is implied and the need for participation for the development of an understanding of the phenomenon is acknowledged.

In nursing research Benner's rigorous approach to data collection and analysis lends credibility to qualitative methodology. Researcher influence in the process is acknowledged from the inception of the research questions and throughout the process using field notes to make explicit underlying assumption. Research findings are verified through involvement of the participants themselves or experts in the field of study (Benner et al., 2009a).

Criticism of Benner's theory

Benner's theory is criticised for its qualitative methodology, vagueness of terms and concepts, elitism and anti-positivism. The non-generalisability of qualitative findings is criticised and the validity of subjective accounts as evidence of expertise questioned (Green and Holloway, 1997; Nelson and McGillion, 2004). Lack of clarity of the meaning of expertise and the ambiguity of intuition is criticised (English, 1993). Others, (Edwards, 2001; Horrocks, 2002, 2004) contest Benner's interpretation and use of Heideggerian concepts.

Nelson (2004) is concerned about elitism and anti-positivism within Benner's theory. Although experienced, some nurses do not become experts or demonstrate the autonomy necessary in moral decision making. Nelson (2004) argues that little consideration is given to the reasons why individuals do not develop autonomy. For instance this could be attributed to lack of opportunity within the remit of their work role. Nelson (2004) also questions the use of positive exemplars, which support an ideal perspective of skilled practice that could have a negative influence on nurses' self-esteem. Furthermore, Benner's portrayal of nursing as a moral practice with an emphasis on emotion as a basis for skilled ethical comportment and expertise is perceived by Nelson (2004) as having been derived from the highly 'particular and controversial' philosophical approach of Charles Taylor. His antagonism towards natural science and the rationality of positivism is construed as a religious quest for ethical practice to protect against the corrupt influence of institutions (Nelson, 2004).

Concern is also expressed about the entrenched anti-positivistic view of the phenomenological stance adopted by Benner that does not reflect modern thinking about science (Paley, 1996, 2002). Nelson (2004) and Paley (1996) call for a more pluralistic ethical perspective within nursing and an end to entrenched thinking.

Furthermore, Paley (2004) suggests that 'embedded cognition can be both intuitive and rational' (Paley, 2004: 7) and that whilst Benner has set a precedent in the study of clinical decision making, her approach is limited. Paley claims that, in view of evidence of the influence of environmental design on clinical cognition, Benner's focus on the development of individual, intuitive expertise is now outdated (Paley, 2004).

Where to find out more

More information about Patricia Benner can be found in

Tomey AM, Alligood MR (eds) (2006) *Nursing Theorists and their Work*. 6th edn. Mosby Elsevier, London

Section Three

How do I know what people need?

Understanding the problem by reviewing the patient's deficits and strengths

Overview

The theorists in the previous sections described the skills and knowledge required to become a nurse. This section focuses on the application of those skills. That is, for the moment, consider nursing as something that is done to somebody else. This idea will be challenged in the next two sections, but for the time being the question is: How do we know what other people need? This section describes those theories that could be considered needs theories. They focus on how to assess somebody and how to plan for these assessed problems.

Virginia Henderson

The section begins with a chapter on Virginia Henderson. Known as the mother of American nursing, Brian Johnstone describes her theory and impact over 50 years of nursing. Henderson developed a clear definition of nursing that was accepted worldwide at the time. Her identification of 14 fundamental needs was pivotal. She advocated university education for all trained nurses back in the 1960s and had clear ideas on the necessity for research to underpin best practice. Like many innovative nurses she was deeply interested in the mechanisms and function of the nurse–patient relationship. Johnstone describes these aspects of Henderson's thinking and the enduring impact it has had.

Madeleine Leininger

The second chapter in this section introduces Madeleine Leininger's ideas. Like many inspirational nurses Leininger's originality came from wide experience coupled with the ability to integrate this knowledge in a practical, coherent and compassionate manner. Her background was in anthropology as well as nursing. Yvonne Christley tells us that Leininger spent two years living with the Gadsup people of Papua New Guinea. While in New Guinea she recognised that the Gadsup culture had some features related to caring that were unique to their culture and some that were shared with other cultures. Leininger's great and enduring contribution is therefore to recognise these features across cultures and society generally. Her theory of transcultural nursing expands our understanding of what different people may need from us.

Ernestine Wiedenbach

Linda Wylie describes Ernestine Wiedenbach's approach to the practice of nursing:

> *Overt action, directed by disciplines' thoughts and feelings toward meeting the patient's need-for-help, constitutes the practice of clinical nursing ... goal-directed, deliberately carried out and patient-centred.*

It is important to recognise that this was just one component of Wiedenbach's description of nursing. Her theory considered that there were four elements to clinical nursing: philosophy, purpose, practice and art. Whilst the practice element is clearly focused on needs Lynda Wylie explains how Wiedenbach understood the need to explain and integrate all these components.

Dorothea Orem

Dorothea Orem's theory is based on the notion that each person has a need for self-care in order to maintain optimal health and wellness. All individuals possess the ability and responsibility to care for themselves and dependants. Kenny Keegan tells us that Orem's theory is separated into three conceptual categories which are: self-care, self-care deficit and nursing system. The goal of nursing is to render the patient or members of his or her family capable of meeting the patient's self-care needs. The nurse's role in helping the patient to achieve or maintain a level of optimal health and wellness is to act as an advocate, redirector, support person and teacher, and to provide an environment conducive to therapeutic development.

Myra Levine

Val Douglas tells us how Levine's Conservation Principles Model provides a robust framework to guide patient care. She explains how Levine's concepts of adaptation, wholeness and conservation can be applied to the nursing process. She introduces the idea of 'provocative facts' which can loosely be described as assessment issues that stand out to the nurse. These issues may be in relation to adaptation, wholeness or conservation. Douglas explains that Levine recommended a systematic method which included the identification of provocative facts and the subsequent development of hypotheses to explain them. The patient assessment establishes provocative facts, which is the first step in the scientific approach to nursing care. The chapter describes how this idea is integrated into the traditional nursing process of assessment, planning, implementation and evaluation.

Nancy Roper, Winifred Logan and Alison Tierney

Possibly the most widely utilised theory in the UK is that of Roper, Logan and Tierney. Their Activities of Living captured something of the essence of nursing in the 1980s. On its introduction it is fair to say it revolutionised nursing practice in the UK. Up until that point Lorraine Duers tells us that nursing was strictly task oriented with 'bowel books' and 'bath books' recording care events. Roper, Logan and Tierney shifted the focus onto the needs of the patient rather than the needs of the ward. This of course is not the full story and Duers fills in the gaps, concluding that the model provides an understandable, common-sense approach to what is a complex activity; that of providing effective nursing care to each individual requiring it. The activities of living are used worldwide and the core texts are consistently translated into several languages.

CHAPTER 11

Virginia Avenel Henderson

Brian Johnston

Virginia Avenel Henderson
1897–1996

Profile

Virginia Henderson has been described as the mother of American nursing and nursing throughout the world. Her definition of nursing and identification of the 14 Fundamental Needs of Patients were accepted worldwide. Her dedicated work in defining the unique role of the nurse can be viewed as pivotal in the development of nursing education, practice and research.

Biography

The world-renowned nurse theorist Virginia Avenel Henderson was often referred to as the Florence Nightingale of the 20th century (Johnson and Webber, 2005). She was born in Kansas City in Missouri USA, on the 30th November 1897, to Lucy Abbott Henderson and Daniel B Henderson. She was the fifth of nine children; one child died infancy (Smith, 1989). When Virginia was four years old the family moved to Bedford County in Virginia. Virginia remained in Kansas City for a few more years before joining the rest of her family. Virginia Henderson's grandfather was the headmaster at Bellevue High School for Boys and Virginia and her siblings lived and were educated at the school. At this time her father was a practising lawyer in Washington DC. The family eventually moved to their own house in 1908 (Smith, 1989).

It was during World War I, when two of her brothers were serving in the forces, that she became interested in caring for wounded servicemen (Parker, 2001). In 1918 she enrolled into the Army School of Nursing at Walter Reed Army Hospital in Washington DC graduating in 1921 (Johnson and Webber, 2005). After consolidation of her nurse training as a staff nurse at the Henry Street Visiting Nurse Service in New York (Marriner Tomey, 1994), Henderson took up a post at Norfolk Hospital, Virginia in 1922 which involved teaching nursing. Henderson continued her own nursing education by graduating with a BSc from the Teachers College at Columbia University in 1932, going on to complete an MA in nurse education in 1934. For a short period Henderson took the post of Teaching Supervisor at the Strong Memorial Hospital in New York and she then returned to Columbia University to teach from 1934 until 1948 (George, 1995). In 1953 Henderson joined Yale University School of Nursing as Research Associate. Following her retirement in the 1970s she continued to work as Research Associate Emeritus until her death in 1996 (Johnson and Webber, 2005).

It was while at Yale that her extensive publications began. Henderson is best known for her definition of nursing and the identification of the 14 Fundamental Needs upon which nursing care is based (Parker, 2001).

Special interest

Henderson was interested in the research and development of nursing education curricula. She highlighted her position on the education of nurses stating:

In order for a nurse to practice as an expert in her own right and use the scientific approach to the improvement of practice, the nurse needs the kind of education available only in colleges and universities.

(Henderson, 1966: 69)

She was particularly interested in interpreting the relationship between the patient and the nurse. This relationship is demonstrated in the three levels that the nurse works with the patient:

- A substitute for the patient

Key dates

1921	Qualified as a nurse
1932	BSc Teachers College, Columbia University
1934	Took up a teaching post at Columbia University. Completed MA in nurse education
1939	Rewrote 4th edition of Bertha Harmer's *Principles and practice of nursing*
1953	Joined the School of Nursing at Yale University.
1955	The fifth edition of the *Principles and practice of nursing* published in which Henderson's definition of nursing appeared
1960	*Basic principles of nursing care* guidance booklet published by the International Council of Nurses
1964	Collaborated with Leo Simmons to survey the existence of nursing research
1966	*The nature of nursing* published
1963–1972	Directed *The Nursing Studies Index* at Yale University School of Nursing

- A helper to the patient
- A partner with the patient.

(Henderson, 1966)

Henderson highlighted the uniqueness of nursing and the importance of the nurse truly understanding the needs of the patient. She is quoted as saying that the nurse requires to:

Get inside the skin of each patient in order to know what help he or she needs from them. The nurse is temporarily the consciousness of the unconscious, the love of life for the suicidal, the leg of the amputee, the eyes of the newly blind, a means of confidence for the young mother, a voice for those too weak to speak, and so on. The activities people ordinarily perform without assistance are breathing, eating, elimination, resting, sleeping and moving, cleaning the body and keeping it warm and properly clothed. Nurses also provide for those activities that make life more than a vegetative process, namely social intercourse, learning, occupations that are recreational and those that are productive in some way.

(Henderson and Nite, 1978: 35–36)

Research was of particular interest to Henderson, and during her work with Simmons in 1964, a number of factors were identified as contributing to why nurses were not engaging as much as they should in research. These included energy being focused on preparing new nurses, and recruitment and retention of nurses, and a lack of sustained support by nursing administrators and physicians.

During her training, Henderson was concerned that nursing was perceived as merely an extension of medicine and as using a non-personal approach. Henderson considered nurse education to be a diluted version of the education that was received by those training to be doctors (Salvage and Kershaw, 1990).

This aspect of her views of the nurse's role is borne out in her description of the roles of nurses which suggests that there is potential for conflict. Firstly, Henderson outlines that nurses have a unique function as independent professionals. Secondly, she advocates that the nurse's role is that of the physician's helper (Aggleton and Chalmers, 1986). This relationship is outlined in a statement by Henderson in 1980.

The nursing history parallels the medical history; the nurse's health assessment, the physician's medical examination; the nursing diagnosis; nursing orders to the plan of medical management; and nursing evaluation to medical evaluation.

(Henderson, 1980: 907)

This is reinforced by Henderson in 1991 when she declared:

It is contention that the nurse is, and should be legally an independent practitioner and able to make independent judgements as long as he, or she, is not diagnosing, prescribing treatment for disease, or making a prognosis, for these are the physician's functions. But the nurse is the authority on basic nursing care.

(Henderson, 1991: 22)

Henderson highlighted that the value of physical nursing care is seen to be key in the role of the nurse. She expressed concern about unqualified staff being overly delegated nursing tasks, she stated:

They [unqualified nurses] may fail to assess the patient's needs adequately but, perhaps more important the qualified nurse, being deprived of the opportunity while giving physical care to assess his needs, may not find any other chance to do so.

(Henderson, 1960: 10–11)

Summary of writings

Henderson was a prolific writer from the late 1930s to the early 1990s, publishing research articles, books and book chapters. Her first publication was in 1939 when she revised the *Textbook of the principles and practice of nursing*, originally written by the Canadian nurse, Bertha Harmer. It was the next edition, published in 1955, that included her definition of nursing:

The unique function of [the] nurse is to assist individuals, sick or well, in the performance of those activities contributing to health, or its recovery (or to a peaceful death), that they would perform unaided if they had the necessary strength, will, or knowledge. And do this in such a way as to help them gain independence as rapidly as possible.

(Harmer and Henderson, 1955: 7)

This text was a crucial text for nurse education providing the foundation for the study of nursing arts (Harmer and Henderson, 1955). Henderson argued that the nursing arts included using science to develop skills related to nursing (Harmer and Henderson, 1955).

Henderson's writing also included the following;

- In collaboration with Simmons in 1964 *The yearbook of modern nursing,* and in 1964 *Nursing research: A survey and assessment* (Simmons and Henderson, 1964).
- In 1960 Henderson was requested by the International Council of Nurses to produce a guide for nurses all over the world. This was called the *Basic principles of nursing care*.
- In 1966 *The nature of nursing: A definition and its implications for practice, research and education* included her introduction of the 14 Fundamental

Needs or components of nursing.

- Between 1963 and 1972 Henderson directed *The nursing studies index* (4 volumes) at Yale University School of Nursing.
- In 1978 with Gladys Nite she revised the sixth edition of *The principles and practice of nursing*.
- In 1991 *The nature of nursing: Reflections after 25 years* was published. Here Henderson reflects on her definition and identification of the 14 Fundamental Needs.

Theory

Henderson has been extremely influential throughout the 20th century. She was inspired and influenced by many other pioneers, particularly Annie Warburton Goodrich who was Dean of the Army School where Henderson started her initial nurse training. Warburton was subsequently the first Dean of the Yale School of Nursing when Henderson joined the faculty in 1953. Henderson commented on her early views of Goodrich:

Whenever she visited our unit she lifted our sights above techniques and routine

(Henderson, 1991: 11)

Other key people in Henderson's career included Bertha Harmer. During her time at Columbia University Henderson was invited to revise the fourth edition of Harmer's textbook and subsequent editions continued to include Harmer's name despite the fact that she died in 1934. At no stage did Henderson meet Harmer (Halloran, 1995).

Another key person was Leo Simmons whom Henderson collaborated with while at Yale. Simmons was an anthropologist and together they produced an extensive piece of work considering the nursing research that had been carried out over 30 states in America (Simmons and Henderson, 1964). It was as a result of this work that it was recognised that there was very limited, specific nursing research. From this Yale University sponsored the development of the *Nursing studies index* which culminated in four volumes of nursing literature (Parker, 2001). Henderson herself suggested that the development of the *Nursing studies index* was her greatest achievement and contribution to nursing (Halloran, 1995).

Henderson was very interested in physiology and was influenced by Caroline Stackpole during her time as a student at Columbia University in the 1920s. Stackpole's work was based around the theory that health was supported by the concept of homeostasis and keeping lymph constant around the cell (Henderson, 1966). Henderson stated:

A definition of nursing should imply an appreciation of the principles of physiological balance.

(Henderson, 1966: 11)

However, Henderson appreciated that any physiological imbalance affects the psychological and emotional balance of a patient.

The concept of health and the promotion of health were areas of interest for Henderson. On the subject of health Henderson stated:

Individuals will achieve or maintain health if they have the necessary strength, will, or knowledge.

(Henderson, 1966: 15)

This notion of education and promotion of health were significant for Henderson and she argued that:

The promotion of health is more important than care of the sick.

(Henderson, 1971: 33)

Henderson was influenced by Maslow's hierarchy of human need published in 1954 which outlined seven levels of need, each requiring to be achieved to provide a source of human motivation. The levels, displayed in a pyramid format with each level building on the previous one, were as follows:

- Physiological needs
- Safety needs
- Needs for love and belonging
- Self-esteem needs
- Learning, or cognitive needs
- Aesthetic needs
- Self-actualisation needs.

(Maslow, 1954)

This concept or framework was a factor in Henderson's development of the 14 Universal Human Needs (Newton, 1991). Henderson's work on needs was an influence on others including Roper, Logan and Tierney in their development of the Activities of Daily Living Model (Roper et al., 2007)

Henderson herself highlighted that she was not setting out to develop a nursing theory, but was attempting to provide clarity on what were the functions of a nurse (Marriner Tomey, 1994). George (1995) argued that Henderson should be described as a needs/problem-orientated theorist.

Henderson did not offer a definition of need, but rather offered her 14 Fundamental Needs of patients requiring nursing care. These are:

1. Breathe normally.
2. Eat and drink adequately.
3. Eliminate body wastes.
4. Move and maintain desirable postures.
5. Sleep and rest.
6. Select suitable clothes; dress and undress.
7. Maintain body temperature within a normal range

Links to other nursing theorists

It can be argued that Virginia Henderson's philosophy of nursing has influenced and is linked to many other nursing theorists particularly those interested in needs, problem solving and interactions with patients including Florence Nightingale (*see Chapter 1*), Dorothea Orem (*see Chapter 14*), Ida Jean Orlando (*see Chapter 22*) and Nancy Roper, Winifred Logan and Alison Tierney (*see Chapter 16*).

References

Aggleton P, Chalmers H (1986) *Nursing models and the nursing process*. Macmillan Education, Basingstoke

Aggleton P, Chalmers H (2000) *Nursing models and nursing practice*. Palgrave, Basingstoke

George JB (1995) *Nursing theories: The base for professional nursing practice*. Prentice Hall International, London

Halloran EJ (1995) *A Virginia Henderson reader: Excellence in nursing*. Springer Publishing Company, New York

Harmer B, Henderson V (1955) *Textbook of the principles and practice on nursing*. Macmillan New York

Henderson V (1960) *Basic principles of nursing care*. International Council of Nurses, Geneva

Henderson V (1964) The nature of nursing. *American Journal of Nursing* **64**: 62–8

Henderson V (1966) *The nature of nursing: A definition and its implications for practice, research, and education*. Macmillan, New York

by adjusting clothing and modifying the environment.
8. Keep the body clean and well groomed and protect the integument.
9. Avoid dangers in the environment and avoid injuring others.
10. Communicate with others in expressing emotions, needs, fears, or opinions.
11. Worship according to one's faith.
12. Work in such a way that there is a sense of accomplishment.
13. Play and participate in various forms of recreation.
14. Learn, discover, or satisfy the curiosity that leads to normal development and health and use the available health facilities.

(Henderson, 1991: 22–3)

Henderson outlined the activities of nurses as components of nursing in relation to meeting the 14 Fundamental Needs (Aggleton and Chalmers, 2000). Salvage and Kershaw (1990) suggest that Henderson's approach to nursing is focused on

...helping with and deciding with, not doing for and deciding for.

(Salvage and Kershaw, 1990: 93)

They argue that this approach was an influence on Orem's development of the Self-Care Model.

Henderson's 14 Fundamental Needs consider the biological, psychological, sociological, and spiritual needs of the individual patient. George (1995) categorises each of the 14 needs: 1–9 are related to physiological needs, 10 and 14 to the psychological needs of communication and learning, 11 to spiritual needs, and 12 and 13 to sociological needs. Salvage and Kershaw suggest that, in comparison to Maslow's Hierarchy of Needs, Henderson's 14 Fundamental Needs are focused more towards physiological and safety needs.

Henderson believed that the role of the nurse will change during the rehabilitation phase. She demonstrated this by the use of pie charts that showed the relationship and dependence of the patient and other professionals and people during their care. As the patient is rehabilitated the role of the nurse is significantly reduced to a minimal slice of pie, with patients and their family or carers forming the largest piece of the pie (Henderson, 1966).

Another influence on Henderson was Ida Orlando who developed the Nursing Process Theory (Marriner Tomey, 1994). Henderson said:

Ida Orlando made me realise how easily the nurse can act on misconceptions of the patient's needs if she does not check her interpretation of them with him.

(Henderson, 1966: 14)

Putting theory into practice

Henderson highlights the importance of the nurse paying attention to and interpreting the verbal and non-verbal information provided by patients (Aggleton and Chalmers. 1986). She reinforces this stating:

It requires a listening ear and constant observation and interpretation of nonverbal behaviour.

(Henderson, 1991: 34)

Henderson's theory is built upon the understanding of the role and function of the nurse and the relationship the nurse has in helping to meet the needs of the patient (Aggleton and Chalmers, 2000). However, it must be said that Henderson herself did not see her work as a theory. Marriner

Tomey and Alligood (2006) suggest that Henderson's work could be viewed as a philosophy of nursing. Nevertheless the concepts that she shared are renowned throughout the world as defining the boundaries for nurses (Johnston and Webber, 2005).

Henderson's philosophy is very much reliant on the participation of patients in meeting their needs, involving a process of interaction or negotiation between the nurse and the patient. This process may not be possible due to the patient's level of dependency at any given time, for example if the patient is comatose (Aggleton and Chalmers, 2000).

Henderson highlights that individuals may require nursing care when they do any activities that support their health, recovery or a peaceful death, relating to the 14 Fundamental Needs. Henderson's approach highlights the model of nursing, which can be argued is a predecessor to the modern nursing process.

Aggleton and Chalmers (2000) explored the way in which Henderson addresses the stages of meeting a patient's needs. The first stage, nursing assessment of a patient, is in two phases. In the first phase the nurse requires to identify with patients if they are able to contribute to the current needs that are not being met. The second phase focuses on the potential causative factors of why these needs are not being met. The second stage is the setting of goals which are set and documented with the patient. These goals should be short-term, intermediate or long-term. Henderson argues that setting these patient-centred goals should be realistic at this care planning stage and considered with the evaluation stage in mind. The nursing intervention stage is focused on process and procedures aimed at meeting the unmet fundamental needs. These nursing interventions can include the administration of medications and treatments that have been prescribed by medical staff. However, according to Aggleton and Chalmers (2000) Henderson's model is not explicit about the actual nursing interventions that should be used.

The final stage of Henderson's model involves the nurse examining or evaluating whether the unmet needs that the nurse identified at the assessment stage have been met by the patient's own resources. The nurse will look at the goals that have been achieved and new goals that need to be set to meet further unmet need (Aggleton and Chalmers, 2000).

George (1995) discusses some limitations to the 14 Fundamental Needs including the limited conceptual links between physiological and other characteristics of being a person, suggesting that the holistic nature of being a person is not fully explored in her work. Also, if the list of needs is taken at face value, then the order of the 14 needs suggests that physiological needs are prioritised ahead of psychological needs.

Henderson's philosophy of nursing was developed well before the modern nursing process. She advocated the planning and evaluation of nursing and importantly the use of documentation (Salvage and Kershaw, 1990). Henderson commented on the nursing process as

...the application of the logical approach to the solution of a problem. The steps are those of the scientific method.

(Henderson, 1980: 906)

Henderson subsequently questioned if the steps within the nursing process were unique to nursing and could be used by any health professional (Henderson, 1980).

Henderson, in her later work, expressed concerns about the success of defining nursing stating:

In spite of the fact that generations of nurses have tried to define it, the nature of nursing remains a question.

(Henderson, 1991: 7)

Henderson V (1971) Health is everybody's business. *Canadian Nurse* **67**: 31–4

Henderson V (1980) Nursing. Yesterday and tomorrow. *Nursing Times* **76**: 905–7

Henderson V (1991) T*he nature of nursing: Reflections after 25 years*. National League for Nursing Press, New York

Henderson V, Nite G (1978) *Principles and practice of nursing* (6th edn). Macmillan, New York

Johnson BM, Webber PB (2005) *An introduction and reasoning in nursing*. Lippincott Williams & Wilkins, Philadelphia

Marriner Tomey A (ed) (1994) *Nursing theorist and their work*. Mosby, Boston

Marriner Tomey A, Alligood MR (eds) (2006) *Nursing theorist and their work*. Mosby Elsevier, St Louis

Maslow AH (1954) *Motivation and personality*. Harper and Ron, New York

Newton C (1991) *The Roper, Logan, Tierney Model in Action*. Macmillan, Basingstoke

Parker M (eds) (2001) *Nursing theories and nursing practice*. F.A. Davis Company, Philadelphia

Roper N Logan W, Tieney AJ (2007) *The Roper, Logan, Tierney model of nursing: Based on activities of living*. Churchill Livingstone, London

Salvage J, Kershaw B (eds) (1990) *Models for nursing 2*. Surban Press, London

Simmons LW, Henderson VA (1964) *Nursing research: A survey and assessment*. Appleton and Lange, New York

Smith J.P (1989) *Virginia Henderson the ninety years*. Scutari Press, Harrow

Where to find out more

There is a vast number of sources to find out more about Virginia Henderson.

- http://currentnursing.com/ nursing_theory/Henderson.htm. *Current Nursing* (a portal for nursing professionals) is a particularly informative website

- Smith JP (1989) *Virginia Henderson: The first ninety years*. Scutari Press, London
This excellent text provides insight into the extraordinary person and world ambassador to nursing.

- Henderson V (1991) *The nature of nursing: A definition and its implication for practice, research, and education: Reflections after 25 years*. National League for Nursing Press, New York
All of Henderson's texts are thought-provoking and relevant to nursing today, but this, her last publication, is one of her most relevant texts

Henderson suggests that if she was to rewrite the nature of nursing she would include nursing theory and the nursing process (Henderson, 1991).

Further influence on nurse education, practice and research

Henderson has had an influence internationally on all areas of nursing including nurse education, practice and research.

In 1960 the International Council for Nurses (ICN) requested that Henderson write a guide for nursing that could be used throughout the world and this led to the publication of *Basic principles of nursing care* (1960). This work became an instant success and has been published in many languages. According to Parker (2001) Henderson's work has been as important in the 20th century as Florence Nightingale's *Notes on nursing* was in the century before.

Henderson's influence on nursing education is remarkable. She pursued the stance that the curriculum for nursing education required to be organised in accordance with the role and functions of the nurse (Marriner Tomey, 1994). This position is notable in that it seeks to differentiate between the roles of nursing and medicine, thereby distinguishing nursing as a profession in its own right:

> *The curriculum must be organised around the nurse's major functions rather than that of the physician.*
>
> (Henderson, 1964: 67)

Henderson suggested that the term 'nurse' should refer only to a person with the correct level of education; someone who had been prepared for nursing in a recognised nursing programme lasting from two and half to three years in duration (Harmer and Henderson, 1955). These nursing programmes would encourage the student to engage critically with biological and physiological sciences, medical sciences and social sciences (Harmer and Henderson, 1955). Henderson (1964) strongly promoted the development of nursing independent practice and nursing assessment skills. Additionally, she pushed for nurse education to be moved from hospital-based training to university-based education, with the schools of nursing being administered by colleges or universities.

Henderson's influence on practice cannot be understated and she was a great advocate for nurses providing excellent basic nursing care. By working in partnership with patients and their families Henderson stressed the importance of the nurse recognising the value of the family unit to the patient. Nurses can work by assessing, planning, implementing and evaluating the 14 Fundamental Needs or components to promote health, wellbeing and independence.

Henderson was a staunch champion for nurses engaging in research that informs their practice (Marriner Tomey, 1994). Her work with Yale University and in particular with Leo Simmons on examining the range of nursing research in a large part of America, gave an opportunity to question why nurses were not engaging in research. It also provided inspiration for nurses to be involved in research activities to inform and improve practice. Henderson spent a considerable part of her long and illustrious career in library science research developing the *Nursing studies index* (Johnson and Webber, 2005). Parker (2001) suggests that Henderson's work compiling nursing research literature was her greatest contribution to nursing.

CHAPTER 12

Madeleine Leininger

Yvonne Christley

Biography

Madeleine Leininger was born on the 13th July 1925 in Sutton, Nebraska in the United States. She commenced her nurse training in 1945 graduating in 1948 with a diploma in nursing from St Anthony's School of Nursing, Colorado. Leininger continued with her academic studies after registration and was awarded a BSc in biological sciences from Benedictine College, Kansas in 1950. This was to be a busy year for Leininger and culminated in the launch of a psychiatric nursing service at St Joseph's Hospital, Nebraska and the development of a nurse education programme for Creighton University, Nebraska (Seitzman and Eichelberger, 2004).

By 1954 Leininger had completed an MSc in psychiatric nursing at the Catholic University of America, Washington. Immediately following the completion her Masters Leininger was appointed as Professor of Nursing and Director of the Graduate Programmes at University of Cincinnati, Ohio where she remained until 1960. While in this post Leininger introduced the first graduate psychiatric nursing programme in the United States (Andrews and Boyle, 2008).

In addition to her already considerable accomplishments Leininger commenced further academic studies completing a PhD in cultural and social anthropology at the University of Washington in 1965. Leininger was the first nurse to complete a PhD in anthropology and was subsequently appointed as the first Professor of Nursing and Anthropology at the University of Colorado. The University of Colorado created this professorship specifically for Leininger. It was during this appointment that Leininger developed the first course in transcultural nursing. Leininger moved to the University of Washington 1969 where she served as Dean of the School of Nursing until 1974 (Tomey and Alligood, 2002).

From 1974 to 1980 Leininger was Dean and Professor of Nursing and Anthropology at the University of Utah, where she founded the first masters and doctoral degrees in transcultural nursing and established the Transcultural Nursing Society and International Association of Human Care. In 1981 she was appointed to the position of Professor of Nursing and Director of the Centre for Health Research where she remained until her retirement as professor emerita in 1995. While at the university she launched the *Journal of Transcultural Nursing* in 1989 and acted as editor until 1995. In 1991 she developed and published the seminal Culture Care Diversity and Universality Theory (Leininger and McFarland, 2002; Tomey and Alligood, 2002).

Leininger is the founder of and one of the most influential leaders of transcultural nursing. She is an internationally renowned scholar, leader, educator and researcher. Leininger is currently retired, however, she remains actively involved in teaching, writing and lecturing on nursing, transcultural nursing and anthropology (Fawcett, 2002).

Special interest

In the 1950s, while working with children with mental health problems, Leininger noticed that children from different cultures expressed differences in they ways in which they liked to receive care. In particular, Leininger

Madeleine Leininger

Born 1925

Profile

Madeleine Leininger is the founder of and one of the most important leaders of transcultural nursing. She is an internationally renowned scholar in both nursing and anthropology. Her vision, leadership, creativity and determination has created, for nurses, a new body of nursing knowledge that recognises the importance of culture and care in establishing meaningful and therapeutic nurse interventions.

Key dates

1950	BSc in biological sciences, Benedictine College, Kansas
1954	MSc in psychiatric nursing, Catholic University of America, Washington Identified and investigated the influences of culture on patients' experiences and expectations of care
1965	Became the first nurse to be awarded a PhD in cultural anthropology and introduced the first educational courses in transcultural nursing
1973	Established the first academic department in transcultural nursing
1974	Established the Transcultural Nursing Society
1978	Introduced the first masters and doctoral courses in transcultural nursing
1989	Established the *Transcultural Nursing Journal*
1991	Published the Culture Care Diversity and Universality Theory
1995	Published *Transcultural nursing: Concepts, theories, research and practices*
2002	Published, in partnership

with Marilyn McFarland, the 3rd edition of *Transcultural nursing: Concepts, theories, research and practices*

2006   Published, in partnership with Marilyn McFarland, the 2nd edition of *Culture care diversity and universality: A worldwide nursing theory*

observed that the psychoanalytic theories and treatments which underpinned the care of children with mental health problems did not appreciate the importance of providing culturally sensitive care. She realised that she and other health professionals lacked insights and understanding of the children's cultural background. Furthermore, she observed that the nursing interventions designed to help these children had little or no impact on those from different cultures. Leininger felt that this was because nurses and other professionals were limited in their ability to respond to the care needs of the children from different cultures because of a lack of cultural understanding (Reynolds, 1993). This experience encouraged Leininger to embark on a lifetime quest to understand the nature and relationship of culture in the provision of effective and therapeutic nursing care.

In order to learn and further her understanding Leininger embarked upon a PhD in anthropology. She was captivated by anthropology and believed that cultural understanding and learning was of vital importance to nursing knowledge and practice. Leininger immersed herself in discovery of culture and culturally orientated caring practices spending two years living with and studying the Gadsup people of Papua New Guinea. While in New Guinea she recognised that the Gadsup culture had features related to caring that were unique to their culture and some that were shared with other cultures (Miller, 2007).

In summary, as a result of the poor cultural understanding observed in clinical practice and the cultural experiences and understanding gained from the Gadsup, Leininger developed transcultural nursing and the supporting Theory of Culture Care Diversity and Universality. In essence Leininger developed her theory by bringing together aspects of nursing and anthropology and continued to use this approach to advance transcultural knowledge and practice throughout her distinguished career.

Summary of writings

Leininger has written and edited 28 books, more than 200 journal articles and contributed to no less than 25 book chapters (Tomey and Alligood, 2002). The most important of all her writings are contained within three groundbreaking works, namely; *Nursing and anthropology: The two worlds to blend* (Leininger, 1970), all three editions of *Transcultural nursing: Concepts, theories, research and practice* (Leininger, 1978; 1995; Leininger and McFarland, 2002) and the seminal *Culture Care Diversity and Universality: A nursing theory* (Leininger, 1991) followed by a second edition in 2006 (Leininger and McFarland, 2006)

Nursing and anthropology: The two worlds to blend (Leininger, 1970) was the first piece of nursing literature to introduce and situate the concepts of culture and care as essential components of meaningful and therapeutic nurse–patient relationships. Her work highlighted important overlaps between understandings derived from anthropology (in particular culture and care) and the development of nursing knowledge and practice, which had been largely neglected by the nursing profession until this point. It was in this book that Leininger laid the foundations for the development of a new discipline in nursing which she named transcultural nursing (Dyson, 2007).

In 1978 Leininger wrote *Transcultural nursing: Concepts, theories, research and practice*. The book contained the theoretical, philosophical and conceptual underpinnings of transcultural nursing and introduced for the first time the significance of the concept of culturally sensitive care to nursing knowledge and practice. The book was a complete shift away from the prevailing focus of nursing on medical symptoms, disease and treatment, and focused nursing knowledge and practice on providing patients with culturally sensitive holistic care. This book remains the definitive source of knowledge for transcultural scholars and is currently in its third edition (Leininger and McFarland, 2002).

By 1991 Leininger produced and published her definitive work *Culture Care Diversity and Universality: A nursing theory* (Leininger, 1991). The Culture Care Diversity and Universality Theory was developed with the intention of providing a theoretical framework for progressing transcultural nursing knowledge and practice. It provides a structure by which nurses can unravel, understand and provide culturally sensitive care to patients, families and communities and is widely regarded as one of the most important nurse innovations for the care of patients from different cultures (Leininger, 2002; Fawcett, 2005; Andrews and Boyle 2008).

Culture Care Diversity and Universality Nursing Theory

Leininger observed as far back as the 1950s that patients from different cultures were not receiving care that was sensitive or acceptable to their cultural background. In order to address these cultural care deficiencies Leininger developed and introduced the concept of transcultural nursing. Transcultural nursing is an approach to nursing which acknowledges the centrality and value of the patient's and the nurse's culture in building effective therapeutic relationships. Leininger asserts that transcultural nursing is characterised by the importance it places on culture; an understanding and appreciation of cultural influences are seen as critical to a successful nurse–patient relationship (Leininger, 2001). The principles of transcultural nursing can also be applied to nursing research and education. In order to comprehensively articulate and explain the significance of transcultural nursing, Leininger (1991) developed and published her Theory of Culture Care Diversity and Universality. *Figure 12.1* provides an overview of the key components of the theory.

The main aim of the theory is to provide a comprehensive framework of transcultural nursing that can be used to ensure patients receive holistic and 'culturally congruent' nursing care. The phrase culturally congruent care was devised by Leininger in the 1960s and refers to nursing care that is both culturally orientated and developed in partnership with the patient and/or family (Leininger, 1978). At the centre of the theory is the assertion that all cultures have customs and traditions associated with caring which need to be identified, understood and acted upon if nurses are to provide holistic nursing care to patients from different cultural backgrounds (Leininger, 1991).

The theory is structured around four key principles (Leininger, 1991):

Care diversity and universality

The first and most important principle of Leininger's theory is the assertion that caring practices can be unique and specific to a particular culture or be shared across many cultures (Baldonado et al., 1998). The caring practices that are unique and practised in a different way from one cultural group to another are referred to as care diversities (differences). The caring practices that are shared across cultures are referred to as care universalities (commonalities). In order to provide culturally appropriate nursing care the similarities and differences in caring practices between cultures need to be unravelled and understood (Leininger, 2007).

World view and social structure

The second key principle of Leininger's theory involves considering experiences of care and caring and how these are influenced by a person's 'world view' and the social structures within which individuals live. The theory describes the concept of world view as the outlook people

Figure 12.1. Culture Care Diversity and Universality Theory: Key components.

Links to other nursing theorists

The Culture Care Diversity and Universality Theory has been linked with and compared to Dorothea Orem's Self-Care Deficiency Theory (*see Chapter 14*) and Jean Watson's Nursing Human Science and Human Care Theory. A key similarity between all these theories is the special emphasis placed on the concept of care and caring in professional nursing practice.

have on life. This outlook or world view is thought to be derived from an individual's experience of culturally defined social structures. Furthermore, the values, beliefs and behaviours associated with care and caring are thought to be embedded in a person's world view and social structures such as language, family, social relations, educational attainment, economic status, and the environmental contexts of cultures, etc. (McFarland and Eipperle, 2008). Care is thought to have different meanings for different cultural groups, which can be detected by examining an individual's world view, social structure, lifestyle and language.

Generic and professional care practices

The third key principle identifies differences in generic or lay approaches to caring and the professional care delivered to patients by nurses. Leininger indicates that the practices of generic or lay care are acquired through cultural learning and are used to enable and support individuals within a family, group or community to resolve health problems, cope with disability or embrace death. Furthermore, the caring practices and meanings associated with care differ between cultural groups.

By contrast the professional care practices associated with nursing are acquired through formal evidence-based conceptualisations of health, disease and wellbeing. This approach to nurse education and preparation fails to take account of culturally orientated caring preferences. As such, patients are exposed to nursing care experiences that may not acknowledge the importance of their caring beliefs, values, and practices, the consequences of which could result in cultural conflict, non-compliance and stress (Leininger and McFarland, 2002).

Transcultural care modes and actions

The fourth and final key principle refers to trancultural care modes and actions. In order to assist nurses to provide care that is culturally orientated the theory includes three transcultural approaches and actions to nursing care, namely:

- *Culture care preservation or maintenance*: this mode of nursing care and action is concerned with safeguarding and maintaining the centrality of the patient's cultural care values, beliefs and expectations within the nurse–patient relationship.
- *Culture care accommodation or negotiation*: this mode of nursing care and action is concerned with the development of innovative and flexible nursing interventions that assist patients from different cultures to adapt to and negotiate their way through the complexities of healthcare delivery and recovery.
- *Culture care repatterning or restructuring*: this mode of nursing care and action is concerned with facilitating opportunities for patients to alter and improve their damaging health behaviours while also valuing those patients' cultural beliefs, values and expectations in relation to care, health and wellbeing.

All these care modes and actions can only be achieved by nurses who have been thoroughly prepared and are competent in transcultural nursing (Reynolds, 1993). The four key overarching principles of Leininger's theory are supported by a number of theoretical assumptions, the most important of which are summarised in *Figure 12.2*.

In summary, the theory demonstrates that care is a core value at the

Care	Cultural care	Care diversities and universalities
• Care is the essence and focus of nursing • Care is an essential component of health, wellbeing, growth, survival, disability and death	• Culturally based care is the most comprehensive and holistic approach to nursing practice • Culturally based care is an essential component of healing, as healing cannot occur in the absence of caring	• Culture care concepts vary between cultures • Some care and caring practices are unique (care diversities) to a particular culture • Some care and caring practices are shared between cultures (care universalities)

Figure 12.2. Key theoretical assumptions.

centre of nursing practice, while also illustrating that care and caring, as perceived and experienced by the patient, is firmly rooted in the individual's cultural background. Furthermore, care and caring practices from a cultural point of view exhibit features that can be unique to an individual culture or be universally shared between cultures. As such, the theory provides nurses and nursing with an opportunity and a challenge to enhance patient care experiences by delivering culturally competent nursing care that is informed by an understanding of the patient's diverse and universal care values, beliefs and expectations.

Putting theory into practice

Transcultural nursing and its underpinning Theory of Culture Care Diversity and Universality have had a profound impact on the provision of nursing interventions that are sensitive to patients' culturally defined values, beliefs and expectations of care (Price and Cordell, 1994). The concept of culturally competent nursing care has gained considerable acceptance in many countries and is considered one of the most effective approaches to caring for the culturally diverse. The far-reaching impacts of transcultural nursing is demonstrated by the extensive body of scholarly articles, research, textbooks, educational curricula and clinical policy and practice guidelines on transcultural nursing. All of these knowledge-generation activities reflect the demand from clinical nurses, researchers, educationalists and students for information that supports the acquisition of the knowledge and skills necessary to understand and practise in culturally competent ways (Shapiro et al., 2006).

Cultural competence in clinical practice is represented in Leininger's theory as a combination of attitudes, communication and practice skills that enable the nurse to work effectively with patients, families or communities from diverse cultures (Dyson, 2007). The culturally competent nurse is able to assess patient care needs in partnership with the patient and based on cultural similarities and differences that might influence the effectiveness of jointly agreed care plans (Leininger, 1991). The Culture Care Diversity and Universality Theory provides three approaches to guide nursing care decisions and actions towards the provision of effective culturally sensitive care to patients. These approaches to nursing practice are culture care preservation or maintenance, culture care accommodation or negotiation and culture care repatterning or restructuring and are illustrated in *Figure 12.3* (A detailed explanation of each of these approaches is provided in the theory section of this chapter.)

References

Andrews M, Boyle J (2008) *Transcultural concepts in nursing care* (5th edn) Lippincott Williams & Wilkins, Philadelphia, London

Andrews M, Hanson P (2003) Religion, culture and nursing, in Andrews M, Boyle J (eds) *Transcultural concepts in nursing care* (4th edn) Lippincott Williams & Wilkins, Philadelphia, London

Baldonado A, Beymer PL, Barnes K, Starsiak D, Nemivant EB, Anonas-Ternate A (1998) Transcultural nursing practice described by registered nurses and baccalaureate nursing students. *Journal of transcultural Nursing* 9(2): 15–25

Cortis JD (2000) Caring as experienced by minority ethnic patients. *International Nursing Review* 47(1): 53–62

de Villiers L, van der Wal D (1995) Putting Leininger's nursing theory culture care diversity and universality into operation in the curriculum. Part 1. *Curationis* 18(4): 56–60

Dyson S (2007) *Fundamental aspects of transcultural nursing*, Quay Books, London

Fawcett J (2002) The nurse theorists: 21st-century updates – Madeleine M Leininger, *Nursing Science Quarterly* 15(2): 131–6

Fawcett J (2005) *Contemporary nursing knowledge: Analysis and evaluation of nursing models and theories* (2nd edn) FA Davis Co, Philadelphia

George TB (2002) Care meanings, expressions, and experiences of those with chronic mental illness. *Archives of Psychiatric Nursing* **16**(1): 25–31

Jeffreys MR (2006) *Teaching cultural competence in nursing and health care: Inquiry, action, and innovation.* Springer, London

Kavanagh KH (1993) Transcultural nursing: Facing the challenges of advocacy and diversity/universality. *Journal of Transcultural Nursing* **5**(1): 4–13

Leininger M (1970) *Nursing and anthropology: Two worlds to blend.* Wiley, London

Leininger M (1978) *Transcultural nursing: Concepts, theories, and practices.* Wiley, Chichester

Leininger M (1991) The Theory of Culture Care Diversity and Universality. *National League for Nursing* **15**: 5-68

Leininger M (1995) *Transcultural nursing: Concepts, theories, research and practices* (2nd edn) McGraw-Hill, London

Leininger M (1996) Culture care theory, research, and practice. *Nursing Science Quarterly* **9**(2): 71–8

Leininger M (2001) Current issues in using anthropology in nursing education and services *Western Journal of Nursing Research* **23**(8): 795–806; discussion 807–11

Leininger M (2002) Culture Care Theory: A major contribution to advance transcultural nursing knowledge and practices *Journal of Transcultural Nursing* **13**(3): 189–92; discussion 200–1

Leininger M (2007) Theoretical questions and concerns: Response from the Theory of Culture Care Diversity

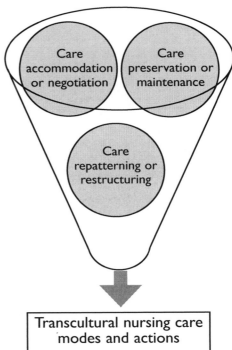

Figure 12.3. Transcultural care modes and actions.

Transcultural care modes – a practice example

Peter, a 26-year-old man was admitted to the intensive care unit (ICU) following a road traffic accident. He had sustained an extensive and diffuse head injury and required mechanical ventilation. Shortly after his arrival in ICU his condition deteriorated and a CT scan revealed that the injury to Peter's brain was catastrophic and irreversible. The consultant in charge of the ICU informed the family that Peter was brain dead and asked their permission to cease all active treatment and allow Peter to die. He also encouraged Peter's family to consider the possibility of organ donation. Peter's family responded with horror at the prospect of ceasing active treatment and threatened to commence legal action if it was halted. Peter remained in the ICU for a further five weeks before he died. He was accompanied at all times by his family and members of his spiritual community, who prayed constantly at his bedside. The nurses in the ICU were concerned at the disturbance Peter's family and friends were causing in the ICU and felt that they interfered with their ability to care for other patients. Some nurses reacted negatively to Peter's family and perceived them as difficult and uncooperative (Andrews and Hanson, 2003).

A transcultural approach to caring for Peter and his family would have equipped the ICU nurses to make sense of and respond to the culturally orientated care needs of this patient and his family. The Culture Care Diversity and Universality Theory provides the following three approaches to guide transcultural nursing actions. Leininger suggests that one or all of these methods can be used to guide nurses in the delivery of culturally competent nursing care. To illustrate, the above example has been applied to three modes of nursing action, which are:

- *Culture care preservation or maintenance*: This mode of nursing action is concerned with providing care that does not conflict with the patient's or family's cultural values, beliefs or expectations of nursing care (Kavanagh, 1993). This approach would have illuminated important information about Peter and his family's religious and moral beliefs. To Peter's family the sanctity of human life was paramount and to them brain death was quite simply not an acceptable description of death. The family were also active members of a Christian spiritual community and believed that the redemption of Peter's soul could only be achieved through prayer (Andrews and Hanson, 2003). Furthermore, they believed that for Peter's soul to depart his body in peace and dignity he should not be left alone. If the ICU nurses had been aware of the importance of Peter's family's spiritual care values and beliefs they would have been better able to understand and respond more empathetically to their care requirements.

- *Culture care accommodation or negotiation*: This mode of nursing action is concerned with providing care that accommodates cultural difference. If cultural difference cannot be completely accommodated then culturally acceptable alternatives are negotiated in partnership with the patient's or family's wishes (George, 2002). The lack of communication between the ICU nurses and family regarding the latter's spiritual care needs inhibited the creation of a culturally considerate and sensitive caring environment for Peter and his family. Furthermore, the ICU nurses could have used this approach to care to negotiate opportunities with the family to meet their spiritual care needs while also ensuring that the disturbance to other patients was kept to a minimum.

- *Culture care re-patterning or restructuring*: This mode of nursing action is concerned with reforming cultural beliefs for effective care. In this example a re-patterning of the ICU nurses' understanding of cultural beliefs and practices and associated spiritual care requirements in end-of-life care is essential (de Villiers and van der Wal, 1995). The provision of meaningful and sensitive end-of-life nursing care to patients and families requires cultural competence and a deep understanding and awareness of the cultural variations associated with death, dying and what constitutes a good death (Cortis, 2000).

The above practice example demonstrates the utility of the Culture Care Diversity and Universality Theory to therapeutic and effective nurse–patient and nurse–family relationships. The provision of culturally appropriate spiritual care to Peter and his family should have been a key priority as he approached death and illuminated the importance of understanding the diverse cultural influences on a patient or family's interpretations and experiences of health, illness and death. The abilities of the nurse to develop effective communication strategies with those from culturally diverse backgrounds is of central importance to the delivery of care that is culturally sensitive and acceptable to the patient, family and the nurse.

Influence

Since its inception in the 1950s, transcultural nursing has influenced and impacted on the development of nursing care knowledge and practice on a worldwide scale. Over more than five decades transcultural nursing has changed practice, education and research and situated culturally competent nursing care as an expected standard for patients, families and communities. Leininger developed the Culture Care Diversity and Universality Theory in 1991 in order to systematically progress transcultural nursing knowledge and practice (Leininger, 2002).

The theory is heralded as a significant advancement in the care of patients from different cultures and continues to be one of the most important resources for discerning and delivering culturally competent patient care. It is the first nursing theory to discover, identify and distinguish care and caring practices that are diverse (different) and as such unique to individual cultural groups from those that are universal (common) and

and Universality perspective *Nursing Science Quarterly* **20**(1): 9–13

Leininger M, McFarland MR (2002) *Transcultural nursing: Concepts, theories, research and practice* (3rd edn) McGraw-Hill, London

Leininger M, McFarland MR (2006) *Culture Care Diversity and Universality: A worldwide nursing theory* (2nd edn) Jones and Bartlett, London

McFarland MR, Eipperle MK (2008) Culture Care Theory: A proposed practice theory guide for nurse practitioners in primary care settings. *Contemporary Nurse* **28**(1-2): 48–63

Miller J (2007) Madeleine Leininger over the years. *Nursing Science Quarterly* **20**(3): 199

Price JL, Cordell B (1994) Cultural diversity and patient teaching. *Journal of Continuing Education in Nursing* **25**(4): 163–6

Reynolds CL (1993) *Madeleine Leininger: Cultural care diversity and universality theory*. Sage Publications, London

Shapiro ML, Miller J, White K (2006) Community transformation through culturally competent nursing leadership: Application of theory of culture care diversity and universality and tri-dimensional leader effectiveness model. *Journal of Transcultural Nursing* **17**(2): 113–18

Sitzman K, Eichelberger L (2004) *Understanding the work of nurse theorists: A creative beginning*. Jones and Bartlett Publishers, London

Tomey AM, Alligood MR (2002) *Nursing theorists and their work* (5th edn) Mosby, London

Zoucha R, Husted GL (2000) The ethical dimensions of delivering culturally congruent nursing and health care. *Issues in Mental Health Nursing* **21**(3): 325–40

Where to find out more

Further information on transcultural nursing and the culture care diversity and universality theory can be found in the following resources:

Websites

- www.tcns.org
This website of the Transcultural Nursing Society provides comprehensive information of relevance to cultural care and practice.

- www.madeleine-leininger.com
This website provides information about transcultural nursing and the work of Madeleine Leininger.

Journals

- *Journal of Transcultural Nursing* – focuses on transcultural nursing theory, practice and research
- *Journal of Multicultural Nursing & Health* – focuses on multiculturalism in health and nurse education

Books

- Andrews M, Boyle J (2008) *Transcultural concepts in nursing care*. Lippincott, London
- Spector R (2004) *Cultural diversity in health and illness*. Prentice Hall Health, London
- Leininger M (2002) *Transcultural nursing: Concepts, theories, research and practices*. McGraw-Hill, London

shared between cultures (Fawcett, 2002). Leininger's theory is considered to be wide ranging and holistic, whilst also centring attention on the specifics of culture. This has been instrumental in assisting nurses and nursing to determine patients' culture care meanings and practices. It continues to be the only nursing theory to examine the complex interplay between care, culture, health, wellbeing and death (Zoucha and Husted, 2000).

Prior to Leininger the principal approach to patient care was through the perspective of the medical model of treatment and cure. Leininger's theory pioneered a move away from the medical model and inspired and equipped nurses and nursing with the tools necessary to determine and develop nursing practices that acknowledge and support the patient's cultural values, beliefs and expectations of care (Leininger, 1996).

Furthermore, the theory significantly influenced and changed the views of the wider nursing profession with respect to the concept of care and caring. Leininger noticed that although the terms care and caring were discussed frequently by nursing scholars and practitioners their precise meaning, value and definition were seriously lacking. The theory actively addresses the significance and value of care to nursing practice, describing care as the essence and central focus of nursing. Additionally the theory reveals the importance of care, caring and culture to effective therapeutic nurse–patient relationships (Leininger, 2002).

Finally, many nurse leaders consider the theory to be the single most significant progression of nursing knowledge of the 20th century and anticipate that it will be of even greater importance in the 21st century (Fawcett, 2002). The reasons for the theory's continued significance and influence relate to global increases in migration and immigration. This has resulted in increases in the number of different cultures nurses can expect to encounter in everyday practice (Andrews and Boyle, 2008). As such, if nurses are to deliver realistic and culturally sensitive effective nursing care it is crucial that they have a comprehensive knowledge and understanding of the impacts and influences of culture on care, health and wellbeing.

Ernestine Wiedenbach

Linda Wylie

Biography

Ernestine Wiedenbach was born in 1900 and is a notable figure in the early development of nursing theory in the USA. She was one of the early nurse theorists who removed nursing from the medical model by placing the patient at the centre of the decision making process.

Born into an affluent German family in 1900, Ernestine's family emigrated to America when she was a young child (Eichelberger, 2009). Ernestine's interest in nursing began whilst being involved in the care given to her grandmother by a private duty nurse and this interest was further cultivated when listening to the experiences of hospital life related by her sister's boyfriend who was a young intern. Therefore, after completing a degree in the liberal arts at Wellesley College in 1922, she enrolled in the Johns Hopkins Hospital School of Nursing, much to the dismay of her parents.

Initially Ernestine was thwarted in her desire to be a nurse by a disagreement with the school's administration (Nickel et al., 1992). As the student representative, Ernestine was expelled for voicing student grievances. Adelaide Nutting, a Johns Hopkins alumna, intervened, however, and contacted Elsie Lawler, the Director of the Johns Hopkins School of Nursing, who allowed Ernestine to continue her nursing studies at that school on the condition that under no circumstances was she to organise or encourage dissent amongst the nursing students. Ernestine complied.

On completion of her nursing studies, on the strength of her Bachelor's Degree, Ernestine was offered a supervisor's role at Johns Hopkins Hospital. Later, on moving to Bellevue Hospital in New York, Ernestine continued her studies at night school obtaining a Master's Degree and a Certificate in Public Health Nursing in 1934. She then moved out of the hospital setting to work with public health nurses in the Association for Improving Conditions of the Poor at the Henry Street Settlement.

Subsequently, Ernestine left clinical nursing altogether to work as a professional writer with the Nursing Information Bureau for the *American Journal of Nursing*. Here she made many important professional contacts whilst developing her writing skills. After the bombing of Pearl Harbour during the Second World War, Ernestine worked with the Nursing Information Bureau to prepare nurses entering the war. She was unable to join them overseas due to a minor cardiac condition.

After the war, Ernestine was persuaded to return to direct patient care by Hazel Corbin, director of the Maternity Center Association of New York. Ernestine enrolled as a student midwife at the School for Midwives. She was 45 years old. After graduating, Ernestine practised as a nurse-midwife at the Maternity Centre Association, as well as developing an academic career by teaching advanced maternity nursing at evening classes. In addition she wrote several articles for professional journals and was an active member of professional nursing organisations.

In 1952, Ernestine was appointed as Director of Graduate Programs at Yale University School of Nursing in Connecticut, developing maternal-newborn health nursing programmes. These commenced in 1956 (Nickel et al., 1992). Shortly after this, in 1958, she wrote her first book *Family-centered*

Profile

Ernestine Wiedenbach developed her theory the Helping Art of Clinical Nursing after a lifetime of experience in nursing and midwifery practice. A key date was 1952 when she was appointed director of Graduate Programs at Yale University School of Nursing in Connecticut, developing maternal-newborn health nursing programmes. Here she came into contact with nurse theorist Ida Orlando Pelletier and philosophers Patricia James and William Dickoff who were influential in encouraging Ernestine to formulate her theory. A key strength of this theory was the move away from a medical model of nursing care to one of identifying the patient's need for help.

Key dates

1922	Began nurse training at Johns Hopkins Hospital School of Nursing
1934	Master's degree
1945	Began midwifery training at School for Midwives, Maternity Center Association, New York
1952	Director of Graduate Programmes at Yale University School of Nursing, Connecticut
1958	*Family-centered maternity nursing* published
1966	Retired

maternity nursing a comprehensive text on obstetric nursing. A series of books and articles followed.

After an active academic career, Ernestine retired in 1966 and moved to Florida. She never married and died at the age of 97 in 1998.

Key texts included:

- *Family-centred maternity nursing* (1967). Maternity care in the States in the middle of the 20th century was moving into the hospital and was becoming increasingly medicalised. This book challenged the conventional medical model of hospital birth from a nursing perspective and suggested new ways to practise with the family as the centre of the care planning process
- *Clinical nursing: A helping art* (1964). This book presents the theory for which Ernestine Wiedenbach is most well-known. During the writing of this book she developed her theory more clearly. The book focuses on the needs of the patient and identifies that the art of nursing is one in which the nurse nurtures or cares for her patients in a motherly fashion.
- *Meeting the realities in clinical teaching* (1969). This book sees the further development of the Helping Art of Clinical Nursing. Wiedenbach discusses the realities of nursing and the need to identify these needs and meet them through careful directing, teaching, coordinating and planning.

Theory

The Helping Art of Clinical Nursing, a philosophical model of nursing practice, was developed by Wiedenbach when she joined the School of Nursing at Yale University. Ida Orlando Pelletier, another nurse theorist, stimulated Ernestine to understand the concept of self and the effect a nurse's thoughts and feelings has on the outcome of her actions (McKee et al., 1998). Patricia James and William Dickoff, who were professors of philosophy at Yale and taught on the nursing programmes, along with other members of faculty, also encouraged Ernestine to develop her theory.

The philosophical theory of the Helping Art of Clinical Nursing was influenced by her many years in both clinical practice and in teaching. James and Dickoff, whilst advising Ernestine in the writing up of her theory in her first book *Clinical nursing: A helping art* (Wiedenbach, 1964) pointed out that what she was writing about was a prescriptive nursing theory and encouraged her to develop the theory more fully in a further book, Meeting the Realities of Clinical Teaching which was published in 1969.

The basis of the Helping Art of Clinical Nursing was an understanding of the use of self and the effect a nurse's thoughts and feelings have on the outcome of her actions. To ensure clear understanding of her theory,

---

Box 1. Terminology

A key element of the Helping Art of Clinical Nursing was in the use of terminology. She therefore defined key concepts to ensure clarity and power to her work.

- The *patient* was defined as any person who has entered the healthcare system and is receiving help of some kind, such as care, teaching or advice. The patient need not be sick since someone receiving health education would therefore qualify as a patient.
- A *need for help* was defined as any measure desired by the patient that has potential to restore or extend the ability to cope with various life situations that affect health and wellness.
- The *nurse* she considered to be a functioning human being with personal thoughts and feelings. These thoughts and feelings are intimately involved not only in what the nurse does but in how he or she does it. These are fundamental to every action undertaken whether by written communication, gesture or action.
- A *person*, whether nurse or patient, is endowed with a unique potential to develop self-sustaining resources. People generally tend towards independence and fulfilment of responsibilities. Self-awareness and self-acceptance are essential to personal integrity and self-worth. Whatever an individual does at any given moment represents the best available judgement for that person at that time.

Ernestine defined key terms as shown in *Box 1*. Her theory, however, considered that there are four elements to clinical nursing, philosophy, purpose, practice and art (Wiedenbach, 1962).

Philosophy

In Ernestine's own words

Philosophy, an attitude toward life and reality that evolves from each nurse's beliefs and code of conduct, motivates the nurse to act, guides her thinking about what she is to do and influences her decisions. It stems from both her culture and her subculture, and is an integral part of her. It is personal in character, unique to each nurse, and expressed in her way of nursing. Philosophy underlines purpose and her purpose reflects philosophy.

(Wiedenbach, 1964: 13)

Ernestine Wiedenbach recognised three essential components to a nursing philosophy:

- Reverence for the gift of life.
- Respect for dignity, worth, autonomy and individuality of a human being.

- Resolution to act dynamically on personally and professionally held beliefs.

Purpose

Purpose – that which the nurse wants to accomplish through what she does – is the overall goal toward which she is striving, and so is constant. It is her reasons for being and doing; it is the why of clinical nursing and transcends the immediate intent of her assignment or task by specifically directing her activities towards the 'good' of her patient.

(Wiedenbach, 1964: 13)

Practice

Overt action, directed by disciplines thoughts and feelings toward meeting the patient's need-for-help, constitutes the practice of clinical nursing...goal-directed, deliberately carried out and patient-centred.

(Wiedenbach, 1964: 23)

Ernestine considered that there are three elements necessary for effective practice, knowledge, judgement and skills, with three additional components of practice directly related to patient care – identification, ministration and validation with coordination indirectly related to it.

Knowledge encompasses all that has been perceived and grasped by the human mind. Knowledge has infinite scope and range. Knowledge may be acquired by the nurse in the academic arena and be useful for directing, teaching, planning and coordinating the care of the patient but is not sufficient to meet his need for help. This knowledge comes through interaction with patients in the real world environment enabling the implementation of skills for the benefit of the patient.

Knowledge may be factual, speculative or practical.

- *Factual*: accepted knowledge that is known to be true.
- *Speculative*: theories and concepts that are put forward to explain phenomena, particularly relevant to the subject areas of the natural sciences, the social sciences and the humanities.
- *Practical*: knowing how to apply factual or speculative knowledge to the situation at hand.

Judgement represents the nurse's potential for making sound decisions after weighing the facts. Judgement is derived from a cognitive process of present knowledge against the personal values achieved through ideals, principles and convictions. Judgement also differentiates facts from assumptions, relating them to cause and effect. Ernestine suggested that judgement is very personal and the nurse will exercise this according to the purpose to be served, the available knowledge, and her reaction to

the prevailing environment at the time, in terms of the time, setting and individuals involved. Decisions that are made in this way may not be sound depending on the degree to which the nurse's emotions and thoughts have been disciplined. Uncontrollable emotions can blot out both knowledge and purpose. Unfounded assumptions can distort facts. Hence the nurse requires as broad a knowledge and experience base as possible, and as great a clarity of purpose as practical, in order to make a sound judgement.

Skills represent the nurse's potential for achieving the required results. Skill covers various and numerous acts which are characterised by 'harmony of movement, expression and intent, by precision and by adroit use of self' (Wiedenbach, 1962). These acts are carried out with a deliberate purpose in mind and are not goals in themselves. These are different from nurse's actions which are carried out as a means to an end rather than the means by which they are reached. Ernestine identified two fundamental skills by which the nurse carries out her role.

- *Procedural*: these skills are considered to be options by which the nurse may identify and meet her patient's need for help.
- *Communication*: these skills are fundamental to identifying to the patient and others the thoughts and feelings the nurse desires to convey whilst caring for her patients.

Identification includes individualised care of patients taking into account their experiences and their own perception of their condition and needs. Ernestine recognised four elements to identification of the patient's need for help.

- Observing behaviours consistent or inconsistent with comfort.
- Exploring the meaning of individual patients' behaviour with them.
- Determining the cause of the discomfort or incapability.
- Determining if patients can resolve their problems or have a need for help.

Ministration is providing the needed help. It requires the identification of the need for help, the selection of an appropriate skill, and acceptance of that skill by the patient. Validation is evidence that the patient's need for help has been met as a result of the help given.

Ernestine identifies one other element in the practice of the Helping Art of Clinical Nursing that indirectly affects the nurse's role. This is coordination, in which the nurse coordinates all the services to the patient to prevent fragmentation of care by consulting and conferring with others to plan future care, and reporting this information both orally and in writing to ensure teamwork.

Links with other nursing theorists

Ida Jean Orlando (*see Chapter 22*) was a key influence in the formulation of Wiedenbach's theory which follows a deliberate rather than automatic nursing approach, and also incorporates the nursing process (McKee et al., 1998).

References

Chinn and Jacobs (1994) *Theory and Nursing; A systematic approach* (4th edn) Mosby, St Louis

Cragin L (2004) The theoretical basis for nurse-midwifery practice in the United States: A critical analysis of three theories. *Journal of Midwifery and Women's Health* **49**(5): 381–7

Eichelberger LW (2009) *Ernestine Wiedenbach*. Available from: http://healthsci.clayton.edu/eichelberger/wiedenbach.htm [Accessed 07.09.09]

Gustafson DC (1988) Signalling behaviour in stage 1 labour to elicit care: A clinical referent for Wiedenbach's need-for-help. *Dissertation Abstracts International* **49**(10): 4230

McKee NJ, Danko M, Heidenreiter TJ, Hunt NE, Marich JE, Marriner-Tomey AM et al. (1998) Ernestine Wiedenbach. The helping art of clinical nursing. In Marriner-Tomey AM (ed) *Nursing theorists and their work* (4th edn) Mosby, St Louis

Nickel S, Geese T, MacLaren A (1992) Ernestine Wiedenbach: Her professional legacy. *Journal of Nurse-Midwifery* **37**: 161–7

Sitzman K, Eichelberger LW (2003) *Understanding the work of the nurse theorists: A creative beginning*. Jones and Bartlett, Boston

Wiedenbach E (1949) Childbirth as

Art

Art is

...the application of knowledge and skill to bring about desired results... Art is individualized action. Nursing art, then, is carried out by the nurse in a one-to-one relationship with the patient, and constitutes the nurse's conscious responses to specifics in the patient's immediate situation.

(Wiedenbach, 1964: 36)

Ernestine considered that the Helping Art of Clinical Nursing is directed towards the achievement of four main goals

- Understanding patients, their condition, situation and need.
- Enhancing their capabilities.
- Improving their condition or situation within the framework of the medical plan for their care.
- Preventing a recurrence of the condition or the development of a new one that has the potential to cause anxiety, disability or distress.

There are three operational processes that influence nursing art – stimulus, preconception and interpretation. Nurse act on the basis of these operations and their actions may be rational, reactionary or deliberative. Stimulus is the patient's presenting behaviour, preconception is an expectation of what the patient may be like, and interpretation is a comparison of perception with expectation or hope. However, perception is based on interpretation of the stimulus and may be misinterpreted by the nurse.

A rational act by the nurse is a response guided by the nurse's immediate perception of patients' behaviour, what they say and do and how they appear (Chinn and Jacobs, 1994). A reactionary act however adds the dimension of emotional feelings of the nurse in response to the patient's behaviour and how the nurse had hoped or expected the patient's behaviour to be. Deliberative action is in stark contrast to both rational and reactionary acts. In carrying out deliberative acts nurses apply the principles of helping, and thus fulfil their purpose, to gain an understanding of what patients mean by the behaviour they are displaying.

The deliberative act is a fundamental part of the Helping Art of Clinical Nursing; Wiedenbach proposed in this theory that this is what constitutes good nursing practice.

Putting theory into practice

Formulating a philosophical model within a profession is fundamental to clarifying focus and direction. Such a model will encourage the profession to identify the basic beliefs of its members. Ernestine Wiedenbach was a keen advocate of the need to articulate a personal professional philosophy. She suggested that the rationale for nursing is that the nurse has come into being to meet the needs of the patient. She therefore identified five essential attributes of a professional person such as a nurse:

- Clarity of purpose.
- Mastery of skill and knowledge required to fulfil the purpose.
- Ability to establish and maintain purposeful working relationships with both professional and nonprofessional others.
- Interest in the advancement of knowledge in the area of interest and in the creation of new knowledge.

- Dedication to the furtherance of the goal of mankind rather than self-aggrandisement.

Wiedenbach's work on personal professional philosophies is still very relevant today. Her view was that philosophy is an attitude towards life which motivates the individual. Identifying one's personal professional philosophy encourages commitment, guides thinking about one's actions and influences the decisions made. Ernestine advocated explicit articulation of an individual's philosophy to enable individuals to examine their beliefs and values and to encourage them to explore the extent by which these beliefs influence their actions and attitudes.

Nursing practice today is based on identifying a patient's need for help. The Helping Art of Clinical Nursing conceptualises nursing as the practice of identification of a patient's need for help through observation of presenting behaviours and symptoms; exploration of the meaning of those symptoms with the patient; determining the cause(s) of discomfort; and determining the patient's ability to resolve the discomfort or indeed if the patient has a need for help from the nurse or other healthcare professionals. Intervention may therefore be required and the nurse facilitates the medical plan of care whilst devising a nursing plan of care in partnership with the patient. In providing care the nurse exercises sound judgement through deliberative, practised and educated recognition of symptoms whilst considering the patient's perception of the situation (Sitzman and Eichelberger, 2003).

Nurses are indeed applying the concepts of the Helping Art of Clinical Nursing far more today than nurses did in the 1950s and 1960s (McKee et al., 1998). Individualised care and the nursing process both encourage nurses to work with their patients. In maternity services midwives are advocating a return to normality and individualised care. Drawing from her many years experience as a midwife, Ernestine published an article *Childbirth as mothers say they like it* in which she notes that mothers wanted childbirth to be as natural as possible (Wiedenbach, 1949), and midwifery to be a supportive role identifying the need for help and stepping in with supportive measures at that point. This is echoed in the recognition that many of the mothers of 21st century are also becoming increasingly aware once again that natural childbirth can be a fulfilling and empowering process. Other areas in which Ernestine led the way in the maternity services was by identifying that mothers wished to be instructed on the process of birth thus demystifying it; by encouraging father participation; and by full participation of the mother in the birth and rooming in with the baby postnatally. This all remains very relevant to present day midwifery practice. Family-centred care was included in the Helping Art of Clinical Nursing, a concept reinvented by the NHS in the 1980s (McKee et al., 1998)

In education also, universities are applying nursing models such as the Helping Art of Clinical Nursing to the education of both nurses and midwives. Ernestine recognised that graduate study would extend nurses' personal limits in caring for patients. She identified that nurse education would improve nursing practice by

- Taking responsibility for the preparation of future practitioners of nursing.
- Arranging for student nurses to gain clinical experience in a wide range of hospital and community areas.
- Working with the students in clinical areas thus linking theory with practice.
- Offering educational opportunities for further study.

Application of the model, the Helping Art of Clinical Nursing, to clinical

mothers say they like it. *Public Health Nursing* **41**: 417–21

Wiedenbach E (1958) *Family-centered maternity nursing.* Putnams, New York

Wiedenbach E (1964) *Clinical nursing: A helping art.* Springer, New York

Wiedenbach E (1967) *Family-centered maternity nursing.* (2nd edn) Putnams, New York

Wiedenbach E (1969) *Meeting the realities in clinical teaching.* Springer, New Yorkr

Where to find out more

The Helping Art of Clinical Nursing is a fundamental theory of nursing and midwifery practice and more information about this theory and its place within the wider concepts of nursing theorists can be found in the following books.

Marriner Tomey AM (ed) (2006) *Nursing theorists and their work* (6th edn) St Louis, Mosby

Sitzman K, Eichelberger LW (2003) *Understanding the work of the nurse theorists: A creative beginning.* Jones and Bartlet, Boston

In addition, the library at Yale University, USA, holds further papers and information.

Other publications by Wiedenbach

Books
Wiedenbach E, Falls CE (1978) *Communication: Key to effective nursing.* Tiresias, New York

Book chapter
Wiedenbach E (1973) The nursing process in maternity nursing. In Clausen JP et al. (eds) *Maternity nursing today.* McGraw-Hill, New York

Articles

Dickoff JJ, James PA, Wiedenbach E (1968) Theory in a practice discipline1: Practice-orientated theory. *Nursing Research* **14**: 415–35

Dickoff JJ, James PA, Wiedenbach E (1968) Theory in a practice discipline 11: Practice-orientated theory. *Nursing Research* **17**: 545–54

Wiedenbach E (1940) Toward educating 130 million people: A history of the nursing information bureau. *American Journal of Nursing* **40**: 13–18

Wiedenbach E (1949) Childbirth as mothers say they like it. *Public Health Nursing* **41**: 417–21

Wiedenbach E (1951) Safeguarding the mother's breasts. *America Journal of Nursing* **51**: 544–8

Wiedenbach E (1960) Nurse-midwifery, purpose, practice and opportunity. *Nursing Outlook* **8**: 256

Wiedenbach E (1963) The helping art of nursing. *American Journal of Nursing* **63**: 54–7

Wiedenbach E (1965) Family nurse practitioner for maternal and child care. *Nursing Outlook* **13**: 50

Wiedenbach E (1968) Genetics and the nurse. Bulletin of the *American College of nurse midwifery* **13**: 8–13

Wiedenbach E (1968) The nurse's role in family planning: A conceptual base for practice. *Nursing Clinics of North America* **3**: 355–65

Wiedenbach E (1970) Nurses' wisdom in nursing theory. *American Journal of Nursing* **70**: 1057–62

practice requires the nurse to have a sound knowledge of physiology and pathophysiology, psychology and sociology, proficiency in clinical skills, and excellent decision making and communication skills. These needs are met in nursing and midwifery educational programmes of study today producing nurses and midwives who provide professional, holistic care to patients and their families.

Wiedenbach's concept of 'need for help' has been also been utilised in research. A study undertaken in 1980 (Gustafson 1988) used this model to determine when a woman in the first stage of birth develops this 'need for help'. Women in the first stage of labour were filmed and, through analysis of their body language and vocalisations, need for help and decreased coping was identified. Midwifery care could then be initiated to support the women at this time.

Influence

Ernestine Wiedenbach's theory, the Helping Art of Clinical Nursing and subsequent publications have been influential in the development of undergraduate and postgraduate nursing and midwifery programmes both in the USA and the UK as she was an early supporter of nurse-midwifery, family-centred maternity care and family nurse practitioners. Her theory was instrumental in legitimising practice-based theory development and, in 1961, the American College of Nurse-Midwives (ACNM) adopted and developed an expanded version of Ernestine's personal philosophy of nursing as the first official ACNM philosophy (Cragin, 2004). The ACNM philosophy is a reference point for all aspects of the profession. Accreditation by the ACNM requires every educational programme to have a clearly defined philosophy as a foundation for curriculum development and evaluation. This philosophy must reflect the ACNM's philosophy as well as that of the university. The ACNM philosophy is also influential on all nurse-midwifery services as this must be considered when writing practice guidelines. The philosophy of a nursing service will identify the views and beliefs about practice thus enabling patients to decide whether the nursing service is compatible with their healthcare needs.

The Helping Art of Clinical Nursing identifies concepts which are much broader in perspective than previous concepts derived from a medically based philosophy of care for patients. This theory begins the process of recognising that patients are far more than their medical condition but must be considered in the concept of their mind and body and the world in which they live. This theory lays the foundation for the nursing process and working in partnership with patients to identify their own perceived needs and thus working towards an agreed goal.

Ernestine Wiedenbach was an influential nurse-midwife within both clinical nursing and midwifery and nurse-midwife education within the USA. Her achievements within clinical practice, professional education, publishing and theory development led her to being awarded as an Associate Professor Emerita, Maternal and Newborn Nursing at Yale University on her retirement in 1966. Over the next decade however she continued to contribute further, by advising and educating maternity nursing students and faculty.

CHAPTER 14

Dorothea Elizabeth Orem

Kenny Keegan

Biography

Dorothea Elizabeth Orem was born in Baltimore, Maryland USA in 1914 and died in 2007 at her residence on Skidaway Island, Savannah, Georgia. She is generally recognised as one of the foremost nursing theorists of the 20th century. She grew up in a traditional working class household; her father was a building site worker and her mother a housewife. Orem attended high school in Baltimore and, following graduation, chose nursing as a career. Orem entered the nurse training at Providence Hospital, Washington, DC and her experiences here were pivotal. It was while in training, she later explained, that she knew 'nursing as nursing'. To illustrate her understanding of what nursing meant to her she cited two instances in particular: Orem first recalled the compassionate care a head nurse had taken of a young patient who had contracted typhoid and suffered a haemorrhage. The other instance, she recalled, was when she witnessed another head nurse's determined effort to relieve a woman's discomfort after surgery.

Her early nursing experience included operating room nursing, private duty nursing (in home and hospital), paediatric and adult medical and surgical units, evening supervisor in the emergency room, and biological science technician. During the 1930s she studied for her Bachelor of Science degree in nursing education in 1939 and her Master of Science degree in nursing education in 1946, both from the Catholic University of America. From 1940 to 1949 Orem held directorship of both the Nursing School and the Department of Nursing at Providence Hospital in Detroit. During the period 1949 to 1957 Orem worked for Indiana State Board of Health where her goal was to upgrade the quality of nursing. It was in this role that she first began developing her theory of nursing. She became aware of the ability of nurses to do nursing, but noted their inability to talk about nursing. She began to ask the questions, 'What do nurses do?', 'Why do they do what they do?' and 'What are the outcomes of their care?' From 1958 to 1960 she worked for United States Department of Health, Education and Welfare. The years 1959 to 1970 saw Orem serve as Acting Dean of the School of Nursing and as an Assistant Professor of Nursing Education at the Catholic University of America. She continued to develop her concept of nursing and self-care during this time.

In 1970 Orem left the Catholic University of America and set up her own consulting firm. In the following 20 years she continued to refine her Self-Care Nursing Development Theory (SCNDT). She first published her seminal *Nursing: Concepts for practice* in 1971 with subsequent editions being published in 1980, 1985, 1991, 1995 and 2001. During this time Orem wrote and published many papers and lectured internationally concerning her nursing insights and views on practice.

She officially 'retired' in 1984 but continued to contribute to the development of nursing as a scientific discipline through refinement of her SCNDT.

The numerous honours bestowed on Orem demonstrate recognition of her unique contribution to the development of nursing theory and science. In 1976, Georgetown University awarded her an honorary Doctor of Science, as did Incarnate Word College of San Antonio, Texas, in 1980. She received

Dorothea Elizabeth Orem
1914–2007

Profile

Orem's Model of Self-Care deficits is particularly apposite to mental health nursing. Orem's emphasis on the nurse and patient working in partnership in a continuum of lessening dependence as the patient gets better mirrors the therapeutic relationship and communication at the heart of mental health nursing practice.

Key dates

1939	BSc in nursing education at Catholic University of America
1946	MSc in nursing education at Catholic University of America
1949	Began working at Indiana State Board of Health with a goal to upgrade the quality of nursing
1958	Started work for US Department of Health, Education and Welfare.
1959	Appointed Acting Dean and Assistant Professor at School of Nursing, Catholic University of America
1970	Set up own consulting firm
1971	*Nursing: Concepts for practice* first published
1976	Awarded honorary Doctor of Science by Georgetown University
1980	Awarded honorary Doctor of Science by Incarnate Word College of San Antonio, Texas
1980	Received Award for Nursing Theory by Catholic University of America
1988	Awarded Doctor of Humane Letters by Illinois Wesleyan University
1992	Received honorary fellowship from the

American Academy of Nursing

1998   Received Doctor of Nursing *honoris causa* from the University of Missouri-Columbia

Links to other nursing theorists

Orem was not influenced by any one person; formal logic and metaphysics were among other disciplines that influenced her work. However, she influenced the work of Virginia Henderson (*see Chapter 11*) and Madeleine Leininger (*see Chapter 12*).

the Catholic University's Alumni Association's Award for Nursing Theory in 1980, Doctor of Humane Letters from Illinois Wesleyan University in 1988, an honorary fellowship from the American Academy of Nursing in 1992, and Doctor of Nursing *honoris causa* from the University of Missouri-Columbia in 1998.

In 70 years as a nurse, her major contribution to the establishment of nursing as a respected autonomous profession, with a firm scientific practice base is unquestioned.

Summary of writings

The essential elements of Orem's Self-Care Deficit Theory first emerged in response to the need to design new nurse education curricula. *Guidelines for developing curricula for the education of practical nurses* was published in 1959 and was Orem's first notable publication. She described this project as identifying the domain and boundaries of nursing as a science and an art in response to a general dissatisfaction with the absence of an organising framework for nursing knowledge (Orem, 1978). In these formative years of her nursing thought, three basic questions guided her search for meaning in nursing (Orem, 2001):

- What do nurses do and what should nurses do as practitioners of nursing?
- Why do nurses do what they do?
- What results from what nurses do as practitioners of nursing?

Orem's ideas were further developed after her input to the Nursing Development Conference Group (NDCG). Founded in 1968, this group was concerned with the advancement of nursing knowledge through identification of nursing as a structured practice-based profession (Hartweg, 1995). Orem (2001) explained that

> ...all of the conceptual elements [of the self-care framework] were formalised and validated as static concepts by 1970.

Orem said that her ideas were primarily the result of reflecting upon her experiences and that she was not influenced by any one person, but formal logic and metaphysics were among other disciplines that influenced her work (Hartweg, 1991).

Orem's understanding of the purpose and process of nursing as expressed in her ideas of self-care continued to evolve throughout the 1960s. In 1971 she published her *Nursing: Concepts of practice* with revisions in further editions published in 1980, 1985, 1991, 1995 and 2001. At the core of this book was her work on her Theory of Self-Care. At its most basic this describes patients as individuals whose normal state is one of independence and the ability to 'self-care' in all daily activities of life. Orem suggested that, when this is compromised through illness or some other disability, nursing should intervene to promote self-care for the individual to be as autonomous as possible.

Nursing theory

Orem outlines five premises of self-evident characteristics of human beings which are guiding principles that underlie her process of conceptualising nursing. They are:

- Human beings require continuous deliberate inputs to themselves and their environments in order to remain alive and function in accord with natural human endowments.

- Human agency, the power to act deliberately, is exercised in the form of care of the self and others in identifying needs for and in making needed inputs.
- Mature human beings experience privations in the form of limitations for action in care of self and others and involve the making of life-sustaining and function-regulating inputs.
- Human agency is exercised in discovering, developing and transmitting to others ways and means to identify needs for and to make inputs to the self and others.
- Groups of human beings with structured relationships cluster tasks and allocate responsibilities for providing care to group members who experience privations for making required deliberate input to self and others

(Orem, 2001)

Orem's theory is based on the notion that each person has a need for self-care in order to maintain optimal health and wellness. All individuals possess the ability and responsibility to care for themselves and dependants. The theory is separated into three conceptual categories which are: self-care, self-care deficit and nursing system (Parse, 1987). The goal of nursing is to render the patient or members of his or her family capable of meeting the patient's self-care needs. The nurse's role in helping the patient to achieve or maintain a level of optimal health and wellness is to act as an advocate, redirector, support person and teacher, and to provide an environment conducive to therapeutic development (Orem, 2001).

Theory of Self-Care

Self-care is the ability to perform activities and meet personal needs with the goal of maintaining biopsychosocial health and wellness. It is also a learned behaviour influenced by the metaparadigm, that is, the broad definition of the concerns of nursing; of person, environment, health and nursing. There are three components: universal self-care needs, developmental self-care needs, and health deviation. The term self-care can refer to both nurses as care givers and patients as providing the level of self-care they are capable of. For example, a patient may be capable of simple personal hygiene tasks such as hand washing but require assistance to bathe (Orem, 2001).

The purpose of self-care is to maintain life, the essential physical, psychological and social functions; to maintain the integrity of functions and development of the person within the framework of conditions that are essential to life. It is based on the presumption that

individuals learn self-care practices through experience, education, culture, scientific knowledge, growth, and development (Parse, 1987). There are three categories of self-care requisites:

- *Universal self-care*: common to all people and includes physiological and social interaction needs (food, air, water, activity and rest, solitude and social interactions, promotion of normalcy, etc.).
- *Developmental self-care*: needs that occur as the individual grows and develops (toilet training, adjustment to new job, new baby, etc.).
- *Health Deviation self-care*: needs produced by disability, illness, or injury.

(Orem, 2001)

Theory of Self-Care Deficit

The term self-care deficit refers to the relationship between self-care agency and therapeutic self-care demands of individuals. This applies to individuals who are completely, or partially, unable to know or to engage in self-care. It specifies when nursing care is needed (e.g. if there is a self-care deficit between what the individual can do and what needs to be done to maintain normal functioning, then nursing care is needed).

Every mature person has the ability to meet self-care needs, but when a person experiences the inability to do so due to limitations, thus exists a self-care deficit.

Individuals benefit from nursing interventions when a health situation inhibits their ability to perform self-care or creates a situation where their abilities are not sufficient to maintain own health and wellness. Nursing action focuses on identification of limitation/deficit and implementing appropriate interventions to meet the needs of person (Orem, 2001).

Orem (2001) describes self-care deficit nursing as a general theory of what nursing is and what nursing should be. As a general theory, it is not an explanation of a particular nursing practice situation. The theory is an expression of a combination of features that are common to all instances of nursing. It addresses the ability of the nurse to aid the person in meeting current and potential self-care demands.

Theory of Nursing Systems

Orem (2001) describes the Theory of Nursing Systems as including the Theory of Self-Care Deficit, and with it the Theory of Self-Care. The Theory of Nursing Systems establishes the structure and the content of nursing practice. It is the theory that articulates the nurse property of nursing agency with the patient properties of therapeutic self-care demand and self-care agency.

Nursing systems are determined by whether the patient's self-care needs are met by the nurse, the patient, or both. Focus is on the person, within or across particular nursing systems. Orem (2001) identifies three types of self-care needs.

- *Wholly compensatory*: Here the nurse provides complete healthcare for the individual (e.g. the unconscious patient).
- *Partially compensatory*: This is where the nurse and patient work together to meet the patient's needs (e.g. a patient with some physical limitations).
- *Supportive-developmental*: This is when the nurse's primary supportive role is patient education, enabling patients to independently address their own self-care needs (e.g. teaching a patient insulin self-injection technique).

As will be demonstrated in the next section, Orem's work has proved to be very popular with her fellow nurses across a wide spectrum of practice and clinical specialties, although *Nursing: Concepts of practice* is a challenging text to the reader both in terms of intellectual rigor and the sheer breadth and depth of the work. The core utility of her theory, enabling nurses to conceptualise the care they give to their patients in a structured, systematic and understandable way both to them, and to the patients they care for, is her crowning and lasting contribution to contemporary nursing practice.

Theory into practice

Orem (2001) suggests the uniqueness of nursing and what differentiates it from other human services such as medicine is the focus on human beings. The role of nursing in society is to enable individuals to develop and exercise their self-care abilities to the extent that they can look after themselves. According to the theory, those whose requirements for self-care exceed their own ability to provide it are said to be in a state of self-care deficit.

The Self-Care Deficit Theory is described by Orem (2001) as a general theory of nursing. That is, a theory of nursing that is applicable across all different clinical and practice environments where people are in need of care. It describes core nursing concepts that are applicable in all nursing situations. The following case study illustrates this point and demonstrates the application of Orem's theory to mental health nursing. (NB all names and places have been changed to protect patient confidentiality, Nursing and Midwifery, 2008).

Case study

John Gordon is a 74-year-old man who was admitted to the local mental health acute ward four days ago. He is a retired police officer who lived with his wife up until her death 14 months ago. His twin daughters (50 years old) are married with their own families, although both live in the same village as John and take turns visiting him on a daily basis. Although describing their father's reaction to the death of their mother as 'devastated' they felt that he had come to terms with this after a period of adjustment and what they describe as 'normal' mourning. They noticed a marked change in their father's behaviour and appearance about a month ago. Normally a man who took pride in his dress and grooming, he began to go for days without shaving or washing, and wore the same scruffy sweater and trousers. He was reluctant to engage in conversation with them and when he did he spoke of having committed a 'terrible crime' and there was an impending court case to deal with this. His daughters also noted he was losing weight and appeared to have no appetite as he refused to let them cook for him and refused to eat any food they brought for him.

John presents as a tall, thin, stooped, softly spoken man who appears pre-occupied. When engaged in conversation he will speak of his 'upcoming trial' reflecting delusional thought processes. He is very reluctant to eat as he feels this will 'go against him when his trial starts'.

John underwent a full physical, psychological and social assessment. Within these parameters John's present demand for self-care and the abilities he has to provide self-care is also assessed. When self-care deficits have been established a nursing system is designed to provide assistance. The nursing interventions to address the goals identified in John's assessment will initially be based on the nursing system identified as partly compensatory. This is because John is not totally dependent on nursing staff to meet his self-care deficits, but does require a high degree of nursing care to meet them.

Physical self-care deficits

John has been losing weight due to disruption in cognitive operations and activities as a result of delusional thinking.

- *Goal*: John will be assisted to maintain adequate nutrition, hydration, and elimination.
- *Nursing interventions*: Commenced on fluid intake/ output chart, bowel function monitored, daily blood pressure, temperature and respiration recorded. Weekly weight and urinalysis recorded.

It may be necessary to alter routines to increase John's control over issues involving food. As a trust relationship develops, more routine procedures may be gradually introduced.

Psychological self-care deficits

John is experiencing delusional thoughts of guilt concerning having committed a serious crime and an upcoming court appearance.

- *Goal:* Provision of safe and secure environment to negate the risk of self-harm or suicide. Demonstrate decreased anxiety level. Respond to reality-based interactions initiated by others. The risk of suicide is increased in males with depression who are socially isolated, have a chronic condition and within the age range of the patient under consideration.
- *Nursing interventions:* John will be placed on close observation which means nursing staff will be aware of his whereabouts at all times and as such maintain his safety. Recognise John's delusions as his perception of the environment. Initially, do not argue with John or try to convince him that the delusions are false or unreal. Interact on the basis of real things; do not dwell on the delusional material. Involve John in one-to-one activities at first, then activities in small groups, and gradually activities in larger groups.

Social self-care deficits

John's normal social routine is based almost entirely on his interaction and support from his daughters and their families. At present this relationship should be maintained and encouraged through flexibility in terms of visiting times and providing the family with ongoing information on John's care and health status. Longer term a plan of psychoeducation for the family regarding John's illness, medication management and relapse prevention should be undertaken

Influence

Parse (1987), in critiquing Orem's work, states that she (Orem) has produced a theory that is strong, and further suggests her work in education, practice and research has facilitated scholars to examine the various aspects of nursing science. Parse concludes that Orem was a pioneer and had the courage to make her ideas public to encourage critical reflection and, as such, advance nursing as a science. Pearson (2008) points to the continuing relevance of Orem's work. He suggests this is demonstrated by the widespread adoption of self-care in health service planning and delivery. He cites that self-care is highlighted in the United Kingdom's National Health Service Plan (Department of Health, 2007), as one of the key building blocks for a patient-centred health service and self-care features as a key component of rehabilitation and long-term care in most advanced economies. This recent report by the UK Department of Health identifies extensive evidence that suggests that supporting self-care can improve health outcomes, increase patient satisfaction and help in deploying the biggest collaborative resource available – patients, their families and communities (Department of Health, 2007).

The pervasiveness of Orem's work is described by Isenberg (2001) who states the theory has been used to guide practice across a wide range of nursing situations in all types of care settings ranging from neonatal intensive care units to nursing home environments. Orem-based nursing has been described in the literature in all kinds of differing clinical environments. Walsh (1989) describes an Orem-based approach to nursing patients with asthma. Mason and Chandley (1990) looked at the efficacy of Orem as applied in a high security forensic special hospital setting. Lukkarinen and Hentinen (1997) describe the application of Orem's theory in patients with coronary disease; Storm and Baumgartner (1987) describe the care of a woman with multiple sclerosis requiring self-ventilation; Urbancic (1992) outlines the application of Orem's theory in the empowerment and support of adult female survivors of childhood incest; and Davis and Underwood (1989) use Orem's self-care framework to explore the ethical issue of informed consent.

References

Davis A, Underwood P (1989) The competency quagmire: Clarification of the nursing perspective concerning the issues of competence and informed consent. *International Journal of Nursing Studies* **26**(3): 271–9

Department of Health (2007) *Research evidence on the effectiveness of self care support (Work in Progress 2005–07)*. London, Department of Health

Hartweg DL (1991) *Dorethea Orem: Self-care deficit theory.* Sagem Newbury Park, CA

Hartweg DL (1995) Dorothea Orem: Self-care deficit theory. In CM McQuiston, AA Webb (eds) *Foundations of nursing theory: Contributions of 12 key theorists* (pp. 139–202). SageThousand Oaks, CA

Isenberg MA (2001) Self-Care Deficit Nursing Theory: Directions for advancing nursing science and professional practice. In Parker M (ed) *Nursing theories and nursing practice* (pp. 179–91) Davies Co, Philadelphia

Lukkarinen H, Hentinen M (1997) Self-care agency and factors related to this agency among patients with coronary heart disease. *International Journal of Nursing Studies* **34**(4): 295–304

Mason T, Chandley M (1990) Nursing models in a special hospital: A critical analysis of efficacy (Research in wards using Orem, Roper, Henderson, Riehl, Rogers and Roy). *Journal of Advanced Nursing* **15**(6): 667–73

Nursing and Midwifery Council (2008) *The Code: Standards of conduct, performance and ethics for nurses and midwives.* NMC, London

Orem D (1978) *A general theory of nursing.* Paper presented at the second annual Nurse Educator Conference, New York, December, 1978

Orem D (2001) *Nursing: Concepts of practice* (6th edn) Mosby, St. Louis

Parse R (1987) *Nursing science. Major paradigms, theories and critiques*. Saunders, Philadelphia

Pearson A (2008) Does self-care agency change between hospital admission and discharge? An Orem-based investigation. *International Journal of Nursing Practice* **14**(1): 1–2

Storm D, Baumgartner R (1992) Achieving self-care in the ventilator-dependent patient: A critical analysis of a case study. *International Journal of Nursing Studies* **24**(2): 95–106

Urbancic J (1992) Empowerment support with adult female survivors of childhood incest: Part II – Application of Orem's methods of helping. *Archives of Psychiatric Nursing* **6**(5): 282–6

Walsh JME (1989) Asthma: The Orem self-care nursing model approach. *Journal of Clinical Practice, Education and Management* **3**(38): 19–21

Where to find out more

- www.scdnt.com

The Self-Deficit Nursing Theory Group's website

From an international perspective Orem's work has disseminated widely all over the world. Her key text *Nursing: Concepts of practice* has been translated into Dutch, French, German, Italian and Spanish. Literature searches will yield nursing papers and research in the application of self-deficit nursing in Australia, Belgium, Denmark, Finland, Germany, Holland, Norway, Portugal, Sweden, Switzerland, United Kingdom, Hong Kong, Thailand, Turkey, Canada, Mexico, United States of America and Puerto Rico (Isenberg 2001).

Orem's influence on the development of modern nursing theory and practice is virtually incalculable. The dissemination of her work worldwide is itself impressive but more impressive is how her general theory of nursing has been taken up by thousands of nurses in a myriad of differing clinical specialities and environments.

Ultimately it has been patients that have benefited from Orem's 70-year endeavour in the field of nursing and nursing theory development. This would doubtless be the proudest legacy of her life's work.

CHAPTER 15

Myra Estrin Levine

Valerie Douglas

Biography

Myra Levine was born in Chicago, the eldest of three children (George, 2002). She had a very close relationship with her other two siblings, a brother and a sister, and Levine developed an interest in nursing due to her father's ill health and his requirement for nursing care.

Levine enjoyed a varied and exciting career both in clinical practice and nurse education. She was awarded a Diploma from Cook County School of Nursing in 1944, a Bachelor of Science from the University of Chicago in 1949, and a Master of Science from Wayne State University in 1962 (George, 2002). Some of her clinical positions included a private duty nurse (1944), a civilian nurse with the US army (1945), director of Drexel Home for Older Adults in Chicago (1950–1951), and a surgical supervisor at both the University of Chicago clinics (1951–1952) and the Henry Ford Hospital in Detroit (1956–1962). She held academic positions in four schools of nursing in Chicago: Cook County School of Nursing (1963–1967), Loyola University (1967–1973), Rush University (1974–1977) and the University of Illinois (1962–1963, 1977–1987). In 1987, Levine was made Professor Emerita, medical and surgical nursing at the University of Illinois (Schaefer, 2006)

She also held the position of visiting professor at two schools of nursing in Israel (Johnson and Webber, 2005). One was at the Ben Gurion University of the Negev and the other was Tel Aviv University. She treasured the professional relationships and friends that she made in Israel and it was there that Levine was conscious of her spiritual heritage and took pride in it (Stafford, 1996).

Levine received several awards including an honorary doctorate in 1992 from Loyola University in Chicago and she was the first person to receive the Sigma Theta Tau Elizabeth Russell Belford excellence in teaching award in 1977 (Schaefer, 2006). She received recognition from the Alpha Lambda Chapter of Sigma Theta Tau in 1990 for her exceptional contribution to nursing. Levine was also made an honorary member of the American mental health aid to Israel in 1976. She was an active member of the Illinois Nurses' Association/American Nurses' Association.

Following her retirement in 1987, Levine remained committed to the development of nursing theory. Myra Levine died on 20th March 1996, she was a wife, mother, nurse, innovative educator, and a dynamic public speaker.

Special interests

In 1950, when Levine was appointed a director of nursing at Drexel Home for Older Adults she had the opportunity of establishing a course for registered nurses (Levine, 1988). This experience had a great impact on her because it was at Drexel Home that she developed an interest in nurse teaching.

Another experience which had a profound effect on Levine was the death of her first born son Benjamin when he was just three days old. In some of her writings, she refers to him as *Benoni*, Hebrew for 'the son of my sorrow' (Levine, 1972, 1988). After Benoni's death, Levine had both an interest and desire to bring comfort to those who were passing through similar circumstances. In 1956, Levine was able to fulfil this desire when she was appointed surgical

Myra Estrin Levine
1920–1996

Profile

Myra Levine is a nursing champion because she has left the nursing profession a legacy through her development of the Conservation Principles Model. The model has an excellent underpinning philosophy and can be used as a framework for nursing practice, research and nurse education programmes.

Key dates

1944	Diploma from Cook County School of Nursing
1944	Private duty nurse
1945	Civilian nurse with the US army
1947–1950	Preclinical instructor in physical sciences Cook County School of Nursing
1949	BSc from the University of Chicago
1950–1951	Director of Drexel Home for Older Adults
1951–1952	Surgical Supervisor, University of Chicago Clinic
1956–1962	Surgical Supervisor, Henry Ford Hospital
1962	MSc in Nursing from Wayne State University
1962–1963	University of Illinois
1963–1967	Cook County School of Nursing
1967–1973	Loyola University, Chicago
1969	The *American Journal of Nursing* book of the year award. Also awarded in 1973.
1974	Visiting Professor, Tel Aviv University, Israel
1974–1977	Rush University, Chicago
1977	Elizabeth Russell Belford Award for excellence in teaching
1977–1987	University of Illinois
1982	Visiting Professor, Tel Aviv University amd Ben Gurion University of the Negev

1987	Professor Emerita, Medical and Surgical Nursing, University of Illinois
1990	Awarded Alpha Lambda Chapter of Sigma Theta Tau for excellence in teaching award
1992	Awarded Honorary doctorate from Loyola University, Chicago

supervisor at the Henry Ford hospital in Detroit. Whilst undertaking this role she always went to the mothers who had lost babies to share in their grief and to let them know they were not alone. Levine (1988) comments that she had been left alone by nurses when she lost Benoni and she promised herself that she would not let this happen to other mothers if she 'had the power to prevent it'. She realised the importance of a holistic approach to care.

Levine was able to combine her interest in teaching and her holistic approach to care when she was appointed as a co-ordinator of clinical nursing at Cook County School of Nursing. This was an era when nurse education and nursing practice were based on a medical model, which included patient assessment, diagnosis, prescribing and treatment (McKenna and Slevin, 2008). Nursing practice and nurse education tended to focus on the disease rather than the whole person. Levine's intention was to develop a medical and surgical curriculum in nursing which was not procedure orientated (George, 2002). She had a deep desire to maintain the 'unique wholeness' of the individual (Stafford, 1996) and in order to do this she developed the Conservation Principles Model which emphasised the importance of maintenance of wholeness through conservation of energy, and structural, personal and social integrity. The term conservation can be defined as 'keeping together' the wholeness of the person (Levine 1973: 13). Levine (1988) suggested that conservation as a 'keeping together' function was a suitable goal for the delivery of nursing care.

The Conservation Principles Model enabled Levine to organise nursing knowledge. Levine claims she

Wanted nurses to learn the science principles a priori instead of in the traditional pattern in which they learned how to, first, and sought the applied science a posteriori.

(Levine, 1988: 227)

A priori is a term used to denote that knowledge comes before experience and a posteriori is knowledge which comes from experience (McKenna and Slevin, 2008).

When Professor Rebecca Bergman, the founder of the School of Nursing at Tel Aviv University invited Levine to Israel, Levine felt that was a good opportunity to become more acquainted with her Jewish heritage. It took Levine three years to arrange the six-month visit to Israel and in September 1973 she arrived (Levine, 1988) with her husband and two children. Within two weeks of arrival the Yom Kippur War had commenced. She was amazed how dedicated the nurses were, working long hours without a complaint or murmur (Levine, 1988). Levine stayed in Israel during the war and gave teaching sessions and workshops at Tel Aviv University (Levine, 1988). During this time she developed a deeper interest in her spiritual roots, roots that influenced her as a person and as a nurse. She believed every nursing act was a 'privileged act of loving' (Stafford, 1996).

Another of Levine's interests was the assembling of a large collection of postage stamps depicting the history of nursing. The stamps were issued by various countries throughout the world and included historical figures such as Florence Nightingale. Levine presented her collection of approximately 550 stamps to the University of Illinois on her retirement in 1987.

These interests and experiences had an impact on Levine, both personally and professionally, they influenced her writings and gave her inspiration for theory development.

Writing

Levine was a prolific writer and was author of books, chapters of books and numerous journal articles. She received the American Journal of the

Year Award for the first and second editions of her book *Introduction to clinical nursing* in 1969 and 1973 (Schaefer, 2006). These books were written for student nurses (Levine, 1973). The second edition of the book focuses on patient-centred nursing care and the four principles of conservation. It includes pathophysiology and psychosocial issues relevant to medical and surgical nursing (Levine, 1973). When the books were submitted for publication, Levine was informed that she was 10 years ahead of her time.

Levine's book, *Renewal for nursing* (1971) was written for registered nurses returning to practice after a break in service. The book includes humorous illustrations; some of these include analogies which are powerful cognitive tools relating new knowledge to familiar concepts (Martin, 2003). This book was translated from English to Hebrew.

Levine's other writings in journals and chapters of books include some of her theories related to the principles of conservation. However, Levine and her husband Edwin, who was an associate professor in Classics, were co-authors of an article entitled *Hippocrates, father of nursing too?* (Levine and Levine 1965). She also wrote an article entitled *Benoni* in which she discusses the impact of the death of her first born son (Levine, 1972).

Levine is one of the few nurse theorists who use verses of Scripture from the Tanakh (Old Testament) within her writing (Levine, 1969, 1996). In her article *The conservation principles: A retrospective*, Levine (1996) refers to Genesis 1:27 in the Tanakh to support her beliefs about the sanctity of life.

And God created man in His own image, in the image of God created He him, male and female created He them.

Levine (1996) suggested that wholeness of each individual is holiness, and the sanctity of life is evident in everyone. She viewed spirituality as one of the dimensions of the whole person which has an integrated interaction with the other dimensions (Martsolf and Mickley, 1998).

Levine gives credit in some of her writings to the theories which were influential in her development of the conservation principles model. These include Erikson's description of wholeness as an open system (Levine, 1973, 1996), Selye's Response to Stress theory (Levine, 1969), Gibson's Perceptual Awareness Concepts (Levine, 1969) and Bates' Model of the External Environment (Levine, 1973).

Levine's theories

The four principles of conservation are the core of Levine's theory. She includes the concepts of adaptation, the internal and external environment, wholeness and integrity within her theory.

Adaptation is the process whereby individuals adjust to the environment in which they live (Levine, 1996). During this process of adaptation an individual retains wholeness within the realities of the internal and external environment (Levine, 1969). From a biological perspective everything within the cells and organs are classed as the internal environment and the external environment is everything outside the body. Levine (1973) refers to the concept of homeostasis and negative and positive feedback mechanisms to explain internal adaptation. She relates negative feedback with auto regulation of the body systems and positive feedback with disruptions to pathological processes (Levine, 1973; Fawcett, 1991).

Levine (1973) uses Bates' classification of the external environment within her theories to emphasise the importance of holism. These are perceptual, operational and conceptual:

- *Perceptual level*: This includes how individuals respond to the environment with their sensory organs. The sensory organs include sight, hearing, touch, taste and smell.
- *Operational level*: This is the aspect of the environment that is not directly perceived but it can physically affect the individual. These aspects include radiation, micro-organisms and pollutants which have no colour or odour.
- *Conceptual level*: This includes cultural patterns and symbols of language, religion, values and beliefs. Levine (1973: 12) states that

Human life is inextricably bound to a life of ideas, of symbolic exchange and of belief, tradition, and judgement which influences behaviours.

These ideas can influence lifestyle and health behaviours. The recognition of the individual's integrated response to the internal environment and the interaction occurring within the external environment is important for the provision of holistic care (Levine, 1973).

Levine's (1973) theories also include three further characteristics of adaptation. These are historicity, specificity and redundancy.

- *Historicity*: This refers to the concept that adaptive responses can be influenced through information conveyed by generations of genes and personal life experience.
- *Specificity*: Each system within an individual's body has different physiological response pathways. For example the pathway of a reflex action (adaptive response) when a person touches a hot stove and the pain makes the person withdraw his or her hand is different from that of the inflammatory response at the site of the injury. Both responses happen in a cascade of complementary reactions (Sitzman and Eichelberger, 2004).

Links with other nursing theorists

Myra Levine and Martha Rogers (*see Chapter 19*) have diverse beliefs regarding the concept of energy but they both agree on the view of a purposeful, person–environment interchange of energy.

References

Delmore BA (2006) Levine's framework in long-term venti-lated patients during the wean-ing process. *Nursing Science Quarterly* **19**(3): 247–8

Fawcett J (1991) Analysis and evaluation of Levine's Conservation Model. In Schaefer KM, Pond JB (eds) *Levine's Conservation Model*. F.A. Davis Company, Philadelphia

George JB (1995) Myra Estrin Levine. In George JB (ed) *Nursing theories. The base for professional nursing prac-tice* (4th edn) Prentice Hall International, London

George JB (2002) The conservation principles: A model for health: Myra Estrin Levine. In George JB (ed) *Nursing theories. The base for professional nursing practice* (5th edn) Prentice Hall, London

Grindley J, Paradowski MB(1991) Developing an undergradu-ate program using Levine's Model. In Schaefer KM, Pond

- *Redundancy*: Some systems may become redundant, temporary and may respond to a corrective action. Stitzman and Eichelberger (2004) provide the example of allergy injections over a period of time to stop the effects of severe allergies by desensitising the immune system. Some systems may become permanently redundant and this may be due to the ageing process (Levine, 1996).

Conservation

The outcome of adaptation is conservation. Levine (1973) states that the term conservation is derived from the Latin word *conservatio* which means to keep together. When individuals adapt to change productively, it means that they are in a state of conservation (Sitzman and Eischelberger, 2004).The nurse has a role to play in relation to conservation. Levine (1973) explains that to keep together means to maintain a correct balance between active nursing interventions and patients' safe limits and ability actively to participate in their own care.

Nursing interventions can influence adaptation from a physical perspective and/or promote renewed social wellbeing. Levine describes four conservation principles of nursing. These are conservation of energy, conservation of structural integrity, conservation of personal integrity and conservation of social integrity. Levine uses the term integrity which means the oneness or wholeness of the individual.

Conservation of energy
Conservation of energy is based on the idea that a person depends on energy balance to carry out activities; illness increases the demand for energy; and energy requirements can be measured by the level of fatigue (Levine, 1991; Fawcett, 1991). Levine applies the concepts of conservation of energy to physiology and altered physiology due to illness. The production and expenditure of energy is a fundamental requirement for all of life's processes (Levine, 1967). In order to carry out daily energy-using activities the human body requires energy-producing nutrients (Levine, 1973). The fuel of energy is nutrients and oxygen, which is transported by the circulatory system (Levine 1973). The disease process can increase the demand for energy. Levine (1973) uses the example of a change in temperature signalling an increase in energy production. She claims that for every degree Fahrenheit rise in body temperature there is a 7% increase in metabolism. Conservation of energy during illness does not necessarily mean minimising all of the patient's activities but encouraging the patient to continue doing the activities which do not cause excessive fatigue.

Conservation of structural integrity
Conservation of structural integrity includes maintaining the structure of the body, preventing physical breakdown, promoting healing, and restoring the structural function of the body (Levine, 1988). Levine (1973) provides examples of the body's defences which help to promote structural integrity. These include inflammatory immune response mechanisms and a reflex action which enables a person to move his or her hand quickly due to a painful stimulus. Levine (1967) suggests that a person may require a surgical intervention to restore or redesign structural integrity. She provides various examples of types of surgery which will result in a revised structure for the person. These include formation of a stoma or the amputation of a limb. Levine (1991) suggests that the process of healing can also be the means by which structural integrity can be restored.

Conservation of personal integrity
Self-identity and self-worth are the foundations of personal integrity. Levine (1991) claims that having a sense of identity and self-worth is a strong

confirmation of wholeness. The body does not exist independently from the mind, emotions and soul (Levine, 1967).   Each person is unique and this is due to his or her own life experiences, and socioeconomic and religious influences. People will also have their own sleeping patterns and personal hygiene habits (Levine, 1967). Respect from nurses is imperative for the self-worth of patients (Levine, 1973).

Conservation of social integrity

Levine (1991) believes that individuals are social human beings and the real meaning of humanity is the result of good relationships with other people. Strength can come from these relationships during a time of illness and anxiety. In a broader context, social integrity of the individual is tied to the capability of social systems (Levine, 1973). Individuals may depend on the social system for housing, benefits and social care.

Wholeness

The concept of wholeness is imbedded in this conceptual model. The word *hal* is an Anglo Saxon word which means whole and the word health is derived from it (Levine, 1991: 242). Levine refers to Erikson's description of wholeness as an open and fluid system. Her belief is that health or wholeness exists when the constant interactions with the environment present no difficulties as this is the assurance of integrity in every dimension of a person's life.

Putting theory into practice

The Conservation Principles Model provides a robust framework to guide patient care. The concepts of adaptation, wholeness and conservation can be applied to the nursing process. In order to illustrate how to put the theory into practice, in the following case study the concepts will be applied to a patient who has sustained a cardiovascular accident (CVA).

Case study

Assessment is the identification of the factors that affect the wholeness or the integrity of the individual. This can be related to actual and potential problems. During the assessment the nurse should take into consideration historicity, specificity and redundancy (George, 2002). The nurse may want to ascertain if the patient has a family history of CVA or heart disease or a personal history of hypertension, heart disease or transient ischaemic attacks (*historicity*). It is also important to know about the patient's present signs and symptoms (*specificity*). The patient could have hemiplegic limbs (*redundancy*) due to the CVA. This redundancy may be temporary and the patient may be able to walk again.

Assessment data would then be collected in relation to the first principle, conservation of energy. This information may include vital signs, oxygen saturations, uptake and use of oxygen, nutritional status, elimination of urine and faeces as well as any other activity of living that requires energy expenditure. The nurse will also assess the patient's ability to carry out activities without excessive fatigue.

Assessment data in relation to the second principle, conservation of structural integrity, could include further information about the CVA. When did it happen? Was there loss of consciousness for a short period? Did the patient experience any headaches or confusion before or following the CVA? Is there any weakness or numbness in any of the limbs, or a hemiparesis? Is the patient incontinent? Pressure ulcer risk assessment or wound assessment is included within structural integrity.

JB (Eds) *Levine's Conservation Model*. F.A. Davis Company, Philadelphia

Johnson BM, Webber PB (2005) *An introduction to theories and reasoning in nursing.* Lippincott Williams and Wilkins, London

Leach MJ (2006) Wound Management: Using Levine's conservation model to guide practice. *Ostomy Wound Management* **52**(8): 74–80. http://www.o-wm.com/article/6024 [accessed 7 May 2009]

Levine ME (1967) The four conservation principles of nursing. *Nursing Forum* **6**: 54–9

Levine ME (1969) The pursuit of wholeness. *American Journal of Nursing* **69**(1): 93–8

Levine ME (1971) *Renewal for nursing*. F.A Davis Company, Philadelphia,

Levine ME (1972) Benoni. *American Journal of Nursing* **72**(3): 466–8

Levine ME (1973) *Introduction to clinical nursing*. F. A. Davis Company, Philadelphia

Levine ME (1988) Myra Levine In: Schorr TM, Zimmerman A (eds) *Making choices, taking chances. Nurse leaders tell their stories*. C.V Mosby Company, St Louis

Levine ME (1991) Introduction to patient-centred nursing care. In Schaefer KM, Pond JB (eds) *Levine's Conservation Model*. FA Davis Company, Philadelphia

Levine M E (1996) The Conservation Principles: A retrospective, *Nursing Science Quarterly* **9**(1): 38–40

Levine E, Levine ME (1965) Hippocrates, father of nursing too? *American Journal of Nursing* **65**(12): 86–8

McKenna H, Slevin O (2008) *Nursing models, theories and practice*. Blackwell, Oxford:

Martin M (2003) "It's like .... You know": The use of analogies and heuristics in teaching introductory statistical methods. *Journal of Statistics Education* 11(2): online. http:www.amstat. org/publications/jse/v11n2/ martin.html (accessed 10 July 2009)

Martsolf DS, Mickley JR (1998) The concept of spirituality in nursing theories. Differing world views and extent of focus. *Journal of Advanced Nursing* **27**: 294–303

Mock V, St. Ours C, Hall S et al. (2007) Using a conceptual model in nursing research – mitigating fatigue in cancer patients. *Journal of Advanced Nursing* **58**(5): 503–12

Pasco A, Halupa D (1991) Chronic pain management In Schaefer KM, Pond JB (eds) *Levine's Conservation Model*. FA Davis Company, Philadelphia

Schaefer KM (1991) Developing a graduate program in nursing: Integrating Levine's philosophy. In Schaeffer KM, Pond JB (eds) *Levine Conservation Model: A framework for nursing practice*. Philadelphia: F A Davis

Schaefer KM (2006) Myra Estrin Levine 1921–1996, The Conservation Model In;Tormey, AM, Alligood MR (eds) *Nursing theorists and their work* (6th edn) F. A. Davis Company, Philadelphia

Sitzman K, Eichelberger LW (2004) *Understanding the work of nurse theorists. A creative beginning*. Jones and Bartlett Publishers, London

Stafford MJ (1996) *In tribute: Myra Estrin Levine, Professor Emerita,MSN, RN, FAAN Journal* article obituary. *Illinosis Nurses Association* Available from: http://web. ebscohost.com/ehost/delivery ?vid=6&hid=6&sid=a5119a6 8-12bd-4a92-93 [accessed 11 June 2009]

The data in relation to the third principle, conservation of personal integrity, may include dietary habits, spiritual needs and the patient's ability to communicate. A patient who has had a CVA may have an altered body image or become frustrated due to not being able to carry out the normal activities of living independently. These feelings may be part of the patient's private self and a patient may be reluctant to share them with a nurse. Patients may be more willing to share information with the nurse regarding their public self (George, 1995).

Assessment data is related to the fourth principle, conservation of social integrity, and may include information about the next of kin and any previous involvement with the social services. Information can be obtained from family members who may be able to provide information which will influence the care management of the patient.

Levine (1973) recommends the use of a scientific approach to nursing care. This is a systematic method which includes the identification of provocative facts, which are established by patient assessment, and the development of a hypothesis. According to Levine (1973) a fact that provokes attention is known as provocative fact. She claims that the identification of provocative facts is the first step in the scientific approach to nursing care. Some of the provocative facts for the patient with a CVA in relation to conservation of energy could be that the patient is weak and fatigued and requires assistance with washing and dressing. The patient is unable to swallow fluids and may become dehydrated. In relation to conservation of structural integrity, a provocative fact could be that the patient has a life-sided hemiparesis and will be unable to mobilise independently. The provocative fact for the conservation of personal integrity is that the patient may feel that he or she will lose self-respect and personal dignity as a result of the CVA. In relation to conservation of social integrity a provocative fact could be than the patient has never been separated from his or her family or experienced hospitalisation, and therefore may feel socially isolated.

Planning care is the next stage. Levine (1973) suggests that following the identification of provocative facts in the scientific approach, the second step is the formulation of a hypothesis. An example of a hypothesis could be 'thickening fluids will enable the patient to swallow'. Levine (1991) suggests that the success of the scientific method depends on the knowledge base of the nurse. Nurses with a good knowledge base are more likely to identify relevant provocative facts and formulate a testable hypothesis (Levine, 1991). However, Levine's framework is very adaptable and goals have been used instead of hypotheses in the application of the model. The goal of nursing care is to promote wholeness (Levine, 1971) and patients should be involved in setting these goals. The multidisciplinary team may also influence goal setting. For example, the speech and language therapist will have assessed the patient's swallowing reflex and the dietitian will have been consulted regarding the dietary needs.

Implementation of the nursing activities or intervention should be based on the four principles of conservation. Levine (1973) suggests that nursing activities should be designed to help successful adaptation whenever possible. In relation to conservation of energy, nursing activities will be related to the balance between energy input and expenditure. This could involve providing the patient with nutrients and preventing the patient becoming dehydrated. The energy output could be commencing passive and active exercises in conjunction with the physiotherapist but this would be balanced with ensuring the patient had adequate rest. In relation to structural integrity, the nursing care may focus on skin care and preventing the formation of decubitus ulcers (pressure ulcers) and hospital-acquired infections. The patient may be taught to adapt to carrying out activities with one hand. One of the nursing actions for personal integrity could be to promote independence by encouraging the patient to feed him or herself. The nurse should involve the patient in decision making when possible, provide privacy and promote the dignity of the patient in every nursing action. Levine (1967) suggests that patient education acknowledges individuals' rights to be assisted in understanding the implications of their illness and their subsequent care. This will include both medical and nursing actions. The nursing action for social integrity could be, keeping the family informed about the patient's progress and if necessary arranging for social services to support both the patient and family during the rehabilitation period.

Evaluation is also important to ensure that outcomes have been met. Levine (1973) points out that evaluation of the care plan comes from constant observation of the patient. She states that if the hypothesis does not achieve its objective then a new hypothesis is formulated. The same principle would be applied if goals were used instead of a hypothesis. The nursing care delivered to the patient within the four conservation principles is evaluated. A special emphasis is placed on the effectiveness of achieving adaptation within these four areas, conservation of energy, structural integrity, personal integrity and social integrity (George, 2002). The effectiveness of achieving adaptation is a very important part of the evaluation for a patient who has sustained a CVA.

Influence

Levine's Conservation Principles Model has influenced nurse education, research and nursing practice. The model was initially developed by Levine as a framework for a nurse education programme (Levine, 1973) when it was found to be a robust framework. The model has influenced other professionals in that it has been used to develop an undergraduate programme (Grindley and Paradowski, 1991) and a graduate programme in nursing (Schaefer, 1991) at a college in Pennsylvania. According to Fawcett (1991) the model has also been used within nurse education programmes in Israel. Grindley and Paradowski (1991) have commented that the model has proved to be flexible in its application and this is one of its major strengths.

Levine's theories have proved testable and specific and have been used as a framework for several research studies. Delmore (2006) used it to evaluate fatigue and protein calorie malnutrition affecting adult, long-term ventilated patients during the weaning process. The model has also been used to guide a randomised controlled clinical trial on the effects of exercise on cancer-related fatigue during chemotherapy or radiation treatment (Mock et al., 2007). The researchers involved commented that Levine's model proved to be a robust framework for guiding this study.

The model has also been used as a framework to provide nursing care for patients in various care settings such as intensive care units, and accident emergency departments. It has also been used for patients who have chronic pain (Pasco and Halupa, 1991) and patients who have wounds. Leach (2006) provides an example of how the four principles of Levine's model were applied to a patient with a venous leg ulcer. The model was found to enhance good nursing practice and embrace the wholeness and health of the individual (Leach, 2006). The model provides an excellent framework for research, education and practice and has inspired many researchers, nurses working in clinical practice, and educationalists. Schaefer (2006) suggests that nurses who use the Conservation Principles Model can explain, predict and deliver patient care.

Where to find out more

- Sitzman K, Eichelberger LW (2004) *Understanding the work of nurse theorists. A creative beginning*. Jones and Bartlett Publishers, London

Sitzman and Eichelberger provide a basic description of Levine's theories in Chapter 11. The content is written in a simple format and is an excellent introduction to nursing theories. The learning activities at the end of the chapter encourage the reader to explore Levine's theories in more depth.

- *Taber's Online Medical Dictionary. Myra Levine's Conservation Model* (21st edn) http://www.tabers. com/taberonline/ub/view/ Tabers/144303/0/MYRA_ LEVINE_C

This online dictionary provides a concise description of Levine's model.

CHAPTER 16

Nancy Roper
1918–2004

Winifred W Logan
Birthdate
Unknown

Alison J Tierney
Birthdate
Unknown

Profile

Roper, Logan and Tierney were pioneers of nursing through their development of a model of nursing that is based on twelve activities of living. Providing a user friendly framework around which nurses can base holistic care delivery, the Roper, Logan and Tierney model is a commonly utilised model of nursing within Europe (Timmins and O'Shea, 2004).

Key dates

1936   Roper commenced sick children nurse training at Booth Hall Hospital, Manchester

1940   Roper commenced general nurse training at Leeds General Infirmary

1976   Roper's PhD monograph *What is nursing?* published

1976–1980   Roper invited Logan and Tierney to collaborate on initial model of nursing

1980   Roper, Logan and Tierney's *Elements of nursing* first published

2001   Final account of the Roper Logan Tierney nursing model published

Nancy Roper, Winifred W Logan and Alison J Tierney

Lorraine Duers

Biography

In 1940 Roper commenced her general nurse training at Leeds General Infirmary. It was during her period of nurse training that she first recognised the commonalities in the nursing care that patients required (these subsequently became what are now known as the activities of living in the Roper-Logan-Tierney Model of Nursing).

In 1976 the results of Roper's PhD research, 'What is nursing?', were published and it was during this time that her model of living and nursing was developed. The earlier work of Henderson (1969) was influential in this process (Roper, 2002). At this point the activities of living were known as the activities of daily living (until it became clear that some of the activities are not carried out on a daily basis, thus the name change).

During the 1970s, Roper invited Logan and Tierney to collaborate and advance her ideas in relation to her initial model of nursing. All three graduated from Edinburgh University and all three worked there during their careers.

In 1980 Roper, Logan and Tierney's *Elements of nursing* was published for the first time with reprints following in 1985, 1990 and 1996. Following the success of their first book, the three continued to publish their work at a steady rate throughout the 1980s, 1990s and into the 21st century. The final account of their nursing model was published in 2001. The potential of the Roper-Logan-Tierney Model of Nursing, since its conception, to influence high quality nursing care provision is demonstrated within this literature.

In 2002, Roper wrote about her recollections of the professional advancement of nursing over a 65-year period. This article enables readers to develop insight into the changes within the field of nursing over this seven-decade period.

In an editorial, following the death of Roper on 5th October 2004, Scott (2004: 1121) said that the influence Nancy Roper had on nursing had been 'profound' and described the co-writer of the Roper-Logan-Tierney (RLT) Model of Nursing as 'a great nursing pioneer'. How fitting it is, therefore, that a chapter within this book is dedicated to this particular pioneer and her co-writers.

Born near Carlisle, in 1918, Nancy Roper trained initially as a registered sick children's nurse from 1936 to 1939 at Booth Hall Hospital, Manchester and then moved on in 1940 to commence a period of training to become a registered general nurse, via Leeds General Infirmary (Scott, 2004). She later became a full-time writer and it was Roper, herself, within a reflective article, named *Sixty-five years of nursing: Selected recollections,* who provides insight into what prompted her to explore, what she considered to be, the core elements of nursing (2002). During her time as a student nurse, Roper disliked being moved from one ward to another. Her opinion was that there were far more commonalities within the various settings, than differences, with regard to obtaining nursing experience (Roper, 2002). Her MPhil research focus, at a later date, therefore, was to answer the question, 'What is nursing?' A monograph of this research indicated benefits to be gained from further development of a model of nursing, based on a model of living (Roper, 1976). With this advancement of her ideas in mind, Roper invited two nurse colleagues, Winifred Logan and Alison Tierney, to collaborate with her in this venture.

Roper, Logan and Tierney had all graduated from the University of Edinburgh, all had worked within the Department of Nursing studies there during their careers, and each had specific knowledge and experience they could offer to the process of expanding upon and reorganising Roper's earlier work to create the RLT Model of Nursing (Roper et al., 1980).

At the time of being invited to join Roper and Tierney, Logan was a nurse educator, who had worked internationally in America, Canada, Iraq and Malaysia (Roper et al., 1980). Logan started her nursing career at the Royal Infirmary of Edinburgh. She later studied for her Masters degree within Columbia University in New York, where other pioneers of nursing, such as Peplau and Henderson, had also studied, and where the nursing process and models of nursing were being deliberated upon. This, according to Marriner Tomey (2001), as cited in Roper et al. (2001), may have led to Logan's interest in creating, along with Roper and Tierney, a new Scottish model of nursing. Logan has held revered nursing positions during her career, including being Executive Director of the International Council of Nurses (ICN), Chief Nursing Officer of the Abu Dhabi Ministry of Health and Senior Lecturer (Roper et al., 1980).

Alison Tierney is a graduate nurse who gained a doctoral degree during the 1970s, at a time when few nurses studied to this level (Roper et al., 1980). When invited to join Roper and Logan, Tierney was working as a lecturer within Edinburgh University and her remit included the development of the foundation course for students, known today as the Common Foundation Programme (CFP). In collaboration with Roper and Logan, Tierney incorporated their new model of nursing into the foundation programme for nursing students within Edinburgh University, and found that it assisted in providing a meaningful and nursing-focused introduction for the learner nurses (Roper et al., 2001). Similar to Logan, Tierney has held revered positions during her career, including that of Director of the Nursing Research Unit at Edinburgh University (Tierney, 1998).

Special interest

Until the early 1980s, within hospital settings, patient care delivery was task oriented. Nurses, according to their rank, were allocated tasks to complete throughout their span of duty, by the 'Nurse in Charge' of the ward. These tasks were then documented in associated 'books'. For example, the 'Bathing book' would indicate which patients were to be assisted with an immersion bath and which patients would be bed-bathed. On completion of the allocated task the nurse would sign the appropriate

book indicating that the task had indeed been carried out. The Nurse in Charge used this information to provide a report on the patient status for the nurses on the next shift.

With the introduction of what became known as 'total patient care', reflecting the RLT Model of Nursing, the 'Bathing book', 'Bowel book' and all the other 'books' relating to individual nursing tasks needing to be completed throughout the day, were replaced by new paperwork relating to the 'holistic' nursing care of the patient. The nurse, rather than merely carrying out tasks set by a more senior member of nursing staff, was now being asked to think about the nursing needs of the individual patient. This provided, for nurses, the opportunity to really get to know their patients as people and not as 'conditions' or a set of tasks needing to be completed. Interestingly, Gullick et al. (2004) undertook a survey of nurses ($n = 620$), working within an Australian hospital, to determine how well organisational models enabled nurses to provide high standards of care. Findings indicated that nurses 'know' their patients better (when allocated a certain number of patients to care for holistically, during their span of duty) and job satisfaction is increased (through a sense of completion in being able to meet patient needs).

Nurses were required to assess, plan, implement and evaluate patient care; a concept identified by Yura and Walsh (1967) as the Nursing Process. The acronym APIE (assessing, planning, implementing, evaluating) became used (nurses related this to the idea that people in the West of Scotland are fond of 'a pie'!). However, The Nursing Process, although outlining the four steps to be considered when providing care for a patient, does not provide information on exactly what should be assessed, how planning can be decided upon, how this plan can be implemented and the form that evaluation should take. The RLT Model of Nursing provides guidance for the nurse as the steps of the nursing process are addressed.

Summary of writings

Roper, Logan and Tierney developed the first model of nursing to originate from the United Kingdom (Marriner Tomey, 2001). During 1965, nurse scholars in America recognised the need for an organising framework for nursing knowledge (Roper, 2002). A Nursing Model Committee was formed, which, in 1968, became known as the Nursing Development Conference Group and the concept of the nursing process and product developed (Nursing Development Conference Group, 1973). The RLT Model began to develop in the 1970s when Nancy Roper, through her MPhil degree studies at the University of Edinburgh, advanced the idea that some sort of framework for nursing practice might allow learner nurses to look past the patient's condition to see the person as a whole. The framework would also assist in the organisation of the student nurse's thinking process in relation to nursing practice (Roper, 1976). Roper's early work was influenced by another nurse theorist, Virginia Henderson (Roper, 1976), who had described 14 components of nursing activities within a model of nursing she had developed (Henderson, 1969). In collaboration with Logan and Tierney, Roper's initial work developed further and the three had their first book published in 1980 (Roper et al., 1980).

Roper (1976) had made reference to the term Activities of Daily Living (ADLs), in her early writing, but later recognised that activities of living may not necessarily be carried out on a daily basis: the term was replaced with the more appropriate 'Activities of Living' (ALs) in the later RLT Model, and eventually 12 ALs were identified. These are identified and discussed later in this chapter. Changes were also made to some of Roper's original activities of living; for example, the activities of talking, hearing, seeing and socialising were combined to become what is now known as the AL of communicating. New ALs were also added to Roper's original list, namely, maintaining a safe environment, controlling body temperature, expressing sexuality, and dying (Roper et al., 1980). Since 1980 there have been three further editions of the book in 1985, 1990 and 1996. Roper et al. (2001), in what they said were their final accounts of the RLT Model, make reference to Reed (1995), who made the point that models should be open to adaptation. Roper et al. conclude their final account with the sentiment:

> *We hope that our nursing model will continue to evolve through its use and adaptation in the future.*
> (Roper et al., 2001: 166)

Theory

Roper et al. (1980) based their model on the idea that humans, in order to function normally, have to carry out a series of everyday activities; their 12 activities of living (ALs):

- Breathing
- Eating and drinking
- Eliminating
- Sleeping
- Mobilising
- Maintaining a safe environment
- Controlling body temperature
- Working and playing
- Expressing sexuality
- Personal cleansing and dressing
- Communicating
- Dying

Some of these activities are considered as essential whereas others improve the quality of life for the individual. In order to live, people need to breathe (AL: Breathing). Breathing, therefore, is an essential activity of living; oxygen is taken from the atmosphere to the cells of the body, via the respiratory and cardiovascular systems. As well as needing oxygen, humans cannot exist without the intake of nutrients and fluids to support the body's cells to function (AL: Eating and drinking). In order to maintain fluid and electrolyte balance within the body, and to excrete unabsorbed residue from ingested food and waste products of metabolism, urine and faeces need to be eliminated (AL: Eliminating). The human being also needs to sleep, as during sleep the growth hormone is released and cells are replenished (AL: Sleeping). Roper et al. (1980) argue that humans have a basic urge to move, as it is through movement that people can explore their environment and exercise their body so that the bodily systems will function efficiently (AL: Mobilising). However, if the person is to survive within their environment, it is necessary to prevent such things as fire, accidents, pollution and spread of infection (AL: Maintaining a safe environment). The control of body temperature, within a relatively narrow range and constant level, is essential for the many chemical processes required for body function (AL: Controlling body temperature). Roper et al. (1980) also recognised that the following ALs can increase the quality of life. In order to gain income and to enjoy their lives during leisure time, humans should work and play (AL: Working and playing) and be able to express their sexuality, personality and attract a mate with whom they can procreate, if they so wish (AL: Expressing sexuality). This links nicely to the AL: Personal cleansing and dressing. Not only will people feel confident if they are dressed and groomed but, Roper et al. (1980) suggest, they will also adhere to their social responsibility to maintain cleanliness. In order to establish and maintain human relationships and exchange information, human beings need also to communicate (AL: Communicating) with others.

The activity of dying is the ultimate action of being alive. Nurses should provide appropriate nursing care for the dying person and his or her relatives, and care for the bereaved, following the death of a loved one (Roper et al., 2001).

Roper, according to Dopson (2004), did not wish the activities of living to be regarded in such a way as to simply provide a checklist for nurses to tick as having been addressed. Therefore, if the RLT Model is to be utilised as intended, the nurse, in addition to assessing ability to carry out the activity of living, has to assess the dependency/independency of the patient in relation to each of the ALs. The patient's lifespan, lifestyle and individuality are all related to the level of dependency/independency. The environment within which people live can further impact on their abilities to carry out the ALs independently, and patient needs arising from increasing dependence must also be met by the nurse.

There are also other factors that may impact on a person's ability to carry out the ALs, for example, their own body's anatomical and physiological performance, psychological, intellectual and emotional wellbeing. The nurse must also take into account, when assessing the patient using the RLT Model, those sociocultural, politico-economic and spiritual factors and each person's own philosophical, ethical and religious beliefs that can impact on how an individual carries out the ALs. The nurses' role can, therefore, vary from giving information to a patient who can then independently carry out the AL, to actually carrying out the activity for patients if they are unable to carry it out themselves (Mooney and O'Brien, 2006).

Additional theory, related to this model, is that once a problem with an individual's ability to carry out the activities has been identified, goals must be set, whereby the problem can be resolved, or if this is not possible at least minimised. Problems can be actual or potential. An actual problem is one that is actually being experienced by the patient, whereas a potential problem is a problem that, if action is taken, may be prevented from becoming an actual problem. This aspect of the theory is explored further below.

Putting theory into practice

The RLT Model of Nursing is reliant on a thorough patient assessment being completed to ascertain the patient's individual needs (Mooney and O'Brien, 2006). Each person is a unique individual and must be treated as such (Nursing and Midwifery Council, 2008). Assessment is one of the first steps of the nursing process, the others being planning, implementation and evaluation. The RLT Model guides the nurse on how to move through these steps. The process of assessment, planning, implementation and evaluation is, according to Tierney (1984), utilised by all disciplines. There is a fifth stage of the nursing process that is sometimes referred to in the literature; the 'nursing diagnosis' stage. At this point the nurse makes a decisive statement about the patient's nursing needs (George, 1995). However, when using the RLT Model, only the assessing, planning, implementing and evaluation phases need to be considered. The way in which the nurse is guided by the RLT Model through the steps of the nursing process is demonstrated below.

Assessment

Nurses are urged by Roper et al. (2001) to view assessment as more than just part of the admission procedure. Their rationale behind this is that when assessment is seen as being just part of the admission procedure it can become delegated to a junior member of staff and interpreted as a form filling exercise. Vital details can be missed, due to the junior member failing to recognise the importance or relevance of the information. Also, at times a thorough assessment of a patient is not possible, or is inappropriate, and recognition of this may prove difficult for junior nurses. If a patient has life-threatening injuries, the assessment priority would be on the ABC of resuscitation (Roper et al., 2001).

Using the RLT Model, outwith the aforementioned situation, the nurse collects and documents the patient's biographical and health data. Rudyard Kipling (1902) in his *Just so stories* wrote about six honest serving men who taught him all he knew, their names being 'What' and 'Why' and 'When' and 'How' and 'Where' and 'Who'. This is a good way of remembering about individuality in the development of a nursing plan. To be able to prepare an individualised nursing care plan the nurse has to consider how, what, when, where, who, and why the activities of living

Links with other nursing theorists

Roper, Logan and Tierney's work has links with Virginia Henderson's Basic Principles of Nursing Care (*see Chapter 11*) and Helen Yura and Mary Walsh's work on the nursing process. See Yura H, Walsh M (1967) *The nursing process: Assessing, planning, implementing and evaluating.* Appleton-Centiury-Crofts, New York.

References

Dopson L (2004) Obituary: Nancy Roper. *Nursing Standard* 19(5): 31

George J (1995) *Nursing theories: The base for professional nursing practice.* Prentice Hall International, London.

Gullick J, Shepherd M, Ronald T (2004) The effect of an organisational model on the standard of care. *Nursing Times* 100(10): 36–9

Henderson V (1969) *Basic principles of nursing care.* International Council of Nurses, Geneva

Kipling R (1902) *Just so stories.* British Library Images Online. Available from: http://www.bl.uk/onlinegallery/onlineex/englit/kipling/index.html [accessed 28 July 2009]

Marriner Tomey A (2001) Foreword. In: Roper N, Logan W, Tierney A (eds) *The Roper-Logan-Tierney Model of Nursing.* Churchill Livingstone, Edinburgh

Marriner Tomey A, Allgood MR (1998) *Nurse theorists and their work* (4th edn) Mosby, St Louis

Mooney M, O'Brien F (2006) Developing a plan of care using the Roper, Logan and Tierney model. *British Journal of Nursing* 15(16): 887–92.

Nursing and Midwifery Council (2008) *The Code: Standards of conduct, performance and ethics for nurses and midwives.* Nursing and Midwifery Council, London

Nursing and Midwifery Council (2009) *Record keeping: Guidance for nurses and midwives.* Nursing and Midwifery Council, London

Nursing Development Conference Group (1973) *Concept formalization in nursing: Process and product.* Little, Brown and Company, Boston

Reed PG (1995) A treatise on nursing knowledge development in the 21st century: Beyond postmodernism. *Advances in Nursing Science* 17(3): 70–84

Roper N (1976) *Clinical experience in nurse education.* Churchill Livingstone, Edinburgh

Roper N (2002) Sixty-five years of nursing: Selected recollections. *British Journal of Nursing* 11(7): 426–8

Roper N, Logan W, Tierney A (1980) *The Elements of Nursing: A model of nursing based on a model of living.* Churchill Livingstone, Edinburgh

Roper N, Logan W, Tierney A (2001) *The Roper-Logan-Tierney Model of Nursing.* Churchill Livingstone, Edinburgh.

Scott H (2004) Nancy Roper (1918–2004) a great nursing pioneer. *British Journal of Nursing* 13(19): 1121

Tierney AJ (1984) A response to Professor Mitchell's 'Simple

are carried out. In terms of how, it is vital to assess how, and how often, the patient carries out the activity. What, when and where the activity is carried out must be assessed, in order that the person's usual routine is maintained as much as is possible during the time of receiving nursing care. If the person needs assistance in carrying out any of the ALs it is useful to know who it is that provides this assistance so that they may become involved in the planning of care for the individual. In addition, the nurse requires information with regard to why the person chooses to carry out the AL in this way. For example, during the night, a patient may choose to sleep in a chair rather than in bed. The patient may have certain beliefs that have led to this situation and developed a knowledge base and an attitude towards this practice. Roper et al. (2001) believe that during the time a person requires nursing care, his or her pattern of living should have minimal disturbance, i.e. usual routines should be maintained. What if it is the pattern of living that has led to the individual needing nursing care in the first place? Roper et al. (2001) advise that appropriate information should be provided to allow the person to make an informed decision on how to proceed with his or her life.

Current problems (actual and potential) in relation to each of the ALs need to be discussed, with the patient/significant others, and documented. The rationale for gaining this information is to prevent what may be a potential problem from becoming an actual problem. Imagine that, on assessment, an identified actual problem for the patient is inability to mobilise independently. A potential problem associated with being immobile is pressure area damage. By identifying this as a potential problem, the nurse can put in place nursing actions to prevent pressure area damage occurring.

While assessing ALs it is important that the nurse records details relating to Roper et al.'s other concepts of their model, for example, the person's dependence/independence status in relation to each activity of living.

Assessment is followed by the development of a nursing plan, wherein goals are set, priorities indicated and nursing interventions (actions) are planned.

Planning

Setting goals for the patient to achieve can be challenging as they need to be Specific, Measurable, Achievable, Relevant and Time restricted (SMART). Consider these two goals for a patient whose mobility has decreased due to fractured femur and decide which one would provide a nurse with the most appropriate information regarding the patient's situation:

- Goal A: Mobility will improve.
- Goal B: [patient name] will be able to walk to and from the toilet to the bed, with the aid of a walking frame and assistance of one nurse, within two days from today.

Goal B informs the nurse of what is expected, it gives details of the distance the patient should be able to walk and the assistance that is required. It also has a time frame, so in two days' time the nurse can evaluate whether or not the goal has been achieved. If it has not been achieved the nurse will have to reconsider whether the goal was realistic in the first place and set a new goal for the coming period of time. The most achievable goals are those set in collaboration with the patient/significant others. People are less likely to feel that care is inappropriate if they actually agreed to the care provision in the first instance. Involvement in the process also gives an element of control to the people affected by whatever has brought them to the point of requiring nursing care.

Implementation

Once a plan has been agreed it can be used to inform nurses of what needs to be done and when it needs to be done. This phase is the practical stage of the nursing process where the written plan is converted into nursing care. Colleagues, therefore, rely on the plan being accurate. Continuous reassessment is ongoing during the implementation phase of the nursing process to assist nurses to deliver appropriate individualised care in a systematic, logical manner and aid in the prevention of inappropriate care or treatment being provided. Nursing action includes doing, recording and delegating.

Evaluation

Without evaluation the effectiveness of the nursing intervention remains unknown. Basically the evaluation stage of the nursing process involves the nurse judging whether or not the goals set during the planning phase have been achieved; for example, did the patient manage to walk to and from the toilet to the bed, with the aid of a walking frame and the assistance of one nurse, within two days of the goal being set? If the goal is achieved then the planning and nursing intervention has been appropriate. If not, reassessment is necessary and so the process begins again.

Influence

Timmins and O'Shea (2004) consider the RLT Model of Nursing to be one of the most commonly utilised within Europe. It is used extensively, nationally and internationally (Scott, 2004). Editions of the Roper-Logan-Tierney Model of nursing have been translated into many languages including Italian, German, Spanish, Estonian, Finnish, Lithuanian, Portuguese and more recently, Japanese (Roper, 2002). Marriner Tomey and Allgood (1998) feature Roper, Logan and Tierney alongside the various American nurse theorists because of the influence the RLT Model has had on the development of nursing as a profession. The RLT Model has the potential to influence patient/relative/significant others' satisfaction with the nursing service. The rationale behind this statement is that the RLT Model encourages the use of a set of nursing orders, ideally kept at the patient's bedside, which direct the nurses in care delivery. Once the appropriate action, indicated by the nursing order, has taken place, the nurse will sign for having delivered the nursing care. This will enable other nurses to know what care the patient has received and when this happened. It will also inform relatives of the care their loved one has been given. This in itself can assist in satisfaction with the nursing service being delivered and prevent complaints in relation to care delivery from arising. This does, however, rely on all of the nurses documenting the care as it is provided to the patient, in accordance with Nursing and Midwifery Council (2009) guidance. Further information regarding RLT Model documentation can be accessed via the appendices within The Roper-Logan-Tierney Model of nursing book (Roper et al., 2001).

Tierney (1998) argues that the RLT Model has helped in the appreciation of just how complex nursing is and has assisted in the move from thinking about ill health to that of health. It has helped to bring the nursing process to life.

guide to the nursing process'. *British Medical Journal* 288: 835–8

Tierney AJ (1998) Nursing models: Extant or extinct. *Journal of Advanced Nursing* 28(1): 77–85

Timmins E, O'Shea J (2004) The Roper-Logan-Tierney (1996) model of nursing as a tool kit for professional development in education. *Nurse Education in Practice* 4: 139–67.

Yura H, Walsh M (1967) *The nursing process: Assessing, planning, implementing, and evaluating*. Catholic University of America, Washington.

Where to find out more

- Department of Health (2007) *The essence of care: Patient-focused benchmarking for health care practitioners*. Available from: www.doh.gov. uk/essenceofcare

- www.healthsci.claytonedu/ eichelberger/nursing.htm
The Clayton State University School of Nursing's nursing theory link page.

- International Council of Nurses (2010) *ICN Advancing Nursing and Health World Wide 1899–2010*. Available from: www.icn. ch

- Transcultural Nursing (2005) *Basic concepts and case studies*. Available from: www. culturaldiversity.org

Section Four

Grand theories

How does this all fit together?

Overview

This section is probably the most difficult. This is because grand theories always fail and so the attempt can seem pointless. Some information always comes along that does not fit. As a consequence it is easy to imagine that this section is not worth engaging with, but this would be a mistake. This section contains much of the truly original and inspiring ideas within nursing theory. Many ideas have been spawned and applied as a consequence of these theorists' grand ventures. They point the way for others to test and apply their ideas. Many of the theorists discussed in other sections owe a debt to the theorists in this one.

A commonality among these theorists is the attempt to integrate aspects of other schools of thought. They are all widely read in areas such as neuroscience, physics and philosophy and therefore see connections others may not. Their attempts to make these connections coherent significantly add to our knowledge base.

Sister Callista Roy

The first chapter is about Sister Callista Roy. Mandy Allison explains how Sister Callista developed a theory of adaptation based on her understanding of neuroscience. Like most of these grand theorists Roy continues to refine her original ideas to incorporate new findings. Her latest version re-defines adaptation to incorporate cosmic philosophical assumptions which she believes will become the basis of developing knowledge. Like Neuman and Newman her assumptions are actually quite behaviourist in practice given that they focus on stimulus response and feedback mechanisms. This may be why, despite her propensity to integrate issues relating to the meaning of life, the model still has practical explanatory value.

Roy was strongly influenced by Hans Selye. Selye was an endocrinologist who was the first to introduce the notion of biological stress in 1936. He coined the term 'general adaptation syndrome' to describe an individual's response to stress. Roy's initial ideas flowed from this concept as did Betty Neuman's.

Betty Neuman

Betty Neuman is the subject of the second chapter in this section. Neuman amalgamated Selye's ideas on stress with philosophical ideas on the purpose of humanity. In this regard she followed de Chardin by believing people were spiritually evolving towards perfection. As such she saw people as adaptive individuals striving for simultaneous growth and homeostasis through the interaction of many interlinked systems. Her systems theory is complex on first glance, but has retained a practical focus which has helped it endure. In 1993 Reed claimed it was one of the three most utilised theories in nursing.

Martha Rogers

In the case of Rogers, her grand theory of everything has arguably influenced every nursing theorist since. As Stuart Milligan writes:

> Few nurses can be considered to have fundamentally challenged the conceptual basis of their profession more than Martha Rogers. For three decades after she first proposed her theory of the Science of Unitary Man, she was a major figure in the field of nursing science, and 15 years after her death, her ideas continue to influence nursing practice, education and research.

Milligan's chapter captures something of the energy and originality of this remarkable woman. Only Rogers could have inspired a 'Golden Slinky' to be a prestigious academic honour (see p 145). Her influence is most notable on the final two theorists in this section.

Margaret Newman

For example, Margaret Newman is another theorist who integrates different philosophies in developing grand theory. Glenn Marland points out that she seems to have synthesised ideas from a variety of sources such as Hegel's dialectical fusion of opposites, Young's theory of human evolution, and Bentov's theory of time as a measure of consciousness. He concludes that the outcome of this synthesis is unique and ground breaking. Newman's approach is based on free thinking philosophical analysis of health and medicine which is grounded in rejection of the prevailing medical model of 1960s America. Whilst in one sense, therefore, Marland suggests she can be considered a woman of her time she can also be viewed as innovative and original, as many of her ideas persist.

Rosemarie Parse

Parse concludes this section. Herself a recipient of the Golden Slinky, Parse continues to update her theory to the extent that the version presented by Angela Kydd here may well have been further amended by the time you read it. This highlights the endless reflection and reinvention of theory that informs and is informed by the evidence-based nursing movement today. This process in itself is what constitutes the pioneering qualities of Parse.

Reference

Reed K (1993) *Notes on nursing theory: Betty Neuman: The Neuman systems model*. Sage, Beverly Hills

CHAPTER 17

Callista L Roy

Mandy Allison

Biography

Dr Sister Callista Roy was born at Los Angeles Country General Hospital on 14th October, 1934, the second of 14 children. She was named after Callistus, Pope and martyr, on whose Saint's day she was born.

At the age of 14 Callista worked first as a pantry girl, then maid, then nursing assistant in a general hospital. Having been raised in a family which held deep religious beliefs and a commitment to God and service, Callista chose to become a nun and entered the Order of the Sisters of Saint Joseph of Carondelet.

In 1963 she gained a Bachelor of Arts in nursing at Mount St Mary's College in Los Angeles and began work as a paediatric nurse. She went on to study for a master's degree in paediatric nursing in 1964. It was at this time, during a seminar, that nurse theorist, Dorothy E Johnson, challenged Roy to develop a theory for nursing. Roy had made comments about the ability of children to adapt when faced with illness and how this might be a suitable concept on which to base a model of nursing. Roy further suggested that the goal of nursing was promoting patient adaptation. Roy took up the challenge and developed her theory of the person as an adaptive system culminating in the Roy Adaptation Model (RAM). Her first publication on the Adaptation Model, 'A conceptual framework for nursing' appeared in *Nursing Outlook* in 1970.

In 1966 Sister Callista commenced teaching both paediatric and maternity nursing at Mount St Mary's College. It was here that she first began to deliver course content based on her own theory. By 1968, she had introduced her ideas about adaptation nursing as the basis of the nursing curriculum. By 1971 she was head of the nursing department at the college and was completing a PhD in sociology at the University of California, Los Angeles. Ten years later, the RAM was being taught in over 30 other schools of nursing across the USA (Lutjens, 1991). By 1987 over 100 000 nurses had graduated from schools using the RAM making it one of the most widely used and most highly developed models (Lutjens, 1991). During this time, Roy also served on the faculty at the University of Portland in Oregon were she helped to establish a Master of Science programme in nursing.

As the RAM gained momentum, Roy accepted invitations to speak on topics related to nursing theory, research, curriculum, clinical practice and professional trends for the future throughout North America and in over 30 other countries including Japan, Puerto Rico, Panama, Mexico and Columbia. Her books have been translated into 12 different languages.

To develop her understanding of the holistic person, especially as an adaptive system, Roy undertook a two-year postdoctoral programme in neuroscience nursing at the University of California in San Francisco in 1983. She then went on to accept the post of Associate Research Nurse in the Department of Neurosurgery at the same university in 1985. Roy's belief that nursing education provided an opportunity to share her convictions about the integration of theory, practice and research led her to accept the post of Professor and Nurse Theorist at the School of Nursing at Boston College in 1987. Here, she continues to develop and update the Roy Adaptation Model as a framework for theory, practice and research in nursing. She also holds a concurrent position as Research Professor in Nursing at Mount St Mary's.

Callista L Roy
Born 1934

Profile

Callista Roy is widely known for developing the Roy Adaptation Model. She is a prolific writer, lecturer, researcher and teacher. Declared a living legend by the American Academy of Nursing, Roy has over 40 years nursing experience. At the age of 75, she is currently Professor and Nurse Theorist at the Boston College School of Nursing in Chestnut Hill, MA.

Key dates

1963 BA in nursing, Mount St Mary's College, Los Angeles

1966 MS in nursing, University of California, Los Angeles

1973 MA in soiciology, self and systems, University of California, Los Angeles

1977 PhD in sociology, University of California, Los Angeles

1978 Became Fellow of the American Academy of Nursing

1983 Became Robert Wood Johnson Clinical Nurse Scholar

1981 Awarded Sigma Theta Tau, International Honor Society, Founder's Award

1987–present Professor and Nurse Theorist, School of Nursing, Boston College

1991 Received Martha Rogers Award for Advancing Nursing Science, National League for Nursing

1995 Awarded Carondelet Medal, Mount St Mary's College for outstanding contributions to education for women

2000 Received Alpha Sigma Nu Jesuit Universities Book Award for Roy Adaptation Model-Based Research: 25

2003	years of contributions to nursing science
2003	Received Doctorate of Humane Letters, 50th Anniversary of the St Anselm's Department of Nursing, Manchester, NH
2006	Honoured at Massachusetts Department of Corrections Volunteer Recognition Ceremony, by Commissioner Dennehy, State House, Boston, MA

Roy is an active member of the Roy Adaptation Association (RAA) which was founded in 1991. Membership of the association is open to students, clinicians, scholars, researchers and institutions. The aim of this society is to seek to advance nursing practice by developing basic and clinical nursing knowledge based on the RAM.

Respected and revered, Roy has received many awards in recognition of her work. These include the National League for Nursing Martha Rogers Award for advancing nursing science in 1991 and the Sigma Theta Tau International Founders Award in 1981 for contributions to professional practice. The Sister Callista Roy Lectureship was established at the Department of Nursing at Mount St Mary's College in Los Angeles and the Roy Knowledge Institute has been established by Boston College PhD in Nursing Programme. Roy has also received the prestigious Outstanding Alumna Award and Carondelet Medal in 1995 from Mount St Mary's for contributions to education for women, ethics and cultural diversity.

Special interest

Roy has shown commitment to research throughout her career and has participated in over 30 research projects to date. Her research interests fall into three main areas:

- Developing the RAM, in particular, conceptualising and measuring coping and other key concepts of the model.
- Expanding the philosophical basis of adaptation nursing.
- Seeking to further define the distinction between veritivity and relativity.

(Roy, 2000a, b, 2007a, b)

Roy believes neuroscience is 'the frontier of knowledge development' (Jones and Roy, 2002). Her research activities include involving families in the cognitive recovery of patients with mild head injury, and nurse coaching as an intervention for patients after ambulatory surgery, (Roy, 1990, 2000c, 2001; Morgillo and Roy, 2005).

Roy believes that research should influence nursing practice and in order to do this conceptual models of nursing should be tested and re-tested (Roy, 1991, 1995, 2003; Jones and Roy, 2002; Roy and Zhan, 2000). This belief drives Roy's interest in developing the role of the nurse and nurse knowledge, particularly emerging nursing knowledge, and practice outcomes (Roy, 2003; Roy and Lindendoll, 2006; Barone et al., 2008).

Summary of writings

Roy is a prolific writer producing many books, contributions to publications and journal articles. Since her first publication in 1970 introducing adaptation as a framework for nursing, she has written and contributed to over 100 titles. Her writing reflects her life's work evolving the RAM, using it to develop nursing practice and pursuing her interest in research into neuroscience.

Roy's research challenges and continually pushes the philosophical boundaries of nursing science and is reflected in her most recent work, the 3rd edition of *The Roy Adaptation Model* (2008a), which seeks to redefine adaptation with the cosmic philosophical and scientific assumptions outlined in the theory section below. Roy believes this will become the basis of the developing knowledge which will make nursing a major social force in this century (Roy, 2008a). This work builds on the theories purported by Roy in other publications (Roy, 1997; 1999, 2000a; 2007b).

Roy's work also shows how the RAM has been used to develop

evidence-based practice for specialised practice areas. These include diabetes management (Whittemore and Roy, 2002); dyspnoea, (Breslin et al., 1992); recovering from head injury (Roy, 1990) and care of the elderly (Roy and Zhan, 2000).

Roy's passion and commitment for developing clinical practice and relating knowledge to practice led to the recent publication of *Nursing knowledge and development of clinical practice* (Roy and Jones, 2006). This book provides evidence on how nursing knowledge can improve nursing practice and overall healthcare delivery, now and in the future. It concentrates on four major themes: the current state of nursing knowledge; the philosophy of nursing knowledge; the integration of nursing knowledge with practice; and examples of the impact on healthcare delivery when nursing knowledge is applied. Roy reiterates the importance of developing nursing knowledge in *Defining international consensus on mentorship in doctoral education* (Roy and Lindendoll, 2006) and previously in *Action plans linking nursing knowledge to practice outcomes, research and theory for nursing practice* (Jones and Roy, 2002).

Theory

Callista Roy's theory has its foundations in her spiritual and philosophical beliefs and educational background (Roy, 1984). This is evident in a model which makes a number of fundamental assumptions, both scientific and philosophical.

These scientific assumptions include the belief that individuals and the earth have common patterns and integral relationships; that individuals and environment transformations are created in human consciousness; and that system relationships include acceptance, protection and fostering of interdependence (Andrews and Roy, 1986)

Philosophical assumptions include: veritivity, the principle of human nature that affirms a common purposefulness of human existence, activity and creativity for the common good; cosmic unity, the view that as a person, individuals have mutual relationships with the world and God; common purposefulness, the belief that all persons and earth have both unity and diversity and find meaning in mutual relations with each other; and relativity, the belief that there is no way to determine objective truth or objective morality, that the truth is that which is meaningful or significant within a given context and feelings are the final guide to action (Roy, 2000a).

Whilst these fundamental statements may seem remote to the nursing process, once the basic principles are grasped, the RAM provides an holistic approach to person-centred nursing care. Furthermore, RAM proves useful as a personal reflection and learning tool (Connerly et al., 1999; Roy, 2003).

The person as an adaptive system

Roy views the 'person' as an adaptive system, a whole comprised of parts which functions as a unit for some purpose (Roy, 1970). She refers to the 'person' but in this model the 'person' includes people as individuals or in groups, families, organisations, communities, nations, and society as a whole.

As a system the person takes in inputs and processes these to produce a response or output. Outputs are viewed as behaviours and can be adaptive or ineffective. Adaptive behaviours are evidence of an effective response to stimuli whilst ineffective behaviours are indications of problems. The point at which a person is able to respond positively is known as the adaptation level (Roberts and Roy, 1981).

A person's behaviour or adaptation level is influenced by the environment

Links to other nursing theorists

Callista Roy's work has links with Dorothy E Johnson's Behavioural System Model.

References

Andrews HA, Roy C (1986) *Essentials of the Roy Adaptation Model*. Appleton Century Crofts, Connecticut

Barone S, Roy C, Frederickson K (2008) Instruments used in Roy Adaptation Model-based research: Review, critique and further directions. *Nursing Science Quarterly* **21**(4): 353–62

Breslin E, Roy C, Robinson C (1992) Physiological research in nursing, dyspnea: Paradigm shift metaparadigm exemplar. *Scholarly Inquiry for Nursing Practice* **6**: 81–109

Buck MH (1984) Self-Concept: Theory and development. In Roy C (ed) *Introduction to Nursing: An Adaptation Model* (pp 255–83) Prentice Hall, New Jersey

Connerley K, Ristau S, Lindberg C, McFarland M (1999) *The Roy Model in nursing practice*. Connecticut, Stamford Appleton Lang

Frederickson K (1993) Translating the Roy Adaptation Model into practice and research. In E Parker (ed) *Patterns of nursing theory in practice* (pp 230–8) NLN Press, New York

Jones D, Roy C (2002) Knowledge Impact Conference 2001: Action Plans Linking Nursing Knowledge to Practice Outcomes. *Research and Theory for Nursing Practice: An International Journal* **6**(1) 63–6

Lutjens LR (1991) *Callista Roy, an adaptation model*. Sage, California

Martinez C (1976) Nursing assessment based on the Roy Adaptation Model. In C Roy (ed) *Introduction to Nursing: An Adaptation Model* (pp 379–85) Prentice Hall, New Jersey

Morgillo S, Roy C (2005) Cognitive behaviour therapy and the Roy Adaptation Model: A discussion of theoretical integration. In SM Freeman, A Freeman (eds) *Cognitive behavior therapy in nursing practice* (pp 3–27). Springer Publishing Company, New York.

Nuwayhid KA (1984) Role function: Theory and development. In C Roy (ed) *Introduction to Nursing: An Adaptation Model* (pp 284–305) Prentice Hall, New Jersey

Randall BM, Tedrow M, Vanlandingham J (1982) *Adaptation nursing: The Roy Conceptual Model made practical*. Mosby, St Louis

Roberts S, Roy C (1981) *Theory construction in nursing: An adaptation model*. Prentice Hall, New Jersey

Roy C (1970) Adaptation: A conceptual framework for nursing. *Nursing Outlook* **18**(3): 43–5

Roy C (1984) The Roy Adaptation Model of Nursing. In Roy C (ed) *An introduction to nursing: An adaptation model* (2nd edn) Prentice Hall, New Jersey

Roy C (1990) Nursing care in theory and practice: Early interventions in brain injury. In Harris R, Burns R, Rees R (eds) *Recovery from brain injury* (pp 95–110) Institute for Learning Difficulties, Adelaide

Roy C (1991) Structure of knowledge: Paradigm, model and research specifications for differentiated practice. *Proceedings of American Academy of Nursing*, Annual Meeting, Kansas City

Roy C (1995) Developing nursing knowledge: Practice issues

(Roberts and Roy, 1981), and this environment consists of the world within and around the person and his or her ability to deal with that world. For example, a factory worker is made redundant and chooses to pursue a career in teaching. She recognises that her current skills are inadequate so goes to university for additional qualifications. The external environmental factor here is her redundancy, whilst the desire to pursue a career in teaching and her ability to identify how to achieve this are internal factors.

Environmental inputs or contributing factors are described by Roy as stimuli. These can be focal, contextual or residual (Roy, 1970). Focal stimuli are those which are most immediate to the person, they can be internal or external, they can also change rapidly to contextual stimuli and vice-versa. Contextual stimuli are all other factors which contribute to a situation; these may also be internal or external. Residual stimuli are subconscious or historical factors that cannot be validated but may have an impact on the situation.

For example, a man is admitted to hospital with a badly broken leg. After his leg has been set and pain relief has been administered, the nurse monitoring his vital signs finds his temperature is slightly raised. She notices his hands shaking and asks if he still has pain but the man explains that hospitals make him nervous. Through the course of her shift the nurse notes that the man's temperature continues to rise and informs the doctor. For the man, initially the focal stimulus is the pain from his broken leg; his raised temperature is a contextual stimulus; and the anxiety is caused by a residual stimulus. As the pain relief kicks in and his temperature continues to rise the pain becomes a contextual stimulus and the rising temperature becomes the focal stimulus. However, his continued nervousness at being in hospital remains a residual stimulus.

How a person deals with these stimuli is identified as the person's coping mechanisms or internal processes (Roy, 1984). These are split into two categories: *the regulator subsystem* and *the cognator subsystem*. Regulator coping mechanisms are automatic, physiological responses through chemical, neural, circulatory or endocrine activity, such as the fight or flight response. The cognator subsystem responds through four cognitive/emotive channels: perceptual/information; processing; learning; and judgement and emotion. These responses can be genetically determined or learned (Santo, 1984).

Both subsystems can manifest in four ways or adaptive modes within a person. These are the *physiological mode*; *self-concept mode*; *role function mode* and *interdependence mode* (Randall et al., 1982).

The *physiological mode* provides physical responses to environmental stimuli. Roy identifies five needs for physical integrity: oxygen, nutrition, elimination, activity and rest, and protection (Roy, 1984). Physical responses can include symptoms such as a raised temperature, heart attack, vomiting and pain.

The *self-concept mode* focuses on psychological, spiritual and psychic identity. Roy believes we all need to know who we are and we require a sense of unity and peace to exist (Roy, 2008a). She also assumes the person is a composite of beliefs and feelings formed by internal perceptions of self and others. This sense of self encompasses the physical self, body sensations and image, and the personal self, including moral, ethical and spiritual beliefs (Buck, 1984).

In the *role function mode*, the person has a desire for social integrity, to know where they 'fit in' and know how to act. Roy has identified three roles: primary, secondary and tertiary (Nuwayhid, 1984). Each role has instrumental and expressive behaviours. How well individuals can fill these roles is an indication of their ability to function. For example, a woman may see her primary role as that of a mother. This involves washing her child,

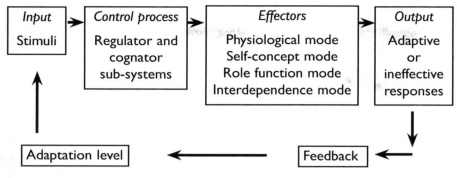

Figure 17.1. Person as an adaptive system.

an instrumental behaviour, and hugging him, an expressive behaviour. She is a teacher (her secondary role) and has always lived in the same village (tertiary role).

The final mode is the *interdependence mode*. Roy assumes that everyone needs to feel secure in nurturing relationships and focuses specifically on relationships with significant others and support systems (Frederickson, 1993). Significant others are identified by the individual, and support systems are all other relationships required to meet interdependence needs. These two types of relationships provide receptive behaviour and contributive behaviour. Assessment of these behaviours provides an indication of the individual's social adaptation (Tedrow, 1984).

Figure 17.1 provides a simplification of the person as an adaptive system.

In summary, Roy's Adaptation Model views the person as an adaptive system with inputs (stimuli/environment); controls (coping mechanisms); effectors (modes); and outputs (adaptive or ineffective responses). The person is constantly growing and developing within a changing environment to fulfil a unique purpose in life (Roy, 2008b). Roy presents health as the process of being and becoming an integrated and fulfilled person. A lack of fulfilment or inability to integrate is considered a lack of health (Martinez, 1976).

Theory into practice and influence

The goal of nursing

Roy views nursing as the science and practice that expands adaptive abilities and enhances person and environment transformation (Roy, 2008a). The goal of nursing therefore is the promotion of adaptation within the four modes (Roy, 2008a). By promoting adaptation the nurse contributes to the person's health and quality of life or enables the person to die with dignity (Connerley et al., 1999).

The nursing process

When using the RAM the nurse is responsible for identifying a person's level of adaptation and coping abilities and for identifying difficulties, the nurse must then help the person adapt to changes in health status by using nursing interventions (Roy, 1984).

There are six nursing steps in the nursing process, which are used to gather information, identify a person's needs, provide nursing care and evaluate care outcomes. These steps are:

- Assessment of behaviour
- Assessment of stimuli

raised from four philosophical perspectives. *Nursing Science Quarterly* **8**: 79–85

Roy C (1997) Future of the Roy Model: Challenge to redefine adaptation. *Nursing Science Quarterly* **10**(1): 42–8

Roy C (1999) *Roy Adaptation Model-based research: 25 years of contributions to nursing science*. Sigma Theta Tau International Centre Nursing Press, Indianapolis

Roy C (2000a) The visible and invisible fields that shape the future of the Nursing Care System. *Nurse Administration Quarterly* **25**(1): 1–12

Roy C (2000b) A theorist envisions the future and speaks to nursing administrators. *Nurse Administration Quarterly* **24**(2): 1–12

Roy C (2000c) Critique: Research on cognitive consequences of treatment for childhood acute lymphoblastic leukemia. *Seminars in Oncology Nursing* **16**(4): 291–4

Roy C (2001) Alterations in cognitive processing. *Neuroscience Nursing*. Norwalk CT: Appleton-Lange, (185–211) and W B Saunders, (275–323)

Roy C (2003) Reflections on nursing research and the Roy Adaptation Model. *Igaju-syoin* [Japanese Journal] **36**(1): 7–11

Roy C (2007a) Update from the future: Thinking of theorist Callista Roy. *Nursing Science Quarterly* **20**(2): 113–16

Roy C (2007b) The Roy Adaptation Model: Historical and philosophical foundations. In ME Moreno et al (eds) *Applicacion Del Model Adaptacion en el Ciclo Vital Humano* (2nd edn) Universidad de La Sabana, Chia, Columbia:

Roy C (2008a) *The Roy Adaptation Model* (3rd edn) Prentice Hall Health, Upper Saddle River New Jersey

Roy C (2008b) Adversity and theory: The broad picture. *Nursing Science Quarterly* **21**(2): 138–9

Roy C, Jones D (eds) (1997) *ENRS Theory Interest Group Knowledge Conference 1996. Developing knowledge for nursing practice: Three philosophical modes for linking theory and practice.* Knowledge: BC Press, Chestnut Hill, MA

Roy C, Jones D (2006) *Nursing knowledge development and clinical practice.* Springer, New York

Roy C, Lindendoll N (2006) Defining international consensus on mentorship in doctoral education. *Journal of Research in Nursing* **11**(4): 345–53

Roy C, Zhan L (2000) The Roy Adaptation Model: A basis for developing knowledge for practice with the elderly. In Parker M (ed) *Nursing theories and nursing practice.* FA Davis, Philadelphia

Santo MK (1984) Major factors influencing adaptation. In C Roy (ed) *Introduction to Nursing: An Adaptation Model* (2nd edn) (pp 64–87) Prentice Hall, New Jersey

Tedrow M P (1984) Interdependence: Theory and development. In C Roy (ed) *Introduction to Nursing: An Adaptation Model* (2nd edn) (pp 306–22) Prentice Hall, New Jersey

Whittemore R, Roy C (2002) Adapting to diabetes mellitus: A theory synthesis. *Nursing Science Quarterly* **15**(4): 311–17

- Nursing diagnosis
- Goal setting
- Intervention
- Evaluation

(Martinez, 1976)

Assessment of behaviour: behaviour is an indicator of how well individuals are adapting or managing to cope with changes to their health status (Roy, 1984). Behaviours are observable or non-observable (Frederickson, 1993). For example, a high temperature is observable and a feeling of dread is non-observable. Areas of concern, or adaptive problems are identified by the nurse or patient as ineffective responses or behaviours that need modification or adaptive behaviours that need reinforcing.

Therefore, the first step of the nursing process is to gather information about the behaviour of the person in each of the four adaptive modes for both the regulator and cognator coping mechanisms. The nurse systematically looks at the responses in each mode using observation, clinical measurement and interview to decide whether they are ineffective or adaptive. The primary concern for the nurse is to address the ineffective behaviour caused by environmental changes which are placing a strain on the person's coping mechanisms (Frederickson, 1993).

Assessment of stimuli (environment): the second step of the nursing process involves the identification of internal and external stimuli that are influencing the person's adaptive behaviours (Lutjens, 1991). They are then organised as: focal, those most immediate confronting the person; contextual, all other stimuli present that are affecting the situation; and residual, those stimuli whose effects on the situation are unclear. The nurse then assesses the environment relative to the behaviour identified in the first assessment step. This is done in collaboration with the person and involves observation, clinical measurement and interview. The aim is to identify problem stimuli to enable goal setting to bring about a change in stimuli or environment to enable the person to cope more effectively.

Nursing diagnosis: step three of the nursing process involves the formulation of statements that interpret data about the adaptation status of the person, including the behaviour and most relevant stimuli (Lutjens, 1991). Roy has identified three methods of making a diagnosis, including summaries about one mode, summaries about stimuli or environment in one mode, or summaries for behaviours in several modes which are affected by the same stimuli (Martinez, 1976). The nurse's aim is to provide a clear summary of ineffective behaviours and stimuli to facilitate goal setting (Roy, 2008a).

Goal setting: the fourth step of the nursing process requires the nurse to establish clear statements for the behavioural outcomes for nursing care, the time-frame of expected behavioural outcomes, and to identify the expected changes in behaviour (Randall et al., 1982). Goals can be long or short-term and, where possible, the nurse should involve the person in developing the goals. The aim is to ensure goals focus on ineffective behaviours in an attempt to change them to adaptive behaviours (Roy, 2008a).

Intervention: the fifth step of the nursing process involves implementing approaches to care based on how best to assist the person to achieve the established goals. The approaches used focus specifically on the management of stimuli affecting the behaviours concerned and the probability of their effectiveness which was identified in goal setting above (Randall et al., 1982).

Evaluation: the sixth and final step of the nursing process involves assessing the effectiveness of the nursing intervention in comparison with the goal established (Roy, 1984). If goals have been achieved they are considered to be effective having brought about a change from ineffective behaviours to adaptive behaviours. If the goals have not been achieved the six-step process is repeated.

Roy (2008a) reiterates the importance of the continuing cycle of the six-step nurse process to overcome ineffective responses and ensure reinforcement of adaptive behaviours. The process should be on-going with all six steps in use for different aspects of care at any given time.

This idea of cyclical and ongoing assessment and intervention has been acknowledged by virtually every theorist since.

Where to find out more

- http://www.bc.edu/bc_org/avp/son/theorist/nurse-theorist.html Callista Roy's web page at Boston College provides links to her studies, work and publications:

- http://www.bc.edu/schools/son/faculty/theorist/Roy_Adaptation_Association.html The Roy Adaptation Association homepage

Betty Neuman
Born 1924

Key dates

1947   Receives RN Diploma.

1957   Completes her first degree at University of California at Los Angeles

1966   MSc from University of California at Los Angeles

1972   Publishes her 'teaching tool' for the first time

1985   Completes her doctoral degree at Pacific Western University

1988   Founds the Neuman Systems Model Trustees Group Inc

1992   Awarded Honorary Doctorate of Letters at Neumann College, Aston

1995   Made Honorary Member of the Fellowship of the American Academy of Nursing

1998   Awarded Honorary Doctorate of Science from Grand Valley State University, Michigan

Betty Neuman
Glenn Marland and Gerry McGhee

Biography

In 1924 Betty Neuman was born into a farming family in the village of Lowell, South Eastern Ohio, USA (Reed, 1993). Her rural upbringing nurtured within her a strong compassion for those in need and this belief has underpinned her philosophy throughout her long career in healthcare (Freese, 2006). Her basic personal philosophy was simply described as 'Helping each other live' (Reed, 1993: 1). In 1947 she received her Registered Nurse (RN) diploma from the Peoples Hospital School of Nursing (now General Hospital) in Akron, Ohio. She then moved to California where she gained a wide range of experience in a variety of nursing roles, involving both care delivery as well as nurse education (Heyman and Wolfe, 2000). In 1957 she attended the University of California at Los Angeles (UCLA) where she completed her degree, with honours, in psychology and public health (Freese, 2006). This achievement was then followed by the successful completion of a Masters degree in Mental Health and Public Health Consultation, also gained through UCLA (Heyman and Wolfe, 2000).

In the 1960s Betty Neuman was considered to be a pioneer within the community mental health profession and it was towards the end of this period when she starting working more in the field of nurse education that she began to develop her model (Freese, 2006). It was in 1970 that she first unveiled a 'teaching tool', developed for an educational programme being designed for UCLA graduate nursing students. The motivation behind her creation was the provision of an overview of the course that would facilitate students, on entering the course, to make more of an informed decision around the nursing specialty most suited to them. Skalski et al. (2006: 70) reports Betty Neuman's view that this educational approach provided a 'holistic framework to organise nursing knowledge'.

Neuman completed a doctoral degree in the field of clinical psychology, awarded by Pacific Western University, in 1985 (Freese, 2006; Reyes et al., 2008). In 1988 Neumann founded a group of trustees who are dedicated to supporting and promoting the model's integrity and development, and guiding its use in the areas of nursing practice, education and research (Reyes et al., 2008). She was awarded an Honorary Doctorate of Letters in 1992 at Neumann College in Aston, Pennsylvania, followed by Honorary Member of the Fellowship of the American Academy of Nursing in 1995 (Reyes et al., 2008). In 1998 the Grand Valley State University in Michigan awarded her an Honorary Doctorate of Science and Neuman has continued to develop and promote her model throughout the healthcare community (Reyes et al., 2008). She continues to lead a very active life working in private practice as a licensed marriage and family therapist (Freese, 2006).

Summary of writing

Betty Neuman has been prolific in a range of professional activities throughout her professional life, including many conference presentations, lectures and consultations, as well as numerous publications on the use of the Neuman's System Model (NSM). Neuman, along with a colleague (Neuman and Young 1972) first published her 'teaching tool' in the 1972 Spring issue of *Nursing Research* where the diagram associated with this development became known as the Betty Neuman healthcare system model and this model, even to the present day, remains largely similar in layout and format (Reed, 1993; Metzger McQuiston et al., 1995). This early work was refined somewhat and in 1974 was published in the first edition of *Conceptual models for nursing practice* by Riehl and Roy (Metzger McQuiston et al., 1995). Neuman edited her first book, *The Neuman's Systems Model: Application to nurse education and practice*, in 1982. In this publication Neuman was joined by 50 authors who described the use of the model in a wide variety of educational and clinical settings (Metzger McQuiston et al., 1995). It was within her second edition in 1989 that Neuman further developed her model by introducing the additional spiritual variable (Reed, 1993; Freese, 2006). A third edition, published in 1995, expanded upon the applicability and relevance of the model moving into the 21st century, emphasising its capacity to cross cultural barriers and multidisciplinary boundaries (Neuman, 1995). In the latest edition Neuman is joined by Jacqueline Fawcett as co-editor and this final edition continues the tradition of the previous publications by providing the most up-to-date examples of the application of the model across education, practice and research settings as well as in administration. Its contributors come from a diverse range of countries including North America, Europe and Asia (Neuman and Fawcett, 2002). In addition to these four editions of her book, Neuman's refinements to her model are evident in a journal article in 1990 as well as three book chapters in 1974, 1980 and 1990 (Fawcett, 2001).

Neuman's theory

Betty Neuman has outlined a range of established theories that have contributed to the creation of her model. Philosophically she was drawn to de Chardin and Marx; the former was said to have first proposed the concept of a 'spiritual evolution' believing that human beings spiritually are ultimately evolving towards perfection (Heyman and Wolfe, 2000), while Marx proposes that the properties of parts are, to a significant degree, determined by the 'larger wholes within organised systems' (Freese, 2006: 319). Other theorists who were important in the creation of Neuman's Systems Model included Selye (1950) who carried out significant work around stress and the defences utilised to minimise the associated adverse experience (Aggleton and Chalmers, 2000). Selye defined stressors as 'tension producing stimuli that can create stress and may be either positive or neutral' (Freese, 2006). Drawing from Seyle's General Adaption System Model, Neuman's theory recognises a non-specific reaction to stress which involves three stages: alarm (the body prepares to deal with a stressor), resistance (the body strives to return to homeostasis or a resting state), and finally exhaustion (body function starts to break down) (Heyman and Wolfe, 2000).

Neuman's Systems Model also borrowed on Gestalt theory, as articulated by Perls (1973), which outlined the importance of homeostasis as a process that allows the organism to maintain equilibrium and therefore, under differing circumstances, its health status (Freese, 2006). It is individuals' 'dynamic interaction' with their environment that determines the nature of their experience and, consequentially, their behaviour (Heyman and Wolfe, 2000: 1). This model also draws on General Systems Theory which evolved from the field of thermodynamics and concerns the flow of energy from one system to another (Heyman and Wolfe, 2000). System theory identifies and focuses on the 'nature of living organisms as open systems' and the interaction between these and the environment (Freese, 2006: 319). Neuman was considerably influenced by work in the field of public health,

Links with other nursing theorists

Betty Neuman is linked with several other nurse theorists, such as Dorothy E Johnson and her Behavioural System Model, Sister Callista Roy (*see Chapter 17*) and Imogene King (*see Chapter 23*), primarily because all four theorists' frameworks and approaches to nursing care practice share a focus on systems (Marriner Tomey, 1989).

and consequently incorporated Capan's associated concepts of primary, secondary and tertiary prevention within her systems model. She considered all these levels of prevention to be important, and that the nursing profession was in an advantageous position to address each of these within working practices (Aggleton and Chalmers, 2000).

These influences all support Neuman's overriding belief that a holistic perspective on human beings is essential, especially in healthcare delivery (Reed, 1993). So important was this concept to her model that she changed the spelling of the term to wholistic in the second edition of her book in 1989 to further emphasise that the term refers to the whole person (Freese, 2006). This holistic perspective is one of a number of 'assumptions' that Neuman makes in relation to her model. These assumptions, or propositions, are statements that link and describe concepts, and are fundamental and inherent to this model (Aylward, 2006). Following on from this, Neuman's understanding of the 'person' was as a 'layered multi-dimensional being' (Heyman and Wolfe, 2000: 2) made up of five subsystems (variables):

- Physical/physiological
- Psychological
- Socio-cultural
- Developmental
- Spiritual.

According to Neuman the individual has inbuilt survival qualities which are unique to that person and are contained within the individual's core, or basic, structure (Aggleton and Chalmers, 2000). The individual's core structure of survival qualities is protected by a series of outer barriers, the first of these being the flexible lines of defence used to cushion the normal line of defence and described as a dynamic barrier. If this becomes penetrated by a stressor and fails to protect the normal line of defence, the lines of resistance become activated. The normal line of defence is considered to be the typical level of stability of the organism over time (Aggleton and Chalmers, 2000). A number of lines of resistance protect the basic core and become active when stressors invade the normal line of defence (Heyman and Wolfe, 2000). According to Neuman (Randel, 1992) the organism can be threatened by three main types of stressors:

- Intrapersonal
- Interpersonal
- Extrapersonal.

Whenever and wherever these stressors are experienced the individual reacts, and such a reaction is normally followed by a period of 'reconstitution' as the person returns to a state of 'wellness'. Nurse intervention is required when the flexible line of defence can no longer protect the normal line of defence, and a breakthrough causes a state of disequilibrium to develop. This flexible line of defence is also referred to as a 'buffer zone' and varies in the amount of protection it can offer. This is dependant upon the inter-relationships of the five system variables or stressors, which determine the degree of reaction of the system to that particular stressor (Haggart, 1993). Neuman's model is considered to be a systems model in that the important emphasis is placed upon the interaction of subparts or subsystems of the organism (Reed, 1993). Neuman sees her concepts of health and wellness as being dependant upon a state of equilibrium existing within the organism, with all parts and subparts being in harmony (Neuman, 1995). Health is on a continuum that ranges from optimal health, at its maximum, through to death (Neuman, 1990). Neuman's model sees the individual in constant

References

Aggleton P, Chalmers H. (2000) *Nursing models and nursing practice* (2nd edn) McMillan Press Ltd, London

August-Brady M (2000) Prevention as intervention. *Journal of Advanced Nursing* **31**(6): 1304–8

Aylward PD (2006) Betty Neuman: The Neuman Systems Model and global applications. In Parker (ed) *Nursing theories and nursing practice*. (2nd edn) F.A. Davis Company, Philadelphia

Burns N, Grove SK (2001) *The practice of nursing research: Conduct, critique and utilization* (4th edn) Philadelphia: W.B. Saunders Company

energy exchange and dynamic interaction with his or her environment (Reed, 1993). According to Aggleton and Chalmers (2000), when working with this model, the nurse is assessing the individual by identifying potential and actual stressors, before going on to consider the presenting client circumstance in terms of:

- *Primary prevention*: Potential risks and hazards that require to be identified and their meaning understood by the patient.
- *Secondary prevention*: Looking at the reaction to stressors as well as internal and external resources that would be useful in resisting these stressors.
- *Tertiary prevention*: Where there is a need to consider the level of stability following a period of treatment and any factors that could lead the individual to relapse back into a state of ill health.

Application of the theory

As noted earlier, the Neuman Systems Model was originally devised to respond to the needs of graduate students within the UCLA (Fawcett, 2001). The model was considered as an educational tool designed to organise better nursing knowledge, and was largely contained within the academic setting. In the subsequent decades the model's application within the practice and research settings has grown considerably (Reed, 1993). Neuman developed and refined a community mental health course for UCLA students, developing her first 'mental health consultation' practice model before the creation of the systems model (Freese, 2006). The model's application to curriculum development remains an important area of its application, and its utility within nurse education programmes is well documented (Fawcett, 1989).

Nelson et al. (1989) describe the use of the Neuman Systems Model, within the Nursing Baccalaureate programme in North America, as inspiring a curriculum that was committed to service and caring through its emphasis on health and primary prevention, client-centred goals and evaluation. The model was particularly valued in ensuring the nursing student had an ability to identify the client perspective of a nursing situation and was clearly able to separate this perspective from his or her own. The model provided guidelines for students, allowing them to more effectively organise the complex multi-phenomena associated with the healthcare field, as they begin to undertake research within this setting.

The use of the Neuman Systems Model within the curriculum will guide future developments in healthcare through its provision of a collaborative model that is client focused as well as providing an emphasis both on primary prevention and the promotion of a more coordinated care management process (Lowry et al., 1995). Stittich et al. (1995) see the Neuman Systems Model as a valuable organising framework to utilise within curriculum planning as the healthcare system adapts to meet the demands of the 21st century. In particular, Stittich et al. (1995) believe that this model will assist future developments in areas such as providing a community healthcare focus, increasing educational opportunities for faculties and students in the provision of services, and providing an increased emphasis within the curriculum on processes such as adaptation to socio-cultural changes. The model itself has been used not only to address the care requirements of individuals, but also can be effectively utilised in assisting families or even whole communities who are undergoing adverse events (Reed, 1993; Ume-Nwagbo et al., 2006). The systems theory, that forms the basis of the Neuman Systems Model, emphasises its use beyond the individual and can directly address the needs of both families and the wider community. This

Fawcett J (1989) Analysis and evaluation of the Neumans System Model. In Neuman (ed) *The Neuman Systems Model*, (2nd edn) Appleton & Lange, Norwalk

Fawcett J (2001) The nurse theorists: 21st century updates – Betty Neuman. *Nursing Science Quarterly* **14**(3): 211–13

Fawcett J (2004) Conceptual models of nursing: International in scope and substance? The case of the Neuman Systems Model. *Nursing Science Quarterly* **17**(1): 50–4

Freese BT (2006) Betty Neuman: 1924–present. In Marriner Tomey A, Alligood MR (eds) *Nursing theorists and their work*. Mosby Elsevier, St Louis

Grant JS, Bean CA (1992) Self-identified needs of informal care givers of head injured adults. *Family and Community Health* **15**(2): 49–58

Haggart H (1993) A critical analysis of Neuman's Systems Model in relation to public health nursing. *Journal of Advanced Nursing* **18**: 1917–22

Heyman P, Wolfe S (2000) *Neuman Systems Model*. Available from: http://www.patheyman. com/esseys/neuman/index.htm [Accessed 01/07/2009]

Kearney MH (1998) Ready-to-wear: Discovering grounded formal theory. *Research in Nursing and Health* **21**: 179–86

Lowry LS, Walker PH, Mirenda R (1995) Through the looking glass back to the future. In Neuman B (ed) *The Neuman Systems Model*. (3rd edn) Appleton & Lange, Norwalk

McCann T, Clarke E (2003) Grounded theory in nursing research: Part 1 – Methodology. *Nurse Researcher* **11**: 7–17

Metzgar McQuinston C, Webb AA (1995) *Foundations of nursing theory: Contributions of 12 theorists*. Sage Publications, Thousand Oaks

Montgomery P, Craig D (1990) Levels of stress and health practices of wives of alcoholics. *Canadian Journal of Nursing Research* 22: 60–70

Nelson LF, Hanson M, McCullagh M (1989) A new Baccalaureate North Dakota-Minnesota Nursing Education Consortium. In Neuman B (ed) *The Neuman Systems Model* (2nd edn) Appleton & Lange, CT

Neuman B (1982) *The Neuman Systems Model: Application to nursing education and practice.* Appleton-Century-Crofts, Norwalk, CT

Neuman B (1990) Health as a continuum based on the Neuman Systems Model. *Nursing Science Quarterly* 3(3): 129–35

Neuman B (ed) (1995) *The Neuman Systems Model.* (3rd edn) Appleton & Lange, Norwalk

Neuman B, Fawcett J (eds) (2002) *The Neuman Systems Model.* (4th edn) Prentice Hall, New Jersey

Neuman B, Newman DML, Holder P (2000) Leadership–scholarship integration: Using the Neuman Systems Model for 21st century professional nursing practice. *Nursing Science Quarterly* 13(1): 60–3

Neuman B, Reed KS (2000) A Neuman Systems Model perspective on nursing in 2050. *Nursing Science Quarterly* 20(2): 111–13

Neuman B, Young R (1972) A model for teaching total person approach to patients' problems. *Nursing Research* 21: 264–9

Parrahoo K (2006) *Nursing research: Principles, process and issues.* (2nd edn) Palgrave McMillan, London

Perls F (1973) *The Gestalt approach: Eye witness to therapy.* Science and Behavior Books, Palo Alto

Randall BP (1992) Nursing theory: The 21st century. *Nursing*

makes its use consistent with health promotion approaches associated with the field of public health (Haggart, 1993).

The Neuman Systems Model is considered, by its originator, to have provided a clear direction to the organisation of nursing activities. In particular, the use of the systematic nursing process approach has provided practical guidance despite the many changes that have affected care delivery over the last three to four decades (Fawcett, 2001). During assessment the nurse should endeavour to establish any significant sources of stress and make an effort to overcome any differences of opinion that may exist between the nurse and her client (Aggleton and Chalmers, 2000). Goal planning, and appropriate strategies to tackle identified problems, must involve negotiation between the nurse and the patient. Care has to be taken to distinguish between immediate, intermediate and future goals, which all must be written in a measurable observable format to allow outcomes to be evaluated effectively (Aggleton and Chalmers, 2000). The Neuman Systems Model considers that intervention is required when a stressor is identified and this model makes particular emphasis on the primary, secondary and tertiary levels of prevention (Aggleton and Chalmers, 2000). Primary intervention, as discussed by August-Brady (2000), is an appropriate intervention to use when a stressor has not penetrated through the normal line of defence to produce symptoms. Such intervention would largely involve health promotion and the education of individual, families and communities (Aggleton and Chalmers, 2000). Once this line of defence becomes penetrated, secondary intervention is required and is designed to achieve wellness through strengthening resistance and thereby promoting reconstitution. Tertiary intervention is required during reconstitution and has the purpose of further protecting client systems through the support of existing strengths and protecting energy levels within the organism. According to August-Brady (2000), using this 'prevention as intervention' approach maintains the important 'holistic' philosophy inherent within nursing practice. It allows for the measurement of effective nursing practice, thereby providing a foundation for evidence-based practice.

Although the model was primarily designed to be used within the field of nursing, Neuman has made it clear that she sees this model being used by a variety of other disciplines (Haggart, 1993). Lois W Lowry, associate professor from the University of South Florida, stated in an interview with Fawcett (2004) that the Neuman Systems Model will continue to be utilised well into the 21st century as it is both broad and flexible, while still reflecting the cultural variability that exists within contemporary populations requiring a caring input. The breadth and flexibility of the model is reflected in its usage across diverse groups and care settings, as well as through its ability to guide nursing across the world and within radically differing healthcare cultures (Freese, 2006). This ability for the model to develop and adapt to future care demands lies in this breadth and flexibility, and involves the ongoing application of research to constantly examine the current and future application of the model.

The Neuman Systems Model has also been regularly identified as having a conceptual framework for research, and studies supporting its concepts are becoming increasingly evident (Reed, 1993). It has the potential to generate nursing theory and its associated concepts are indeed very relevant today (Freese, 2006). Neuman herself firmly believes that the model needs to change and develop or it could easily become stagnant (Fawcett, 2001). Skalski et al. (2006) cite several studies involving the Neuman Systems Model that have examined a variety of research areas such as the needs of cancer patients and their families (Reed, 1993); levels of stress and health practices of wives of alcoholics (Montgomery and Craig, 1990); self-identified needs of informal care givers of head injured adults (Grant and Bean, 1992); and the experiences of family members of persons with Huntington's disease (Semple, 1995).

Theories in general are not definitive explanations but simply interpretations of phenomena and can be classified at three distinct levels, and the terms used to label these levels can vary. At the highest theory level terms used include grand theory, formal or scientific theory and laws; at the intermediate level are middle-range or substantive theory; and at the lower level of the hierarchy is tentative theory (Kearney, 1998; Burns and Grove, 2001; McCann and Clarke, 2003; Parahoo, 2006). The Institute for the Study of the Neuman Systems Model has commenced work to derive and test middle range theories based on the model (Freese, 2006). The Neuman model provides a clear direction for the researcher who is intent on examining stressors, and in explaining factors that influence such stressors within a holistic open systems framework.

Influence

Betty Neuman, and her systems model, have had a considerable influence on healthcare over the last three decades. Her strong compassion for her fellow human beings has underpinned the philosophy of the model and its development (Freese, 2006). From its earliest emergence the theory has been well received by the nursing profession as evidenced by its wide use within all areas of the discipline, and is it increasingly being adopted beyond the nursing profession (Reyes et al., 2008). Work to improve the model is ongoing and its relevance to a wide variety of healthcare cultures across the world is becoming increasingly more apparent. More than 50 countries world wide have adopted the model within both education and practice, and the Neuman Systems Model is one of the three most adopted theoretical frameworks in existence (Reed, 1993). Nurses from these differing cultures have published their experiences of using the model within their varying organisations and find the breadth and flexibility of the framework helpful in their approach to the delivery of care (Neuman and Reed, 2000).

The model has received some criticism in that many concepts are not defined to an adequate level, and its accuracy in representing human beings and their interaction with the environment has been questioned. However, despite these apparent inadequacies, the model provides those in healthcare delivery and education with an excellent framework within which to examine and conceptualise stress and prevention (Heyman and Wolfe, 2000). The importance of the model's use in the future is highlighted by Neuman et al. (2000) in terms of leadership and scholarship. Worldwide trends in the care of clients within the community make it vital that healthcare avoids the fragmentation of services, but rather plans for the integration of resources. Neuman et al. (2000) explain how, in this new era, leadership and scholarship must be seen as essential to each other and to the delivery of this care. The Neuman Systems Model will greatly assist in the avoidance of fragmentation and provide a clear sense of direction for effective leadership, and the effective organisation and integration of these services.

Neuman continues to develop, expand and clarify the model, and in so doing she sees her current role as that of facilitator and networker in how the model is applied and utilised. This involves her spending considerable time and effort in helping others work with, and more effectively apply, the model to their particular healthcare setting (Metzger McQuiston et al., 1995). It was with this requirement in mind that Neuman in 1988 organised the Neuman System Model Trustees Group, Inc, to ensure the integrity of the model as well as advancing its continuous development (Reed, 1993).

Science Quarterly **5**(4): 176–84

Reed KS (1993) *Betty Neuman: The Neuman Systems Model.* Sage Publications, Newbury Park

Reyes JR, Ricana R, Rico RP, Rimas MF, Rosales A (2008) *Betty Neuman's Systems Model.* Available at: http://nursingthe-ories.blogspot.com/2008/07/betty-neumans.html [Accessed 01/07/2009]

Semple OD (1995) The experiences of family members of persons with Huntington's disease. *Perspectives* **19**(4): 7–12

Seyle H (1950) *The physiology and pathology of exposure to stress.* ACTA, Monreal

Skalski CA DiGerolamo L Gigliiotti (2006) Stressors in five client populations: Neuman Systems Model-based literature review. *Journal of Advanced Nursing* **56**(1): 69–78

Stittich EM, Flores FC, Nuttall P (1995) Cultural considerations in a Neuman-based curriculum. In Neuman (ed) *The Neuman Systems Model.* Appleton & Lange, Norwalk

Ume-Nwagbo PN, DeWan SA, Lowry LW (2006) Using the Neuman Systems Model for best practices. *Nursing Science Quarterly* **19**(1): 31–5

Where to find out more

- http://www.neumansystemsmodel.org
- http://www.patheyman.com/essays/neuman/implications.htm

Key dates

1936   Received her nursing diploma

1937   Bachelor of Science Degree

1945   Masters Degree

1954   Doctorate

1937–1951   Held various posts in Public Health Nursing and Visiting Nursing in Michigan, Connecticut and Arizona

1954   Appointed head of the Division of Nursing at New York University

1963–1965   Edited *Journal of Nursing Science*

1970   Publication of *An introduction to the theoretical basis of nursing*

1975   Retired from New York University

1996   Inducted into the American Nurses Association Hall of Fame

Links with other nursing theorists

Martha Rogers' work links with that of Rosemarie Parse (*see* Chapter 21).

CHAPTER 19

Martha Elizabeth Rogers
Stuart Milligan

Biography

Few nurses can be considered to have fundamentally challenged the conceptual basis of their profession more than Martha Rogers. For three decades after she first proposed her theory of the Science of Unitary Man, Rogers was a major figure in the field of nursing science, and since her death, her ideas continue to influence nursing practice, education and research. Opinion may be divided over the ultimate merits of the grand theory she conceived (and in particular, its applicability in practice), but her conceptual originality and unflinching pursuit of a unique theoretical framework for nursing are unchallenged (Gunther, 2006a).

Martha Elizabeth Rogers was born in Dallas, Texas on 12th May, 1914, a birth date she shared with Florence Nightingale, born 94 years earlier. After an early foray into science studies, she entered nursing school and received her nursing diploma in 1936. She was later to admit, 'I liked going to school; I knew I didn't know enough' (Butcher, 2007a), and in the 17 years that followed, she gained Batchelors Degree, Masters and Doctoral awards. Importantly, Rogers chose not to place narrow limits on her learning. By the time she took up the position of Head of the Division of Nursing at New York University in 1954, she was not only an experienced nurse but also well versed in the sciences, arts and humanities (Donaldson, 2004). It was undoubtedly this broad and eclectic knowledge base that enabled Martha Rogers to formulate a radically new theoretical basis for nursing.

Rogers was a respected nurse administrator, leader, educator and researcher (Tomasson, 1994; Donaldson, 2004). She was also a passionate advocate for the nursing profession and a supporter of various nursing organisations. However, it is as a nursing scholar and theorist that she is best known. Her theory of the Science of Unitary Man (later revised to the Science of Unitary Human Beings) was her greatest contribution. However she contributed much forward thinking in other fields including nurse education policy and nursing in space (Rogers et al., 1994).

Between 1963 and 1965 she was editor of the *Journal of Nursing Science*, and she continued as Head of Division at New York University until she retired in 1975 (Gunther, 2006a). Thereafter she continued to lecture and write until her death, at the age of 79, in 1994.

Consistent with a lifetime spent at the forefront of nursing theory, Rogers' influence has continued to be felt since her death (Rogers et al., 1994). In 1996, she was inducted into the American Nurses Association (ANA) Hall of Fame. Her citation reads:

Over a long and productive career, she demonstrated leadership skill and a futuristic vision that improved nursing education, practice, and research in the United States and internationally.

(ANA, 1996).

Today, Rogerian science continues to be promoted and refined, most notably by the Society of Rogerian Scholars. Her advocacy in support of the independence of nursing is relevant to ongoing debates about the role of Nurse Practitioners and (in the US) Physicians' Assistants (Freda, 2007).

Her concepts of resonancy and patterning are finding new applications in models of the effects of complementary therapies such as guided imagery and Reiki (Butcher and Parker, 1998; Ring, 2009b). New Rogerian science-based nursing theories continue to be developed (Malinski, 2006), and papers on Rogerian theory and research are published regularly in *Visions: The Journal of Rogerian Nursing Science, Advances in Nursing Science, Nursing Science Quarterly* and a range of other nursing journals in the US, the UK and around the world.

Special interest

In an interview given in 1988, Rogers revealed the motivation behind her efforts to develop a new grand theory of nursing (New York University, 1988a). In her own words, she wondered, 'What are people like?' and 'What do we need to know in order to serve them?' She was convinced that 'People needed knowledgeable nursing, and we have not been providing it'. She was determined not to base her world view on other basic sciences such as medicine or psychology. Instead, she took as her starting point, the assertion of Florence Nightingale that the focus of nursing should be the person in his or her world.

Working from this premise, Rogers redefined nursing as a basic science equal to those it had been traditionally viewed to be derived from. She was later to remark,

> *Nursing then becomes a noun (meaning the body of knowledge) and the practice of nursing becomes the use of that knowledge for human betterment.*

> (New York University, 1988a)

In this respect, Rogers became an early advocate of the creation of a unique body of nursing knowledge, separate from those of other disciplines (Smith, 2007). She also called for the development of unique research methodologies to facilitate applied nursing research, a call still being echoed in contemporary writing (Malinski, 2006).

In many ways, Rogers' theories and emerging 'world view' of nursing reflected the generation in which she lived. She grew up in an American society emerging from post-war austerity and beginning to re-evaluate its beliefs, values and priorities. This was the psychedelic generation which encouraged rule-breaking and exploration of the psychological, spiritual and para-normal. Indeed, Rogers' 'unitary man' can be seen partly as a precursor of the 'whole person' of today's holistic nursing models.

One unique way in which Rogers' vision and forward thinking were demonstrated was through her advocacy of the contribution of nursing to the field of space travel. She wrote and lectured enthusiastically on the unique challenge space exploration presented to the emerging science of nursing (Rogers, 1992). In 1988 she predicted that 'Nurse astronets' would be working in outer space within a decade, and in 1992 she was appointed the first honorary board member of the Space Nursing Society (New York University, 1988b; Corbett, 2007). In reality, that prediction of nurses in space by 1998 was a little premature. Nevertheless, the International Space Station is already equipped with a health maintenance facility, and it seems only a matter of time before Rogers' dream is realised (Sheehy, 1999).

Summary of writings

In the course of her career, Rogers wrote three books which, according to the American Nurses Association, 'enriched the learning experience and

References

Alligood MR, Fawcett J (2004) An interpretive study of Martha Rogers' conception of pattern. *Visions: The Journal of Rogerian Nursing Science* **12**(1): 8–13

American Nurses Association (1996) *Martha Elizabeth Rogers (1914–1944) 1996 inductee*. Available from: http://nursingworld.org/FunctionalMenuCategories/AboutANA/WhereWeComeFrom_1/allofFame/19962000Inductees/rogeme5577.aspx [accessed 27th July 2009]

Barrett EAM (2006) What is nursing science? In: Andrist LC, Nicholas PK, Wolf KA (eds) *A history of nursing ideas*. Jones and Bartlett Publishers, Boston.

Biley FC (1995) *An introduction to Martha Rogers and the science of unitary human beings*. Available from: http://www.societyofrogerianscholars.org/biley.html [accessed 29th July 2009]

Biley FC, Sayre-Adams J, Wright S (2001) Providing a conceptual framework for practice. In: Sayre-Adams J, Wright S (eds) *Therapeutic touch: Theory and practice* (2nd edn). Churchill Livingstone, London

Butcher HK (2002) Living in the heart of helicy: An inquiry into the meaning of compassion and unpredictability within Rogers' nursing science. *Visions: The Journal of Rogerian Nursing Science* **10**(1): 6–22

Butcher HK (2006) Unitary pattern-based praxis: A nexus of Rogerian cosmology, philosophy, and science. *Visions: The Journal of Rogerian Nursing Science* **14**(2): 8–33

Butcher HK (2007a) *A portrait of Martha E Rogers*. Available from: http://rogeriannursingscience.wikispaces.com/

influenced the direction of nursing research for countless students' (ANA, 1996). In an interview in 1987, she explained that the first two books enabled her to develop and refine the theories which were eventually to be presented in the third (New York University, 1988a).

Educational revolution in nursing was published in 1961, while Rogers was developing a new, five-year nursing curriculum at New York University. In this provocative text she set out her vision of a profession with its own, unique body of theoretical knowledge and equal academic standing with sociology, psychology and medicine. This new scientific discipline of nursing was to be taught in universities, and was to have baccalaureate, masters and doctoral programmes. In expounding these ideas, Rogers became an early and powerful advocate of the professionalisation of nursing (Donaldson, 2004).

In *Reveille in nursing* (published in 1964), Rogers issued a renewed wake-up call to the profession. She asserted that 'professional education requires rigorous intellectual training' (quoted in Philips, 2000), and once again called for the movement of nursing education into institutions of higher education (Barrett, 2006).

Rogers' most influential work, *An introduction to the theoretical basis of nursing*, was published in 1970. Described as 'marking a new era in nursing science', the book signalled a radical departure from traditional nursing theories (Hektor, 1989). In her own foreword, Rogers explained her motivation to be 'a deep-seated conviction of the critical need for nursing practice to be underwritten by substantive knowledge so that human beings may benefit' (Rogers, 1970 : vii).

In the grand theory she first referred to as the Science of Unitary Man, Rogers signalled a paradigmatic shift towards a view of nursing derived more from cosmology than medicine (George, 2001). According to Rogers, human beings were 'integral, irreducible, pan-dimensional energy fields … evolving rhythmically and unpredictably toward infinite diversity and innovativeness' (Butcher, 2007b). The place of nursing was to engage with the whole man (Rodgers later used the word 'human') in a mutual journey towards maximum health potential.

In a later interview (in 1988), Rogers admitted that 'there are a number of pages in that 1970 book, if somebody ripped them out, would improve the book' (New York University, 1988a). However, it remains a milestone of nursing literature, 'elegant in its simplicity, sophisticated in its presentation, and erudite as its author' (Meleis and Scheetz, 2006: 623).

After 1970, Rogers wrote numerous book chapters, research papers and other articles, many expounding and refining the Science of Unitary Human Beings (Malinski, 2006). Although she promised she would, she never did revise *An introduction to the theoretical basis of nursing* (Wright, 2007). However, to read her magnum opus today, flawed as it is, is to gain insight into a mind well versed in history, philosophy, art and science, well used to intense intellectual debate, and craving explanation and understanding of the world around it. Rogers' attention to detail is apparent in her meticulous charting of human history, but her originality of thought is what particularly shines through. As she presents her conceptual model, in all its abstract complexity, the reader is caught up in a whirlwind of thinking which still seems radical today.

Theory

Martha Rogers' Science of Unitary Human Beings is ranked among the grand theories of modern nursing (Gunther, 2006a). It was conceived in the 1960s, first published in 1970, and continuously refined up to the 1990s and beyond (Gunther, 2006a). The fundamental principles on which the

Science of Unitary Human Beings is established are the nature of energy fields and the continuous process which links people and their environment (Gunther, 2006a). According to Rogers, each person can be thought of as occupying an energy field, the boundaries of which uniquely define that individual (Rogers, 1970: 90). Man is then seen as a pan-dimensional but irreducible, indivisible, unified whole, 'evolving rhythmically along life's longitudinal axis' (Rogers, 1970: 93). Human energy fields are not fixed but in a continuous state of flux, and importantly, they extend beyond the traditionally accepted boundaries of the human body. The environment is also an energy field, and is continuous with each human energy field. Furthermore, individual human energy fields have the potential to be continuous with each other, for instance when a nursing intervention is taking place.

On the basis of these assumptions, Rogers developed her principles of homeodynamics. These are principles that govern the behaviour of systems, both human and environmental, and which enable us to describe, explain and predict a range of events relevant to nursing practice (Rogers, 1970: 96). In its 1970 manifestation, Rogers' theory incorporated four homeodynamic principles:

- resonancy
- helicy
- reciprocy
- synchrony.

In later versions, reciprocy and synchrony were subsumed within helicy, and the principle of integrality introduced (Gunther, 2006a). Fundamental to the homeodynamic principles was the concept of patterning: the way in which energy fields are manifest or expressed.

Homeodynamics describe the way the human body maintains its equilibrium through the constantly changing balance between inter-related physiological and metabolic processes. Resonancy describes the nature of the flow of energy between man and his environment. It is wave-like, rhythmic, continuous and unending. In a later version of the model, Rogers referred to the frequency of wave patterns as continually changing, increasing from lower to higher (Wright, 2007).

Related to the principle of *resonancy* is the concept of patterning, which describes the aspect of the energy field which is manifest in the identifiable features (and experiences, perceptions, behaviours and qualities) displayed by any individual (Gunther, 2006b). Examples of manifestations of patterning are sense of self, illness and healing (Gunther, 2006a). A thorough understanding of patterning is essential to the practical application of Rogerian nursing science (Alligood and Fawcett, 2004).

The second of Rogers homeodynamic principles, *helicy*, relates to the unpredictable, evolving nature of energy fields (Butcher, 2002). According to Rogerian theory, human and environmental energy fields change continuously, becoming progressively more innovative and diverse. This process results in the manifestation of increasingly complex and diverse patterning. There is a repeating, spiral element in helicy which is manifest in rhythmic phenomena such as changes in sleep pattern and changing perceptions of the passage of time (Rogers, 1970: 100; Ring, 2009a).

If helicy is the nature of change, the third principle, *integrality*, is the process by which change takes place (Gunther, 2006b). Integrality is based on the assumption that the human field is integral or consistent with the environmental field. When there is a continuous field between human and environment, changes in one field can be brought about by changes in the other. For instance, when a nurse modifies the environment in which a

[accessed 27th July 2009]

Butcher HK (2007b) *Rogerian cosmology and philosophy.* Available from: http://rogerian-nursingscience.wikispaces.com/ [accessed 27th July 2009]

Butcher HK, Parker NI (1998) Guided imagery with Rogers' science of unitary human beings: An experimental study. *Nursing Science Quarterly* **1**(3): 103–10

Castledine G (1995) Will the nurse practitioner be a mini doctor or a maxi nurse? *British Journal of Nursing* **4**(16): 938–9

Corbett K (2007) *Dr. Martha Rogers' influence: Founding of Space Nursing Society.* Available from: http://www.spacenursingsociety.net/aboutus.html [accessed 8th November 2009]

Corner J (2008) Working with difficult symptoms. In: Payne S, Seymour J, Ingleton C (eds) *Palliative care nursing: Principles and evidence for practice* (2nd edn). Open University Press, Buckingham

Cowling WR (1993) Unitary knowing in nursing practice. *Nursing Science Quarterly* **6**(4): 201–7

Cowling WR (1997) Pattern appreciation: The unitary science/practice of reaching for essence. In: Madrid M (ed) *Patterns of Rogerian knowing.* Jones and Bartlett Publishers, Boston

Cowling WR (2001) Unitary appreciative inquiry. *Advances in Nursing Science* **23**(4): 32–48

Cowling W (2008) An essay on women, despair, and healing: A personal narrative. *Advances in Nursing Science* **31**(3): 249–58

Cox (2003) Theory and exemplars of advanced practice. Spiritual intervention. *Complementary Therapies in Nursing and Midwifery* **9**: 30–4

Donaldson R (2004) Finding aid for the Martha Rogers papers, *1931–1996: Biographical sketch. Foundation of New York State Nurses - Bellevue Alumnae Centre for Nursing History*. Available from: http://foundationnysnurses.org/bellevue/guidetoarchivalrecords/collections/MC12fa.php [accessed 22 July 2009]

Erci B (2007) Nursing theories applied to vulnerable populations: Examples from Turkey. In: De Chesnay M (ed) *Caring for the vulnerable: Perspectives in nursing theory, practice and research* (2nd edn). Jones and Bartlett Publishers, Boston

Fawcett J, Alligood MR (2003) The science of unitary human beings: Analysis of qualitative research approaches. *Visions: The Journal of Rogerian Nursing Science* **11**(1): 7–20

Freda MC (2007) A role model of leadership in and advocacy for nursing. *Nursing Forum* **24**(3/4): 9–13

George JB (2001) Science of Unitary Human Beings: Martha E. Rogers. In: George JB (ed) *Nursing theories: The base for professional nursing practice*. (5th edn) Prentice Hall, New Jersey

Gunther MA (2006a) Martha E. Rogers: Unitary human beings. In: Marriner Tomey A, Alligood MR (eds) *Nursing theorists and their work* (6th edn). Mosby, St Louis

Gunther M (2006b) Rogers' science of unitary human beings in nursing practice. In: Alligood MR, Marriner Tomey A (eds) *Nursing theory: Utilization and application* (3rd edn). Mosby, St Louis

Hardin SR, Husse L, Steele L (2003) Spirituality as integrality among chronic heart failure patients: A pilot study. *Visions: The Journal of Rogerian Nursing Science* **11**(1): 43–53.

Hektor LM (1989) Martha Rogers: A life history. *Nursing Science Quarterly* **2**: 63–73

patient is cared for, there is the potential for a change in the patient's 'state of being' (Biley, 1995; Rasmussen and Edvardsson, 2007).

The Science of Unitary Human Beings has been criticised for its heavy reliance on abstract concepts and a perceived difficulty proving the validity of its precepts. Critics have also pointed to the absence of any elements of caring theory (Watson and Smith, 2002). The evolution of Rogerian science over the past 40 years has gone some way to address these and other concerns (Wright, 2007). However, what Rogers attempted, and to a certain extent achieved, was a shift away from a traditional approach to nursing, based on illness and disease, to a focus on a unified concept of human functioning where the whole person ('and their world') is the object and the purpose of care (New York University, 1988a; George, 2001).

Rogers' theorising was not confined to the theoretical base and science of nursing. She also influenced thinking on nurse education, nursing services, nursing roles and nursing research (Gunther, 2006a). She advocated the replacement of hospital training with a five-year university degree, and was instrumental in developing higher level nursing programmes. She supported the creation of independent nurse practitioner roles, advocated the siting of nurse-led services in schools and communities, and even developed a conceptual model of the role of nurses in outer space (Rogers et al., 1994).

Putting theory into practice

As discussed, Rogerian science has been criticised for being overly abstract and difficult to apply in practice. However, two elements of Rogers' original theory which are claimed to translate particularly successfully into practice are pattern appraisal and patterning/mutual patterning activities. Pattern appraisal is the comprehensive assessment of the individual within his or her world (New York University, 1988a). In the course of the appraisal, the practitioner considers environmental and human energy field patterns, rhythms, dissonance and harmony (Masters, 2005). The tools used are the senses, feelings, intuition, reflection and validation with both self and the individual patient or client (Erci, 2007).

Patterning activities are the 'interventions' of unitary nursing practice. However, Rogers proposed that these should not be solely led by the practitioner but should generally be mutually determined and delivered. Examples might include healing, meditation, imagery, humour, touch, therapeutic touch, teaching, journaling, guided reminiscence and modification of surroundings (Masters, 2005; Gunther, 2006b).

Evaluation is a third area where Rogerian theory can translate well into nursing practice. The focus for Rogerian evaluation is not the measurement of narrow mechanistic parameters but once again the recording of manifestations of field including harmony and dissonance. This might be achieved through the recognition of pain, fear, worry, low mood or family tensions (Erci, 2007), but might equally be appreciated through attention to concepts such as serenity and at-homeness (Rasmussen and Edvardsson, 2007; Rushing, 2008).

A final, albeit indirect way in which the Science of Unitary Human Beings continues to influence nursing practice is through refinement and extension of the original theories. Some examples of theories which have built on the work of Martha Rogers include Newman's Health as Expanding Consciousness and Parse's Theory of Creativity, Actualisation and Empathy (Gunther, 2006a) as discussed in the following chapters..

Looking at nursing care as a whole, two interesting areas of practice where Rogerian thought either has already been, or might be expected to be relevant are complementary therapies and palliative care. Wald (2006) believed that Martha Rogers was instrumental in bringing complementary therapies into wider use, and 'adding to the spiritual dimensions of care'. What Rogers contributed was a theoretical context within which so-called 'healing' practices could be considered and evaluated. Hence, therapies such as guided imagery, medical acupuncture, reiki and, most famously, therapeutic touch have each found a comfortable, conceptual home within Rogers' theories (Butcher and Parker 1998; Biley et al., 2001; Walling, 2006; Ring 2009b)

Rogerian theory also has some relevance to palliative care and the care of the dying. Palliative care, since its modern inception in the hospice movement of the 1960s, has been concerned with the care of the whole person and with bringing about healing, even in the absence of a cure (Milligan and Potts, 2009). Several aspects of palliative care including symptom management, the creation of healing environments, and support for the bereaved are approached in a way that is consistent with a unitary world view. For example, current, integrative approaches to breathlessness management advocate an assessment process which has much in common with Rogers' pattern appraisal or Cowling's unitary knowing, concentrating as it does on the lived experience of breathlessness rather than reductionist measures such as peak flow rate or oxygen saturation (Corner, 2008; Cowling, 1993, 1997, 2001). To give another example, it is proposed that there is potential for healing in giving attention to atmosphere as a component of the palliative care environment (Rasmussen and Edvardsson, 2007). Finally, some nurses are utilising unitary theory to understand what happens when people suffer loss. For instance, Todaro-Franceschi (2006) has devised interventions that utilise synchronicity (meaningful coincidence) associated with grieving as a means of promoting personal transformation and recovery of well-being among bereaved people.

Influence

In her lifetime and in the years since her death, Martha Rogers can be seen to have had a major influence in several areas of nursing including education, research and practice (Gunther, 2006a). Perhaps not surprisingly, her greatest impact has been felt in the United States. However, her views about the position of nursing within society, and her theories about the unitary nature of man have translated well into many other countries (Wright, 2007).

Rogers maintained the view, throughout her lifetime, that nursing should be taught by nurses, and that it should be taught in universities (Rogers et al., 1994). She was not alone in demanding these changes. However, hers was one of the loudest and most persistent voices, and she must be given some of the credit for the fact that in many countries around the world today, degree-level nursing courses, taught by nurses are becoming established.

Rogers consistently called for research to further understand the phenomena she sought to describe. In *An introduction to the theoretical basis of nursing* she emphasised the importance of studying the patient in his or her environment as the basis for nursing knowledge. And in an interview in 1978 she called for further research into the science of nursing and applied research to test the application of the Science of Unitary Human Beings in practice (New York University, 1988b). Today, the influence of Rogers in nursing research continues with the emergence of new Rogerian research methods (Gunther, 2006a; Malinski, 2006). These tend to be predominantly descriptive and to be characterised by personal involvement (of the researcher), intensive interviewing, self-reflection, openness to new discovery, willingness to change direction and complex content analysis of large volumes of descriptive data (Fawcett and Alligood, 2003).

Of course like any other theorist, Rodgers has her detractors. As already mentioned, her theories have been criticised for being over-abstract and

Malinski V (2006) Rogerian science-based nursing theories. *Nursing Science Quarterly* **19**(7): 7–12

Masters K (2005) Framework for professional nursing practice. In: Masters K (ed) *Role development in professional nursing practice*. Jones and Bartlett Publishers, Boston

Meleis A, Scheetz S (2006) Abstracts of writing in nursing theory, 1960–1984. In: Meleis A I (ed) *Theoretical nursing: Development and progress* (4th edn). Lippincott Williams & Wilkins, Philadelphia

Milligan S, Potts S (2009) The history of palliative care. In: Stevens E, Jackson S, Milligan M (eds) *Palliative nursing: Across the spectrum of care*. Wiley-Blackwell, Chichester.

New York University (1988a) *Martha Rogers interviewed by Jacqueline Fawcett* (Part 1). Available from:. http://www.youtube.com/watch?v=V1XN3rPKndE [accessed 26th July 2009]

New York University (1988b) *Martha Rogers interviewed by Jacqueline Fawcett* (Part 2). Available from: http://www.youtube.com/watch?v=f6qWm8sGut0&feature=related [Accessed 26th July 2009]

Phillips JR (2000) Rogerian nursing science and research: A healing process for nursing. *Nursing Science Quarterly* **13**: 196–201.

Rasmussen BH, Edvardsson D (2007) The influence of environment in palliative care: Supporting or hindering experiences of "at-homeness". *Contemporary Nurse* **21**(1): 119–31

Ring ME (2009a) An exploration of the perception of time from the perspective of the science of unitary human beings. *Nursing Science Quarterly* **22**: 8–12

Ring ME (2009b) Reiki and changes in pattern manifestations. *Nursing Science Quarterly* **22**(3): 250–8

Rogers ME (1961) *Educational revolution in nursing*. Macmillan, New York.

Rogers ME (1964) *Reveille in nursing*. F.A. Davis Company, Philadelphia

Rogers ME (1970) *An introduction to the theoretical basis of nursing*. F.A. Davis Company, Philadelphia

Rogers ME (1992) Nursing science and the space age. *Nursing Science Quarterly* **5**(1): 27–34

Rogers ME, Malinski VM, Phillips JR, Manhart EA (1994) Martha E. Rogers: *Her life and her work*. F. A. Davis Company, Philadeplphia

Rushing AM (2008) The unitary life pattern of persons experiencing serenity in recovery from alcohol and drug addiction. *Advances in Nursing Science* **31**(3): 198–210

Sarner 1 (2002) Therapeutic touch. In: Shermer M, Linse P (eds) *The skeptic encyclopaedia of pseudoscience*. ABC-CLIO, California.

Sheehy SB (1999) Emergency care in space: Interview with two astronauts. *Journal of Emergency Nursing* **25**(6): 474–7

Smith LS (2007) Said another way: Is nursing an academic discipline? *Nursing Forum* **35**(1): 25–9

Todaro-Franceschi V (2006) Synchronicity related to dead loved ones as a natural healing modality. *Spirituality and Health International* **7**(3): 151–61

Tomasson RE (1994) Martha Rogers, 79, an author of books on nursing theory [Obituary]. *New York Times* **18 March**: 8

Wald F (2006) Foreword. In: Ferrell BR, Coyle N (eds)

impossible to prove. The assertion that nursing should be regarded as an independent science with its own body of knowledge has been challenged, for instance by Castledine (1995) and others. And she has been accused, with Dolores Krieger (the principal exponent of the practice of therapeutic touch), of promoting a belief system bordering on theosophy (Sarner, 2002). Certainly ' views were radical for their time, but in areas such as healing and spirituality, they still have relevance for contemporary nursing practice (Cox, 2003; Hardin et al., 2003; Cowling, 2008).

Perhaps Rogers will be remembered most for her re-establishment of a world view for nursing which focused on people in their environment rather than disease and treatment (Butcher, 2006; New York University, 1988a). In her 1970 book, she asserted two fundamental assumptions:

Man is a unified whole possessing his own integrity and manifesting characteristics more than and different from the sum of his parts.

and

Man and environment are continuously exchanging matter and energy with one another.

In the 1970s, these assertions contributed to the paradigm shift which Rogers and others achieved. Today, they continue to resonate, particularly in fields of nursing where holistic practice plays a fundamental part.

CHAPTER 20

Margaret Newman

Glenn Marland

Biography

Margaret Newman was born on the 10th of October, 1933 in Memphis Tennessee. She felt a vocational call to nursing inspired by being the primary carer of her mother who had amyotrophic lateral sclerosis (Newman, 2009), a form of motor neurone disease. This experience was developmental (Marchione, 1993); significantly, she observed that her mother, although physically incapacitated, saw herself like any other person and did not regard herself as being ill (Newman, 1986). Newman's first educational qualification after leaving school, however, was a bachelor's degree in Home Economics and English from Baylor University in Waco Texas in 1954 (Marriner-Tomey and Alligood, 2006).

It was not until 1962, when she was 29 years old, that she gained a Bachelor's Degree in Nursing from the University of Tennessee in Memphis (Marriner-Tomey and Alligood, 2006). One year later, she began graduate study in medical/surgical nursing at the University of California in San Francisco, receiving a Masters Degree in 1964 (Newman, 2009). Immediately after, she served in a joint capacity as director of nursing of a clinical research centre and assistant Professor of Nursing at the University of Tennessee in Memphis (Newman, 2009). She then began a decade of teaching and doctoral study at the New York University, gaining a PhD in 1971 (Newman, 2009). During this formative time in the development of her ideas about nursing theory, she was a student and colleague of Martha Rogers, with whom she debated the relationship between health and illness. Eventually, she came to the realisation that both states are manifestations of a single 'unitary' process (Newman, 1986). She was also influenced by Martha Roger's conceptualisation of 'pattern', a term the latter used to sum up the person's unique way of interacting with his or her environment and of the need to see the person as unitary rather than being broken into parts, for example, as in biological systems.

By 1977 she had taken up the post of Professor at Penn State University (Newman, 2009). Her research study in movement, time and consciousness coincided with an invitation to speak at a nursing theory conference in New York in 1978. At this conference her ideas of illness as part of health and the need for nurses to identify the person's 'life pattern' for what it means to that person were first presented (Marchione, 1993). Her theory of Health as Expanding Consciousness also began to take shape (Newman, 2009). By 1979 these ideas had already been published in a book chapter (Newman, 1979). This theory was further developed with the assistance of research students when, in 1984, she took up the position of Nurse Theorist at the University of Minnesota, before retiring from teaching in 1996 (Newman, 2009). Marchione (1993) lists other influences on the continuing genesis of Newman's theory as the biomedical engineer, Itzhak Bentov (1978); the philosopher, Teilhard de Chardin (1959); the physicist, David Bohm (1980); the mathematician, Arthur Young (1976a, 1976b); and the physician, Richard Moss (1981).

Newman has received many honours and accolades. She is a fellow of the American Academy of Nursing, and outstanding alumni of the University of Texas and New York University, where she also gained the Distinguished Scholar Award (Newman, 2009). She gained the Founders' Award for Excellence in Nursing Research from Sigma Theta Tau international and

Profile

Newman is radical in scope and vision, not leaning on conventional concepts of health and disease but courageously breaking new ground. Her theory is extraordinarily prescient of current best practice. Person-centredness, the patient as expert, partnership working and recovery-orientated practice are all echoed in her work.

Key dates

1962   BSc in Nursing from the University of Tennessee in Memphis

1971   Awarded PhD by New York University.

1978   First publicly articulated the ideas which were to form her Theory of Health as Expanding Consciousness at a conference in New York City

1979   Ideas about health published in a book chapter entitled *Towards a theory of health*

2008   Listed as a Living Legend by American Academy of Nursing

Links with other nursing theorists

Newman acknowledges the inspiration of Martha Rogers (*see Chapter 20*), specifically Roger's view of the unitary self and her use of the term 'pattern' to mean individuals' unique ways of interacting with their environment.

the E Louise Grant Award for Nursing Excellence, University of Minnesota (Newman, 2009). In 2008 she was listed as a Living Legend by the American Academy of Nursing and is listed in *Who's who in America* (Marquis, 2009).

Special interest

Newman's distinctive contribution rests in her creation of a grand theory that not only explains nursing but also places nursing in the context of a radical view of health and illness. She calls for a revolution which demands a 180 degree turn in thinking (Newman, 2008). As a grand theory it can only be judged in its own terms. Although she seems to have synthesised ideas from a variety of sources such as Hegel's dialectical fusion of opposites, Young's theory of human evolution, and Bentov's theory of time as a measure of consciousness (Marriner Tomey and Alligood, 1989), the outcome of this synthesis is unique and ground breaking. Her approach is based on a free thinking philosophical analysis, which rejects the taken-for-granted assumptions of health and medicine, but which was nevertheless popularised in 1960s America. So in one sense she was very much a woman of her time. The ideas underpinning her theory, however, have not gone away but persist in modern practice. Perhaps an unease with the dichotomous view of health and illness as opposites is also persisting. The problem though is that when the values of a health theory are judged against conventional medical notions of health they invalidate assumptions such as those underpinning Newman's theory because they are alien and incompatible. In other words it is not congruent with the reality of medicine and therefore may be undervalued.

Summary of writings

Newman's first published work, in the journal *Nursing Forum* in 1966, was entitled 'Identifying patient needs in short span nurse–patient relationships'. She first articulated her ideas about the meaning of health in 1979 in her book *Theory development in nursing*. Her seminal work, *Health as Expanding Consciousness*, was published in 1986 with a second edition in 1994. She now admits (Newman, 2008) that her early writings placed emphasis on control of the environment and separation of concepts and hence unwittingly were influenced by traditional positivistic scientific method. Her most recent book, summing up the potential impact of her theory in practice, was published in 2008 and is entitled *Transforming presence: The difference that nursing makes*. In this book she strives to reflect consistently the dynamic and holistic nature of the theory of Health as Expanding Consciousness. In the preface she recalls part of her speech made at the Nursing Theory Conference in New York in 1978.

> *The responsibility of the nurse is not to make people well or to prevent their getting sick but to assist people to recognise the power that is within them to move to higher levels of consciousness.*
>
> (Newman 2008: xvi)

It is this notion that has come to fulfilment in her later work and has been developed throughout her literary career.

Theory

In order to understand Newman's theory, it is necessary to know about each of the assumptions on which it is based. The focus of her work has been on the meaning of health (Newman, 2005), which forms the cornerstone of

References

Awa M, Yamashita M (2008) Persons' experience of HIV/AIDS in Japan: Application of Margaret Newman's theory. *Authors Journal, International Council of Nurses* 454–61

Bentov I (1978) *Stalking the wild pendulum*. Dutton, New York

Berry D (2004) An emerging model of behavior change in women maintaining weight loss. *Nursing Science Quarterly* **17**(3): 242–52

Bohm D (1980) *Wholeness and the implicate order*. Routledge, London

the theory. Her conceptualisation of health is a radical, even revolutionary departure from the health as opposed to disease model of medicine; it is a new paradigm of health (Newman, 1986). Her views (Newman, 2005), however have emerged from, and are akin to those of Rogers (1970) by whom she was inspired. Rogers saw health and illness as being equal expressions of the life process in a 'unitary' human being. Newman (1986) sees disease and non-disease as reflections of the whole and not as discrete separate entities. Health is a manifestation of the evolving pattern of a person's interaction with his or her environment. The paradigm shift therefore is:

- From treatment of disease symptoms to a search for a pattern.
- From viewing disease as negative to regarding it as part of the self-organising process of expanding consciousness.

To appreciate Newman's conceptualisation of health, therefore, it is necessary to know what she means by 'pattern' and 'health as expanding consciousness'. Each person develops and is constantly developing his or her own unique way of coping with life and navigating through life experiences. This way of coping is not haphazard or random, however, and although it is dynamic it evolves into rhythm and configurations, which become identifiable as patterns (Newman, 1986). Particular events and people may have major significance in these patterns. Pattern consists of relationships with other people and with oneself and the environment (Newman, 2005). Newman particularly emphasises the effect of time on the shaping of these patterns because they are temporal and dynamic in nature. Newman (1986), perhaps inspired by Teilhard de Chardin (1959) and Young (1976a, 1976b), takes this idea further to assume that consciousness, or the pattern of the whole for each individual, is co-existent in the universe from rocks to spirit and from animals to humans.

Newman's concept of health is unconventional and may be counter-intuitive for many. What medicine defines as disease Newman sees as a significant opportunity for new life choices and for the development of a variation of previous patterns of living. It may be that this creates opportunities for increased freedom and awareness of human potential (Newman, 2005). Life is seen as a process of expanding consciousness (Newman, 2005) as originally proposed by Bentov (1978). Each person's unique pattern is his or her consciousness based on life experiences. In this way people are not less whole when they become ill, sick or diseased but will be challenged to cope, that is, to adapt their pattern of living. Pattern is dependent on relationship, for example hydrogen in combination with oxygen produces water, which is different from each of its components (Newman, 2005). In the same way the person's pattern is determined by and dependent on relationships with other people and things. Pattern is dependent on a subjective sense of meaning and therefore is essentially phenomenological. It is the relationships deemed important to each person that shape his or her pattern.

Putting theory into practice

Interestingly, Newman (2005) does not regard her view of nursing as new but one which many experienced nurses may have followed intuitively.

The thing that makes a difference in practice is the caring creative presence of the nurse, in recognising the pattern of the whole.

(Newman 2005: 9)

Newman (2008) describes the nurse as a co-participant in a caring, pattern-recognising relationship with the patient which can become a transforming

of relating in a paradigm of wholeness. *Image: Journal of Nursing Scholarship*

Newman M (2005) Giving Human Health In Picard C (ed) *Giving Voice to what we know.* Th...

Forensic Nursing 01–08

Marchione J (1993) *Margaret Newman: Health as Expanding Consciousness.* Sage Publications, London

Marquis (2009) *Who's Who in America.* Available from: http://www.marquiswhoswho. com [accessed 28th June 2009]

Marriner Tomey A, Alligood M (1989) *Nursing theorists and their work* (2nd edn). Elsevier Health Sciences, St Louis

Marriner Tomey A, Alligood M (2006) *Nursing theorists and their work.* Mosby/Elsevier, St. Louis

Moch SD (1990) Health within the experience of breast cancer. *Journal of Advanced Nursing* 15(12): 1426–35. Available online: Cinahl Plus with Full Text [accessed 8 Feb 2010]

Moss R (1981) *The I that is we.* Celestial Arts, Millbrae CA

Newman M (ed) (1979) *Theory development in nursing.* F. A. Davis, Philadelphia

Newman M (1986) *Health as Expanding Consciousness.* Mosby, St Louis

Newman M (1994) *Health as Expanding Consciousness.* (2nd edn) New York, National League for Nursing Press

Newman M, Sime A, Corcoran-Perry S (1991) The focus of the discipline of nursing. *Advances in Nursing Science* 14(1): 1–6

Newman M (1999) The rhythm

nal of 227–30

aring in the
Experience.
, Jones D (eds)
*oice to what we
: Margaret Newman's
eory of Health as Expanding
Consciousness in nursing edu-
cation, practice and research*
(pp 3–10) Jones and Bartlett.
Sudbury MA

Newman M (2008) *Transforming
presence: The difference that
nursing makes*. FA Davis,
Philadelphia

Newman M (2009) *Health as
Expanding Consciousness*.
Available from: http://
healthasexpandingconscious-
ness.org

Newman MA. Moch SD (1991)
Life patterns of persons with
coronary heart disease. *Nursing
Science Quarterly* 4(4): 161–7

Picard C, Jones D (2005) *Giving
voice to what we Know:
Margaret Newman's Theory
of Health as Expanding
Consciousness in nursing edu-
cation, practice and research*.
Jones and Bartlett, Sudbury,
MA

Rogers M (1970) *An introduction
to the theoretical basis of nursing*. F.A. Davis, Philadelphia

Teilhard de Chardin P (1959) *The
phenomenon of man*. Harper
and Brothers, New York

Vandemark L (2006) Awareness of
self and expanding consciousness: jusing nursing theories to
prepare nurse-therapists.*Issues
in Mental Health Nursing*
27(6): 605–15

Young A (1976a) T*he geometry of
meaning*. Robert Briggs, San
Francisco

Young A (1976b) *The reflexive
universe: Evolution of consciousness*. Robert Briggs, San
Francisco

presence. She also does not see theory, research and practice as separate disciplines but as being inextricably linked by the nurse. This integration is what she refers to as praxis.

The nurse's task initially is to recognise his or her own pattern (Newman, 1986), which can be equated to self-awareness (Vandemark, 2006). The nurse then has to find ways to recognise the person's (patient's) pattern. Newman (2005: 5) gives this example:

It involves connecting with the patient by making very specific observations about the patient's condition (for example, 'you're looking tired')…. On one occasion the only thing I could come up with was, 'Reading the want ads, huh?' The comment opened up a wealth of expressed concerns of the patient about her physical condition and her future job capabilities, concerns that she had not revealed to any other professional because, as she said, 'They didn't ask me.' The comment was personal and specific and said, 'I'm talking to you, buster!' Compare that to the nurse's common greeting to the patient of, 'How are you this morning?'

She also recommends that the North American Nursing Diagnostic Association (NANDA) assessment framework can be used to help pattern identification (Newman, 1986). This framework consists of the dimensions of exchanging, communicating, valuing, relating, choosing, moving, perceiving, feeling and knowing.

A useful worked care plan example is given by Marchione (1993) showing the emerging pattern of Ms X, a patient who first presented with right arm and breast oedema. It is worthwhile to examine this example because it reflects an incomplete and stifled application of Newman's theory bound up in the here and now of the patient's situation. Indeed Marchione (1993) points out that this example, although useful in showing an application of the NANDA framework, gives a snapshot impression and not the assessment of change and movement of pattern over time that matches better with Newman's theory. The initially fuzzy and indistinct impression gained by the nurse of the person's pattern takes shape through time and through continued caring interactions. Nurses may use, for example, a life story approach to elicit pattern and then reflect their impressions back to the person to check for validity. Discussions about significant events and people may also be shown in a diagram giving nurses a visual impression of the patient's story, which can be shared with the patient to seek further clarification and elaboration. Newman (2005) suggests that this kind of process leads to insight which, in turn, will lead to decisions as to what action patients should take to best cope with their current situation.

The timing and pacing of patient–nurse interactions need to show sensitivity to patients and be driven by their needs; and this has been described as the rhythm of the interpersonal relationship (Newman, 1999). The patient may discard old ways of coping and Newman sees this new direction as a manifestation of expanding consciousness. Assessment is based on a knowing of the patient based on a mutual process; a view from within, not a cold and detached clinical knowing from without. The concepts of health and caring are inextricably linked (Newman, 2005). Newman sees caring in the human health experience as the 'true crux of the nursing discipline' (Newman et al., 1991). She regards the concept of caring as dependent on that of health because she sees caring as being about undivided wholeness and transformation towards expanding consciousness with the highest level of consciousness being love (Newman, 2005).

Research based on Health as Expanding Consciousness has concerned either pattern recognition or the identification of critical choice points in a person's life that have led to an unfolding of expanding consciousness

(Newman, 2005). For example, Moch (1990), in a qualitative study of women with breast cancer, found that the women developed an increased sense of closeness and receptivity to others. A study by Newman and Moch (1991) of people with coronary heart disease found that the relationships of participants in the study became more characterised by caring and sensitivity towards others. Newman's approach to research is constructivist, whereby the nurse becomes part of the theory (Newman, 1994). This is another example of an integration being what she describes as 'praxis', a process where the nurse, in relationship with the patient, becomes part of the process (Picard and Jones, 2005).

Influence

Health as Expanding Consciousness has been influential in shaping practice and research but also, more significantly, the integration of nursing theory, research and practice. Many publications in journals and books authored by nurses throughout the world and in a variety of clinical settings, have acknowledged that the work has been guided by the theory of Health as Expanding Consciousness. For example:

- Awa and Yamashita's (2008) work into the experience of HIV/AIDS in Japan.
- Berry's (2004) application of Health as Expanding Consciousness to behaviour change in women maintaining weight loss.
- Hayes and Jones's (2007) application of Health as Expanding Consciousness and pattern recognition in a forensic setting.

Newman's theory has also been inspirational to those who continue to be uneasy and dissatisfied with conventional concepts of health and illness, for example, Baroja's rejection of traditional medicine (Fraser, 2008).

Where to find out more

- http://healthasexpandingcon-sciousness.org

This is Margaret Newman's own website, which is a good, easily accessible primary source.

- Marchione J (1993) *Margaret Newman: Health as Expanding Consciousness*. Sage Publications, London

Marchione's notes are useful for providing worked examples, although her explanation of the Theory of Health as Expanding Consciousness lacks clarity and may be off putting for anyone reading about Newman's work for the first time.

CHAPTER 21

Rosemarie Rizzo Parse

Born
Date unknown

Profile

Parse has contributed greatly to a unique theory of nursing that is grounded in the human sciences and concentrates on the lived experience of the individual and his or her significant others. Parse's Theory of Humanbecoming was not designed as a nursing process, as it does not seek to solve problems. The experience is that of individuals who determine the decisions they wish to make, and the nurse, in harmony with the patient's feelings, may guide the way. The theory espouses person-centredness, quality of life and human dignity as perceived by patients, their families and the wider community.

Key dates

1981 Original theory published in *Man-living-health: A theory for nursing*
1987 The Totality Paradigm and the Simultaneity Paradigm presented
1992 Theory was renamed as the Humanbecoming Theory
1993–2006 Professor at Loyola University Chicago
2001 Lifetime Achievement Award for her contribution to nursing
2007 Became Consulting and Visiting Scholar New York University College of Nusing
1988 Founded *Nursing Science Quarterly*

Rosemarie Rizzo Parse

Angela Kydd

Biography

Rosemarie Parse has a long and illustrious career in nursing theory and practice, research, teaching, administration and writing. She is however most famous for her work as a nurse theorist. She provides a human science, rather than natural science, context for nursing theory, research and practice. Her original theory of Man-Living-Health was first published in the 1980s (Parse, 1981). She has redefined, developed and renamed her work over the years into the Human Becoming Theory (Parse, 1992), and in the late 1990s her theory of Human Becoming evolved into a school of thought (Parse, 1998). Parse founded the Institute of Human Becoming in Pittsburgh, which is an international consortium for Parse scholars, where she runs classes for scholars wishing to have detailed tuition on her theory. She has inspired nurses, student nurses and healthcare professionals to understand people and their universe in a unique way. Further revisions to her work included removing the space between the words human and becoming and her current Humanbecoming Theory was coined (Parse, 2007).

Rosemarie Parse is a Distinguished Professor Emeritus at Loyola University Chicago. She initiated the nursing theory-guided practice expert panel of the American Academy of Nursing, which she chaired in 2007 and is now a Fellow of the organisation. She founded and is the current editor of *Nursing Science Quarterly* which provides a forum for nurse researchers to publish their work on issues pertaining to nursing practice, research and theory development. She is also president of Discovery International which sponsors international nursing theory conferences.

Rosemarie Parse attained a Masters and Doctorate from the University of Pittsburgh and between 1983 and 1993 she was a member of the faculty of the University of Pittsburgh, Dean of the Nursing School at Duquesne University and Professor and Coordinator of the Centre for Nursing Research at Hunter College of the City University of New York. She was Professor at Loyola University Chicago from 1993 to 2006. In January 2007 she became a Consultant and Visiting Scholar at the New York University College of Nursing. She has been a visiting professor at many universities in the United States and around the world.

Throughout her career, Rosemarie Parse has made a tremendous contribution to the profession of nursing. In addition to her Humanbecoming Theory, she has developed her unique 'paradoxical' models of leading–following, teaching–learning, mentoring, and family, that are used worldwide. She has chaired over 30 doctoral dissertations, and provided mentorship to over 100 research students.

Parse is a world renowned speaker who has presented her work at over 300 conferences in more than 30 countries on five continents. Her works have been translated into many languages, and she regularly consults throughout the world on educational programmes in nursing. She also lectures to a wide range of professional disciplines in healthcare settings who are utilising her work as a guide to research, practice, leadership, education and regulation of quality standards.

For such works, Parse has received numerous awards. She has been given two Lifetime Achievement Awards (one from the Midwest Nursing

Research Society and one from the Asian Nurses' Association). In addition she was honoured with the Martha E Rogers Golden Slinky Award by the Society of Rogerian Scholars.

Summary of writings

Parse has researched and published articles in a range of journals on a variety of topics. Examples include qualitative research studies on the lived experiences of health and quality of life; emotions such as hope, contentment, sorrow, and laughter; feelings of being respected, of contentment, and of quality of life; the art of nursing; patients' rights and quality of life for the oldest old and people with dementia. She has also written on research methodologies, leadership, nursing administration and management, the use of language, publishing and building on knowledge through qualitative research.

Parse is also a prolific writer for *Nursing Science Quarterly*, which she founded and of which she is the current editor. The journal gives easy access to the rationale for changes and refinements to her theory, to the wider work she has done and to studies that have followed her Humanbecoming Theory.

Parse also has written the following books:

- *Nursing fundamentals* (1974).
- *Man-Living-Health: A theory of nursing* (The first publication on her theory) (1981).
- *Nursing science: Major paradigms, theories and critiques* (1987).
- *The human becoming school of thought: A perspective for nurses and other health professionals* (1998).
- *Illuminations: The Human Becoming Theory in practice and research* (1995 first edition, 1999).
- *Hope: An international human becoming perspective* (1999).
- *Qualitative inquiry: The path of sciencing* (2001).
- *Community: A human becoming perspective* (2003).

Introduction to the theory

The theory is complex, contains a great deal of newly coined words, is dynamic and continues to be refined. In the 1980s Parse put forward a theory of nursing, and with revisions, refinements and new knowledge, she developed this theory into a research methodology and later into a school of thought. Indeed Parse is in the process of further refining her work and it is therefore not possible to do full justice to this work in one book chapter.

What is possible however is to provide an outline of the original theory and point out the major changes that have occurred since it was first published in 1981. As an introduction to the theory, it is important to point out that as Parse draws heavily on the existential-phenomenology literature in her theory, and uses neologisms (words she has coined or compounded), the language that she uses may be difficult for the uninitiated student. Given that the reader may be new to philosophical and research terminology and in order to make this chapter comprehensible to the novice student, a basic meaning is given for such terminology. In outlining such a complex piece of work in a simplistic manner, much of the philosophical underpinning and reasoning will be missing, but it is hoped that the reader will be inspired to explore the tenets of this work in more detail.

At this stage it may be helpful to briefly define three words relevant to the description of Parse's theory:

- *Ontology*: The underpinning assumptions of a particular viewpoint, paradigm or theory. These assumptions state the fundamental values and beliefs of the proponents of the theory.
- *Epistemology*: The theory of knowledge with a critical look at what constitutes the validity of sources of knowledge within a world view.
- *Methodology*: A systematic way of carrying out a piece of research in order to explore or to explain a phenomenon and/or the procedures and processes used to generate such knowledge.

The reader must be aware that this is a crude way of presenting work, and the translations offered by the author may not be as precise as Parse originally intended. However, the justification of such a method is in the intention. This is purely to present the theory in an easy-to-comprehend manner in order to encourage and inspire the student to follow the recommended reading.

It is also recommended that the student reads *Chapter 19* on Martha Rogers before this chapter, as Parse based her work on the theory put forward by Rogers. A further recommendation is that the student read the section below on application of the theory to practice in order to see how the theory works. Whilst the theory is not easy to comprehend, and Parse does have critics for the complexity of her work (for example, Johnson, 1999), those who have studied her work and used her theory have found that Parse's work has great resonance in both their practice and their studies. It is actually in the examples given below on the application of the theory to practice that the reader can clearly see the benefits of following the Humanbecoming Theory. These examples give credit to the pioneering and unique methods of Rosemarie Parse.

The theory

Parse argues persuasively that nursing is not a natural science (medical model) but a human science. Her theory set out to address the limitations of the traditional

Links with other nursing theorists

Parse's main link with other theorists is with Martha Rogers (*see Chapter 19*). Her theory also has links with Madeleine Leiniger's Culture Care Diversity and Universality Theory (*see Chapter 12*), Jean Watson's Human Caring Theory, Margaret Newman's Theory of Health (*see Chapter 20*), Anne Boykin and Savina Schoenhofer's Nursing as Caring Theory, Mary Jane Smith and Patricia Liehr's Middle Range Theory for Nursing and Tom Kitwood's Person-Centred Care.

Parse is one of the new world view nursing theorists, along with Jean Watson and Martha Rogers.

natural sciences in nursing and to embrace the human sciences. Parse (1981) outlines the limitations of the traditional stance:

- The value priorities of the person are subordinated to a set of norms defined by medical science.
- The nurse rather than the person is considered the expert on health.
- The meaning of the lived experiences is not the focus of nursing.
- The potential contributions of nursing as a unique discipline are not recognised.

The major concepts of Parse's theory are to allow individuals to work in unison with their internal and external environment. In this way each unique individual creates unique patterns (habits, coping behaviours) within themselves and their world or universe (Parse, 1999a). The main role of the nurse is to be there (have a presence, be actively listening to what the individual's hopes and dreams and fears are). Parse's theory addresses the individual and the focus emphasises caring and healing rather than illness (Wesley, 1995). According to Parse, health is more a process of becoming, a unique human lived experience rather than a reaction to external realities.

She first published her theory in 1981 as the Man-Living-Health Theory, which was compiled by building on the work of Rogers (1970) and existential philosophers such as Heidegger, Sartre and Merleau-Ponty. From these influences Parse constructed the nine assumptions that made up her Man-Living-Health Theory, which later evolved into her Humanbecoming Theory. These nine philosophical assumptions formed the ontology of her theory. From these assumptions three major themes or principles emerged; meaning, rhythmicity and transcendence (explained in detail below) and each principle has three related concepts.

All of the nine assumptions include at least one element from Roger's Theory of Unitary Man in conjunction with at least one of the tenets from existentialist philosophy. The focus of existentialism is the human experience, and in synthesising these two bodies of influence, Parse demonstrates the inextricable connection between individuals and their environments; between individuals' construction of health in their worlds and the worlds of others; and individuals' understanding of their freedom to be, and the possibilities they have to become, in a complicated world. The nine assumptions consist of four on being human and five on becoming. Each assumption has three principles and each principle has three related concepts. For an explanatory table, see Parse (2008: 370).

The nine assumptions (Parse, 1999a: 5) are:

1. The human is coexisting whilst co-constructing rhythmical patterns with the universe.
2. The human is an open being, freely choosing meaning in situation, bearing responsibility for decisions.
3. The human is a living unity co-constructing patterns of relating.
4. The human is transcending multidimensionally with the possibilities.
5. Becoming is an open process, experienced by the human.
6. Becoming is a rhythmical co-constructing human–universe process.
7. Becoming is the human's pattern of relating value priorities.
8. Becoming is an intersubjective process of transcending with the possibilities.
9. Becoming is human evolving.

The principles

The assumptions are structured around three principles, each with three concepts, underpinning the assumptions. The principles illustrate the concept of paradox as a fundamental part of being human. Parse (1999a: 6) states that the paradoxes are not problems to be solved but are part of the fundamental rhythm of life. The principles are meaning, rhythmicity, and transcendence.

Principle 1: Meaning

Structuring meaning is the imaging and valuing of languaging.

> *Concepts: Structuring meaning multidimensionally is cocreating reality through [the concepts of] languaging of valuing and imaging.*
>
> (Parse, 1981: 69)

This principle means that people are active in creating what is real for them through self-expression and through living their values in a chosen way. They create meanings based on the present and these meanings can and do change with experiences as new situations arise. Individuals constantly evolve and in doing so expand their possibilities.

Principle 2: Rythmicity

> *Concepts: Cocreating rhythmical patterns of relating is living with the paradoxical unity of [the concepts of] revealing–concealing and enabling–limiting while connecting–separating.*
>
> (Parse, 1981: 69)

This principle means that people live in a rhythm and develop patterns of living as they interact with their environment and others. The patterns are naturally paradoxical and encompass apparent opposites. It means that in living moment-to-moment individuals can show part of themselves in a revealing–concealing manner. They might show a part of themselves as opportunities, and limitations emerge in moving with and apart from others.

Principle 3. Transcendence

> *Concepts: Cotranscending with the possibles is [the concepts of] powering unique ways of originating in the process of transforming.*
>
> (Parse, 1981: 69)

This principle means that moving beyond the here and now moment is forging a unique personal path for oneself in the midst of ambiguity and continuous change.

Development of the Humanbecoming Theory

In 1987 Parse identified the two world views or paradigms of totality (natural science) and simultaneity (human science). The totality paradigm views man as a sum of parts – a bio-psycho-social-spiritual being who adapts to the environment and has health as a state of physical, mental and social well-being. The simultaneity paradigm, initiated in the work of Martha Rogers (1970) and developed by Parse (1987, 1995) emphasises that nursing is a distinct human science. This view holds the person as a unique being in a mutual process with his or her environment, and sees health as a value to that individual. The simultaneity paradigm stresses that the individual is much more than a sum of parts. Parse utilises a creative synthesis of existentialism (the human experience – in that human existence is given – but what individuals make of it – their essence – is up to them)

References

Daly J (1999) The lived experience of suffering. In Parse R (ed) *Illuminations: The Human Becoming Theory in practice and research* (pp.243–68). Jones and Bartlett Publishers and National League for Nursing, Sudbury Massachusetts

Edwards S (2000) Critical review of RR Parse's the humanbecoming school of thought. A perspective for nurses and other health professionals. *Journal of Advanced Nursing* **30**(8): 532–7

Johnson M (1999) Observations on positivism and pseudoscience in qualitative nursing research. *Journal of Advanced Nursing* **30**(1): 67–73

McCarthy C, Aquino-Russell C (2009) A comparison of two nursing theories in practice: Peplau and Parse. *Nursing Science Quarterly* **22**(1): 34–40

McKenna H (1997) *Nursing theories and models*. Routledge, London

Parker M (2001) *Nursing theories and nursing practice*. Davies, Philadelphia

Parse R (1974) *Nursing fundamentals*. Medical Examination, Flushing, New York

Parse R (1981) *Man-Living-Health: A theory of nursing*. Wiley, New York

Parse R (1987) *Nursing science: Major paradigms, theories and critiques*. Saunders, Philadelphia

Parse R (1992) Human Becoming: Parse's theory of nursing. *Nursing Science Quarterly* **5** (1): 35–42

Parse RR (ed) (1995) *Illuminations: The human becoming theory in practice and research*. National League for Nursing Press, New York

Parse R (1998) *The Human Becoming School of Thought: A perspective for nurses and other health professionals*. Sage Publications, London

Parse R (ed) (1999a) *Illuminations: The Human Becoming Theory in practice and research* (2nd edn) Jones and Bartlett Publishers and National League for Nursing, Sudbury Massachusetts

Parse R (1999b) *Hope: An international human becoming perspective*. Jones and Bartlett, Boston

Parse R (2001) *Qualitative inquiry: The path of sciencing*. Jones and Bartlett Publishers and National League for Nursing, Sudbury Massachusetts

and phenomenology (the individual's lived experience as seen through their eyes) to justify her theory as unique for nursing (Sarter, 2004).

Further changes took place in 1992 as Parse changed her terminology. The name of the theory was officially changed to the Human Becoming Theory. The word man was removed after the change in the dictionary definition of the word from its former meaning of 'humankind', and the word 'human' was substituted. The word 'health' was substituted by the word 'becoming' and Parse also replaced the word 'environment' with the word 'universe'. Parse's Human Becoming Theory was grounded in the original nine assumptions of her theory, but she refined and redefined some of her original works to include a research methodology. Human becoming reflected living a human life. That is, through living, one is becoming. No other aspects of the theory were changed, but the assumptions underpinning the research methodology were specified for the first time (Parse, 1992).

There are three principles to the practice methodology, and these come from the original three principles, which in 1998 came with reframed language; illuminating meaning, synchronising rhythms and mobilising transcendence (Parse, 1998). Further revisions from 1998 onwards (Parse, 2008) involved removing the space between the words and the Humanbecoming school of thought was created.

The ontological stance of Parse's research methodology

- Humans are indivisible. They cannot be broken in a sum of parts. Humanbecoming means that individuals freely choose personal meaning with their situation, living experiences and their prioritised values.
- Humans are unpredictable. Humanbecoming involves the individual configuring rhythmical patterns of relating with their humanuniverse (or world).
3. Humans are ever changing. Humanbecoming involves individuals cotranscending illimitably (going beyond boundaries) in order to encounter emerging possibilities.

Parse highlights the complexity and uniqueness of each individual. Individuals gain meaning from their experiences of the world, the rhythmical patterns of living with paradoxes and the cotranscending, or going beyond the actual, to an understanding of what can be. How individuals react to circumstances cannot be predicted and this is why nurses need to listen to patients to find out what is going on for them at that point in their lives. Individuals are forever changing as they participate with their universe whilst shaping and creating their own way of being (Parse, 2007).

Whilst the model seems complex on the first introduction to this work, further reading, such as Edwards (2000) and McCarthy and Aquino-Russell (2009) will serve to provide more detail on the humanbecoming school of thought and practice methodology.

Criticisms

All nursing theorists have their critics; reviews of the criticisms levied are provided in an excellent book by McKenna (1997). Such criticisms include that there are too many nursing theories; nurses cannot, nor should have to know all of them; the jargon used is rife within theories, making them hard to understand; and American theories are not always transferable to the UK. Yet some believe that complexity is essential for work to be significant with McKenna (1997) stating that the works of Rogers, Parse and Newman provide a radical view of nursing within the simultaneity paradigm. The view is radical in that there is no optimum health, health is how one experiences and copes with the experiences of personal living. Therefore the goals of nursing centre on quality of life from the individual's perspective.

Putting theory into practice

Parse's Humanbecoming Theory is not easily understood until applied to practice. The accounts of Parsian nurses below illustrate how much richer and rewarding the process of nursing and/or nursing research can be when using the Humanbecoming Theory. In being in the presence of the individual and trying to see the world from his or her stance, the actions and interactions between both the nurse and the individual take on a new meaning and serve to eradicate the unequal power base of the powerful nurse/accepting patient relationship. In addition, the theory enables the nurse and/or the researcher to explore behaviours that cannot be classified as in the totality paradigm because the issue is more than just a 'biopsychosocioculturalspiritual being' who can be understood by studying the parts. The focus of the simultaneity paradigm is much greater than the sum of its parts.

To understand this in a more meaningful way, it is useful to discuss the works of nurses and researchers who have used Parse's theory and methodology.

One example comes from the work of Daly (1999) who studied the experience of suffering. He gives a detailed account of how Parse's research methodology suited the nature of the topic he wanted to explore – how people cope with suffering. He identified nine propositions which emerged from the study, and from these three core concepts were extracted:

Paralyzing anguish with glimpses of precious possibilities
Entanglements of engaging–disengaging
Struggling in pursuit of fortification

(Daly, 1999:253)

The core concepts serve to highlight how individuals find meaning, live rhythmical patterns of paradoxes and looks for possibilities within their lives at any given time.

A second example by Welch (2004) gives a beautifully written account of how he discovered the works of Parse as he struggled to find a research method for his doctoral study on depression in Australian men. He clearly identifies the difficulties he had in trying to utilise the Parsian theory and he decided to apply to the Institute of Human Becoming in Pittsburgh to learn about the theory. He stated that the Humanbecoming Theory appealed to him, but he struggled initially because he found he retained a focus on the depression and not the day-to-day living of the individuals as they managed their lives. He also had problems with the theory as he felt he was 'drowning in thick descriptions densely packed with meaning that was beyond my reach' (Welch, 2004: 204). However, Welch goes on to say that as he studied the theory in detail and learned from both Parse and her Parsian scholars, he realised that in 'being' with his participants, rather than asking them questions about their depression, he could witness

...the rhythms of their stories of joy amid sorrow, hope surfacing with despair, disquiet with serenity, aloneness with togetherness, and struggle with resolve to endure. I marvelled silently at the power of stories to convey...the complexities and ambiguities of human existence.

(Welch, 2004: 205)

A third example is taken from Parse's international study on hope (Parse,

Parse R (2003) *Community: A human becoming perspective*. Jones and Bartlett Publishers and National League for Nursing, Sudbury Massachusetts

Parse R (2007) The humanbecoming school of thought in 2050. *Nursing Science Quarterly* **20**(4): 308–11

Parse R (2008) The humanbecoming leading–following model. *Nursing Science Quarterly* **21**(4): 369–75

Pearson A ,Vaughan B, Fitzgerald M (2003) *Nursing models for practice* (2nd edn) Butterworth Heinemann, Edinburgh

Reed G, Shearer N, Nicoll L (2004) *Perspectives on nursing theory* (4th edn) Lippincott Williams & Wilkins, London

Rogers M (1970) *An introduction to the theoretical basis of nursing*. Davis, Philadelphia

Sartar B (2004) Philosophical sources of nursing theory. In: Reed G, Shearer N, Nicoll L (eds) *Perspectives on nursing theory* (4th edn, pp 305–20) Lippincott Williams & Wilkins, London

Upright C (2009) *Exploring persons' experiences of keeping in touch with loved ones who have died*. A thesis submitted in partial fulfilment of the requirements for the Degree of Master of nursing in policy and practice. Faculty of Human and Social Development, University of Victoria, Canada.Available from: www.nursing.uvic.ca/research/documents/Upright_Christine.pdf [Accessed on October 31st 2009]

Welch A (2004) The researcher's reflection on the research process. *Nursing Science Quarterly* **17**(3): 201–7

Wesley R (1995) *Nursing theories and models* (2nd edn) Springhouse Corporation, Pennsylvania

Where to find out more

Books

Every major book on nursing theories and models cites Parse's work. Examples include:
- Wesley (1995)
- McKenna (1997)
- Reed et al. (2004)

for a brief overview
- Pearson et al. (2003)
- Parker (2001)

for more detailed accounts. However, for an in depth exploration of both the theory and how this can be instigated in practice:
- *Illuminations: The Human Becoming Theory in practice and research* (Parse, 1999a)

Journal

Additional information on the practical use of the theory in research can be found in articles in
- *Nursing Science Quarterly*.

Websites

- http://www.humanbecoming. org
- http://www.nurses.info/nurs-ing_theory_person_parse_rose-marie.htm
- http://www.discovery internationalonline.com

1999b). This work answered critics who state that qualitative research cannot be generalisable to whole populations and can only be used to gain insights into the specific population studied. Parse took the ontological stance of her research methodology that humans are indivisible, unpredictable and everchanging to collect and collate five insights about human experiences from 13 studies conducted in nine different countries.

A fourth practical application is from a doctoral thesis by Upright (2009) who sought a method to explore the phenomenon of keeping in touch with loved ones who have died. In her rationale for selecting Parse's methodology, Upright stated that in interviewing bereaved people about how they maintained communication with someone dear who has died, requires the researcher to engage with participants by listening to their stories about their experiences. Such a method cannot be divided into parts, and the results will be more than merely the sum of the parts (Upright, 2009). Initially, Upright (2009) felt that her work would be impossible, but it demonstrated the connectedness bereaved people still felt with their lost loved one who had died. She used a descriptive, exploratory methodology and within the framework of the Humanbecoming Theory, she focused on the experiences of individuals who kept in touch in some way with a person who had died. Her study served to recommend to nurses and nurse teachers that whilst end of life was addressed as a topic, it was and is an ongoing process for some individuals and that continued connectedness with a dead loved one is a consoling and deeply personal experience.

Influences

The influences of any work are fascinating. Unravelling influences can be pure conjecture unless verified by the architect of the work in discussion. Parse has many acknowledged influences, the first being the work of Martha Rogers (1970) on which her theory is mostly based (see *Chapter 19*). The principles and concepts she has adapted from Roger's works are the principles of helicy, complementality and resonancy, and the concepts of energy field, openness, pattern and organisation, and four-dimensionality (for details see *Chapter 19*). The concepts and tenets from existential phenomenology come from the influences of Heidegger, Sartre and Merleau-Ponty. Coconstitution, coexistence and situated freedom are the concepts, and the tenets are intentionality and human subjectivity (Pearson et al., 2003).

Tracing the influences back, Martha Rogers is reported to have had many influences for her Unitary Human Beings Model from an eclectic set of disciplines, namely anthropology, psychology, sociology, astronomy, religion, philosophy, history, biology, physics, mathematics and literature (Wesley, 1995).

Section Five

What do you want me to do to help?

Working in partnership

Overview

The idea that nursing entails *doing* something to somebody was introduced and examined in the first three sections. The detail of what that may be was further expanded in the grand theories of Section Four. This section alters the focus again by putting the recipient of care at the centre of investigation. Instead of doing things to people, these theorists aim to do things with them. Instead of caring for people, they care about them. The distinction is subtle and potentially confusing. Often, in order to care about people, you may have to care for them. The difference is foundational however. For these theorists interventions are not seen as ends in themselves but steps on a journey of recovery.

Again a disclaimer is required at this point. It should be remembered that all the theorists discussed so far in this book would most likely agree that the interventions they propose are steps on the road to recovery. They would also broadly agree that the person should be at the centre of care. It is only for the purpose of structuring an overall text that the theorists have been separated in this way. However, the theorists discussed in this section have explicitly put the person at the centre of their models and have developed theory from this starting point. This is what distinguishes them.

Ida Orlando

Ida Orlando begins the section. Her theory is interesting as the underpinning philosophy is arguably more behaviourist than the others discussed here. Her language is very much that of stimulus and response, directing the nurse–patient relationship towards the elimination of need. Boyd Thomson explains that this is only part of the process, however. Reflection plays a significant role and Orlando's theory is founded on the centrality of the person in need. Good nursing follows structured recognition and reaction to this principle. Thomson makes clear the links between Orlando's 'dynamic nurse–patient phenomenon' and the broader person-centred care movement.

Imogene King

Imogene King also has partnership at the heart of her theory. Billy Mathers describes that the essence of her theory entailed the nurse and patient working together to define and reach goals that they set together. Mathers illustrates this process through case study examples. He also shows how King attempted to extend partnership principles beyond nursing by creating a common language among all nurses that would enhance the wider multidisciplinary process. It is interesting that, like Casey in *Chapter 25*, King chose classification to do this, as there can be a tendency to assume that classification is the antithesis of person centred care. Both King and Casey demonstrate that this is not so.

Moyra Allen

Moyra Allen extends the principle of person-centred care to the unit of the family. That is, she sees the base unit of partnership as the family, not the individual. Kathleen Duffy describes Allen's enduring impact on Canadian nursing. Again it can be seen that Allen is as much inspirational leader as theorist. Allen had a clear vision of how nursing should go forward. Instead of accepting the general view at the time that nursing should expand its medical role, Allen instead saw the role of the nurse as promoting healthy development of families throughout their life span. This health promotion agenda was research based and founded on clear theoretical ideas of health, family, learning and collaboration. This credibility was extended as her own research provided clear evidence that utilising her model was more beneficial than not.

Anne Casey

The power of evidence is further demonstrated by Anne Casey. Like Allen, Casey embraced a series of concepts that had been developing over the previous years and integrated them into 'family-centred care', now considered to be the central tenet of children's nursing. Most of the literature underpinning her ideas was North American, but she adapted the ideas for the UK and then demonstrated their efficacy. Raymond Duffy tells us how her theory developed and, like Allen, shows how the central unit of the family provides the base unit of effective nursing: 'the care of children, well or sick, is best carried out by their families with varying degrees of help from suitably qualified members of the healthcare team whenever necessary' (Casey, 1988).

Hildegard Peplau

Hildegard Peplau asked difficult questions of the nursing profession. To this end she rejected questions of what is it that nurses do now, but rather questioned what nurses could do in the future. She clearly saw nursing as a work in progress with a continual need to look forward. Phil Barker includes Peplau as one of the major influences on his own theory and she is referred to as the 'ship's surgeon' in the book on the Tidal Model. Margaret Brown tells us that the term is used to indicate her quick wit and ability to reach incisively the crux of an intellectual argument. Peplau's theory examines the development and maintenance of the nurse–patient relationship, the roles of the nurse and how nurses can learn about nursing. She described the key elements in nursing as 'the nurse, the patient and what goes on between them'. The development and maintenance of the nurse–patient relationship depends on the nurse understanding the importance of these elements. Margaret Brown articulates these elements and provides clear evidence as to why Peplau's theory of interpersonal nursing still underpins much of what is good about nursing today.

Philip Barker

Phil Barker is probably the most influential mental health nurse in the Western world at present. His Tidal Model, developed in conjunction with Poppy Buchanan Barker, underpins the ideas inherent in recovery that are taught to all UK undergraduate mental health nurses. Allan Donnell describes Barker's theory in the final chapter. The Tidal Model was developed from a four year study at Newcastle University on the 'need for nursing'. This study sought to answer the question, 'What are psychiatric nurses needed for?' The answer is best articulated here by Donnell, who uses the power of metaphor to illustrate Barker's use of it. A summary does not do the theory justice, but the following core beliefs are central:

- Recovery is possible.
- Change is inevitable.
- Ultimately people know what is best for them.
- Persons possess all the resources they need to begin the recovery journey.

- The person is the teacher and we, the helpers, are the pupils.
- We need to be creatively curious to learn what needs to be done to help the person.

In the Tidal Model people are the experts on their problems of living and the nurse's role is to provide an environment in which healing can happen.

Reference

Casey A (1988) A partnership with child and family. *Senior Nurse* **8**(4): 8–9

CHAPTER 22

Ida Orlando
Boyd Thomson

Profile

Ida Orlando has motivated the development of patient-centered care through her paradigm 'The dynamic nurse–patient phenomenon'. This paradigm echos contemporary work by Carl Rogers and has a strong resonance with current developments in values-based care, a tidal model approach and the development of a dynamic reflective practicioner.

Key dates

1947	Diploma in Nursing, New York Medical College
1951	BSc Public Health, Teachers College, Columbia University, New York
1954	MA Teachers College, Columbia University, New York
1958	Appointed Associate Professor Yale, New Haven, CT
1950s	Development of the dynamic nurse–patient phenomenon
1961	Publication of *The Dynamic Nurse–Patient Relationship*
1962	Appointed Director of Research, McLean Hospital, Belmont, MA
1972	Publication of *The Discipline and Teaching of the Nursing Process*
1972	Appointed Board Member, Harvard Community Health Plan

Biography

Ida Orlando developed her theory of a dynamic nurse–patient phenomenon in the 1950s following research on the concept of the integration of mental health into the basic nurse curriculum at Yale University. Born of Italian descent in 1926, Orlando was a first generation American. Following her school education she attended the New York Medical College (Lower 5th Avenue Hospital School of Nursing) attaining her Diploma in Nursing. Continuing her academic studies she attended St John's University, Brooklyn, New York where she attained a BSc in Public Health Nursing and an MA in Mental Health Nursing from Teachers College, Columbia University, New York.

Orlando became an Associate Professor at Yale School of Nursing with the post of Director of the Graduate Program in Mental Health Psychiatric Nursing. It was whilst in this post at Yale that she became project investigator for a National Institute of Mental Health grant entitled 'Integration of mental health concepts in a basic nursing curriculum'. From this research her theory/paradigm of the dynamic nurse–patient phenomenon was developed appearing in publication in her 1961 book, *The dynamic nurse–patient relationship*. She moved to the post of Director of a research project entitled 'Two systems of nursing in a psychiatric hospital' at McLean Hospital in Belmont, Massachusetts where she continued the development of her theory. The results of this research and its impact on the developing theory are contained in her 1972 book, *The discipline and teaching of nursing processes*. Following completion of this work, Orlando held many different positions in the Boston area, being married to Robert Pelletier and living in Boston. These posts included being a board member of Harvard Community Health Plan and serving as both a national and international consultant. She was a frequent lecturer and conducted numerous seminars on the nursing process. Orlando's work and theory are still commonly used in nursing schools in America. Although less well known and utilised in the UK, her model has a strong resonance with much of current thinking in nursing, in particular mental health nursing, and the care approaches emanating from this. A sad loss to nursing, she died on November 28th, 2007.

The dynamic nurse–patient phenomenon

Orlando's paradigm of this phenomenon came from observations she recorded of interactions between nurses and patients. In trying to categorise these interactions she found that this could only be done under the headings of 'good' or 'bad' nursing. Reflecting on this she identified that both the formulations for 'good' and 'bad' nursing were contained in the records (Orlando, 1961). From these observations she formulated the deliberative nursing process.

Orlando's paradigm focuses around the context of a dynamic nurse-patient phenomenon highlighted through key concepts such as: patient behaviour, nurse response, nurse action and patient reaction (*Figure 22.1*).

A key factor in the model is the differentiation between actions carried out by nurses, which are automatic and designed to meet service needs, protocols or directives, and those that are aimed at individualised, person-centred identification of specific patient needs leading to an integrated, reciprocal care provision system. Orlando proposed that this system consisted of three key stages.

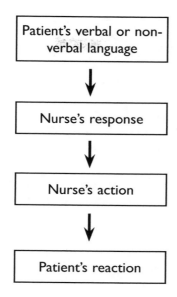

Figure 22.1. The dynamic nurse-patient phenomenon.

Stage 1: The nursing process is set in motion by the patient's behaviour

All patient behaviour, verbal (a patient's use of language) or non-verbal (includes paralinguistics, physiological symptoms, motor activity, and nonverbal communication), no matter how insignificant, must be considered an expression of a need for help and should be validated. If a patient's behaviour is not effectively assessed by the nurse then a major problem in giving care would arise, leading to a nurse–patient relationship failure. Over time, it becomes more difficult to establish rapport with the patient if behaviour is not determined. Communicating effectively is vital to achieve the patient's cooperation in regaining health.

Stage 2: The patient's behaviour stimulates a nurse reaction

In this stage, the beginning of the nurse–patient relationship takes place. It is important to correctly evaluate the behaviour of the patient using the following nurse reaction steps to achieve a positive feedback response from the patient. The steps are:

- The nurse perceives a behaviour.
- The perception leads to an automatic thought.
- The thought produces an automatic feeling.
- The nurse shares reactions with the patient to ascertain whether the perceptions are accurate or inaccurate.

The nurse consciously deliberates about personal reactions and patient input in order to produce professional deliberative actions based on objective assessment rather than automatic reactions.

Stage 3. Critical consideration of ways of implementing the nurse's action

When providing care, nursing action can be either automatic or deliberative.

Automatic reactions stem from nursing behaviours that are performed to satisfy a service requirement, protocol or directive rather than the patient's need for help. For example, the nurse who gives medication to a patient because it is ordered by the physician, without seeking consent or discussing the need for the medication with the patient, is engaging in automatic, non-deliberative behaviour. The reason for giving the medication has more to do with following medical orders (automatically) than with the patient's immediate expressed need for help.

Deliberative reaction is a 'disciplined professional response'. It can be argued that all nursing actions aimed at helping a client could be considered deliberative. However, correct identification of actions from the nurse's assessment should be determined to achieve reciprocal help between nurse and patient. The aim is to promote concordance and partnership rather than mere compliance without involvement. The following criteria should be considered.

- Deliberative actions result from the correct identification of patient needs by validation of the nurse's reaction to patient behaviour.
- The nurse explores the meaning of the action with the patient and its relevance to meeting his or her need.
- The nurse validates the action's effectiveness immediately after compelling it.
- The nurse is freed from extraneous influences unrelated to the patient's need.
- Reflective evaluation to determine if the action helped the client by addressing the need as determined by both the nurse and the client in the immediate situation is essential.

(Orlando, 1972)

This is represented in *Figure 22.2*:

From this it is clear that Orlando proposes a number of paradigm concepts:

- Uniqueness of individual communication.
- An individual's abilities to meet his or her needs is not a constant state but is variable at different times and in different circumstances.
- Being without emotional or physical discomfort contributes to a healthy state.
- A sense of well-being contributes to a healthy state.

- Repeated experiences of feeling helped rather than isolated culminate in a greater improvement.
- Within nursing contact, both nurse and patient will perceive, think, feel and respond in the immediate situation. However previous experience can impact on this.
- Any aspect of care, if done automatically, even though its intention is to be therapeutic, can be distressing to the patient.

(George, 2002)

Orlando proposes therefore that nursing is a distinct profession

...providing direct assistance to individuals in whatever setting they are found for the purpose of avoiding, relieving, diminishing, or curing the individual's sense of helplessness.

(Orlando, 1972)

The role of the nurse is to find out and meet the patient's immediate need for help. The patient's presenting behaviour may be a plea for help. However, the help needed may not be what it appears to be to the nurse. Nurses require to use their perception, thoughts about the perception, or the feelings engendered from their thoughts to explore with patients the meaning of their behaviour. This process helps the nurse discover the nature of the distress and, objectively, what help the patient needs (Schmieding, 2002). Orlando's theory continues to be an effective practice theory by keeping the nurse's focus on the patient. It is clear, concise, and easy to use whilst providing the overall framework for nursing. However, it does not preclude the use of other theories in the care of the patient.

Professional nursing is therefore conceptualised as finding out and meeting the client's immediate need for help, reacting to this in an explorative, reflective, reciprocal way to meet that need and minimising mental and physical distress whilst promoting a sense of partnership and hope.

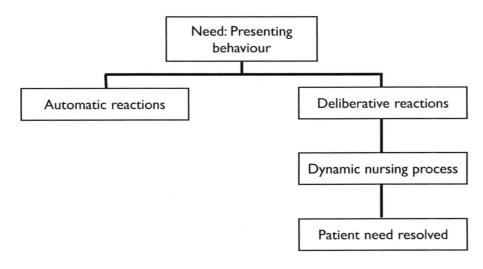

Figure 22.2. Orlando's deliberative reaction.

Table 22.1. Synergy between patient-centred care and the dynamic nurse–patient phenomenon

Patient-centred care	Dynamic nurse–patient phenomenon
Compassion, empathy and responsiveness to needs, values and expressed preferences	Uniqueness of individual communication. Repeated experiences of feeling helped rather than isolated culminate in a greater improvement
Information, communication and education	An individual's ability to meet his or her needs is not a constant state but is variable at different times and in different circumstances. Any aspect of care if done automatically, even though its intention is to be therapeutic, can be distressing to the patient
Physical comfort	Being without physical discomfort contributes to a healthy state
Emotional support, relieving fear and anxiety	Being without emotional discomfort contributes to a healthy state. A sense of well-being contributes to a healthy state. Any aspect of care if done automatically, even though its intention is to be therapeutic, can be distressing to the patient

Links to practice

One key development that mirrors Orlando's thoughts is that of patient-centred care. Although it has many definitions, one of the most widely well accepted is produced by the Institute of Medicine who propose it to be

...providing care that is respectful of and responsive to individual patient preferences, needs and values and ensuring that patient values guide all clinical decisions.

(Institute of Medicine, 2001)

This is in agreement with Orlando's core concept of the correct, validated identification of the patient's individual problems as being essential in the resolution of patient needs. The synergy between these two approaches clearly identifies that the foundation of best practice is built on the twin edifices of being mindful of the patient's lived experience and validating needs and nursing actions. This synergy can be seen in *Table 22.1*.

Both these approaches indicate the need for a reflective system through which an unbiased and non-assuming approach is facilitated, thereby negating the tendency of nurses to be dependent on paternalistic and habitual practice. It empowers patients, allowing them to determine their own needs, and encourages reflection, self-awareness and personal and professional growth in the nurses who participate in it (Ellis, 1999). Inappropriate care stems from an emphasis on system processes at the expense of the uniqueness of the individual patient (Peraino, 2005). The patient must be viewed as the centre of our activity. The patient's satisfaction is the goal of both patient-centred care and the dynamic nurse–patient phenomenon. If the test or treatment is right for that individual patient, with whatever problem, as opposed to that for all patients with a particular diagnosis, then quality care underpinned by these approaches will be achieved.

Orlando's work, although developed in the 1950s, gives clear rationales for what is viewed as the quintessence of current best practice.

Closely related to this is the area of person-centred care. At the time when Orlando was developing her paradigm, in 1957, Carl Rogers was developing and writing his contemporary work on the core conditions which were required to bring about therapeutic change. Rogers' approach was a radical departure from the authoritarian assumption that professional experts could and should help by solving others' problems for them, with the expectation that clients would then somehow be better able to solve their own problems (Rogers, 1957). This again resonates well with Orlando as it proposes the move away from automatic actions based on authoritarian practice to the more reciprocal, validated deliberative actions that recognise the person as the central focus of care. Rogers identified three key concepts in his work, these being:

Empathy: Rogers proposed that if this condition is in place the counsellor is '... experiencing an accurate, empathic understanding of the client's awareness of his own experience.' He stressed the importance of the counsellor showing this understanding to the client. This is in direct agreement with the theory of deliberative actions proposed by Orlando where the nurse explores patients' perceptions of their problems and validates their understandings arising from this.

Unconditional positive regard: This means that the counsellor is accepting and absolutely non-judgemental of the client. Rogers said the counsellor is accepting of all the parts of the client; it is the opposite of saying 'You are bad in these ways, good in those.' It is completely unconditional in that there is no element of, 'I only like you if you are thus and so...' Again this is very similar to the approach required when exploring the patient's behaviours/needs as proposed by Orlando.

Congruence: Rogers defined this as meaning that the counsellor, in the confines of the therapeutic relationship, is a 'congruent, genuine and integrated person'. He said it means that counsellors do not either intentionally

Links with other nursing theorists

Ida Orlando's work has links with Philip Barker (*see Chapter 27*).

References

Barker P, Barker PB (2005) *The Tidal Model. A guide for mental health profession-als*. Brunner Routledge Paul, Sussex

Brooker D (2004) What is person centred care for people with dementia? *Journal of Dementia Care* **9**(3): 33–7

Ellis S (1999) The patient-centred care model: Holistic/multi-professional/reflective care. *British Journal of Nursing* **8**(5): 296–301

George JB (2002) Nursing process ciscipline: Ida Jean Orlando. In George JB (ed) *Nursing theories: The base for professional nursing practice* (5th edn, pp 189pp 189-208208). Prentice Hall, Upper Saddle River, New Jersey

Institute of Medicine (2001) Crossing the quality chasm: A new health system for the 21st Century. In Moon J (ed) *Reflection in learning and professional development: Theory and practice*. Kogan Page, London

Moon JA (1999) *Reflection in learning and professional development: Theory and practice*. Routledge Falmer, London

or unintentionally hide behind a façade or front; that they actually are the person they are feeling themselves to be at the time. This is in agreement with Orlando's proposal that the best care is derived from the relationship between nurse and patient and not from automatic actions (Rogers, 1957).

The work of Rogers was more recently developed by Brooker (2004) who elaborated on the definition of the core concepts of PCA as:

- Respecting and valuing the individual as a full member of society.
- Providing individualised places of care that are in tune with people's changing needs.
- Understanding the perspective of the person.
- Providing a supportive social psychology in order to help people live a life where they can experience relative well-being.

These in many ways mirror the ideas contained in Orlando's work revolving around the concepts of uniqueness, the changing nature of need, the effect of relationships and actions and the centrality of the person.

A key link of Orlando's work to current practice is that of the drive towards a recovery focus of care and the development of value-based practice, particularly in the field of mental health nursing. The values base for mental health nursing contains, amongst other elements:

- Relationships supported by good communication skills at the heart of practice and maximising time to build relationships and challenging systems that detract from this. This would appear to be in line with Orlando's development of deliberative reactions and the need for shared reflections.
- Respect for diversity of values and placing the values of individual users at the centre of practice. This is, again, a clear link to the development of deliberative reactions. Listening to what people say and not basing practice on assumptions about what people need, and seeing the person as the 'expert' in his or her experience. This is a clear reflection of Orlando's ideas on establishing correctly the patient's problems.
- Promoting recovery and inspiring hope – building on people's strengths and aspirations. This can be connected to the variation in people's ability to deal with their needs and the promotion of self-worth as identified by Orlando

Values-based practice means:

- Working in a positive and constructive way with differences and diversity of values.
- Putting the values, views and understandings of individual service users and carers at the centre of everything we do.
- Understanding and using our own values and beliefs in a positive way.
- Respecting the values of the other people we work with and being open and receptive to their views.

(Nurse Education for Scotland, 2007)

These can all be directly linked to the explorative, reflective and reciprocal elements of Orlando's dynamic nurse–patient phenomenon.

Another key link to the developments in practice is the close affinity between Orlando's paradigm and key elements of the Tidal Model for Nursing developed by Phil Barker (Barker and Barker, 2005) (*Chapter 27*).

The Tidal Model is a philosophical approach that focuses on a journey of discovery of mental health for a client in partnership with his or her nurse.

It involves listening to people, and identifying in their own words some of the meaning of their lives (Barker and Barker, 2005). This is in synergy with Orlando's work where problem identification and deliberative actions are identified and shared goals set in a consultative partnership between nurse and patient. The Tidal Model emphasises that the discovery of mental health for an individual is a unique experience as its meaning varies from one person to another. The aim is that people will discover what mental health means for them – as unique persons. This is in agreement with the uniqueness of the dynamic nurse–patient phenomenon for each patient as reflected in its elements of the uniqueness of individual communication and an individual's ability to meet his or her needs not being a constant state but variable at different times and in different circumstances. The Tidal Model recognises that 'quality' nursing care focuses on a special kind of relationship with users and their families. The person's needs change from day to day and problems are not fixed. Problems of living are fluid and changeable (Barker, 2000). Effective care needs to be based on a realisation of the changing nature of people and their life circumstances, a key focus of the dynamic nurse–patient phenomenon. Both of these approaches have arisen from studies of the power relationship between nurses and the people in their care. Both have sought to define how nurses might help empower users and carers and to clarify what kind of 'care' people need from nurses.

Currently in nursing and nurse education a major emphasis is on developing a more reflective approach to care provision in order to develop an environment conducive to the growth of dynamic nursing. Moon (1999) defines this reflective practice as being

...a set of abilities and skills, to indicate the taking of a critical stance, an orientation to problem solving or state of mind.

It is appropriate to recognise here that this key need for reflection, appropriate problem solving and a change of mindset from automatic actions were all recognised as essential concepts by Orlando in the development of her paradigm. In this Orlando recognised in the 1950s what others wrote about in the 1990s that practice is more than just knowing, it requires understanding as it occurs in situations of uncertainty (Moon, 1999). These meta-cognitive skills allow analysis, synthesis, critical judgement and evaluation – the key aims that Orlando desired from her dynamic nurse–patient phenomenon. Both Orlando and Donald Schön (1983), a key writer on reflection, agree that approaches to care require thinking again, in a new way, about a problem we have encountered.

Although Orlando's paradigm was developed around 50 years ago much of contemporary nursing practice developments resonate strongly with the core values of her work by placing communication and the patient at the centre of good professional nursing. Currently these approaches are seen as being at the heart of quality improvement and the achievement of best possible individual outcomes for the patient.

Ida Orlando was in many ways ahead of her time. Her work was developed within a background of medically orientated, autocratic, often authoritarian practice and challenged the nursing profession to think and act in an entirely new way. Her work, although not always recognised, has had a major influence on developments in care and is now at the forefront in terms of concept base of what is viewed as professional best practice.

Nurse Education for Scotland (2007) *The 10 essential shared capabilities for mental health practice. Learning materials (Scotland).* NHS Scotland

Orlando IJ (1961) *The dynamic nurse-patient relationship.* National League for Nursing, Atlanta, GA

Orlando IJ (1972) *The discipline and teaching of nursing processes.* Sage, Thousand Oaks California

Peraino RA (2005) *The consumer's guide to medical mistakes.* Vantage Press, New York

Rogers C (1957) The necessary and sufficient conditions of therapeutic personality change. *Journal of Consulting Psychology* **21**(2): 95–103

Schmieding NJ (2002) Ida Jean Orlando (Pelletier): Nursing Process Theory. In Tomey AM, Alligood MR (eds) *Nurse theorists and their work* (5th edn, pp 399–417) Mosby, St Louis

Schön D (1983) *The reflective practitioner. How professionals think in action.* Temple Smith, London

Where to find out more

Further information about Ida Orlando can be found in:

Tomey AM, Alligood MR (2006) Nurse theorists and their work (6th edn pp 431–51). Mosby Elsevier, St. Louis

Schmieding NJ (2002). Orlando's nursing process theory in nursing practice. In MR Alligood, AM Tomey (eds) *Nursing theory utilization and application* (2nd edn pp. 315–37). Mosby, St Louis

CHAPTER 23

Imogene King
1923–2007

Profile

The ethos behind King's conceptual system is very much one of nurse and patient working together and in collaboration in order to achieve patient goals. In this she was a trendsetter; in the 21st century we now take such ideas for granted but in King's day these notions were revolutionary.

Key dates

1945   Received nursing diploma from St John's Hospital School of Nursing, St Louis, MO

1948   Batchelors degree, St Louis University, MO

1957   Masters degree, St Louis University, MO

1961   Doctor of Education, Teachers College, Columbia University, New York

1980   Received an honorary Doctor of Philosophy degree from Southern Illinois University

1989   Became Sigma Theta Tau International Virginia Henderson Fellow

1989   Received the Elizabeth Russell Belford Founders Award for Excellence in Education

1996   Received the American Nurses Association (ANA) Jessie M Scott Award

2004   Inducted into the ANA Hall of Fame

Imogene King
Billy Mathers

Biography

Imogene King was born in West Point, Iowa, USA. She received her diploma in nursing from St John's Hospital School of Nursing in St Louis, Missouri, in 1945. Thereafter she studied for her Bachelor's degree in nursing in 1948 and Master's degree in nursing in 1957 from Saint Louis University. In 1961, after studying under Mildred Montag at the Teachers College, Columbia University, she graduated with a Doctor of Education degree. In 1980, she received an honorary Doctor of Philosophy degree from Southern Illinois University.

Imogene taught at many universities and held academic positions at Loyola University, Chicago, Ohio State University and University of South Florida where she was appointed Professor Emeritus. She served as Assistant Chief of Research Grants Branch, Division of Nursing, Washington, DC from 1966 to 1968. King served as a consultant and lecturer for the University of Miami's doctoral programme and other graduate and clinical programmes and regularly presented at international conferences between 1978 and 1996.

King was a Sigma Theta Tau International Virginia Henderson Fellow and received the Elizabeth Russell Belford Founders Award for Excellence in Education in 1989. King, an American Academy of Nursing Fellow, received the American Nursing Association (ANA) Jessie Scott Award at the 1996 ANA convention for her contributions to nursing practice, education, and research and for demonstrating the relationships between these components.

Murray and Baier (1996) recall Imogene King as a nurse who, for over 50 years, participated in the movement to establish the unique discipline of nursing. The same authors regard her as an internationally renowned academic who has been hugely influential in the advancement of nursing theory worldwide.

King's contributions to the North American Nursing Diagnosis Association (NANDA) lasted for over 40 years. She was a participant at the First National Conference on the Classification of Nursing Diagnoses in St Louis in 1973. In 1982, the work of the NANDA nurse theorist group began and Imogene King was part of the group that presented an organising framework for nursing diagnoses called Patterns of Unitary Man (Humans), to NANDA and the Taxonomy Committee. Nursing diagnosis was eventually included as a component of the nursing process. Universally recognised as a leader in nursing theory development and theory-based nursing practice, King made a lasting impact on nursing education, practice and research. She worked with nurses worldwide on her many foreign visits, in order to develop nursing as a profession through practice, scholarship and education.

Away from professional life, King was a keen artist and golfer, although it is true say that nursing was her lifelong passion. She published her last article in 2007 in the *International Journal of Nursing Terminologies and Classification* and died in Pasadena, California on Christmas Eve of the same year.

Special interest

Imogene King's special interest was to propose a common nursing language for communication among members of the nursing community worldwide. The development of nursing as an emerging profession in the 20th century indicated the need for such a universal language. King worked towards common nursing classification and terminology systems. Her Theory of Goal Attainment helped pave the way for the nursing process to provide a method for synthesis of nursing data, information, and knowledge. She strove for a common nursing language that would unify nurses of all disciplines. Her dream was that by means of nursing theory and technology, global communication would be enhanced for nurses as part of the interdisciplinary team process.

Writings

Imogene King's publishing career spanned nearly 40 years. As a result it is not be possible to document all of her writings in this chapter, so a selection of her chief publications will be outlined.

She first described her 'conceptual system' in the journal *Nursing Research* in 1968. She developed these ideas further in the first of several books which was published three years later in which she described her General Systems Framework Theory (King, 1971). This theory emphasises the importance of the interaction between nurses and patients. She views this interaction as an open system that is in constant interaction with a variety of environmental factors. She built on this theory by describing in more detail how the goals that have been set can be measured (King, 1988). Later, she further developed her ideas in *Nursing Science Quarterly*, outlining the nurse's role in the general goal of bringing a person closer to a healthy state (King, 1997).

Although these concepts were King's main legacy she was also interested in nurse education and she recorded some of her ideas in *Curriculum and instruction in nursing* (King, 1986). Her writings also inspired and informed the creation of the nursing process (Yura and Walsh, 1983). This has had a major impact upon nursing worldwide as it provides a framework for basic nursing care.

Theory

The conceptual system has three interacting systems; the personal, the interpersonal, and the social. The nurse and the patient interact towards a goal. The end-point of this interaction, which occurs over time, is transaction, at which the individual's goal is accomplished and the goal is attained based on King's transaction process model (Parker, 2001).

The most intimate level of the three systems is the personal system, which is comprised of individuals. An obvious example of personal systems would be individual nurses and patients. The second level of systems would be interpersonal systems, or groups. These are generally small groups, for example, a family. The largest systems are social systems, for example, universities and hospitals.

The Theory of Goal Attainment, which lies at the heart of King's theory of nursing, exists in the context of her conceptual framework. The essence of goal attainment theory is that the nurse and patient work together to define and reach goals that they set together. The patient and nurse each perceive, judge, and act, and together react to and interact with each other. At the end of this process of communication and perceiving, if a goal has been set, a transaction is said to have occurred. The nurse and patient also

Links with other nursing theorists

King's contributions to North American Nursing Diagnosis Association (NANDA) lasted for over 40 years. In this she worked very closely with other nursing theorists such as Dorothea Orem (*see Chapter 14*), Dorothy Johnson, Martha Rogers (*see Chapter 19*), Virginia Henderson (*see Chapter 11*) and Callista Roy (*see Chapter 17*). She also has links with Hildegard Peplau (*see Chapter 26*).

decide on a way to work towards the goal that has been decided upon, and put into action the plan that has been agreed upon. King believes that the main function of nursing is to increase or to restore the health of the patient. So then, transactions should occur to set goals related to the health of the patient. After transactions have occurred and goals have been defined by the nurse and patient together, both parties work toward the stated goals. This may involve interactions with other systems, such as other healthcare workers, the patient's family, or larger systems.

After the transaction has occurred, and the goal has been set, according to King it is important for good documentation to be practised by the nurse. She believes that documenting the goal can help to summarise and simplify the process of goal attainment. This will make it easier for nurses to communicate with each other and other healthcare workers involved in the process. It also helps to provide a way to determine if the goal is achieved. This assessment of whether or not the goal has been accomplished is an important factor in the end stage in King's Goal Attainment Theory (Murray and Baier, 1996).

Many people believe King's Theory of Goal Attainment to be a productive and empowering way for nurses and patients to interact. It could be argued that it stands in sharp contrast to the potentially paternalistic medical model which has traditionally been predominant in healthcare. The medical model works by making a professional diagnosis of the patient's problem and then offering the antidote. In recent years attempts have been made to make the medical model more empowering for the patient by offering a range of alternatives, such as which medication the patient might prefer, where appropriate. King's theory is an attempt to put the patient at the heart of his or her own care as equal partners with the nurse and other health professionals. In this way, she appears to have been something of a trendsetter, as patient and service groups are becoming increasingly more influential in the 21st century, ensuring that patients' voices are heard throughout their treatment. Some people have questioned how well King's model applies to patients with serious ill health, as it is necessary for the patient to be able to build a relationship with the nurse in order to agree goals, and to work towards attainment of these goals. Others contend that King's theory can be applied to all groups because a large portion of communication involves nonverbal behaviour, so being able to communicate through spoken language is not a prerequisite for transactions to occur.

King was of the opinion that many nurses actually use the Theory of Goal Attainment when interacting on a daily basis with patients, although they sometimes do not recognise it as such. King believed, however, that it is very important for nurses to have an understanding of the theoretical basis for their behaviours and nursing actions. Nurses basing their behaviour on King's theory would engage patients in discussion to set goals and agree on the ways they are both going to work towards these goals. The nurse would also document both the goals and the steps being taken towards them, and then review the goals to determine if they had been successfully achieved.

King's Theory of Goal Attainment and her conceptual framework have been applied in many different situations. Literature documents its application across various age groups, from infants through children and adults to the elderly. It has been applied to various patient groups including patients with cancer, diabetes, and HIV (Williams, 2001). It has also been used as a tool to address the concerns of various patients including those expressing concerns about birth, body weight, and stress. It has also been applied in various healthcare settings, such as hospitals, clinics, and nursing homes (Williams, 2001).

King's theory can work well with patients with mental health problems as can be observed below. It has many similarities to one of the best-known mental health nursing models, introduced by Hildegard Peplau (1952). Peplau was one of the first to suggest what the essence of mental health nursing might be. She described this as being essentially a partnership and relationship between patient and nurse. In this respect King and Peplau can be seen to be in tandem. However, there are differences in their approaches as Peplau describes the patients 'needs' and King refers to 'goals'. This is because Peplau was mainly influenced by the humanistic school of psychology and King by the behaviourist school. Peplau was influenced by Rogers' work in client-centred therapy (Rogers, 2002) and thus used the term 'needs' rather than 'goals' which is more associated with behavioural ideology.

Putting King's model into practice

It has been suggested that King's model is adaptable to many areas of nursing care. The following two case studies outline its use with a patient with diabetes and a patient with depression. Their care will be considered using King's three systems; personal, interpersonal and social.

Case study I

Stuart Forsyth (18) has been newly diagnosed with diabetes during his stay in hospital for treatment for a chest infection. His nurse, Gordon, is preparing him for discharge back to the family home where Stuart lives with his parents and 15-year-old sister. Using King's model, Gordon starts by building a rapport with Stuart (King's personal system). After gaining Stuart's trust over a period of a few days, he then begins to discuss with Stuart his goals for the future. Stuart's chest infection has now cleared and Gordon and Stuart agree that his main goal is to manage his diabetes safely whilst at home with the family. With Stuart's agreement, Gordon starts by providing Stuart with education on diabetes. This includes the practical implications of self-administration of insulin on a daily basis and the importance of glucose monitoring.

King's 'interpersonal' system involved in this instance would be Stuart's family. Gordon would meet with Stuart's family to ensure that they also were provided with information on the management of diabetes including medication administration. The family would be recruited as carers and potential 'experts' in Stuart's care. One of the potential benefits of family involvement is that the family can be available at all times of the day and, where family dynamics are positive, can have close proximity to the patient in a way that health professionals can never achieve. This makes family members a potentially key component in the care of patients who are unwell.

The 'social' component of Stuart's care would be community-based health professionals such as the district nurse and general practitioner. Gordon would be in contact with the district nurse before discharge to arrange a meeting with himself and Stuart to confirm the goals agreed and how these goals could be achieved after discharge. The 'social' aspect of the model would also include the supply of insulin which would be provided by obtaining regular prescriptions from Stuart's general practitioner. A strategy would be worked out with Stuart to cover events when help was not available from the district nurse, such as contacting the general practitioner or practice nurse and phoning the diabetes 'help line'. Gordon would ensure that Stuart's family was also appraised of these arrangements so that Stuart's 'goal' of safely managing his diabetes in the community can be achieved. Regular evaluations with the district nurse would be arranged to monitor the progress of Stuart's goals and make any necessary adjustments.

Case study 2

District nurse Catriona has received a referral from the local hospital asking her to visit Heather Murdoch, a 69-year-old widow who has spent a short time in hospital to receive treatment for a leg wound after a minor household accident. The 'personal' stage of the relationship commences after Catriona is asked to visit Heather to dress her leg wound on a weekly basis. After the first meeting, a rapport has been built up between Heather and Catriona and on the second visit, they begin to discuss Heather's goals. It becomes apparent that Heather is feeling anxious and is wary of going out any further than the local grocery store. Heather lost her husband two years before and this has had a profound effect on her as they went everywhere together. Her anxiety means that previous social activities like helping out as a volunteer at the local hospital shop is now impossible. One of the goals jointly identified by Heather and Catriona is the resumption of her hospital shop duties. They agree a strategy for reducing Heather's anxiety levels, which in the short-term include learning some relaxation exercises and going out together to the local shop for household items.

The 'interpersonal' stage commences when Catriona, with Heather's permission, invites Moira, one of Heather's former work colleagues at the hospital shop, to visit. During this visit, Catriona suggests that Moira might call to accompany Heather to the hospital shop. This companionship might reduce Heather's anxiety levels enough to allow her to resume her voluntary work. It is agreed that the two workers will travel to the hospital shop initially for one day per week and if this goes well the visits will be increased as appropriate. At the same time, Catriona, again with Heather's permission, contacts her daughter who lives 50 miles away, to keep her informed of her mother's progress.

References

Barker P (2003) *Psychiatric and mental health nursing: The craft of caring*. Hodder Arnold, London

King IM (1968) A conceptual frame of reference for nursing. *Nursing Research* **17**: 27–31

King IM (1971) *Toward a theory for nursing: General concepts of human behavior*. John Wiley, New York.

King IM (1981) *A theory for nursing: Systems, concepts, process*. Wiley, New York, NY

King IM (1986). *Curriculum and instruction in nursing*. Appleton-Century-Crofts, Norwalk, CT

King IM (1988) Measuring health goal attainment in patients. In CF Waltz, OL Strickland (eds) *Measurement of nursing outcomes: Measuring client outcomes*. Springer, New York

King IM (1997). King's theory of goal attainment in practice. *Nursing Science Quarterly* 10: 180–5

Murray RLE, Baier M (1996) King's Conceptual Framework ppplied to a transitional living program. *Perspectives in Psychiatric Care* **32**: 15–20

Parker ME (2001) *Nursing theories and nursing practice*. FA Davis Company, Philadelphia PA

Peplau HE (1952) *Interpersonal relations in nursing*. GP Putnam & Sons, New York

Rogers C (1980) *A way of being*. Houghton Mifflin, Boston

Rogers CR (2002) *Client centred therapy*. Constable, London

Williams LA (2001) Imogene Kings Interacting Systems Theory: Application in emergency and rural nursing. *Journal of Rural Nursing and Health Care* 2:1.

Yura H, Walsh MB (1983) *The nursing process: Assessing, planning, implementing, evaluating* (4th edn). Appleton-Century-Crofts, Norwalk, CT

Where to find out more

- http//currentnursing.com/ nursing-theory/goalattainment-theory.htm

This website gives detailed information about Imogene King's nursing theory and its application to practice.

The 'social' stage or system commences when Catriona arranges an appointment for Heather with her general practitioner and accompanies her to the surgery. Beforehand, she has given the general practitioner an update on Heather's situation. The doctor prescribes a small dose of anxiolytic medication as a short intervention and explains that if Heather's symptoms of anxiety persist for longer then one of the newer antidepressants might be considered as these are known to be helpful for some forms of anxiety. Catriona evaluates Heather's care on a two weekly basis, involving Heather herself, Moira and the general practitioner examining whether or not the goal has been met.

The influence of King and her theory

Imogene King first practised at a time when nurses were seen to be the 'handmaiden' of medical staff and very much in the role of assistant to the doctor. Her work in developing her theory helped to establish nursing as an emerging profession in its own right and encouraged other nurses to look upon themselves as health professionals with their own knowledge base. King's nursing theories helped to promote research knowledge development in nursing. Her nursing career supported theoretical development for nurse educators, practitioners and nurse researchers. She had a long interest in nursing languages such as conceptual systems and classification systems. This included an expansion of her comparison of her Theory of Goal Attainment with the nursing process steps by Yura and Walsh (1983) to include expected outcomes and measurable actual outcomes. She was aware of the need to view goals as measurable outcomes with standardised terms as well as to link her nursing theory to nursing outcomes research. She was a champion of technology and nursing informatics and evidence-based practice, and was keen for her theory to integrate new worldwide knowledge in these areas.

It has been shown that King's conceptual model centres around goals for the patient's future health and well-being being set by the patient and nurse working in partnership. Whilst this is a common concept for nurses today, this was novel in King's day where the medical model prevailed. These ideas were to help form the basis of the nursing process of assessment, planning, implementation and evaluation. Nurses are familiar with the idea of setting goals or objectives in the planning stage of the nursing process and King's conceptual system was a pre-curser to this. The 'nursing process' is universally used by nurses of all disciplines in different settings worldwide so it can be acknowledged that King's embryonic ideas around goal setting have had a profound effect on nursing and nurses ever since.

King's theory is very much in line with current thinking in nursing in general, and in mental health nursing in particular. For example, Barker (2003) encourages mental health nurses to listen to the patient's 'life narrative'. This means the patient's own story, such as life events which may have been instrumental to the onset of their current mental health problems and ways which they have found to manage these problems. This acknowledges that patients have a big part to play in their own recovery and the nurse should learn from the patient as much as the patient should learn from the nurse. The possible influence of King can be seen in her establishment of the idea of the nurse–patient partnership.

CHAPTER 24

Moyra Allen

Kathleen Duffy

Biography

Moyra Allen was a Canadian nurse and professor. She was best known for her forward thinking view on nursing as she sought to transform the nature and the image of the profession within Canada in the 1970s. According to Allen, the main goal of nursing was to form a partnership with the person and his or her family to foster health. From that perspective, she, along with colleagues from the McGill University School of Nursing, developed a model best known today as the McGill Model of Nursing. This model is currently used in a number of healthcare organisations in many provinces in Canada and in parts of the US, and its sphere of influence continues to grow.

Allen undertook her initial nurse education at Montreal General Hospital School of Nursing, Quebec, Canada. She went on to obtain a Bachelor of Nursing from McGill University in Quebec, a Masters degree in education from the University of Chicago, Illinois and a Doctorate in Education and Sociology from Stanford University, California. During her lifetime she had strong affiliations with McGill University, working there most of her career. In 1958, she was appointed associate professor within the School of Nursing and became Acting Director of the School shortly before she retired in 1984.

In 1966 and 1967 Allen was co-founder and then president of the United Nurses of Montreal, the first union for English-speaking nurses in Montreal. In 1969, as Director of Nursing Research at McGill University, she founded and became editor of the first scholarly journal of nursing research published in Canada entitled *Nursing Papers*. This journal is now called the *Canadian Journal of Nursing Research*. Innovative at the time, it promoted the distribution of nursing research knowledge throughout Canada.

Allen was known worldwide for her work with the World Health Organization (WHO) evaluating educational programmes in nursing. Between 1971 and 1973 she travelled extensively as a consultant for the WHO, working directly with educators in South America, Africa and India.

During her lifetime Allen received many honours for her contribution to the nursing profession. In 1979, she was awarded the Canadian Nurses Association Jeanne Mance Award, given to individuals who have made significant and innovative contributions to the health of Canadians. In 1983 she received the l'Insigne du Mérite from the Order of Nurses of Québec in recognition of service to her home province. In 1986, she was appointed an Officer of the Order of Canada for her contribution to nursing in Canada and abroad. After she retired she continued to receive accolades from her peers. She received Honorary Doctorates from McMaster University, Ontario in 1984 and another from the University of Montreal in 1990. In 1994, shortly before her death, she received the Ethel Johns Award of the Canadian Association of University Schools of Nursing, in recognition of her major contribution to Canadian university nurse education.

Profile

Moyra Allen transformed the concept of nursing within the Canadian healthcare system in the 1970s. She championed the health-promoting role of the nurse within family-centred care. She developed the McGill Model of Nursing and inspired practitioners to implement and evaluate this model in practice.

Key dates

1943	Graduated with a Diploma in Nursing at Montreal General Hospital School of Nursing, Quebec, Canada
1952	Awarded Masters Degree in Education, University of Chicago
1967	Received Doctorate in Education and Sociology from Stanford University, California
1969	Founded the first scholarly Canadian nursing journal *Nursing Papers* (now the *Canadian Journal of Nursing Research*)
1973	Won five-year National Health Service award and established a research unit at the McGill School of Nursing, Quebec, Canada
1984	Honorary Doctorate from McMaster University, Ontario
1986	Appointed an Officer of the Order of Canada for her contribution to nursing in Canada
1990	Honorary Doctorate from University of Montreal

Summary of writings

Over her lifetime Allen published a number of papers with either a theoretical or a research focus relating to the McGill Model. Allen and Reidy's report in 1971 of the evaluation of the new nursing programme at Ryerson Polytechnical Institute in Toronto provides a glimpse of the origins of the McGill Model of Nursing. In this report Allen and her colleague describe two patterns of teaching and learning behaviour displayed by nursing graduates – a traditional approach, which was medically focused, and a more patient-centred behaviour which Allen termed the 'situation-responsive' approach.

Publications that followed (Allen, 1974, 1977a) focused on outlining the theoretical perspectives of the evolving McGill Model. In these publications Allen concentrated on describing her vision of the contribution of nursing to healthcare in Canada and advocated an expanded role for the nurse with the individual and family in the area of health promotion. Once the central concepts of the McGill Model had been developed they were tested in practice. In 1980 Allen and colleagues (1980a, b) published a two-part research report associated with a comparative evaluation of the model in practice. The research findings indicated improved patient outcomes arising from this nursing approach. As the model gained an acceptance as a useful framework for nursing practice Allen published details of it for the wider nursing audience in the *Journal of Advanced Nursing* and book chapters within texts such as *Recent advances in nursing: Primary care nursing* in 1981 and 1983 respectively.

Posthumously, a paper co-edited by her colleague Warner, comprehensively detailing the McGill Model was published in 2002, and is believed to be the last article written by Allen prior to her death in 1996. For other papers and details of conference proceedings associated with Moyra Allen readers should examine Warner (2002).

Theory

The McGill Model of Nursing was first conceived in response to an identified gap in the Canadian healthcare system. In the 1960s, a new approach to healthcare delivery was implemented in Canada: a universal health insurance plan subsidised through public funding. This reform created an increased demand for healthcare services by the public and was seen as an opportunity to expand nursing roles and services. One school of thought promoted the expansion of nursing into medical-type services. Allen had a different view. She viewed the nurse's role within the healthcare system as unique and active and complementary to, rather than a replacement for, other professions. She advocated the expansion of nursing within the field of health promotion. From grounded theory analysis of observations of individuals and families who were dealing with illness in a variety of settings, Allen generated a theoretical perspective about the role of the nurse in promoting healthy development of families throughout their life span (Gottlieb and Rowat, 1987). The main concepts of the model emerged as health, family, learning and collaboration.

Health

Within the McGill Model of Nursing, health is a central concept and the focus of nursing practice. Allen argued that nurses should not define health in terms of disease or illness but rather support the individual and family to focus on the health aspects of situations. Using the McGill approach to encourage active participation in learning about health, nurses empower people to find healthy ways of coping with conditions. This enables the individual and family to modify and change, with a view to achieving optimum functioning. The McGill Model is especially concerned with the development of healthy families – not with illness and disease.

Family

The concept of family is fundamental within the McGill Model. Central to Allen's theoretical perspective was the premise that health behaviours – ways of coping, living and developing – are social phenomena, learned from a family or social group. Allen postulated that through 'life events', e.g. preparing for a new baby, coping with unemployment, living with a chronic illness, etc., interest in and concern for health is frequently manifested. Consequently, even though only one person or member of the family may be experiencing the life event, a nurse using the McGill Model perceives the individual in a wider, family affected context (Allen and Warner, 2002).

Learning

The perspective on learning that guides this model of nursing is Bandura's Social Cognitive Learning Theory (Bandura, 1977, 1986). Social Cognitive Learning Theory is based on the idea that people learn by watching what others do. This is known as observational learning or modelling. Allen's perspective was that health beliefs, attitudes and practices are learned with the family which is considered the primary socialising unit. Therefore, in order for McGill-orientated nurses to maintain, strengthen, and develop patient's health, they require to actively engage the patient and family in the learning process.

Collaboration

Collaborative relationships between professionals and patients are viewed as essential within the

McGill Model. The model advocates the participation of both nurse and individual/family in working collaboratively on health situations. Their collaboration features periods of assessment, planning, implementation and evaluation.

Assessment

This process acknowledges that one family member's situation influences, and is influenced by, all other family members. During assessment the nurse identifies the specific concerns of the individual and family in a broad context so as to derive an overall view of the current health situation. Using the McGill Model the nurse acknowledges the patient and family as the primary source of information relevant to the situation. The nurse's aim in assessment is to identify the individual/family's enabling qualities and behaviours that are productive to health. The role of the nurse is, then, to provide a supportive milieu as background and enter into negotiation with the patient and family to plan and implement care.

Planning and implementation

Assuming a collaborative approach to the situation, the nurse and individual/family share responsibility for planning and implementing care within the McGill Model. The focus during planning is to build on the patient's and family's strengths and capacities, for example their motivation, knowledge, skills and social support. When the nurse and individual/family have set goals and devised means of achieving these, the plan is tried out. During the implementation phase, the patient and family's major role is to become active learners. The nurse's major role is to tailor the learning activities to the patient and family's needs. The nurse's role during implementation is determined by the family's potential for engaging with health-promoting activities. Alert to cues suggesting nursing roles that support learning in the situation, the nurse at various times during the process may help the family to focus, act as an awareness raiser or role model, or motivate or stimulate the family to develop their health potential. Allen acknowledged that in some situations individuals and/or families may not be able to actively participate in planning and implementation, for example, during acute illness or severe emotional distress. She also accepted that sensory deficits, lack of fluency in language and beliefs about the respective roles of the patient and health professional could influence how the nurse proceeds (Allen and Warner, 2002).

Evaluation

The McGill Model advocates an open approach to evaluation. A critical feature of the model is that both patient and nurse review progress in light of their collaboratively established goals. In contrast to some models that look at outcomes in terms of whether or not the nurse's objectives are achieved, in the McGill Model it is the individual and family's responses that validate the process. The nurse gathers evidence on individual/family responses and outcomes but does not attribute values to them. Evaluation is based on the individual and family's satisfaction with the outcomes.

Readers who wish to explore this model further should note that over the decades the model has been referred to in the literature by a number of titles including the 'Situation-Responsive Nursing Model', the 'Complemental Model', the 'Allen Model', the 'Developmental Model of Health and Nursing' and the 'McGill Model'.

Links with other nursing theorists

Moyra Allen's works links to Margaret Newman's Theory of Health Model (*see Chapter 20*).

References

Allen M (1974) The expanding role of the nurse: Her preparation and practice (editorial). *Nursing Papers* **2**: 2–4

Allen M (1977a) Comparative theories of the expanded role in nursing and implications for nursing practice: A working paper. *Nursing Papers* **9**(2): 38–45

Allen M (1977b) *Evaluation of education programmes in nursing.* World Health Organization, Geneva, Switzerland

Allen M (1981) The health dimension in nursing practice: Notes on nursing in primary health care. *Journal of Advanced Nursing* **6**: 153–5

Allen M (1983) Primary care nursing: Research in action. In: Hockley L (ed) *Recent advances in nursing: Primary care nursing.* Churchill Livinstone, Edinburgh

Allen M, Fraser-Smith N, Gottlieb L (1980a) *Models of nursing practice in a changing heath care system: A comparative study in three ambulatory settings. Part 1: Research report.* McGill University School of Nursing, Montreal, Canada

Allen M, Fraser-Smith N, Gottlieb L (1980b) *Models of nursing practice in a changing heath care system: A comparative study in three ambulatory settings. Part 2: Appendices.* McGill University School of Nursing, Montreal, Canada

Allen M, Reidy M (1971) *Learning to nurse: The first five years of the Ryerson nursing program.* Registered Nurses Association of Ontario, Toronto, Canada

Allen M, Warner M (2002) A developmental model of health and nursing. *Journal of Family Nursing* **8**(2): 96–135

Bandura A (1977) *Social learn-*

Putting theory into practice

An important test of any theoretical model is how useful nurses find the theory in practice. Over the years, the McGill Model has been developed, refined, tested and implemented in various practice settings and has gained widespread acceptance in Canada and elsewhere as a useful framework for nursing practice.

Following the generation of the theoretical aspects of the model, research was undertaken by Allen and colleagues to further refine and expand elements of the model. In the early 1970s, the faculty of medicine at McGill University had established family medicine units in some of the teaching hospitals affiliated to the university. In one of the hospitals – Montreal General Hospital – nursing came solely under the remit of the director of nursing rather than medical staff and it was here in 1974 that the opportunity arose for Allen to mount a demonstration site for the McGill Model. For the purpose of evaluation of the model, two other family medicine units were selected for comparison. A faculty member of McGill School of Nursing worked with the nurses in the demonstration site to facilitate the introduction and monitor the implementation of the new nursing model. No such educational intervention was taken within the other two family medicine units. Data were collected over 14 months using mixed methods including tape-recorded observations of nurse–patient interactions, interviews with nurses, and interviews and questionnaires with patients (Allen et al., 1980a, b). The evaluation demonstrated significant differences between the units. Patients in the demonstration unit indicated that their nurses had tried to help them cope with a significantly greater percentage of health problems than did patients in each of the two comparison sites. This positive response following the introduction of the McGill approach led to a second and eventually a third demonstration as further testing grounds for the model.

The second funded demonstration site was a freestanding, nurse-managed community health centre located in an affluent suburb of Montreal. The centre was known as the Health Workshop. This larger project was evaluated by a research team of which Allen was a member. Data were gathered by observation of nurse–patient interactions followed by interviews with both the nurse and the patient. Although funding was discontinued prior to the final evaluation phase, which related to patient outcomes, aspects of data collection identifying nursing functions and the styles of nursing adopted within the Health Workshop were reported (Allen et al., 1980a, b). The data that were gathered revealed the variety of roles and activities that nurses undertook in structuring learning experiences for individuals and families. These included the nurse as focuser, stimulator, resource provider, integrator, awareness raiser, role model, instructor, guide, coach, encourager, reinforcer and reviewer. In-depth qualitative analysis enabled Allen and colleagues to identify more fully the impact of factors such as motivation, resources and family organisation on an individual/family's health potential. Consequently the importance of the nurse's ability to assess individual/family health potential was reinforced to the research team.

The third demonstration was mounted in a less advantaged rural area of Quebec comprising two towns, one French the other English. This was again a nurse-managed community health centre, also called the Health Workshop. Using similar methodologies as in the previous demonstration sites the main concepts of the model – health, family, learning and collaboration – were supported.

As well as supportive qualitative evidence, all three demonstration projects showed statistically significant positive client outcomes arising from the use of the McGill nursing approach. These included reduced stress, increased satisfaction, improved problem solving and increased involvement in health learning and the applicability of the model for practice was supported.

A number of Masters and PhD level thesis works applying the theory to practice provide consistent support for the theory. Gottlieb and Rowat (1987) report that graduates of the nursing programmes within McGill University have taken the model into varying practice setting such as ambulatory care, paediatric intensive care units and community settings. This has allowed for ongoing evaluation of the model's usefulness in guiding nursing practice. Similar to the findings in these other studies, Monteith and Ford-Gilboe's (2002) research undertaken with families of pre-school children concluded that the use of the McGill Model to guide practice was an appropriate means of supporting family health promotion efforts.

Influence

Moyra Allen's influence within nursing practice, education and research has been wide reaching and enduring. She envisioned nursing as having a unique, active and complementary role in providing healthcare; consequently, the McGill Model of Nursing was developed and refined under her guidance. This model is currently used in a number of healthcare organisations in Canada and beyond and its sphere of influence continues to grow.

Allen transformed nurse education within Canada. The main concepts of the McGill Model of Nursing, health, family, learning and collaboration, became key threads in each level of the under- and post-graduate nursing programmes at McGill School of Nursing. Her evaluation of education programmes in nursing for the World Health Organization contributed to changes in nursing education (Allen, 1977b). The proposals within the paper were adopted by the Canadian Association of University Schools of Nursing for accreditation of baccalaureate programmes in nursing. As Stuart (2002) highlights, her criteria for accreditation and evaluation are still in use in university schools of nursing across Canada today. In 1976, Allen created and initiated the generic Masters programme in nursing at McGill University for science and arts graduates with no previous nursing education. This programme is well known across Canada for its unique and dynamic entry to nursing. Students of the generic Masters programme undertake an intensive 10-month qualifying academic year, followed by a two-year graduate programme. Over the years, the McGill University health community has recognised this programme as preparing highly qualified nurses for practice, research and education.

In 1974, Allen and Joan Gilchrist the director of the School of Nursing at McGill University applied and received funding to establish a research unit in nursing and healthcare. By 1977, with Allen as director of the unit, 25 professionals from 10 disciplines were involved in five major research projects associated with the research unit. Three of these were directly linked to evaluating the McGill Model in practice (Stuart, 2002). Posthumously, Allen has continued to influence nursing scholars and researchers. From the mid-1980s to the present McGill's nursing graduates and faculty members have, through research inspired by the McGill Model, actively shaped the philosophy and practice of nursing in many of Montreal's hospitals and community health centres and in settings in both Canada and the US. Recent papers such as Gottlieb and Gottlieb's (2007) 'reconceptualisation' of aspects of the McGill Model are testament to Allen's enduring influence.

ing theory. Prentice Hall, Englewood Cliffs, New Jersey

Bandura A (1986) *Social foundations of thought and action*. Prentice Hall, Englewood Cliffs, New Jersey

Gottlieb LN, Gottlieb B (2007) The developmental/health framework within the McGill model of nursing. *Advances in Nursing Science* **30**(1): E43–57

Gottlieb L, Rowat K (1987) The McGill model of nursing: A practice-derived model. *Advances in Nursing Science* **9**(4): 51–61

Monteith B, Ford-Gilboe M (2002) The relationships among mother's resilience, family health work, and mother's health-promoting lifestyle practices in families with preschool children. *Journal of Family Nursing* **8**(4): 383–407

Stuart M (2002) F Moyra Allen: A life in Nursing, 1921–1996. *Journal of Family Nursing* **8**(2): 157–65

Warner M (2002) Publications of Dr. F. Moyra Allen. *Journal of Family Nursing* **8**(2): 166–8

Where to find out more

Gottlieb L, Rowat K (1987) The McGill model of nursing: A practice-derived model. *Advances in Nursing Science* **9**(4): 51–61

Stuart M (2002) F. Moyra Allen: A life in Nursing, 1921–1996, *Journal of Family Nursing* **8**(2): 157–65.

Anne Casey
Born 1951

Key dates

1975   Emigrated to the UK. Undertook Registered Sick Children's Nursing at Great Ormond Street Hospital for Children, London

1988   *A partnership with child and family* published.

1991   *Using a nursing model in curriculum planning* published

1996   Appointed Editor of the RCN Publication *Paediatric Nursing* a position she held until 2009

1996   Appointed advisor to the Royal College of Nursing. Developed an interest in health informatics terminology standards

2002   Appointed Fellow of the Royal College of Nursing

Acknowledgement
I would like to thank Anne Casey for answering my questions and sharing her thoughts with me, as this work neared completion.

Anne Casey
F J Raymond Duffy

Biography

Anne Casey is a New Zealand-trained nurse, now based in England. She left New Zealand in 1975 and when she arrived in London she worked in Evelina Children's Hospital at Southwark Bridge, which was part of Guy's Hospital. While there she was persuaded to undertake the Registered Sick Children's Nursing programme at Great Ormond Street Hospital for Children, London. In the 1980s Anne developed a model of nursing which was solely designed for use in paediatric nursing. The model embraced a series of concepts that had been developing over the previous 30 years to become what is now considered to be the central tenet of children's nursing, 'family centred-care' (Coleman, 2002). Anne Casey's Model for Paediatric Nursing was developed whilst she was working with the Paediatric Oncology Unit at Great Ormond Street Hospital in London, and was published initially in 1988, when she was working as a nurse teacher there. The focus of the model is on working in partnership with children and their families, and was one of the earliest attempts to develop a model of practice, which was appropriate to the UK and specifically tailored to suit child health nursing

In October 2002, she became a Fellow of the Royal College of Nursing (RCN) in the UK, for her services to paediatric nursing and to health informatics. She was also the editor of the UK journal, *Paediatric Nursing*, from 1996 until May 2009.

Casey is also currently a nurse advisor for the RCN with a particular interest in information technology (IT) and its impact on nursing. She has been the RCN lead on several IT-related consultations relating to the development of professional nursing content for electronic records and communications. Anne was a very active member of SNOMED-CT (Systematized Nomenclature of Medicine – Clinical Terms). SNOMED is a comprehensive clinical terminology, originally created by the College of American Pathologists (CAP). It is now owned, maintained, and distributed by the International Health Terminology Standards Development Organisation (IHTSDO), a not-for-profit organisation in Denmark. The aim of SNOMED-CT is to provide a consistent way to index, store, retrieve, and aggregate clinical data across specialties and sites of care. The nomenclature also helps when organising the content of medical records, reducing the variability in the way data are captured, encoded and used for clinical care of patients and research. She is currently the Chair of the International Health Terminology Standards Development Organisation (IHTSDO) Nursing Special Interest Group. She has also been Chair of the Standards Working Group and Honorary Secretary of the Association of Common European Nursing Diagnoses Interventions and Outcomes (ACENDIO). Previously, she was also a member of the Strategic Advisory Group for Nursing Information systems to the UK Department of Health (SAGNIS). Casey has had a very active role in national and international nursing informatics, terminology and informatics standards groups, a role which she continues today. She has also been a director and trustee of The Children's Trust, Tadworth and Chair of their Clinical Advisory Committee.

Summary of writings

In 1988 Anne Casey and her co-author Sarah Mobbs published a paper in the *Nursing Times* called 'Partnership in practice'. It contained an outline of what is regarded as the first model of nursing developed solely for UK paediatric nursing, originally published as a discussion paper. Later that year, the model was published in near complete form in the journal *Senior Nurse* (Casey, 1988). The building of the model is described here and although this paper is short, it is clear that the model embraces a number of concepts that are now recognised as the basis of contemporary family-centred paediatric care. Unlike other models, Casey's model is not theory-only based, but draws heavily on her experiences both as a paediatric oncology nurse and as a paediatric nurse teacher. Having developed a 'working' model, Casey and her colleagues went on to make use of the model to re-develop the Registered Sick Children's Nurse Curriculum at Great Ormond Street Hospital for Children in London. In 1991, she published a highly influential chapter in a new textbook, *Curriculum planning in nursing education* edited by Stella Pendleton and Alan Myles. In her chapter, Casey reinforces the details of the Partnership Model of Paediatric Nursing and describes how the model was used to underpin a number of aspects of the curriculum, for example the aims and content, the organisation of content, and organisation of the learning experiences, teaching and learning, and assessment. The publication of this piece in particular, has a strong influence elsewhere in the UK, as many nursing schools set about adapting and altering their paediatric curriculums to meet the requirements of Project 2000 nurse education (English National Board for Nursing Midwifery and Health Visiting, 1989). The adoption of the Partnership Model of Paediatric Nursing as a key element of the Registered Sick Children's Nurse curriculum and further developments in the theory, practice and adoption of family-centred care in the USA and Canada led to family-centred care being the accepted norm by 2002 (Coleman, 2002). Since its publication, Casey has revisited the model on a number of occasions (Casey, 1993, 1995, 2006, 2010), but the central focus on the child at the centre of a partnership of care that involves the family and its role in providing care to the child has remained unchanged.

Alongside her publications on the model Anne has published on a considerable number of topics as editor of the UK journal *Paediatric Nursing*. She also has an extensive list of publications concerning the use and development of terminology standards in healthcare informatics. The aim of her work has been to help in the creation of consistent ways to index, store, retrieve, and aggregate nursing diagnoses and other nurse-derived data across specialties and sites of care. Anne is a recognised national and international expert nurse in this field.

Theory

In the UK, prior to the 1960s, a network of sick children's hospitals existed. These hospitals were created originally in the 19th century, to deal with the high prevalence of childhood infectious diseases. The need to base care on rigid regimes of asepsis and cross infection prevention strategies had meant that the emphasis of care in those institutions up until that point, had been on physical care, with little importance being attached to the psychological or social welfare of children (Coleman, 2002). By the 1980s societal attitudes had changed considerably and there was a growing consensus among paediatric nurses that family-centred care, which took account of the wider needs of children, was a good way to work. This view was supported by the Court Report (Department of Health and Social Security, 1976) and was further emphasised and endorsed in both the Children's Act (Department of

Links with other nursing theorists

Dorothea Orem (*see Chapter 14*) who argued that all nursing care should be viewed as a means of helping individuals to achieve their potential for self-care.

John Bowlby (1969, 1973) who argued that that the child's emotional bond to the family caregivers was a biological response that ensured their survival. The attachments that children form in early childhood, have implications for that person's capacity to form trusting relationships throughout their life. The behaviour involved in developing an attachment to a caregiver is one that can be observed in adults in times of stress and anxiety.

James Robertson (1952), a social worker and psychoanalyst, who had recorded the impact that separation from their parents had on young children.

References

Baker S (1995) Family centred care: A theory practice dilemma. *Paediatric Nursing* **7**(6): 17–20

Bowlby J (1969) *Attachment: Attachment and loss* (Vol 1). Hogarth Press, London

Bowlby J (1973) *Separation: Anxiety and anger: Attachment and loss* (Vol 2). Hogarth Press, London

Bruce B, Ritchie J (1997) Nurses' practices and perceptions of family centred care. *Journal of Paediatric Nursing* **12**(4): 214–22.

Callery P, Smith L (1991) A study of role negotiation between nurses and the parents of hospitalised children. *Journal of Advanced Nursing* **16**: 772–81

Casey A (1988) A Partnership With Child and Family. *Senior Nurse* **8**(4): 8–9

Casey A (1991) Using a nursing model in curriculum planning. In Pendleton S, Myles Y (eds) *Curriculum planning in nursing education: Practical applications*. Edward Arnold, London.

Casey A (1993) The development and use of the Partnership Model of Nursing Care. In Glasper EA, Tucker A (eds) *Advances in child health nursing*. Scutari Press, London

Casey A (1995) Partnership nursing: Influences on involvement of informal carers. *Journal of*

Health, 1989) and the Welfare of Children and Young People in Hospital Report (Department of Health, 1991). However, there was no clear vision of what family-centred care meant in practice (Coleman, 2002). Against this backdrop, Casey was convinced that the time was right for the development of a model that described family-centred paediatric practice. Casey's Model of Nursing was developed during the period from 1984 (when Casey was participating in a full-time nurse teaching course at the Royal College of Nursing in London) to 1988 when she was teaching with Sarah Mobbs and Kieron Spires at Great Ormond Street (Casey and Mobbs, 1988). Her ideas were initially published in the *Senior Nurse* in April 1988 in a near complete form, originally for discussion and further validation. At the time Casey had been working with the Paediatric Oncology Unit at the Great Ormond Street Hospital and at publication, she was a nurse teacher at the Charles West School of Nursing, based at the hospital. The model began as an attempt to describe child- and family-centred paediatric nursing practice and as a mechanism to promote better use of the nursing process (Yura and Walsh, 1967). Later it also became a key driver behind the re-development of the Registered Sick Children's Nurse (RSCN) curriculum at the school, a process which Casey describes in some depth in Chapter 3 of Pendleton and Myles (Casey, 1991).

The philosophy on which the model was based stated that:

The care of children, well or sick, is best carried out by their families with varying degrees of help from suitably qualified members of the health care team whenever necessary.

(Casey, 1988)

As the model developed this initial statement was adjusted, but the model remained grounded in respecting the central focus, the child, and the value of the parents' expertise. Another key concept within the model is the view that is taken by the paediatric nurse of the family. Casey (1988, 1993) stresses that although the family structure, the relationships within it and the dynamics of those relationships, are relevant factors for nurses to consider, the nurse need only be concerned about these, insofar as they impact on the family's ability to meet the child's needs. Families are not the patient or the client, as family centred-care might suggest, the key considerations for the nurse are always the needs and rights of the child.

The focus of the model is on working in partnership with the child and his or her family. The philosophy is that the best people to care for the child is the family, assisted by a variety of professional staff when necessary to meet the needs of the child. She identifies two types of care. The first is family care, that is the usual care delivered by the family to meet the child's everyday needs. A paediatric nurse or other health professional would only deliver this care in the absence of the parents or other family carers. The second type of care described is nursing care and this becomes complementary to family care and is the 'extra' care the child requires related to his or her specific health needs. Depending on the age and ability of the child and the ability and willingness of the parents, much of this 'extra care' may be carried out by the child him or herself or by the family. The nurses' role then becomes an enabling one, in which the professional's task is to support and educate the child and family towards independence. *Figure 25.1* summarises this process.

To achieve this goal within the model, Casey considered five concepts: the child, the family, the environment, health and the nurse. Casey herself states that she based her definitions on what she had learned and practised in paediatric oncology where true partnerships were a reality and therefore could be transferable to other areas of paediatric practice.

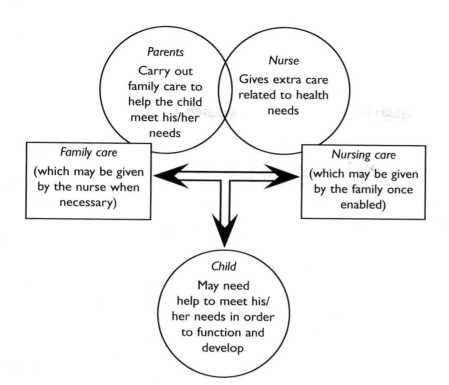

Figure 25.1: Casey's (1988) Partnership Model of Paediatric Nursing (adapted from an illustration by K. Spires).

The child is defined as a unique individual who is functioning, growing and developing – physically, emotionally, socially and spiritually. In order to survive, grow and develop children need care in the form of protection, sustenance, stimulation and love. Most of the child's needs are met initially by the family and that care is termed family care (Casey, 1991). The family is defined as the group that takes responsibility for helping the child meet his or her needs. The family mediates between the child and his or her environment (Casey, 1991).

The environment can be defined as '… all stimuli from external sources that are absorbed and processed by the child' (Weiczoreck and Natapoff, 1981). The environment must be safe and suitable for the child and may be influenced by cultural, social, psychological and physical variables. The child's environment not only affects growth and development, it can also influence the child's physical and mental health.

Health is defined in a very functional manner within the model. Casey (1988) states that good health is taken to mean optimum physical and mental well-being. As she says, '…the child who is healthy and well cared for will have the best opportunity to achieve his or her full potential' (Casey, 1988). Ill-health is seen as any physical, psychological or social dysfunction that affects growth and development. These dysfunctions can be the result of disease, injury, congenital illness or a failure of care.

The model is based on the underlying notion that for most childhood illnesses the family will manage to cope at home, however if they cannot provide all the care that is needed, then help will be sought from outside. Nursing then is seen as just one form of assistance.

Within the model, nursing is defined in terms of actions and Casey admits to being influenced in this by Orem (1985). In this model appropriate paediatric nursing activities become:

- Child care, family care and nursing care that help to meet the child's needs. Nursing care is only the 'extra' care required beyond that which can be achieved by the child and the family to address a health problem or to assist the child in achieving his or her full potential.
- Supporting the child and family in order that they cope and continue to function.

Advanced Nursing **22**: 1058–62.

Casey A (2006) Assessing and planning care in partnership. In: Glasper A, Richardson J (eds) *A textbook of children and young people's nursing.* Elsevier, Edinburgh

Casey A (2010) Assessing and planning care in partnership. In Glasper EA, Richardson J (eds) *A textbook of children's and young people's nursing* (2nd edn). Elsevier, Edinburgh

Casey A, Mobbs S (1988) Partnership in practice. *Nursing Times* **84**(4): 67–8

Casey A, Spisla C, Konicek D, Warren JJ (2006) Practical definition of SNOMED CT concepts: The case of education, advice and counselling. *Studies in Health Technology and Informatics* **122**: 742–5

Chalmers HA (1989) Theories and models of nursing and the nursing process. *Recent Advances in Nursing* **24**: 32–46

Coleman V (2002) The evolving concept of family-centred care. In Smith L, Coleman V, Bradshaw M (eds) *Family-centred care: Concept, theory and practice.* Palgrave,

Basingstoke

Coyne I (1996) Parent participation: A concept analysis.
Journal of Advanced Nursing
23: 733–40

Department of Health (1989) *An
introduction to the Children's
Act, 1989*. HMSO, London

Department of Health (1991)
*Welfare of children and young
people in hospital*. HMSO,
London

Department of Health and Social
Security (1976) *Fit for the
future: The Court Report*.
HMSO, London

English National Board for Nursing
Midwifery and Health Visiting
(1989) *Project 2000 – A New
Preparation for Practice.
Guidelines and Criteria for
Course Development and the
Formation of Collaborative
Links Between Approved
Training Institutions Within the
NHS and Centres of Higher
Education*. ENB, London

Foster RL, Varni JW (2002)
Measuring the quality of children's postoperative pain management: Initial Validation of
the Child/Parent Total Quality
Pain Management (TQPMTM)
instruments. *Journal of Pain
and Symptom Management* **23**:
201–10

Franck L, Callery P (2004)
Re-thinking family-centred care
across the continuum of children's healthcare. *Child: Care,
Health and Development* **30**(3):
265–77

Glasper A (1990) A planned
approach to nursing children.
In Salvage J, Kershaw B (eds)
Models for Nursing 2. Scutari
Press, London

Gottlieb L, Rowatt K (1987) The
McGill Model of Nursing:
A practice derived model.
Advances in Nursing Sciences
9(4): 51–61

Hardiker NR, Hoy D, Casey A
(2000) Standards for nursing
terminology. *Journal of the*

- Teaching knowledge and skills to help the child and family towards independence.
- Referring the child on to other members of the caring team when this is necessary.

Putting theory into practice

Casey's model could be viewed as part of a process of growth of knowledge about the concepts underpinning contemporary paediatric nursing which is family-centred. Casey focused on reaffirming the central role of the child, parental involvement, parental participation and the establishment of formal/informal carer partnerships. Others have examined the negotiation of carer roles and the empowerment of families (Marriott, 1990; Callery and Smith, 1991; Valentine 1998). This accumulation of knowledge about translating theory to practice has led to the movement away from special units for child care, to the encouragement of both child and parental participation wherever children require nursing care. The focus of paediatric nursing has changed from examining family stress and dysfunction, to one which explores families' strengths and needs. Child and family-centred care in the 21st century requires nurses to work collaboratively with families with the focus now being understanding the development of collaborative relationships (Coleman, 2002). Despite this work, some barriers to partnership working still need to be overcome. For example Bruce and Ritchie (1997)and Savage (2000) point out that in current nursing curricula there is still an emphasis on knowledge attainment rather than on the development of the skills required to practise child and family-centred nursing. They suggest the need for the development of more advanced communication skills in counselling, interviewing, interpersonal relationships and family dynamics if child and family-centred care is to be promoted and enhanced in the future.

Family-centred nursing is based on a belief that the family is integral to the care of the child and therefore involves nurses perceiving the care of families as part of their role. Casey's model sees partnership with the child as being of primary importance. The child and family are an interdependent unit of care (an approach often labelled 'family systems nursing') and parent participation is viewed as the norm. In the model the role of parents is fully acknowledged, with the child and the family becoming the focus of care, assisted by the paediatric nurse. Partnership nursing infers an equality of relationship, which, at the far end of the spectrum, would mean the care being led by the child and his or her parents. Parents are considered the experts in the care of their child, with nurses adopting a more consultative role. There are specific attributes that support this concept, namely, collaboration, negotiation, empowerment, support through teaching and advocacy, and open and honest sharing (Smith et al., 2002). The extent to which each of these attributes is utilised depends on the skill of the nurse in facilitating the family's and child's wishes.

Casey, in 1995, undertook some further analysis of 'partnership' working and in this later work she identified three styles of communication that were apparent when interviewing and visiting paediatric nurses and their charges in hospital.

- Style 1: Some paediatric nurses are authoritative and controlling. They do assess parental wishes and do allow them to become involved in care but only on their terms and only when granted permission.
- Style 2: Some paediatric nurses are non-communicating and still continue the old tradition of excluding parents, making assumptions about the family's wishes, needs and abilities.
- Style 3: Some paediatric nurses do communicate and negotiate with

the child and parents, these are skilled nurses willing to share their knowledge and expertise and listen to families.

Casey clearly identifies the few nurses exhibiting style 3 as being truly collaborative, illustrating at first hand that although paediatric nurses were aware of the Partnership Model that they were utilising, it had still not been fully embraced by them all and some resistance to the core concept, that care may be best provided by the family, still existed.

There also remains a problematic issue surrounding the lack of skills that nurses have in negotiation, empowerment and teaching that may mean that the Partnership Model may be used functionally rather than in the truly holistic manner intended by Casey and other supporters of this style of children's healthcare. There is evidence from several studies that nurses understand child and family-centred care but do not use their skills to put it into practice (Baker, 1995; Bruce and Ritchie, 1997; Simons et al., 2001).

It has been suggested that despite its title, the Partnership Model contradicts its aim, by focusing on the child, with the family only fulfilling a care function (Coyne, 1996). Casey is quite clear that in her opinion the child was always at the centre and what she was describing was a partnership with the child and also the family that is one method of delivering family-centred care. The partnership is not with the parents alone as some nurses interpret. As Foster and Varni (2002) point out, it cannot be assumed that the child's perspective is the same as the parent's. In fact it may be desirable for the child's perspective to differ, because this is indicative of the child gaining autonomy and independence. Franck and Callery (2004), in their critical review of common concepts and issues in family-centred care, point out that the difference between 'child-centred' and 'family-centred' care is one of emphasis: neither term can exclude the other because child-centred care must take account of the social environment in which children live and family-centred care must be primarily concerned with the health of children.

Influence

One of the goals of many nursing models is the provision of high quality care based on an identified body of knowledge. Models should also provide a useful means of promoting continuity of care between different care environments (Chalmers, 1989). The widespread adoption of Casey's model in a short period of time, is the key to understanding the influence that this model has had. Family-centred care in nursing is based on a body of primarily North American literature which can be traced back to the early 1980s (O'Sullivan Burchard et al., 2004). Casey's work in both developing and promoting the use of her Partnership Model as a functional method for adapting the principles and concepts embraced in family-centred care, has had a significant impact on embedding family-centred care as the central style of care delivered by UK paediatric nurses. By 1990, family-centred care had clearly been accepted as the most influential philosophy for future paediatric nursing (Glasper, 1990). Casey's model quickly followed as the most influential model in the UK, possibly as a result of her chapter in Pendleton and Myles (Casey, 1991), which illustrated how the model could be used as an integral part of a paediatric nursing curriculum. As a result it was adopted by a number of Registered Sick Children's Nurse training institutions. During the same period other models of family-centred care were being developed in Canada in particular, where the McGill Model (see *Chapter 24*) (Gottlieb and Rowatt, 1987) and the Calgary Model (Wright and Leahey, 1994) emerged, but these had considerably less influence on UK paediatric nursing than did Casey's work.

The success of the model and in her later role as the editor of the RCN's publication *Paediatric Nursing* from 1996 until May 2009 has meant that

American Medical Informatics Association **7**(6): 523–8

Marriott S (1990) Parent power. *Nursing Times* **86**(34): 65

Matney S, Warren JJ, Casey A (2009) Educating a health terminologist. *Studies in Health Technology Information* 146: 577–81

Orem D (1985) *Nursing: Concepts of practice.* McGraw Hill, New York

O'Sullivan Burchard DJH, Clavierole A, Mitchell R, Walford C, Whyte DA (2004) Family nursing in Scotland. *Journal of Family Nursing* **10**: 323–37

Robertson J (1952) *Film: A two year old goes to hospital.* Tavistock Clinic and Institute, London

Savage E (2000) Family nursing: Minimising discontinuity for hospitalized children and their families. *Paediatric Nursing* **12**(2): 33–7

Simons J, Franck L, Roberson E (2001) Parent involvement in children's pain care: Views of parents and nurses. *Journal of Advanced Nursing* **36**: 591–9

Smith L, Coleman V, Bradshaw M (2002) Family-centred care: A practice continuum. In Smith L, Coleman V, Bradshaw M (eds) *Family-centred care: Concept, theory and practice.* Palgrave, Basingstoke

Valentine F (1998) Empowerment: Family centred care. *Paediatric Nursing* **10**(1): 24–7

Weiczoreck R, Natapoff J (1981) *A conceptual approach to the nursing of children.* J.B. Lippincott, Philadelphia

Wright LM, Leahey M (1994) *Nurses and families: A guide to family assessment and intervention* (2nd edn). F.A. Davis, Philadelphia

Yura H, Walsh M (1967) *The nursing process.* Appleton Century Crofts, Norwalk CT

Where to find out more

If you are interested in the most influential writings regarding the Partnership Model of Paediatric Practice then you should read:

Casey A (1988) A partnership with child and family. *Senior Nurse* **8**(4): 8–9

Casey A (1991) Using a nursing model in curriculum planning. In Pendleton S, Myles Y (eds) *Curriculum planning in nursing education: Practical applications*. Edward Arnold, London

Anne Casey's most recent writing regarding partnership working in paediatric nursing can be found in:

Casey A (2010) Assessing and planning care in partnership. In Glasper EA, Richardson J (eds) *A textbook of children's and young people's nursing* (2nd edn). Elsevier, Edinburgh

If you are interested in her work around health informatics then you may want to look at her most recent work which gives some insight into the range of her expertise in this field:

Casey A (2010) Global challenges of electronic records for nursing. In Cowen P, Moorehead S (eds) *Current issues in nursing* (8th edn). Mosby Year-Book, St Louis

Anne Casey has been a figurehead for paediatric nursing in the UK. As editor, and later as a Fellow of the Royal College of Nursing, she has been a long time champion of paediatric nursing, contributing significantly to debates about pre- and post-registration children's nursing education, Registered Sick Children's Nurse competencies, child protection legislation, and a host of other issues of relevance to paediatric nursing policy and practice throughout this period.

Much of the work she is involved in now, relates to advancing the use of health information and communications technology in clinical care and clinical research. In her current role as a health informatics advisor, she has continually promoted the need for nurses to become more involved in creating information systems and technology that take account of their real needs. A recurring interest in this area for Casey is a desire to see nursing terminologies harmonised across both informatics systems and across countries to further improve the clinical usefulness of information technology to nurses (Hardiker et al., 2000, Casey et al., 2006, Matney et al., 2009).

CHAPTER 26

Hildegard E Peplau

Margaret M Brown

Hildegard Peplau
1909–1999

Profile

Hildegard E Peplau led the way in many aspects of practice, education and theory development in nursing; her Theory of Interpersonal Relations has proved timeless. She articulated a framework for partnerships with patients, families and communities and recovery towards health that remains the essence of nursing today.

Biography

The 'mother of psychiatric nursing', as Hildegard Peplau was known, died in 1999, aged 89 years. Peplau had, until the end of her long life, taught, mentored, challenged and inspired generations of nurses.

Peplau was the first nurse, since Florence Nightingale, to publish a theory for the development of nursing (Forchuk, 1993). Her book, *Interpersonal relations in nursing*, published in 1952, was a watershed for nurses; at this time any major publisher would have demanded that a doctor should be co-author of an academic text such as this (Calloway, 2002). This seminal text has been reprinted repeatedly and has 'truly stood the test of time' (Clay, 1988: vii).

Hildegard Peplau was born in Reading, Pennsylvania, to immigrant parents who, although born in Poland, were of German descent. She was the second of six children; three girls and three boys. Her parents did not encourage her during her school years and she felt they actively opposed her learning (Calloway, 2002). Peplau saw nursing as one of the few occupations available to her, as a woman who would need to support herself financially, and which would allow her to escape the narrow confines of her home life (Calloway, 2002). She left home to train as a nurse on her 19th birthday and graduated from Pottsdown School of Nursing in 1931. Her appetite for learning was unabated, however, and she moved on to receive a BA in Interpersonal Psychology in 1943 from Bennington College, Vermont, while she was employed there as the school nurse. Soon afterwards American involvement in World War Two saw her join the US Army Nursing Corps, where she worked for part of the war in England. At the end of her army service her daughter was born and despite the difficulties for a single mother at that time, she raised her with some secrecy and the support of her brother and sister (Calloway, 2002).

After the war, in 1947, she gained an MA in Psychiatric Nursing and in 1953 a Doctor of Education in Curriculum Development from Teachers College, Columbia University, New York. At the same time she worked towards her Certification in Psychoanalysis for Teachers at the William Allanson White Institute in New York (Calloway, 2002).

In 1954 she moved to Rutgers University, New Jersey where she created the first graduate programme to prepare nurses to be clinical specialists in psychiatric nursing. She taught there for 20 years and retired as professor emeritus in 1974. During this period she also served as president and executive director of the American Nurses Association and was a board member of the International Council of Nursing (O'Toole and Welt, 1994).

During her career in practice she worked as a private home nurse, a theatre nurse, an army nurse and in wards in both general and psychiatric hospitals. She also maintained a private psychotherapy practice from 1958 until she retired (O'Toole and Welt, 1994).

Peplau's professional life spanned around 70 years (Peplau, 2008). Hers was not always a comfortable career, she had high standards and a single-minded vision of her own; this did not always endear her to colleagues (Calloway, 2002). In her later years she suffered constant pain following a

Key dates

1931	Qualified as a nurse
1943	BA in Interpersonal Psychology, Bennington College, Vermont
1943	Inducted into the Army Nurse Corps
1947	MA in Psychiatric Nursing, Columbia University, New York
1952	*Interpersonal relations in nursing* published
1953	Doctor of Education, Columbia University, New York
1959	Shortlisted for an academy award (Oscar) in the feature length documentary category, with the film *The Nurse Patient Relationship*
1973	Professor Emeritus at Rutgers University, New York
1992	Received the award named after her by the American Nurses Association; the Hildegard Peplau Award.
1998	Inducted into the Hall of Fame of the American Nurses Association
2008	Named one of 20 most influential nurses in Britain

Links with other nursing theorists

Peplau shares with Florence Nightingale (*see Chapter 1*) a focus on a rigorous, science-based approach to the practice and education of nursing (Gastmans, 1998). It is suggested that Peplau's theory was also expanded and developed by nurse theorists such as Imogene King (*see Chapter 23*), Josephine Paterson and Loretta Zderad (*see Chapter 7*) and Joyce Travelbee (Porr, 2009).

Barbara Carper's (*see Chapter 6*) aesthetic way of knowing in nursing (Carper, 1978) has been used with Peplau's theory to help nurses recognise interpersonal patterns; to make sense and meaning from their observations and provide a context for aesthetic knowing.

Philip Barker and Poppy Buchanan Barker (*see Chapter 27*) used Peplau's theory as part of the underpinnings in the development of the Tidal Model (Barker and Buchanan-Barker, 2005).

road accident and this may have contributed to her increasing impatience with the world of nursing. She felt that change was simply not happening fast enough. However, despite her pain and health problems, she continued to mentor, teach and supervise throughout her retirement.

Special interest

Peplau was truly interested in all aspects of nursing; in particular she focused on interpersonal relations between the nurse and patient. Above all she was a life-long learner and teacher. She had a special interest in psychiatric nursing but her impact was much greater and wider than this field (Johnson and Webber, 2005). The main focus in her early theory was often related to patients being in hospital for a medical or surgical intervention. It should be remembered that Peplau's theory was developed within the American healthcare system of the 1940s and 1950s where most nursing took place within hospitals. Patients would have stayed for much longer than they do today and nursing was still heavily influenced by medicine. In fact it was not Peplau's initial intent to develop a theory, but rather to write about the ideas she had that could improve nursing practice and the interpersonal relations between nurse and patient (Forchuk, 1993).

Peplau developed her interest in psychiatric nursing while she was a student at Bennington College in the early 1940s, where she studied with famous figures from the new psychotherapeutic movement in American psychiatry such as Erich Fromm, Frieda Fromm-Reichman, and particularly, Harry Stack Sullivan. These well-known theorists based their work on the understanding of people, particularly those with mental health problems, through their interactions and interpersonal relations with others. This intensive study of these leading figures in psychiatry and psychology led to her work on interpersonal relations in nursing. This interest was further developed by her experience in the School of Military Neuropsychiatry in England during her World War Two service (O'Toole and Welt, 1994).

Peplau was deeply interested in the difficulties faced by a person with mental health problems and she believed these were rooted in communication and relationships. She was clear that the role of the nurse was to offer patients experiences that helped them feel understood and respected and to give them the opportunity to relate to others (Peplau, 1989a). Peplau's theory of interpersonal relations shone a beacon on the inestimable value of the nurse–patient relationship and the building and maintaining of that relationship. She believed firmly that nurses could make a difference in the context of their interpersonal relationships with their patients. This nurse–patient relationship is described as beginning with two people who are essentially different, with their own ideas, values and goals. When that relationship is fully developed, the two people are working together towards a common understanding of the challenges faced by the patient. Because of the two-way nature of this relationship, self-awareness and knowledge on the nurse's part is essential (Peplau, 1989a).

Peplau was keen that nurses should continually develop their knowledge and skill and started building her theory with two assumptions; in other words, ideas she assumed were true. These are explicit throughout her work and are considered an essential aspect of developing any theory, as they can influence or change the meanings or concepts identified (Johnson and Webber, 2005). The first of these assumptions was that the kind of nurse a person becomes makes a significant difference to what patients will learn through the course of their illness. The second was that both in practice and education it is important to develop the skills to deal with interpersonal challenges (Peplau, 1952/1988). Above all she believed that the nurse needs to understand the meaning of the illness experience to patients; the value of their lived experience.

In contrast to the forward thinking theoretical stance of Peplau the world of psychiatric nursing at that time was more likely to be reflected in the British nursing text for 'mental nursing' from the same period. This text had 39 contributors; only two were nurses, the majority of were doctors. The work of the mental nurse as delineated here is in clear contrast to that of Peplau's theory,

> *It is still highly controversial to what extent nurses should participate in the more psychological forms of treatment.*
>
> (Partridge and McCowan, 1954: 333)

Peplau was scientific and analytical in her approach to learning and she used process recordings of her student nurses' interactions with their patients. These process recordings consisted of carefully written data, containing every detail of the interaction between the nurse and patient. Using this data, she identified the verbal and non-verbal communications between the nurse and patient and explored the developing understanding of the student nurses. A later innovation of Peplau's was to use first audio then video recording of these interactions. What was missing from them, however, was the patient's interpretation of the interaction; there is no doubt that her theory was in advance of its time but perhaps also of its time.

Her theory development has been described as both inductive and deductive as she used her own clinical work, and that of her students, to develop the theory that she then tested in the clinical setting. She also used the existing concepts and theories from other related areas, including those of Harry Stack Sullivan in particular (Forchuk, 1993). She explained her theory development as a three-step process that involves the nurses observing and naming concepts in practice, using available knowledge; interpreting and gathering more information that may extend or change the initial ideas and then using the knowledge to design an intervention for practice (O'Toole and Welt, 1994).

Peplau also had a deep interest and strong views about the profession of nursing, believing that it could only develop fully through clinical practice. She argued for nurse education to be controlled by nurses but in colleges and universities, not in nursing schools. She encouraged the development of nursing theory related to practice as a means of supporting this vision (Calloway, 2002). In American nurse education, she also led the way in the preparation of psychiatric nurses to Masters degree level. Before her innovative and challenging education programme, the Masters preparation would focus on administration or educational aspects of nursing. She insisted on a clinical focus that saw her students spending 16 to 20 hours a week in clinical work

with patients in state mental hospitals (Smoyak, 2009). In effect, it seems that Peplau's special interest was really nursing in all its forms and guises.

Summary of writings

In 1948, Peplau completed her seminal work *Interpersonal relations in nursing*. Her book was published in 1952 and has since appeared in nine languages and was re-printed in 1988 to real acclaim (Clay, 1988). This book has been viewed as one of the factors that proved transformational in progressing nursing from being a skilled occupation to a profession (Peplau, 2008). It contains a framework of concepts that form the basis of psychodynamic nursing (Peplau, 1952/1988). It could be seen as instrumental in changing the role of the patient from being an object of care, to a partner with the nurse in the care experience; a radical view at that time.

Peplau published papers and gave presentations on a variety of topics of interest to nursing; including issues related to practice, education, theory and research.

In practice, for example, she advocated the view that while nurses engage in many technical processes, it is the interaction with the nurse not the procedure being carried out, that brings real benefit to the patient. She suggested that nursing is above all a goal-directed, therapeutic interpersonal process and she is clear in all her writing that nurses can always do more to enable and facilitate the patient's movement towards health (Peplau, 1952/1988).

She wrote widely about communication within the nurse–patient relationship. She viewed the use of verbal communication as supremely important and advocated two main principles; one being clarity and the other continuity or coherence. She also cautioned against 'social talk' as if the nurse was speaking with friends and family. She believed communication with patients was too important to engage in without a therapeutic aim (Peplau, 1952/1988).

Peplau published a number of papers on psychiatric nurse education including subjects such as experiential teaching or how to promote learning through experience (Peplau, 1989b). Peplau's own teaching methods used constant questioning and analysis of actions, language and observations and how these could contribute to nursing knowledge (Calloway, 2002).

She also produced papers and spoke at conferences on key concepts such as loneliness (Peplau, 1989c), anxiety (Peplau, 1989d), and the learning process (Peplau, 1989e). She adopted a qualitative research approach to these concepts, using them to develop and explore behaviours and interventions for nursing practice (O'Toole and Welt, 1994).

She continued to extend her ideas and theory until her death and published and presented her ideas to a national and international audience. Many of her early papers were published in obscure or difficult to access locations. However, in 1989 two of her graduate students, Anita Werner O'Toole and Sheila Rouslin Welt edited a selection of her works from 1953 to 1989 and these form a body of work indicative of Peplau's thinking about nurses and nursing (O'Toole and Welt, 1994)

Theory

This section describes Peplau's original Theory of the Nurse–Patient Relationship which is largely unchanged more than 60 years later.

Peplau's theory examines the development and maintenance of the nurse–patient relationship, the roles of the nurse and how nurses can learn about nursing. She described the key elements in nursing as 'the nurse, the patient and what goes on between them' (Peplau, 1989a: 5). The development and maintenance of the nurse–patient relationship depends on the nurse understanding the importance of these elements.

The nurse–patient relationship is characterised by four interlocking phases and each phase may have overlapping roles and functions. Within each phase there are therapeutic tasks identified for the nurse and expected responses from the patient (Peplau, 1952/1988).

The orientation phase

This is the period where the nurse and patient meet as strangers, often with expectations of each other that may be the result of previous life experiences. The patient presents to the nurse with a felt need for healthcare; the patient may, or may not, recognise that need. Patients may act in ways that seem to be challenging in order to establish if they can trust the nurse with their healthcare.

The therapeutic tasks in this phase are to build trust with patients and establish a therapeutic and dynamic environment where they can begin to identify their needs. This phase is seen as essential in order to help patients integrate their current illness into their life experience (Peplau, 1952/1988).

The identification phase

In this phase the patient starts to develop trust and will begin to respond selectively to the nurse who is perceived to offer the help that is needed. The patient then begins to identify his or her problems and issues with the nurse. During this stage the expectations of the patient can be clarified and the patient's feelings can be explored. These feelings can be powerful and can lead to the person feeling helpless and dependant.

The therapeutic task for the nurse is to ensure that the patient is given the space and time to express these feelings and have these addressed within a non-judgemental relationship. The nurse should be able to accept people as they are and, for example, so-called 'attention seeking behaviour' in a patient should be understood as a normal response to powerlessness (Peplau, 1952/1988). The nurse would then try and work with the person to change these negative feelings for those that are more creative and productive.

The exploitation phase

During this phase patients derive full value from the care given by the nurse and the services available to them. This is a period of intense change and Peplau likens it to adolescence where there is a similar need to learn how to balance dependence and independence.

The therapeutic task for the nurse is to work with the patient to try and

References

Barker P, Buchanan-Barker P (2005) *The Tidal Model: A Guide for Mental Health Professionals*. Brunner-Routledge, Hove

Beeber LS, Bourbonniere M (1998) The concept of interpersonal pattern in Peplau's Theory of Nursing. *Journal of Psychiatric and Mental Health Nursing* **5**: 187–92

Buchanan-Barker P (2004) The Tidal Model: Uncommon sense. *Mental Health Nursing* **24**(3): 6–10

Calloway BJ (2002) *Hildegard Peplau: Psychiatric Nurse of the Century*. Springer Publishing Company: New York

Carper BA (1978) Fundamental patterns of knowing in nursing. *Advances in Nursing Science* **1**: 13–23

Clay T (1988) Foreword. In Peplau HE (ed) *Interpersonal relations in nursing*. Macmillan Education, Hampshire

Department of Health (2006) *The Chief Nursing Officer's Review of Mental Health Nursing*. Department of Health, London

help him or her balance these needs for dependence and independence. The nurse will also continue to meet new needs as they emerge. In essence this phase is where the patient begins to move towards the future and recovery.

The resolution phase

This phase is a period where the patient can be encouraged to be independent and leads to the termination of this professional relationship. During this phase patients feel their needs are being met and begin to aspire to goals they have identified for themselves. They can now apply new skills in problem solving and interpersonal communication. The therapeutic task here is for the nurse to manage the shift in decision making and goal setting to the patient.

Nursing defined

In defining her ideas about nursing, Peplau firmly rejected the idea that 'nursing is what it now does' (Peplau, 1988: 4), and that merely examining current nursing activity does not allow real innovation and development of nursing theory and practice. She continually advocates in her writing that we should not ask, 'What is it that nurses do now?', but rather, 'What can nurses do in the future?' She clearly saw nursing as a work in progress with a continual need to look forward.

She described nursing as not just working with patients but also with families and communities; advocating in particular the importance of collaboration and partnership with all those involved in care (Peplau, 1952/1988).

Nurses, working within Peplau's theoretical framework, may assume a number of different roles within their relationship with their patients. These roles will change to meet the patient's needs at any given time throughout the relationship and include:

- *Stranger*. When the nurse meets with the patient for the first time; both bring with them preconceived ideas and previous experiences.
- *Technical expert*. To understand and provide professional interventions.
- *Resource person*. To give specific and appropriate information to help patients understand the situation they are in.
- *Surrogate*. To replace others from the patient's past, such as the mother. The nurse can help the person examine feelings related to prior relationships and re-focus these as necessary.
- *Counsellor*. To listen to patients as they talk about what has led them to this situation and what their feeling are.

Other roles are identified, but the number and type of these are only limited by the nurse's knowledge, skill and capabilities.

Health defined

Peplau asks many questions about health; in particular about nurses' knowledge of what health is, since if they have difficulty defining this then they cannot know how to support it. Peplau argues that definitions of health lack clarity, therefore, within this theory, health is clearly defined as a,

...forward movement of personality and other ongoing processes in the direction of creative, constructive, productive personal and community living.

(Peplau, 1988: 12)

Douglass JL, Sowell RL, Phillips KD (2003) Using Peplau's theory to examine the psychosocial factors associated with HIV-infected women's difficulty in taking their medications. *Journal of Theory Construction and Testing* **7**(1): 10–17

Forchuk C, Brown B (1989) Establishing a nurse–client relationship: What helps? *Journal of Psychosocial Nursing and Mental Health Services* **27**(2): 30–4

Forchuk C (1992) The orientation phase of the nurse–client relationship: How long does it take? *Perspectives in Psychiatric Care* **28**(4): 7–10

Forchuk C (1993) *Hildegarde E. Peplau Interpersonal Nursing Theory – Notes on nursing theories*. Sage Publications, Newbury Park, CA

Forchuk C (1995a) Uniqueness within the nurse–client relationship. *Archives of Psychiatric Nursing* **9**(1): 34–9

Forchuk C (1995b) Development of a nurse–client relationship: What helps? *Journal of the American Psychiatric Nurses Association* **1**(5): 146–51

Forchuk C, Westwall J, Martin M, Bamber-Azzapardi W, Kosterewa-Tolman D, Hux M (1998a) Factors influencing movement of chronic psychiatric patients from the orientation to the working phase of the nurse–client relationship on an inpatient unit. *Perspectives in Psychiatric Care* **34**(1): 36–43

Forchuk C, Jewell J, Schofield R, Sircelj M, Valledor T (1998b) From hospital to community: Bridging therapeutic relationships. *Journal of Psychiatric and Mental Health Nursing* **5**: 197–202

Forchuk C, Westwall J, Martin M, Bamber-Azzapardi W, Kosterewa-Tolman D, Hux M (2000) The developing nurse–client relationship: Nurses' perspectives. *Journal of the American Psychiatric Nurses Association* **6**(1): 3–10

Forchuk C, Martin ML, Chan YL, Jensen E (2005) Therapeutic relationships: From psychiatric hospital to community. *Journal of Psychiatric and Mental Health Nursing* **12**: 556–64

Gastmans C (1998) Interpersonal relations in nursing: A philosophical–ethical analysis of the work of Hildegard E Peplau. *Journal of Advanced Nursing* **28**(6): 1312–19

Johnson BM, Webber PB (2005) *An introduction to theory and reasoning in nursing.* Lippincott, Williams and Wilkins, Philadelphia

Marchese K (2006) Using Peplau's Theory of Interpersonal Relations to guide the education of patients undergoing urinary diversion. *Urologic Nursing* **26**(5): 363–70

Moore R (2001) A framework for telephone nursing. *Nursing Times* **97**(16): 36

McNaughton DB (2005) A naturalistic test of Peplau's theory in home visiting. *Public Health Nursing* **22**(5): 429–38

NHS Scotland (2006) *Rights, relationships and recovery: The Report of the National Review of Mental Health Nursing in Scotland.* Scottish Government, Edinburgh

O'Toole AW, Welt SR (eds) (1994) *Hildegard E Peplau, selected works: Interpersonal Theory in nursing.* Macmillan Press: Hampshire

Partridge M, McCowan PK (eds) (1954) *A handbook for mental nurses.* Bailliere, Tindall and Cox, London

Pearson A (2008) Dead poets, nursing theorists and contemporary nursing practice. *International Journal of Nursing Practice* **14**: 79–80

Peplau HE (1952/1988) *Interpersonal relations in nursing.* MacMillan Education,

Peplau also describes two conditions necessary for health; these are the ability to meet both physiological demands and interpersonal conditions that are both individual and social (Peplau, 1952/1988). The nurse's role in promoting and maintaining health, therefore, is not only to study the effectiveness of the interventions they offer. They must also understand the skills needed to help people resolve their difficulties, and continue to develop new skills to meet future problems.

Putting theory into practice

Peplau's theory has been used almost continually since she first published her book in 1952. The implementation of the theory into practice has occurred in most nursing specialities and a number of countries. Peplau's theory of psychodynamic nursing is considered suitable for all specialities, not just mental health (Forchuk, 1993).

Peplau's theory predates the nursing process but it can guide all aspects of assessment, planning, intervening and evaluating practice. Assessment begins by determining the stage of the interpersonal relationship that has been reached. It involves the nurse being aware of the communication patterns of the patient. The nurse uses skilled observation and is self-aware and reflective in order to gather as much information as possible about the current situation. This includes being aware of any pre-conceptions that may interfere with the development of the relationship (Forchuk, 1993). The patient's previous experiences, level of anxiety and current ability to learn are also assessed (Marchese, 2006).

Planning of care is carried out in partnership with the patient, taking into account the current phase of the nurse–patient relationship. If the relationship is in the orientation period, for example, the patient may wish the nurse to take the lead in planning care; in the resolution phase the patient would expect to take the lead role (Peplau, 1952/1988). Interventions are developed that are appropriate to the patient's needs at the time and may include, for example, developing trust in the early stages of the relationship, moving to education on concordance with medication as the patient progresses to recovery. Evaluation of the effectiveness of the nursing care provided is continuous through using process recording of the patient's response to each intervention and interaction (Peplau, 1952/1988).

Research into Peplau's theory has been sporadic, but papers continue to appear in nursing journals and these explore her theory in a variety of practice specialities. The most extensive research has been carried out by Cheryl Forchuk in Canada, and has included the development of a tool to identify which stage of the relationship the nurse and patient have reached, enabling the nurse to map the phases of the relationship as it progresses (Forchuk and Brown, 1989). This mapping ensures the nurse is aware both of the patient's needs and the appropriate therapeutic tasks to be addressed. Forchuk examined the orientation phase of the nurse–patient relationship in particular and identified how long it could take to progress through this stage, identifying the factors involved in this process (Forchuk, 1992). Other studies have examined specific aspects of Peplau's theory. These included measuring the uniqueness of the nurse–patient relationship (Forchuk, 1995a), the development of the nurse–patient relationship (Forchuk, 1995b), progress through the phases of the relationship (Forchuk et al., 1998a), and exploring the perspectives of the nurse in relation to Peplau's theory (Forchuk et al., 2000).

The changing setting and context for mental healthcare was also used as an opportunity to use Peplau's theory as the framework to develop a research-based, case management project that planned to integrate people with a long history of psychiatric hospital care into the community (Forchuk et al., 1998b). This approach was grounded in the interpersonal relations among a group of hospital and community staff and the patients who were being discharged from hospital. The study, called 'From hospital to community: Bridging therapeutic relationships' (Forchuk et al., 1998b), showed that this theoretical approach improved the quality of life for the people involved and was an economical approach to the transition process. Forchuk developed this approach further as a model for practice called the Transitional Discharge Model (Forchuk et al., 2005).

Others who have implemented Peplau's theory in practice, include the newly formed NHS direct system in West Yorkshire, that used Peplau's theory as a framework for practice. This theory was chosen because each care episode can be a very brief interaction for the nurse telephone advisors and it is essential that they are able to construct a partnership quickly in order to identify patients' problems and meet their needs (Moore, 2001). The paper also describes how the nurses adopted a range of roles, as described by Peplau's theory; especially important for these nurses were the roles of stranger and resource person, reflective of the purpose of the service they provide.

Douglass, Sowell and Phillips (2003) used Peplau's theory as a framework for an investigation into the factors that affect medication adherence in women who are HIV positive and taking HIV medication. Their results supported the propositions of Peplau's theory as they found a positive correlation between the women's adherence to their medication regime and a positive therapeutic relationship with their care providers.

In a study of the educational needs of patients who required urinary diversion following a diagnosis of cancer, Peplau's theory was used to construct a planned educational programme. The results of this study emphasise the importance of the nurse–patient relationship in achieving positive outcomes for the patient. An awareness of the patient's readiness to learn was a key factor in the success of the educational programme (Marchese, 2006).

McNaughton (2005) explored the use of Peplau's theory, using a case study design, with five pairs of public health nurses and pre-natal women in their care. She found that the theory supported the work of these nurses and they found it to be a useful guide for practice.

Influence

Peplau's theory continues to influence nursing, and mental health nursing in particular. Her work is known throughout the world and underpins current thinking in a variety of ways. One of the key ways identified by Forchuk (1993), is that the focus for nurses should be on their own self-awareness and constant reflection, not just on the patient's experiences but on their own self-development. This emphasis on reflection and self-awareness for nurses increasingly underpins education and clinical practice.

Peplau's theory is evident throughout mental health nursing in Britain today and has echoes in two of the most important recently published documents for mental health nursing. Both the Chief Nursing Officer's *Review of mental health nursing in England* (Department of Health, 2006) and, in Scotland, the *Report of the national review of mental health nursing* (NHS Scotland, 2006) clearly emphasise the fundamental role of the therapeutic relationship in all aspects of nursing care. The key tenets of Peplau's theory, self-awareness, interpersonal skills and the formation and maintenance of the therapeutic relationship, resonate throughout both documents.

Peplau was a pioneer in the education of nurses and developed programmes for both undergraduate and postgraduate courses (Johnson and

Hampshire

Peplau HE (1989a) Interpersonal relationships in psychiatric nursing. In O'Toole AW, Welt SR (eds) *Hildegard E Peplau selected works; Interpersonal Theory in Nursing*. MacMillan Press, Hampshire

Peplau HE (1989b) What is experiential teaching? In O'Toole AW, Welt SR (eds) *Hildegard E Peplau selected works; Interpersonal Theory in Nursing*. MacMillan Press, Hampshire

Peplau HE (1989c) Loneliness. In O'Toole AW, Welt SR (eds) *Hildegard E Peplau selected works; Interpersonal Theory in Nursing*. MacMillan Press, Hampshire

Peplau HE (1989d)Theoretical constructs: Anxiety, self, and hallucinations. In O'Toole AW, Welt SR (eds) *Hildegard E Peplau selected works; Interpersonal Theory in Nursing*. MacMillan Press, Hampshire

Peplau HE (1989e) Process and concept of learning. In O'Toole AW, Welt SR (eds) *Hildegard E Peplau selected works; Interpersonal Theory in Nursing*. MacMillan Press, Hampshire

Peplau LA (2008) Human welfare is advanced by nursing (Letter) *Nursing Times* **104**(49): 14

Porr C (2009) Mindful attentiveness: Rekindling the nurse-patient relationship. *Journal of Clinical Nursing* **26**(3): 150–3

Reynolds W, Lauder W, Sharkey S, MacIvers S, Veitch T, Cameron D (2004) The effects of a transitional discharge model for psychiatric patients. *Journal of Psychiatric and Mental Health Nursing* **11**: 82–8

Smoyak SA (2009) The United States Context. In Barker, P (ed) *Psychiatric and mental health nursing: The craft of caring*. Edward Arnold Ltd, London

Where to find out more

Hildegard E Peplau (1952/1988) *Interpersonal relations in nursing*. MacMillan, UK
This book was re-printed in 2000 and 2004.

Barbara Calloway (2002) *Hildegard Peplau: Psychiatric Nurse of the Century*. Springer, New York

This is a comprehensive biography of Peplau's life and work.

http://publish.uwo.ca/%7Ecforchuk/peplau/abotjrn.html
The Nursing Theorist Homepage provides information about Peplau's life and work.

Webber, 2005). She was among the first nurse educators to identify the need to make the content of nursing programmes explicit; exploring concepts, patterns and theories based on scientific exploration and examination (O'Toole and Welt, 1994). She is identified as having provided a stimulus to the work of other theorists in nursing, such as Henderson, Johnson and King (Johnson and Webber, 2005). Others have been more explicit in their debt to her. For example the Transitional Discharge Model was developed through the Bridges to Discharge Project (Forchuk et al., 1998b), and based on Peplau's theory.

Phil Barker includes Peplau as one of the major influences on his own theory building of the Tidal Model and she is called the 'ship's surgeon' in the book on the model. The term is used to indicate her quick wit and ability to reach incisively the crux of an intellectual argument (Barker and Buchanan-Barker, 2005). The Tidal Model is said to develop many of Peplau's ideas on interpersonal relationships, clarifying further what mental health nurses should be doing (Buchanan-Barker, 2004).

Peplau's legacy, therefore, continues to the present day and where better to finish than with the words of her daughter, Letitia Anne Peplau, a Professor of Psychology at the University of California:

My mother believed in nurses' ability to advance human welfare through theory development, research and practice. She was very proud to be a nurse.

(Peplau, 2008: 14)

CHAPTER 27

Philip J Barker

Allan Donnell

Philip J Barker
Born 1946

Profile

Phil Barker was the first Professor of Mental Health Nursing in the United Kingdom. His work has had huge influence on the development of Mental Health Nursing both in the UK and internationally. In the development of the Tidal Model, Barker has produced a values-based, person-centred model of nursing which guides and develops modern mental health nursing practice.

Biography

Philip J Barker was the United Kingdom's first Professor of Psychiatric Nursing Practice and he held this post at the University of Newcastle, England, from 1993 to 2002. Phil Barker and his wife Poppy Buchanan-Barker are directors of Clan Unity Mental Health Recovery Consultancy and are co-authors of the Tidal Model.

Phil Barker began his career working as a nursing assistant in a large psychiatric hospital in Scotland. His interest in mental health was first sparked in the 1960s when, as a fine art student, he learned of the work of his fellow countryman RD Laing, a psychiatrist who developed a radical, humanist approach to working with people in psychosis.

Later Barker went on to explore behavioural, cognitive and family therapy, alongside his enduring interest in humanistic approaches to care. His doctoral thesis studied women and their experiences of manic depression, and his early published works develop his ideas on assessment and working with people experiencing severe and enduring mental health problems (Barker, 1987).

He later rejected such language as disempowering and his early work, although heavily influenced by the cognitive and behavioural schools, already began to grapple with the difficulties of 'knowing the person' and 'holistic' approaches to nursing (Barker, 1985). His work is philosophical and poetic in nature, rooted in the Celtic tradition of story telling and the 'craft of caring'.

Poppy Buchanan-Barker has a background in social work and has spent many years working as a counsellor with families, people in suicidal crisis and people with substance abuse problems. Here she learned the value of self-confidence, well-being and the need for people to feel good about themselves. Barker and Buchanan-Barker's experiences and conversations together have contributed to the development of the Tidal Model – a humanistic and values-based approach to working alongside people experiencing mental health problems.

In recent years much of their time has been devoted to promoting the Tidal Model, which is an approach to mental health nursing based on hearing the authentic voice of the person. This model is based on a distillation of the ideas of Phil and Poppy over their lifetimes in the field of health and social care. There are now many mental health nurses in all corners of the world advocating and using the Tidal Model as an anchor to their work.

Key dates

1985   First edition of *Patient assessment in psychiatric nursing* published

1987   Completed Doctoral Studies at University of Abertay, Scotland

1993   Appointed Professor of Psychiatric Nursing Practice, University of Newcastle

1999   Published *What are psychiatric nurses needed for?* a paper that was to lead to the development of the Tidal Model

Special interest

Barker believes that it is almost impossible to discuss any complex theory without the use of metaphor and stories (Barker, 2002). This section therefore begins with a story, which, although perhaps apocryphal, might be a useful illustration of several important points about the model and a metaphor itself for the development of the Tidal Model.

An art critic was interviewing the famous artist Pablo Picasso in a café

in the south of France. The critic asked Picasso if he could have a napkin that the artist had been doodling on. Picasso agreed but asked in payment the sum of 10 000 Francs. 'That's ridiculous,' said the critic 'to charge such a sum for a few minutes work!' Picasso looks him in the eye and says, 'My friend, it took me 80 years to draw that.'

Various versions of this story can be found but they all serve to make the same point. Experience is priceless and turns knowledge into wisdom. Within the Tidal Model lies the essence of many important and influential theories and concepts from the fields of mental health nursing, humanistic and cognitive-behavioural psychology, epistemology, philosophy and wisdom from many other sources. These interests, held over a long and distinguished nursing career, have all helped craft the Tidal Model and have all been interests of Barker as reflected in his writings. However, the real and abiding interest of the man and the nurse is how can we help people learn and recover from mental distress?

Within the field of nursing, Barker cites Hildegard Peplau as one of his major influences. Peplau, often called the 'mother of psychiatric nursing', encouraged Barker to 'look beyond the delimiting parameters of the patient label and to consider what it might mean to be the person' (Barker, 1999: 78).

Peplau's interpersonal theory of nursing and her understanding of the therapeutic relationship as a journey taken by the nurse and patient from being distant strangers, to a point where rapport exists and therapeutic helping can begin, mirrors the collaborative relationship outlined in the Tidal Model.

Peplau also highlights the power of metaphor and story telling and the importance of careful attending to what patients say and how they say it. Barker once asked Peplau to sum up her thoughts on what was important in mental health nursing and she replied, 'People make themselves up as they talk!' (Barker, 1999: 122)

The person's story, told in his or her own voice is the key to finding solutions to the individual's mental health problems.

The model emphasises ordinary communication as the medium for identifying where the person is at — most nurses do not have formal psychotherapeutic training but this does not prevent them from being able to transform the ordinary into an extraordinary and powerful form of helping.

(Buchanan-Barker, 2004)

Barker traces the roots of the Tidal Model back to Florence Nightingale who believed that the role of the nurse was not to heal but to create the best possible conditions for healing to take place by nature or by God. Barker creates the term 'trephotaxic nursing' to describe this view of

nursing, which emphasises setting the right conditions for growth and development. (Barker, 1999: 31).

In a study of the Tidal Model as experienced by patients, Cook et al. (2005) suggest that 'empowering interactions, in which the person is genuinely regarded as the expert in their own lives, enhance therapeutic outcomes'. In the Tidal Model the person is the expert on his or her problems of living and the nurse's role is to provide an environment in which healing can happen.

The Tidal Model has been described as a 'deeply collaborative, person-centred, narrative-based theory' (Barker and Buchanan-Barker, 2005: 213). It emphasises solution-focused approaches to problems of living, the importance of the lived experience and an appreciation of the potential for healing that lies within the re-authoring of the narrative (Brookes, 2006). These concepts have long been of special interest to Barker and it might be useful to explore them further before discussing the model itself.

Collaboration and partnership working are buzz words in mental health and social care but Barker means more than including the client or patient in his or her care. Collaboration is about travelling with the person and, together, trying to make sense of the journey. The Tidal Model assumes that the person's narrative is developed through collaboration with the nurse.

The story that becomes the basis of the therapeutic discourse is not a private monologue, but rather is a story jointly authored through a seamless series of conversations.

(Barker and Buchanan-Barker, 2005: 27)

Barker's interest in and commitment to collaborative working is highlighted by the many articles, books and conference presentations he has worked on together with people who have experienced mental distress and have first hand knowledge of mental health services.

Barker's interest in solution-focused approaches and on finding creative and individual ways of helping people manage their problems of living owes much to the work of Steve de Shazer who developed Solution Focused Therapy. This approach has several ideas central to the Tidal Model. Ideas such as, 'keeping it simple', 'change is inevitable' and 'therapy as co-operative endeavour' (De Shazer, 1985), suggest that the focus should be on the solution rather than the problem. De Shazer also suggests that the therapist and the patient construct meanings together and that complex problems need not have complex solutions. Once again these ideas are central to the Tidal Model.

Finally Barker's interest in 'person-centredness' is also evident in the Tidal Model. This means putting the person and his or her world at the heart of the care process. Often care is organised around the needs of the service or to conform to a model of practice that demands that certain things have to be done in a particular way and at a particular time. The Tidal Model's approach is to encourage an exploration of the person's world as he or she sees it. The nurse is encouraged to stay focused on the person's definition of a desired outcome.

Summary of writings

Barker has published 14 books, over 50 book chapters and more than 150 academic papers (Brookes, 2006). A clear and readable account of the Tidal Model is given in Barker and Buchanan-Barker (2005). To find out more about Barker's ideas on mental health nursing a good start might be Barker (1999). To read about the lived experience of 'madness' and the predicaments of those who 'use' mental health services see Barker et al. (1999a).

Phil Barker has also edited a basic but comprehensive textbook for mental health nursing students. This book has become recommended reading on many pre-registration Diploma and Degree programmes. A second edition of this book has recently been published (Barker, 2009).

Theory

The Tidal Model was developed from a four year study at Newcastle University on the 'need for nursing'. This study used grounded theory and action research to explore and clarify the roles and functions of mental health nurses and to answer the question, 'What are psychiatric nurses needed for?' (Barker et al., 1999b).

This study, and other work by Barker at that time, highlighted the centrality of the person's experience – as he or she experience it – and the relationship between the nurse and the 'person in care', as being the foundation of good mental health nursing. The studies found that both professionals and 'people as patients' were keen for nurses to be able to relate in an ordinary everyday way. (Stevenson et al., 2002)

The Tidal Model is values driven. Our values are the compass on the voyage – showing us the right direction and helping us steer our ship safely onwards. The values of the Tidal Model are congruent with modern mental health nursing practice but, like much of the model, have echoes of older wisdom. Barker suggests that nurses must at least display some 'common decency' in their encounters with people who need care. The Tidal Model asks users to subscribe to some key principles before adopting the model, these he calls engagement beliefs.

These engagement beliefs or core values are:

- Recovery is possible.
- Change is inevitable.
- Ultimately people know what is best for them.
- Persons possess all the resources they need to begin the recovery journey.
- The person is the teacher and we, the helpers, are the pupils.
- We need to be creatively curious to learn what needs to be done to help the person.

As well as these core values, the Tidal Model asks us to consider the person inhabiting three dimensions. These elements of personhood are inter-related and the three-dimensional picture is made up of each of them – they are 'self', 'world', and 'others'. This rather confusing triad can be understood as people's internal maps of reality and what they need to feel personally safe and secure (self), how they relate to others and how others can help them (other) and what meanings they place on the events in their lives – how they

Links with other nursing theorists

Florence Nightingale (*see Chapter 1*) and Hildegard Peplau (*see Chapter 26*).

construct and make sense of their surroundings (world). A holistic assessment based on these three key areas helps the nurse and the person explore and construct the narrative to describe the person's predicament (Barker and Buchanan-Barker, 2007).

The central metaphor of the Tidal Model is of course water and the sea. Tides ebb and flow and this can be equated with the cyclical rhythmic nature of life itself. The inhalation and exhalation of breath, the circadian rhythm of waking and sleeping and the need for activity and rest are all examples of this ebb and flow. Life is a journey taken on the ocean of experience. At critical points on the journey people may experience storms, be lost at sea, may become shipwrecked or may be boarded by pirates (Barker and Buchanan-Barker, 2005: 10). These terms are used to describe various psychiatric and emotional disturbances such as being overwhelmed by problems, losing direction, facing emotional breakdown and being subjected to abuse. At times people may need rescuing and they may need a safe haven for a while before they can regain their sea legs and continue their voyage – perhaps with a newly repaired and refitted vessel.

The metaphor of water is a strong one as it reflects the language people often use when describing mental distress, 'I was all washed up', 'drowning in a sea of problems', 'out of my depth', and so on. However, it is important to remember that the metaphors that people use and the stories they tell themselves are personal. The name is not the object, and if people choose to use different language we should accept this.

The model begins with the assumption that the person in distress is experiencing 'problems in living' and that these problems are the proper focus for nursing. Problems of living involve the 'myriad ways that people feel about themselves and others, and their associated beliefs about life in general' (Barker and Buchanan-Barker, 2005: 101). This essentially pragmatic approach respects the lived experience of the individual and does not seek to explain these problems in terms of diagnoses, social inadequacy, psychopathology or bio-chemical imbalances.

Nursing in the Tidal Model is involved in helping to reconstruct the person's narrative along with the person. The nurse is primarily concerned with how individual people articulate their problems and concerns. The words, concepts and metaphors people use to describe their predicaments are much more important than the label attached by the psychiatrist or therapist. Barker argues that medical diagnoses and nursing diagnoses may be useful for some purposes (such as research or service planning) but that the proper focus of nursing care lies with individuals, their human concerns and their perception of the problem rather than directly with the disease or disorder they are experiencing (Barker, 2003: 117).

Evaluation of the model as a useful tool for nursing care is an important aspect of reviewing the utility of the model in practice and there have been several important papers written on the model within different care settings (Cook et al., 2005; Lafferty and Davidson, 2006). The nature of most of these evaluations is essentially qualitative, focusing on the person's experience of the model or the nurse's experience and not on measurable outcomes or behaviours. This is congruent with Barker's ideas on the nature of knowledge and truth (Barker, 1999: 46), but it does mean that the evaluation of the model as one that is useful for practice must essentially be subjective, based on whether you think the model is congruent with the values of mental health nursing in the 21st century.

Putting the theory into practice.

Ultimately any nursing model must be useful in directing and shaping the process of nursing. The process of nursing or 'nursing process' consists of four elements – assessment, planning, implementation and evaluation. (Christensen and Kenney, 1990). This systematic approach to nursing can be used to explore the basic elements of any nursing care and is a useful way of describing the model in practice.

Assessment in the Tidal Model begins with the nurse exploring problems of living with the person during an interview conducted using the 'holistic assessment form'. It is important that this is done as soon as possible after entry to the service and that participation is actively encouraged. The form is completed by nurses and service users together and where possible patients write this, or are helped to write it in their own words (Barker and Buchanan-Barker, 2005).

The assessment begins by a careful explanation of the process and nurses should offer patients a copy of the assessment together with an invitation to record this in their own hand. The process could begin, after making the person comfortable, with the nurse offering the following explanation.

> *We are really interested in your understanding of what's been happening to you recently and how it has been affecting you. We use this assessment – the holistic assessment [offer copy] – to get a summary of all of this down on paper. We use this as a jumping off point for your care plan, trying to make sure that we offer the kind of help you need right now. Do you feel OK about beginning this now?*
>
> (Barker and Buchanan-Barker, 2005:108)

Following permission, the nurse continues by asking why the person has come to the service and explores, by means of a semi-structured interview, how the problem began. The nurse may begin the interview with a question such as

> *So, what has brought you here today?*

The nurse should respectfully listen to the person's story clarifying as necessary by using supplementary questions or by paraphrasing and summarising the person's answers. This should lead into an exploration of the problem's origins. The nurse asks:

When did you first notice, or become aware, of this?

The next set of questions focus on the effect the problem has had on the person's life and how the person felt in the beginning about the problem. It is suggested that a useful way of introducing these questions is by briefly summarising the origins of the problem. In this way the nurse can check out his or her understanding of the person's problem and it also shows to the person that the nurse has been listening carefully. Following this brief summary the nurse could usefully ask:

So how did that affect you at first?

or

So, what effect did that have on you, and your life in general?

These questions may encourage people to talk about the emotional impact of their problems on their life but if they do not it is important to ask further supplementary questions to elicit this. The nurse might ask

And how did you feel about that at the time?

or

How did you feel about that in the beginning?

By now the nurse should have some understanding of how the problem began for the person and how it affected the person at that time. Now the nurse should try to bring the situation up to date. Once again this is a good place to briefly summarise responses to date to check out if both parties are on the same wavelength and that the person is happy to carry on with the interview.

Up to this point the assessment has explored how the problem affected the person at first, how this changed over time and how the problem appears now. The assessment also looks at how the problem has affected the person's relationship with others and asks the person to attempt to clarify the meaning of the problems as he or she sees it.

This approach highlights the person-centredness of the model and is radically different from the focus of a diagnostic interview which seeks to clarify the problem by classifying it under a pre-determined label.

To summarise, the holistic assessment seeks to clarify:

- What does the person believe his or her needs are?
- What is the scale of these problems/needs – how big are they?
- What aspects of the person's life might play a part in helping to resolve such problems, or meet such needs?
- What needs to happen to bring about what the person would regard as positive change?

(Barker and Buchanan-Barker, 2005: 103)

The planning stage of the nursing process involves setting goals and prioritising areas of concern with the person. The Tidal Model suggests

References

Barker P (1985) *Patient assessment in psychiatric nursing* (1st edn) Croon Helm, London UK

Barker P (1987) *An evaluation of specific nursing interventions in the management of patients suffering from manic depressive psychosis.* Unpublished doctoral thesis, University of Abertay, Dundee, Scotland

Barker P (1999) *The philosophy and practice of psychiatric nursing.* Churchill Livingstone, Edinburgh UK

Barker P (2002) Tidal Model - The healing power of metaphor within the patient's narrative. *Journal of Psychosocial Nursing and Mental Health Services* **40**(7): 42–50

Barker P (2003) *Psychiatric and mental health nursing – The craft of caring.* Arnold, London UK

Barker P (2009) *Psychiatric and mental health nursing – The craft of caring.* Arnold, London

Barker P, Buchanan-Barker P (2005) *The Tidal Model – A guide for mental health professionals.* Routledge, London UK

Barker P, Buchanan-Barker P (2007) *The Tidal Model – Mental health reclamation and recovery.* Clan Unity International, Fife UK

Barker P, Buchanan-Barker P (2008) The Tidal Commitments: Extending the value base of mental health recovery. *Journal of Psychiatric and Mental Health Nursing* **15**: 93–100

Barker P, Campbell P, Davidson B (eds) (1999a) *From the ashes of experience – Reflections on madness, survival and growth.* Whurr Publishers, London UK

Barker P, Jackson S, Stevenson C (1999b) *What are psychiatric nurses needed for? Developing a theory of essential nursing practice*. Journal of Psychiatric and Mental Health Nursing **6**: 273–82

Brookes N (2006) Phil Barker – Tidal Model of Mental Health Recovery. In Marriner Tomey A, Alligood MR (eds) *Nursing theorists and their work*. C V Mosby, St Louis USA

Buchanan-Barker P (2004) The Tidal Model – Uncommon sense. *Mental Health Nursing* **24**(3): 6–11

Christensen PJ, Kenney JW (1990) *Nursing process application of conceptual models*. C V Mosby, St Louis USA

Cook NR, Phillips BN, Sadler D (2005) The Tidal Model as experienced by patients and nurses in a regional forensic unit. *Journal of Psychiatric and Mental Health Nursing* **12**: 536–40

Lafferty S, Davidson R (2006) Putting the person first. *Mental Health Today* **Mar**: 31–4

Stevenson C, Barker P, Fletcher E (2002) Judgement days; developing an evaluation for an innovative nursing model. *Journal of Psychiatric and Mental Health Nursing* **9**: 271–2

that this may be done in times of crisis where the focus is on the need for finding immediate support, or at times of transition where the person needs help to move from one care setting to another – perhaps from hospital to the community, and also at times when there is a need for ongoing or developmental care – where the need is for health promotion and personal growth (Barker and Buchanan-Barker, 2007).

The planning stage is inextricably linked to the implementation phase and Barker suggests several useful tools to assist the person and the nurse to explore areas of concern and, in collaboration, develop strategies to deal with them.

At times of crisis the person's personal safety and security is of utmost importance and the main focus of risk assessment within the Tidal Model is to develop a collaborative approach to risk management through the development of a personal security plan by the primary nurse and the person. This plan should be simple and it should identify what the person might do to prevent any potential harm to self or others, and what the nurse needs to do to help the person achieve personal security.

All planning and implementation should be collaborative, and regular one-to-one sessions between the person and the nurse help establish a therapeutic relationship. These sessions should take place regularly and although beginning informally they should over time, begin to develop a focus on the primary concerns of the person. Once again the model has tools to help structure the one-to-one sessions. The focus is on dealing with problems of living, but may also incorporate longer term or more intensive support which focuses on developing an understanding of the sources of problems or their key influences (Barker and Buchanan-Barker, 2007: 32).

In addition to the one-to-one sessions, the model encourages the use of group work to share the common experience of being human. Group work has a long and respected history within mental healthcare but nurses are often reluctant to tackle it. It is sometimes seen as something specialised or as an add-on to the real work of nursing. Barker is clear that nurses can and should use the vehicle of group work to provide a supportive social structure for individualised care (Barker and Buchanan-Barker, 2005: 161).

The final stage of the nursing process is evaluation and the Tidal Model once again emphasises the collaborative and person-centred approach to evaluation. Through the medium of the one-to-one sessions the person and the nurse review problems and concerns and evaluate 'What needs to be done now? By asking the questions, 'What will I do next' and 'How can the team help?', the person explores with the nurse whether the problem has been solved in a way that is acceptable to the person or whether more work needs to be done. The important issue here is that it is the person who decides when the problem is solved – this may not always be congruent with the psychiatrist's diagnosis but it will confirm that the diagnosis is no longer a problem for living.

Influence

Mental health nursing is constantly adapting to professional, political and cultural concerns of the day. At the time of writing, there are some who see the future of mental health nurses secured by developing extended roles as prescribers of medication or of therapy, or by trained nurses becoming managers and arbiters of care provided by 'healthcare workers'.

Superficially, the economic argument for this is easy to make if you assume that care is a menial and unskilled task. Barker refutes this and his influence in the field of mental health nursing is to put care and caring at the core of professional competence. Barker encourages nurses to stay at the 'care face' and develop the inter-personal and human skills of nursing.

This is not an argument against nurses developing as therapists or becoming experts in other fields, but central to any definition of nursing is the notion that nurses perform extraordinary things in very ordinary ways.

The Tidal Model gives value and professional credibility to nurses, and it provides a framework to direct programmes of preparation for nurses, as well as providing a way of re-focusing nursing in clinical settings to become more responsive to people's needs. The model has been adopted in many different types of mental health nursing services all over the world and it is now helping student nurses in many undergraduate courses make sense of the 'craft of caring'.

Recently the authors of the Model have elaborated on its core values to provide a set of 'tidal competencies' (Buchanan-Barker and Barker, 2008). This work will surely prove influential in the debate surrounding competency-based programmes for mental health nurses.

Influence flows both from the model and to it, and the model will continue to develop and grow with the help of all who are involved with it. The recovery movement and the rise of 'patient power' are set to radically alter our notions of mental illness and mental health and how nurses need to respond to problems of living. Just as the disability movement and gay pride have changed our notions of 'disability' and 'sexual deviance' – so perhaps the Tidal Model and the concepts of recovery and reclamation will in time change our notions of madness.

Where to find out more

● www.tidal-model.com

At this official website for the Tidal Model you can learn more about the model from Phil Barker and Poppy Buchanan-Barker.

● www.clan-unity.co.uk

Clan Unity is an organisation, set up by Phil Barker and Poppy Buchanan-Barker to support professionals and people in mental distress.

Index

O

P